T0322014

Building High Integrity Applications with SPARK

Software is pervasive in our lives. We are accustomed to dealing with the failures of much of that software – restarting an application is a very familiar solution. Such solutions are unacceptable when the software controls our cars, airplanes, and medical devices or manages our private information. These applications must run without error. SPARK provides a means, on the basis of mathematical proof, to guarantee that a program has no errors. This book provides an introduction to SPARK 2014 for students and developers wishing to master the basic concepts for building systems with SPARK.

SPARK is a formally defined programming language and a set of verification tools specifically designed to support the development of software used in high integrity applications. Using SPARK, developers can formally verify properties of their code such as information flow, freedom from runtime errors, functional correctness, security properties, and safety properties.

John W. McCormick is a professor of computer science at the University of Northern Iowa. He began his career at the State University of New York in 1979. He has served as secretary, treasurer, and chair of the Association for Computer Machinery Special Interest Group on Ada. In 1993 John was awarded the Chancellor's Award for Excellence in Teaching. He received the Special Interest Group on Ada Distinguished Service Award in 2002, as well as the Outstanding Ada Community Contributions Award in 2008. His additional awards include the Special Interest Group on Ada Best Paper and Presentation Award and the Ada Europe Best Presentation Award.

Peter C. Chapin is a professor of computer information systems at Vermont Technical College (VTC). Peter started at VTC in 1986 as an instructor in the Department of Electrical and Computer Engineering Technology teaching courses on microcontrollers and C programming. Since 2009 Peter has been Software Director of VTC's CubeSat Laboratory where he has worked with students using Ada and SPARK to program small-scale nano-satellites. VTC successfully launched a working CubeSat satellite into low Earth orbit on November 19, 2013. It is the first CubeSat programmed using SPARK.

Building High Integrity Applications with SPARK

JOHN W. McCORMICK

University of Northern Iowa

PETER C. CHAPIN

Vermont Technical College

CAMBRIDGE
UNIVERSITY PRESS

Shaftesbury Road, Cambridge CB2 8EA, United Kingdom

One Liberty Plaza, 20th Floor, New York, NY 10006, USA

477 Williamstown Road, Port Melbourne, VIC 3207, Australia

314–321, 3rd Floor, Plot 3, Splendor Forum, Jasola District Centre, New Delhi – 110025, India

103 Penang Road, #05–06/07, Visioncrest Commercial, Singapore 238467

Cambridge University Press is part of Cambridge University Press & Assessment, a department of the University of Cambridge.

We share the University's mission to contribute to society through the pursuit of education, learning and research at the highest international levels of excellence.

www.cambridge.org
Information on this title: www.cambridge.org/9781107040731

© John W. McCormick and Peter C. Chapin 2015

This publication is in copyright. Subject to statutory exception and to the provisions of relevant collective licensing agreements, no reproduction of any part may take place without the written permission of Cambridge University Press & Assessment.

First published 2015

A catalogue record for this publication is available from the British Library

Library of Congress Cataloging-in-Publication data
McCormick, John W., 1948–
Building high integrity applications with SPARK / John W. McCormick, University of Northern Iowa, Peter C. Chapin, Vermont Technical College.
pages cm
Includes bibliographical references and index.
ISBN 978-1-107-04073-1 (alk. paper)
1. SPARK (Computer program language) 2. Fault-tolerant computing.
I. Chapin, Peter C. II. Title.
QA76.73.S59M38 2015
004.2–dc23   2015014814

ISBN   978-1-107-04073-1   Hardback
ISBN   978-1-107-65684-0   Paperback

Additional resources for this publication at www.cambridge.org/us/academic/subjects/computer-science/programming-languages-and-applied-logic/building-high-integrity-applications-spark.

Cambridge University Press & Assessment has no responsibility for the persistence or accuracy of URLs for external or third-party internet websites referred to in this publication and does not guarantee that any content on such websites is, or will remain, accurate or appropriate.

Contents

Preface   *page* ix

1 Introduction and Overview   1

  1.1 Obtaining Software Quality   2
  1.2 What Is SPARK?   8
  1.3 SPARK Tools   10
  1.4 SPARK Example   12
  Summary   16
  Exercises   16

2 The Basic SPARK Language   18

  2.1 Control Structures   21
  2.2 Subprograms   27
  2.3 Data Types   32
  2.4 Subprograms, More Options   57
  Summary   64
  Exercises   65

3 Programming in the Large   68

  3.1 Definition Packages   69
  3.2 Utility Packages   71
  3.3 Type Packages   73
  3.4 Variable Packages   83
  3.5 Child Packages   87
  3.6 Elaboration   93
  Summary   95
  Exercises   96

4 Dependency Contracts   99

4.1 Data Dependency Contracts   100
4.2 Flow Dependency Contracts   104
4.3 Managing State   110
4.4 Default Initialization   124
4.5 Synthesis of Dependency Contracts   127
Summary   130
Exercises   132

5 Mathematical Background   135

5.1 Propositional Logic   135
5.2 Logical Equivalence   139
5.3 Arguments and Inference   141
5.4 Predicate Logic   144
Summary   150
Exercises   151

6 Proof   155

6.1 Runtime Errors   155
6.2 Contracts   162
6.3 Assert and Assume   189
6.4 Loop Invariants   201
6.5 Loop Variants   211
6.6 Discriminants   216
6.7 Generics   224
6.8 Suppression of Checks   235
Summary   240
Exercises   243

7 Interfacing with Spark   247

7.1 Spark and Ada   247
7.2 Spark and C   261
7.3 External Subsystems   269
Summary   282
Exercises   283

8 Software Engineering with Spark   286

8.1 Conversion of Spark 2005   286
8.2 Legacy Ada Software   291
8.3 Creating New Software   296

8.4 Proof and Testing   307
8.5 Case Study: Time Stamp Server   310
Summary   325

9 Advanced Techniques   326

9.1 Ghost Entities   326
9.2 Proof of Transitive Properties   330
9.3 Proof Debugging   336
9.4 SPARK Internals   347

Notes   355
References   359
Index   363

Preface

SPARK is a formally defined programming language and a set of verification tools specifically designed to support the development of high integrity software. Using SPARK, developers can formally verify properties of their code such as

- information flow,
- freedom from runtime errors,
- functional correctness,
- security policies, and
- safety policies.

SPARK meets the requirements of all high integrity software safety standards, including DO-178B/C (and the Formal Methods supplement DO-333), CENELEC 50128, IEC 61508, and DEFSTAN 00-56. SPARK can be used to support software assurance at the highest levels specified in the Common Criteria Information Technology Security Evaluation standard.

It has been twenty years since the first proof of a nontrivial system was written in SPARK (Chapman and Schanda, 2014). The 27,000 lines of SPARK code for SHOLIS, a system that assists with the safe operation of helicopters at sea, generated nearly 9,000 verification conditions (VCs). Of these VCs, 75.5% were proven automatically by the SPARK tools. The remaining VCs were proven by hand using an interactive proof assistance tool. Fast-forward to 2011 when the NATS iFACTS enroute air traffic control system went online in the United Kingdom. The 529,000 lines of SPARK code were proven to be "crash proof." The SPARK tools had improved to the point where 98.76% of the 152,927 VCs were proven automatically. Most of the remaining proofs were accomplished by the addition of user-defined rules, leaving only 200 proofs to be done "by review."

Although SPARK and other proof tools have significant successes, their use is still limited. Many software engineers presume that the intellectual challenges of proof are too high to consider using these technologies on their projects. Therefore, an important goal in the design of the latest version of SPARK, called SPARK 2014, was to provide a less demanding approach for working with proof tools. The first step toward this goal was the arrival of Ada 2012 with its new syntax for contracts. We no longer need to write SPARK assertions as special comments in the Ada code. The subset of Ada that is legal as SPARK language has grown to encompass a larger subset of Ada, giving developers a much richer set of constructs from which to develop their code.

The real power of SPARK 2014 is under the hood. The new set of SPARK tools is integrated with the front end of the GNAT compiler. This merger allows the SPARK tools to make direct use of the many code analyses performed by the GNAT compiler. Also, the new tools use an entirely new proof system based on the Why3 software verification system (Bobot et al., 2011). Why3 manages a collection of modern satisfiability modulo theory (SMT) provers such as Alt-Ergo (OCamlPro, 2014), CVC4 (New York University, 2014), YICES (Dutertre, 2014), and Z3 (Bjørner, 2012) that complete the actual proving of the contracts in our program. These underlying proof tools can handle far more situations than the original SPARK prover. Do not be put off by this high-powered mathematical foundation; you do not need knowledge of these low-level proof tools to use SPARK.

Another significant improvement in SPARK 2014 is the integration of proof and testing techniques. The Ada 2012 assertions in a SPARK program can be checked dynamically by running test cases. Alternatively, these assertions can be proven correct by the SPARK proof tools. Such a mixed verification approach allows us to incrementally increase the level of formality in our programs. Having the ability to combine testing and proof also allows us to more easily verify programs written in a mixture of languages.

It is useful to distinguish between SPARK as a programming language and the SPARK tools that perform the analysis and proof of program properties. The removal of difficult-to-analyze features such as access types and exceptions makes the SPARK 2014 language a subset of Ada 2012. Yet, the SPARK 2014 language also extends Ada 2012 with additional pragmas and aspects. The SPARK language is described in the SPARK *2014 Reference Manual* (SPARK Team, 2014a) and could potentially be implemented by many Ada compiler vendors.

At the time of this writing, Altran/AdaCore's implementation of SPARK is the only one that exists. Details of their implementation are described in the SPARK *2014 Toolset User's Guide* (SPARK Team, 2014b). Because there is only one implementation of SPARK, it is easy to assume that SPARK is really the union of behaviors described in the reference manual and user's guide. However, it is possible that another implementation of SPARK may arise that implements the language in the reference manual while providing a different user experience.

As a convenience to the reader, in this book we have at times conflated SPARK the language and SPARK as implemented by Altran/AdaCore. With only one implementation of SPARK available, this approach seems reasonable, and it has the advantage of streamlining the presentation. For example, SPARK_Mode, described in Section 7.1.1, provides a way of identifying which parts of a program are SPARK. Technically, SPARK_Mode is a feature of Altran/AdaCore's implementation and not part of the SPARK language itself. Another implementation of SPARK could conceivably use a different mechanism for identifying SPARK code.

It is also important to understand that while the SPARK language is relatively static, the tools are rapidly evolving. As the tools mature they are able to automatically complete more proofs faster than before. You may find that recent versions of the tools do not require as many hints and assertions as older versions. In particular, some examples in this book may be provable by newer tools with fewer assertions required than we use here.

The SPARK language includes the Ada 2012 constructs necessary for object oriented programming: tagged types, type extensions, dispatching operations, abstract types, and interface types. Contract notations are provided for ensuring that any operations applied to a superclass instance are also valid for instances of a subclass (the Liskov Substitution Principle). We have elected not to cover the object-oriented aspects of SPARK programming in this book.

Chapter Synopses

Chapter 1 provides an overview of high integrity software and some approaches commonly used to create high-quality software. The SPARK language and tool set are described in the context of reducing defect rates.

Chapter 2 introduces the basic subset of Ada 2012 that constitutes the SPARK language. SPARK's decision and loop structures will be familiar to all programmers. Subprograms come in two forms: functions and procedures. A significant portion of this chapter is devoted to types. Ada allows us to define our own simple and complex types. Using these types, we can create accurate models of the real world and provide valuable information to the SPARK tools so we can identify errors before the program is executed.

Chapter 3 is about the package. Packages facilitate the construction of large programs. We use packages to support separation of concerns, encapsulation, information hiding, and more. A SPARK program consists of a main subprogram that uses services provided by packages.

Chapter 4 provides the first look at contracts – assertions about the program's behavior that must be implemented correctly by the developer. Dependency contracts provide the means to verify data dependencies and information flow dependencies in our programs. Incorrect implementation of data dependencies or flow of information can lead to security violations. The SPARK tools can check that the implementation conforms to the requirements of these contracts. This analysis offers two major services. First, it verifies that uninitialized data is never used. Second, it verifies that all results computed by the program participate in some way in the program's eventual output – that is, all computations are effective.

Chapter 5 provides a review of basic discrete mathematics useful in reading and writing contracts. Propositional and predicate logic provide the fundamental notions needed for expressing the assertions in contracts that specify functional behavior. The existential (there exists) and universal (for all) quantifiers of predicate logic are crucial in stating assertions about collections. Although not necessary to use the SPARK tools, we give a basic introduction to arguments and their validity. The verification conditions (VCs) generated by the SPARK proof tools are arguments that must be proven valid to ensure that our implementation fulfills the contracts. We leave it to the SPARK tools to do the actual proofs.

Chapter 6 describes how to use the SPARK tools to prove behavioral properties of a program. The first step is the proof that our program is free of runtime errors – that is, no exceptions can ever be raised. By including contracts such as preconditions and postconditions with each subprogram, we state the desired functionality. We can use the SPARK tools to show that these contracts are always honored, and thus, our code implements that functionality. In an ideal world, the tools would need only our code to verify it is free of runtime errors and meets all of its contracts. In reality, the tools are not yet smart enough to accomplish that verification alone. When a proof fails in a situation where we believe our code to be correct, we need to give the tool some additional information it can use to complete its proof. This information comes in the form of additional assertions.

Chapter 7 explores the issues around building programs that are not completely written in SPARK. It is often infeasible or even undesirable to write an entire program in SPARK. Some portions of the program may need to be in full Ada to take advantage of Ada features that are not available in SPARK such as access types and exceptions. It may be necessary for SPARK programs to call third-party libraries written in full Ada or in some other programming language such as C. Of course, SPARK's assurances of correctness cannot be formally guaranteed when the execution of a program flows into the non-SPARK components.

Chapter 8 provides an overview of SPARK in the context of a software engineering process. We describe three common usages: conversion of SPARK 2005 programs to SPARK 2014, analysis or conversion of existing Ada programs, and development of new SPARK programs from scratch. We introduce the INFORMED design method for SPARK and discuss how testing and proof may be used in combination. Finally, we present a case study of developing an application using the INFORMED process.

In Chapter 9 we examine some advanced techniques for proving properties of SPARK programs including ghost entities and proof of transitive properties. We discuss the approaches we found useful for debugging proofs and provide a number of guidelines for completing difficult proofs. Finally, we give a brief tour of the internal workings of SPARK and suggestions for learning more.

Tools

Currently, the partnership of Altran and AdaCore provides the only implementation of SPARK 2014. They provide two versions. SPARK GPL with the corresponding GNAT GPL Ada compiler is available for free to software developers and students at http://www.libre.adacore.com. SPARK Pro with the corresponding GNAT Pro Ada compiler is intended for industrial, military, and commercial developers. Information on subscriptions to these professional tools is available at http://www.adacore.com.

Web Resources

A Web site with the complete source code for all of the examples and some of the exercises in the book may be found at http://www.cambridge.org/us/academic/subjects/computer-science/programming-languages-and-applied-logic/building-high-integrity-applications-spark.

The *Ada 2012 Language Reference Manual* and the *Rationale for Ada 2012* are available at http://www.ada-auth.org/standards/12rm/html/RM-TTL.html and http://www.ada-auth.org/standards/12rat/html/Rat12-TTL.html.

The *GNAT Reference Manual* and the *GNAT User's Guide* are available at http://docs.adacore.com/gnat_rm-docs/html/gnat_rm.html and http://docs.adacore.com/gnat_ugn-docs/html/gnat_ugn.html.

The SPARK *2014 Reference Manual* and the SPARK *2014 Toolset User's Guide* are available at http://docs.adacore.com/spark2014-docs/html/lrm and http://docs.adacore.com/spark2014-docs/html/ug.

Additional resources for Ada 2012 and SPARK may be found at http://university.adacore.com, https://www.linkedin.com/groups/Ada-Programming-Language-114211/about, and https://www.linkedin.com/groups/SPARK-User-Community-2082712/about

You can keep up with the latest SPARK developments at http://www.spark-2014.org.

Acknowledgments

We would like to thank the many SPARK 2014 developers at AdaCore and Altran who helped us with all of the nuances of the language and tools. We appreciate their work in reading and commenting on several drafts of this book. This book is much better as a result of their efforts. We also thank those individuals in industry who use SPARK on real projects for their feedback. Their comments, corrections, and suggestions have enormously improved and enriched this book. We are grateful to (in alphabetical order) Stefan Berghofer, Roderick Chapman, Arnaud Charlet, Robert Dorn, Claire Dross, Pavlos Efstathopoulos, Johannes Kanig, David Lesens, Stuart Matthews, Yannick Moy, Florian Schanda, and Tucker Taft.

Anyone who has written a textbook can appreciate the amount of time and effort involved and anyone related to a textbook author can tell you at whose expense that time is spent. John thanks his wife Naomi for her support and understanding. Peter thanks his wife Sharon for her patience and his students for their interest in SPARK.

John W. McCormick
University of Northern Iowa
mccormick@cs.uni.edu

Peter C. Chapin
Vermont Technical College
PChapin@vtc.vsc.edu

1

Introduction and Overview

Software is critical to many aspects of our lives. It comes in many forms. The applications we install and run on our computers and smart phones are easily recognized as software. Other software, such as that controlling the amount of fuel injected into a car's engine, is not so obvious to its users. Much of the software we use lacks adequate quality. A report by the National Institute of Standards and Technology (NIST, 2002) indicated that poor quality software costs the United States economy more than $60 billion per year. There is no evidence to support any improvement in software quality in the decade since that report was written.

Most of us expect our software to fail. We are never surprised and rarely complain when our e-mail program locks up or the font changes we made to our word processing document are lost. The typical "solution" to a software problem of turning the device off and then on again is so encultured that it is often applied to problems outside of the realm of computers and software. Even our humor reflects this view of quality. A classic joke is the software executive's statement to the auto industry, "If GM had kept up with the computing industry we would all be driving $25 cars that got 1,000 miles per gallon," followed by the car maker's list of additional features that would come with such a vehicle:

1. For no apparent reason, your car would crash twice a day.
2. Occasionally, your engine would quit on the highway. You would have to coast over to the side of the road, close all of the windows, turn off the ignition, restart the car, and then reopen the windows before you could continue.
3. Occasionally, executing a maneuver, such as slowing down after completion of a right turn of exactly 97 degrees, would cause your engine to shut

down and refuse to restart, in which case you would have to reinstall the engine.

4. Occasionally, your car would lock you out and refuse to let you in until you simultaneously lift the door handle, turn the key, and kick the door (an operation requiring the use of three of your four limbs).

Why do we not care about quality? The simple answer is that defective software works "well enough." We are willing to spend a few hours finding a work-around to a defect in our software to use those features that do work correctly. Should the doctor using robotic surgery tools, the pilot flying a fly-by-wire aircraft, or the operators of a nuclear power plant be satisfied with "well enough"? In these domains, software quality does matter. These are examples of *high-integrity applications* – those in which failure has a high impact on humans, organizations, or the environment. However, we would argue that software quality matters in every domain. Everyone wants their software to work. Perhaps the biggest need for quality today is in the software security arena. In his newsletter article, *Security Changes Everything*, Watts Humphrey (2006b) wrote: "It is now common for software defects to disrupt transportation, cause utility failures, enable identity theft, and even result in physical injury or death. The ways that hackers, criminals, and terrorists can exploit the defects in our software are growing faster than the current patch-and-fix strategy can handle."

1.1 Obtaining Software Quality

The classic definition of the quality of a product focuses on the consumer's needs, expectations, and preferences. Customer satisfaction depends on a number of characteristics, some of which contribute very little to the functionality of the product.

Manufacturers have a different view of product quality. They are concerned with the design, engineering, and manufacturing of products. Quality is assessed by conformance to specifications and standards and is improved by removing defects. In this book, we concentrate on this defect aspect of quality.

> This is because the cost and time spent in removing software defects currently consumes such a large proportion of our efforts that it overwhelms everything else, often even reducing our ability to meet functional needs. To make meaningful improvements in security, usability, maintainability, productivity, predictability, quality, and almost any other "-ility," we must reduce the defect problem to manageable proportions. Only then can we devote sufficient resources to other aspects of quality. (Humphrey, 2006a)

Table 1.1. The software CMM (Paulk, 2009)

Level	Focus	Characteristics
1, Initial	None	*Ad hoc* or chaotic.
2, Repeatable	Project Management	The necessary process discipline is in place to repeat earlier successes on projects with similar applications.
3, Defined	Software Engineering	The software process for both management and engineering activities is documented, standardized, and integrated into a set of standard software processes for the organization.
4, Managed	Quality Processes	Detailed measures of the software process and product quality are collected. Both the software process and products are quantitatively understood and controlled.
5, Optimizing	Continuous Improvement	Continuous process improvement is enabled by feedback from the process and from piloting innovative ideas and technologies.

1.1.1 *Defect Rates*

In traditional manufacturing, quality is assured by controlling the manufacturing process. Statistical tools are used to analyze the production process and predict and correct deviations that may result in unacceptable products. Statistical process control was pioneered by Walter A. Shewhart in 1924 to reduce the frequency of failures of telephone transmission equipment manufactured by the Western Electric Company. After World War II, W. Edwards Deming introduced statistical process control methods to Japanese industry. The resulting quality of Japanese-manufactured products remains a benchmark for the rest of the world.

In 1987, the Software Engineering Institute (SEI), led by the work of Watts Humphrey, brought forth the notion that statistical process control could be applied to the software engineering process. SEI defined the Capability Maturity Model for Software (Software CMM) in 1991.[1] The Software CMM defines the five levels of process maturity described in Table 1.1. Each level provides a set of process improvement priorities.

There is a good deal of evidence to support the assertion that using better processes as defined by the Software CMM leads to programs with fewer defects. Figure 1.1 shows the typical rate of defects delivered in projects as

Table 1.2. Origin of defects

Study	Design and coding	Requirements and specification	Other
Beizer (1990)	89%	9%	2%
NIST (2002)	58%	30%	12%
Jones (2012, 2013)	60%	20%	20%

a function of the Software CMM level. The average rate of 1.05 defects per thousand lines of code (KLOC) obtained by engineers working at CMM level 5 appears to be a low number. However, this rate must be considered in the context of the large size of most sophisticated projects. It suggests that the typical million lines of code in an aircraft's flight management system is delivered with more than 1,000 defects. A NASA report on Toyota Camry's unintended acceleration describes the examination of 280,000 lines of code in the car's engine control module (NASA, 2011). Assuming this code was developed under the highest CMM level, the data in Figure 1.1 suggests that this code might contain nearly 300 defects. These numbers are too large for high integrity software.

To prevent or detect and remove defects before a software application is released, it is useful to understand where defects originate. Table 1.2 shows the estimates from three studies on the origins of defects in software. This data indicates that the majority of defects are created during the design and coding phases of development.

Verification and validation are names given to processes and techniques commonly used to assure software quality. Software *verification* is the process of showing that the software meets its written specification. This definition is

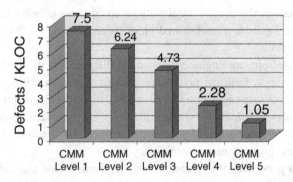

Figure 1.1. Delivered defects by CMM level (data from Jones [2000] and Davis and Mullaney [2003]).

commonly illustrated by the question, "Are we building the *product right?*" Verification is a means of demonstrating correctness. We use verification to locate and remove the defects from our design and implementation, the compiler, operating systems, and hardware on which we execute our application – defects that constitute the majority of those classified in Table 1.2.

Software *validation* is the process of evaluating an application to ensure that it actually meets the users' needs – that the specification was correct. This definition is commonly illustrated by the question, "Are we building the *right product?*" Validation is important in showing that we remove the defects originating in our specification (the third column of Table 1.2).

1.1.2 *Software Testing*

The verification strategies used to achieve the defect rates shown in Figure 1.1 are typically based on software testing. An in-depth coverage of software testing is beyond the scope of this book. For additional information, see Ammann and Offutt (2008), Black (2007), Jorgensen (2008), Kaner, Falk, and Nguyen (1999), or the classic testing book by Beizer (1990). There are two fundamental approaches to testing: black-box testing and white-box testing.

Black-box testing is based solely on the behavior of the program without any knowledge of coding details. It is also called behavioral testing or functional testing. Test cases are created from requirements given in the specification for the application. Black-box testing is usually performed on complete systems or large subsystems. It is often performed by people who did not write the software under test. These testers frequently have more knowledge of the application domain than of software engineering. There are many black-box testing tactics, including Black (2007):

- Equivalence classes and boundary value testing
- Use case, live data, and decision table testing
- State transition table testing
- Domain testing
- Orthogonal array and all pairs testing
- Reactive and exploratory testing

As black-box tests are derived entirely from the specification, they provide a means of verifying that our design, implementation, compiler, operating system, and hardware work together to successfully realize the specification. Black-box testing does not directly provide validation that our specification is correct. However, the testers' domain expertise is a valuable resource in finding errors in the specification during testing.

White-box testing is based on the actual instructions within the application. It is also called *glass-box testing* or *structural testing*. White-box tests are created from the possible sequences of execution of statements in the application. White-box testing is usually performed by programmers and may be applied to small units (unit testing) as well as to a combination of units (integration testing). The two basic tactics of white-box testing are control-flow testing and data-flow testing.

Control-flow tests are usually designed to achieve a particular level of coverage of the code. Commonly used code coverage tactics include:

- statement coverage;
- condition coverage;
- multicondition coverage;
- multicondition decision coverage;
- modified condition/decision coverage (MC/DC); and
- path coverage.

Data-flow tests add another dimension to control-flow testing. In addition to testing how control flows through the program, data-flow testing checks the order in which variables are set and used.

1.1.3 *Improving Defect Rates*

There are at least three reasons why testing alone cannot meet current and future quality needs. First, complete testing is almost always impossible. Suppose we would like to use black-box testing to verify that a function correctly adds two 32-bit integers. Exhaustive testing of this function requires 2^{64} combinations of two integers – far too many to actually test. With white-box testing, we would like to test every possible path through the program. As the number of possible paths through a program increases exponentially with the number of branch instructions, complete path coverage testing of a small program requires a huge effort and is impossible for most realistic-size programs. Good testing is a matter of selecting a subset of possible data for black-box tests and the determination of the most likely execution paths for white-box testing. That brings us to the second reason that testing alone cannot achieve the quality we need. Users always find innovative, unintended ways to use applications. We probably did not test the data entered or the paths executed by those "creative" uses of our application. Third, we now face a new category of user: one who is hostile. Our applications are under attack by criminals, hackers, and terrorists. These people actively search for untested data and untested execution paths to exploit. As a result, we find ourselves updating our applications each time a security vulnerability is discovered and patched.

Watts Humphrey (2004) has suggested four alternative strategies for achieving defect rates below those obtained at Software CMM level 5.

Clean Room: This process was developed by Harlan Mills, Michael Dyer, and Richard Linger (1987) at IBM in the mid-1980s with a focus on defect prevention rather than defect removal. Defect prevention is obtained through a combination of manually applied formal methods in requirements and design followed by statistical testing. Quality results are ten times better than Software CMM level 5 results.

Team Software Process (TSP): A process-based approach for defect prevention developed by Watts Humphrey (2000). Quality results are more than ten times better than Software CMM level 5 results.

Correct by Construction (CbyC): A software development process developed by Praxis Critical Systems (Amey, 2002; Hall and Chapman, 2002). CbyC makes use of formal methods throughout the life cycle and uses SPARK for strong static verification of code. Quality results are 50 to 100 times better than Software CMM level 5 results (Croxford and Chapman, 2005).

CbyC in a TSP Environment: A process combining the formal methods of CbyC utilizing SPARK with the process improvements of the Team Software Process.

Both clean room and CbyC are based on formal methods. *Formal methods* are mathematically based techniques for the development of software. A formal specification provides a precise, unambiguous description of an application's functionality. Later in the development cycle, the formal specification may be used to verify its implementation in software. Although there has been much work over the years, formal methods remain poorly accepted by industrial practitioners. Reasons cited for this limited use include claims that formal methods extend the development cycle, require difficult mathematics, and have limited tool support (Knight et al., 1997).

In this book we introduce you to the SPARK programming language and how it may be used to create high-integrity applications that can be formally verified. Contrary to the claim that formal methods increase development time, the use of SPARK has been shown to decrease the development cycle by reducing testing time by 80 percent (Amey, 2002). A goal of this book is to show that with the tools provided by SPARK, the mathematics involved is not beyond the typical software engineer. We do not attempt to cover formal specification or the software development processes defined by CbyC or TSP in which SPARK can play a critical role in producing high assurance, reliable applications.

1.2 What Is SPARK?

SPARK is a programming language and a set of verification tools specifically designed to support the development of software used in high-integrity applications. SPARK was originally designed with formally defined semantics (Marsh and O'Neill, 1994). *Semantics* refer to the meaning of instructions in a programming language. The semantics of a language describe the behavior that a computer follows when executing a program in that language. *Formally defined* means that SPARK's semantics underwent rigorous mathematical study. Such study is important in ensuring that the behavior of a SPARK program is unambiguous. This deterministic behavior allows us to analyze a SPARK program without actually executing it, a process called *static verification* or *formal verification*.

The information provided by the static verification of a SPARK program can range from the detection of simple coding errors such as a failure to properly initialize a variable to a proof that the program is correct. *Correct* in this context means that the program meets its specification. Although such correctness proofs are invaluable, they provide no validation that a specification is correct. If the formal requirements erroneously state that our autopilot software shall keep the aircraft upside down in the southern hemisphere, we can analyze our SPARK program to prove that it will indeed flip our plane as it crosses the equator on a flight from the United States to Brazil. We still need validation through testing or other means to show that we are building the right application.

In addition, verification of a SPARK program cannot find defects in the compiler used to translate it into machine code. Nor will SPARK find defects in the operating system or hardware on which it runs. We still need some verification testing to show that it runs correctly with the given operating system and hardware. But with a full analysis of our SPARK program, we can eliminate most of the verification testing for defects in the design and implementation of our application – the defects that constitute the majority of those listed in Table 1.2.

SPARK is based on the Ada programming language. SPARK's designers selected a restricted, well-defined, unambiguous subset of the Ada language to eliminate features that cannot be statically analyzed. They extended the language with a set of assertions to support modular, formal verification.

SPARK has evolved substantially over its lifetime. The first three versions, called SPARK 83, SPARK 95, and SPARK 2005, are based on the corresponding

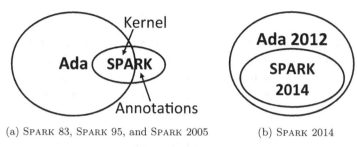

(a) SPARK 83, SPARK 95, and SPARK 2005   (b) SPARK 2014

Figure 1.2. Relationships between Ada and SPARK.

versions of Ada (Ada 83, Ada 95, and Ada 2005). This book describes the current version – SPARK 2014 – which is based on Ada 2012.

The complete set of goals for SPARK 2014 is available in the *SPARK 2014 Reference Manual* (SPARK Team, 2014a). Some of the more important goals include the following:

- The SPARK 2014 language shall embody the largest subset of Ada 2012 to which it is currently practical to apply automatic formal verification.
  Prior to this version, SPARK executable statements were a small subset of Ada called the *Spark kernel*. A special non-Ada syntax was used to write *annotations* – formal statements used for the static verification of the program. SPARK 2014 uses the syntax available in Ada 2012 to write both executable statements and static verification statements called *assertions*. Preconditions, postconditions, and loop invariants are examples of assertions we shall look at in detail. The two Venn diagrams in Figure 1.2 illustrate the relationships between Ada and SPARK.
- SPARK 2014 shall provide counterparts of all language features and analysis modes provided in SPARK 83/95/2005.
- SPARK 2014 shall have executable semantics for preconditions, postconditions, and other assertions. All such expressions may be executed, proven, or both.
- SPARK 2014 shall support verification through a combination of testing and proof. Our programs can be written as a mix of SPARK 2014, unrestricted Ada 2012, and other languages. We can formally verify or use testing to verify those parts written in SPARK 2014. We must use testing to verify those parts not written in SPARK 2014.

Throughout this book, we use the name SPARK to refer to SPARK 2014.

1.3 SPARK Tools

SPARK comes with a set of tools for developing SPARK programs. A full description of the tools is available in the *SPARK 2014 Toolset User's Guide* (SPARK Team, 2014b). In this section we list and provide a very brief summary of these tools. More detailed descriptions of each tool are given in later chapters when appropriate.

1.3.1 *GNAT Compiler*

The GNAT compiler performs the tasks of a typical compiler:

- Checks that the program is in conformance with all of the Ada syntax and semantic rules.
- Generates the executable code.

The *SPARK 2014 Toolset User's Guide* (SPARK Team, 2014b) recommends that our first step in developing a SPARK program is to use the GNAT compiler *semantic check* tool to ensure that the code is valid Ada. Once we have completed the formal verification of our SPARK program, our final step is to use the GNAT compiler to generate the executable code.

For testing purposes, we can request that the compiler generate machine code to check any assertions (preconditions, postconditions, etc.) while the program is running. Should any assertion be found false, the exception Assertion_Error is raised. This capability allows us to perform tests of our assertions prior to proving them.

1.3.2 *GNATprove*

GNATprove is the verification tool for SPARK. It may be run in three different modes:

Check: Checks that a program unit contains only the subset of Ada that is defined for SPARK.
Flow: Performs a flow analysis of SPARK code. This analysis consists of two parts: a *data-flow analysis* that considers the initialization of variables and the data dependences of subprograms and an *information-flow* analysis that considers the dependencies or couplings between the values being passed into and out of a subprogram.[2]
Proof: Performs a formal verification of the SPARK code. Formal verification will point out any code that might raise a runtime error such as division by zero, assignment to a variable that is out of range of the type of the variable, incorrect indexing of arrays, or overflow of an arithmetic

expression. If the SPARK code contains assertions expressing functional properties of the code, they are verified.

The assertions in the SPARK code that GNATprove verifies are logical statements. A *logical statement* is a meaningful declarative sentence that is either true or false. The term logical statement is often shortened to *statement*. A statement cannot be true at one point in time and false at another time. Here, for example, are two simple logical statements, one true and one false:

• Sodium Azide is a poison.
• New York City is the capital of New York state.

Our assertions will often involve existential (there exists) or universal (for all) quantifiers as in the following examples:

• There exists a human with two heads.
• All men are mortal.

To convince ourselves that the first of these quantified statements is true, we need to find at least one person with two heads. If we can find one man that is immortal, we can feel comfortable that the second quantified statement is false. In later chapters you will learn how to write logical statements for SPARK assertions.

GNATprove analyzes the SPARK code and our assertions to produce a number of logical statements. A *theorem* is a statement that has been proven (to be true). The logical statements produced by GNATprove are *conjectures* – statements that are believed to be true but not yet proven. SPARK calls these conjectures *verification conditions* or *VCs*. We say that a VC is *discharged* when we have shown it to be true. If we discharge all the VCs generated by GNATprove, we can have confidence that our SPARK program is correct.

If you took a discrete mathematics course, you studied different approaches for proving logical statements. It takes skill and time to manually prove a logical statement. GNATprove produces too many VCs to be proven by hand. Fortunately, there are a number of proof tools available to perform the necessary proofs. GNATprove makes use of two proof tools called Alt-Ergo (OCamlPro, 2014) and CVC4 (New York University, 2014). Other tools that GNATprove may use include YICES (Dutertre, 2014) and Z3 (Bjørner, 2012).

1.3.3 *GNATtest*

Formal verification provides us with the greatest confidence that our program meets its specification. However, it is not always possible to formally verify all parts of a program. There are a number of reasons why some subprograms cannot be formally verified:

- We may not be able to express formally the desired properties of a subprogram. Take, for example, a program that takes in a large amount of seismic data, performs a set of sophisticated mathematical transformations on that data, and displays a graphical picture for the geophysicist on the basis of the results of the transformations. Although we can formally specify the mathematical transformations, it is unlikely we can formally specify the graphical output.
- We may need to use a programming language feature not amenable to formal verification. For example, we may need to make use of pointers to solve a particular subproblem.
- It may not be cost effective to apply formal verification to some components in our program. We might have a module from a previous project that has been verified by other means, but we do not have the budget to reverify it. Sometimes it may be more cost effective to test a simple subprogram than to formally specify and formally verify it.

Testing is the primary method used to verify subprograms that are not amenable to formal verification. We also recommend that some testing be performed on code prior to formal verification with proof tools. In addition to finding errors in the code, such testing may also reveal errors in the assertions. GNATtest is a tool based on AUnit that creates unit-test skeletons and test drivers for valid Ada program units. Test cases for GNATtest may even be written directly in the Ada code.

SPARK was designed to allow engineers to mix formal verification using GNATprove with testing using GNATtest. Formal verification provides more confidence at lower cost, while testing allows verification of portions of the code for which formal specifications are not feasible. Ada contracts on subprograms provide the mechanism for combining proof and testing.

1.4 SPARK Example

To give you a feel for what SPARK code looks like, we end this chapter with an example. Our example is of a SPARK implementation of the selection sort algorithm derived from the Ada code given in Dale and McCormick (2007). Do not be worried about the details yet – we spend the rest of the book describing them. We encapsulate all of the details of the selection sort in a package. We discuss packages in detail in Chapter 3. SPARK packages are written in two parts: a specification that defines what the package contains and a body that contains the actual implementation. Here is the specification of a package containing a sort procedure that sorts an array of integers:

```
1    pragma Spark_Mode (On);
2    package Sorters is
3
4      type Array_Type is array ( Positive range <>) of Integer;
5
6      function Perm (A : in Array_Type;
7                    B : in Array_Type) return Boolean
8      -- Returns True if A is a permutation of B
9        with Global => null,
10            Ghost => True,
11            Import => True;
12
13      procedure Selection_Sort (Values : in out Array_Type)
14      -- Sorts the elements in the array Values in ascending order
15        with Depends => (Values => Values),
16            Pre      => Values'Length >= 1 and then
17                        Values'Last   <= Positive'Last,
18            Post     => (for all J in Values' First  ..  Values' Last - 1 =>
19                        Values (J) <= Values (J + 1)) and then
20                        Perm (Values'Old, Values );
21    end Sorters ;
```

The first line of this specification is a *pragma*, which is a directive to the GNAT compiler and GNATprove. In this example, the pragma informs GNATprove that this package specification should be checked to ensure that it contains only constructs that are in the SPARK subset of Ada. Line 4 defines an array type that is indexed by positive whole numbers and contains integer elements. The <> symbol indicates that the first and last index values are not specified. Such an array type is called an unconstrained array type. We discuss arrays in detail in Chapter 2.

SPARK has two forms of subprograms: the procedure and the function. Lines 13 through 20 specify the selection sort procedure. On line 13 we see that this procedure takes a single parameter, Values, that is an array of the type defined in line 4. The notation **in out** tells us that the array Values is passed into the procedure (**in**), possibly modified, and returned back to the caller (**out**). We discuss subprograms in detail in Chapter 2.

Lines 15 through 20 are the formal *contracts* for this procedure. A SPARK contract is a type of assertion and is based on an Ada construct called an aspect. An *aspect* describes a property of an entity. In this case the entity is the procedure Selection_Sort . The aspect Depends describes the information flow in the procedure. Here, the new array is derived from the information in the original array. The aspect Pre is a precondition. Here we specify that the array passed into this subprogram contains at least one value and its last index is less than the largest possible positive integer. The final aspect, Post, is a postcondition stating that after the procedure completes its execution, the values will be in ascending order (each value in the array is less than or equal to the value that follows it), and the array will be a permutation of the original array (this ensures that the result contains the same values as the original array).

Lines 6 through 11 specify a function that is given two array parameters, A and B, and returns True if one array is a permutation of the other and False otherwise. The notation **in** tells us that each array is passed into the function and not modified by it. The aspect Global tells us that this function does not access any global data. The aspect Ghost indicates that this function will only be used during static verification of the code; it need not be compiled into machine code that might be executed. Finally, the aspect Import indicates that we have not written an implementation of this function. We discuss functions in Chapter 2 and ghost functions in Chapter 9 and complete the formal proof of correctness of this selection sort in Section 9.2.

Now let us look at a program that uses our selection sort program. The following program reads integers from the standard input file, calls the selection sort procedure, and displays the sorted array.

```
1    pragma SPARK_Mode (Off);
2    with Ada.Text_IO;
3    with Ada.Integer_Text_IO;
4    with Sorters;
5    procedure Sort_Demo is
6
7        Max : constant Integer := 50;
8        subtype Index_Type is Integer range 1 .. Max;
9        subtype Count_Type is Integer range 0 .. Max;
10       subtype My_Array_Type is Sorters.Array_Type (Index_Type);
11
12       List  : My_Array_Type;    -- A list of integers
13       Count : Count_Type;       -- Number of values in List
14       Value : Integer;          -- One input value
15
16   begin
17       Ada.Text_IO.Put_Line (Item => "Enter up to 50 integers, enter 0 to end");
18       Count := 0;  -- Initially , there are no numbers in List
19       loop -- Each iteration, get one number
20           Ada.Integer_Text_IO.Get (Item => Value);
```

```
21          exit when Value = 0;      -- Exit loop on sentinel value
22          Count := Count + 1;
23          List (Count) := Value;    -- Put Value into the array List
24       end loop;
25
26       -- Sort the first Count values in the array List
27       Sorters . Selection_Sort  (Values => List (1 .. Count));
28
29       Ada.Text_IO.Put_Line (Item => "Here are the sorted numbers");
30       for J in 1 .. Count loop
31          Ada.Integer_Text_IO .Put (Item  => List (J),
32                                    Width => 8);
33          Ada.Text_IO.New_Line;
34       end loop;
35    end Sort_Demo;
```

The first line of this program is a pragma telling the tools that this code is not written in the SPARK subset of Ada. Thus, although we can formally verify the selection sort procedure, we will need to verify this code some other way. We reviewed this code and conducted a number of test runs to convince ourselves that this code is correct.

Lines 2 through 4 tell what outside resources are needed by this program. Here, we need operations from the Ada library to do input and output with strings (the package Ada.Text_IO) and integers (the package Ada.Integer_Text_IO). We also need the package Sorters that we specified earlier.

Lines 8 through 10 define three subtypes. Subtypes allow us to derive a more specialized or restricted domain from an existing type. For example, the subtype Index_Type has a domain limited to whole numbers between 1 and 50. The subtype My_Array_Type constrains the array type from the Sorters package such that the first index is 1 and the last index is 50. We will discuss types and subtypes in detail in Chapter 2.

Lines 12 through 14 define three variables for the program. List is an array of 50 integers (indexed from 1 to 50), Count is a whole number between 0 and 50, and Value is a whole number.

Lines 17 through 34 are the executable statements of our program. We will discuss the details of all these statements in Chapter 2. Even without detailed knowledge, you can probably follow the three major steps: a sentinel controlled loop to read integers, a call to the selection sort procedure, and a loop to display the resulting array.

One task remains. We need to write the SPARK code that implements the selection sort. This code goes into the body of package Sorters. We will complete this body and prove it is correct in Section 9.2.

Summary

- High integrity applications are those whose failure has a high impact on humans, organizations, or the environment. Software quality is extremely important in such applications.
- Software quality should matter in all applications.
- The conformance of software to specifications and standards is an important, but not the only, aspect of software quality.
- A software defect is a difference between the behavior of the software and its specification.
- A correct program has no defects.
- The better the process used to develop software, the lower the defect rate.
- Testing alone is not adequate for developing high integrity software.
- Formal methods provide a means for producing software with fewer defects than that verified with testing.
- SPARK is a programming language specifically designed to support the development of software used in high integrity applications. It is an unambiguous subset of the Ada programming language.
- Static analysis is the examination of software without executing it. Static verification can only be done on programs written in unambiguous languages such as SPARK.
- The information provided by a static verification of a SPARK program can range from the detection of simple coding errors to a proof that the program is correct.
- GNATprove is the tool used to carry out the static verification of a SPARK program.
- An Ada compiler is used to translate a SPARK program into machine language instructions.
- Aspects are used to specify properties of entities.
- The Depends aspect describes what values a calculated result depends on.
- The Pre and Post aspects describe preconditions and postconditions.

Exercises

1.1 Describe a defect you have observed in software you use and how you manage to get around that defect.

1.2 If the Toyota Camry engineers worked at CMM level 3, how many defects should we expect in the 280,000 lines of code in the car's engine control module?

1.3 If the typical million lines of code in a flight management system might contain more than 1,000 defects, why are there not more reports of airplanes falling from the sky as a result of software failures?

1.4 Which of the software testing techniques described in this chapter have you used to verify programs you have written?

1.5 What is the difference between software verification and software validation?

1.6 Why is testing alone not adequate to meet current and future software quality needs?

1.7 Define the term *semantics* in relation to software development.

1.8 True or false: SPARK is a subset of Ada.

1.9 Name and give a brief description of each of GNATprove's three modes.

1.10 Define *logical statement*.

1.11 Give an example of a logical statement that is true. Give an example of a logical statement that is false.

1.12 Determine whether the following existential statements are true or false:
   a. Some men live to be 100 years old.
   b. Some women live to be 200 years old.
   c. There is some number whose square root is exactly half the value of the number.

1.13 Determine whether the following universal statements are true or false:
   a. All men live to be 100 years old.
   b. The square of any number is positive.
   c. Every mammal has a tail.

1.14 Define *theorem* and *conjecture*.

1.15 Define *verification condition* (VC).

1.16 What is meant by *discharging* a VC?

1.17 What is a *pragma*?

1.18 What is an *aspect*?

1.19 Define *precondition* and *postcondition*.

2

The Basic SPARK Language

SPARK is a programming language based on Ada. The syntax and semantics of the Ada language are defined in the *Ada Reference Manual* (ARM, 2012). The SPARK *Reference Manual* (SPARK Team, 2014a) contains the specification of the subset of Ada used in SPARK and the aspects that are SPARK specific. As stated in Chapter 1, a major goal of SPARK 2014 was to embody the largest possible subset of Ada 2012 amenable to formal analysis. The following Ada 2012 features are not currently supported by SPARK:

- Aliasing of names; no object may be referenced by multiple names
- Pointers (access types) and dynamic memory allocation
- Goto statements
- Expressions or functions with side effects
- Exception handlers
- Controlled types; types that provide fine control of object creation, assignment, and destruction
- Tasking/multithreading (will be included in future releases)

This chapter and Chapter 3 cover many, but not all, of the features of Ada 2012 available in SPARK. We discuss those features that are most relevant to SPARK and the examples used in this book. We assume that the reader has little, if any, knowledge of Ada. Barnes (2014) presents a comprehensive description of the Ada programming language. Ben-Ari (2009) does an excellent job describing the aspects of Ada relevant to software engineering. Dale, Weems, and McCormick (2000) provide an introduction to Ada for novice programmers. Ada implementations of the common data structures can be found in Dale and McCormick (2007). There are also many Ada language resources available online that you may find useful while reading this chapter, including material by English (2001), Riehle (2003), and Wikibooks (2014).

Let us start with a simple example that illustrates the basic structure of an Ada program. The following program prompts the user to enter two integers and displays their average.

```
1   with Ada.Text_IO;
2   with Ada.Integer_Text_IO ;
3   with Ada.Float_Text_IO;
4   procedure Average is
5      -- Display the average of two integers  entered  by  the  user
6      A :  Integer ;    -- The first  integer
7      B :  Integer ;    -- The second integer
8      M : Float ;        -- The average of the two integers
9   begin
10     Ada.Text_IO.Put_Line (Item => "Enter two integers." );
11     Ada.Integer_Text_IO . Get (Item => A);
12     Ada.Integer_Text_IO . Get (Item => B);
13     Ada.Text_IO.New_Line;
14
15     M := Float (A + B) / 2.0;
16
17     Ada.Text_IO.Put (Item => "The Average of your two numbers is " );
18     Ada.Float_Text_IO . Put (Item => M,
19                          Fore => 1,
20                          Aft  => 2,
21                          Exp  => 0);
22     Ada.Text_IO.New_Line;
23   end Average;
```

The first three lines of the program are *context items*. Together, these three context items make up the *context clause* of the program. The three *with clauses* specify the library units our program requires. In this example, we use input and output operations from three different library units: one for the input and output of strings and characters (Ada.Text_IO), one for the input and output of integers (Ada.Integer_Text_IO), and one for the input and output of floating point real numbers (Ada.Float_Text_IO). The bold words in all our examples are *reserved words*. You can find a list of all seventy-three reserved words in section 2.9 of the ARM (2012).

Following the context clause is the specification of our program on line 4. In this example, the specification consists of the name Average and no parameters. The name is repeated in the last line that marks the end of this program unit. Comments start with two adjacent hyphens and extend to the end of the line. In our listings, comments are formatted in italics.

Following the program unit's specification is the *declarative part* (lines 5–8). In our example, we declared three variables. Variables A and B are declared to be of type Integer, a language-defined whole number type with an implementation-defined range. Variable M is declared to be of type Float, a language-defined floating point number type with an implementation-defined precision and range. The initial value of all three variables is not defined.

The executable statements of the program follow the reserved word **begin**. All but one of the executable statements in our example are calls to procedures (subprograms) defined in various library packages. In the first statement, we call the procedure Put_Line in the library package Ada.Text_IO.

Except for procedure New_Line, all of the procedures called in the example require parameters. Ada provides both *named* and *positional* parameter association. You are probably very familiar with positional parameter association in which the formal and actual parameters are associated by their position in the parameter list. With named parameter association, the order of parameters in our call is irrelevant. Our example uses named association to match up the formal and actual parameters. To use named association, we give the name of the formal parameter followed by the arrow symbol, =>, followed by the actual parameter. In our call to procedure Put_Line, the formal parameter is Item and the actual parameter is the string literal of our prompt. When there is only a single parameter, named parameter association provides little useful information. When there are multiple parameters, however, as in the call to Ada.Float_Text_IO.Put, named parameter association provides information that makes both reading and writing the call easier. The formal parameters Fore, Aft, and Exp in this call supply information on how to format the real number. Details on the formatting of real numbers are given in section A.10.9 of the ARM (2012).

The only statement in our example that is not a procedure call is the assignment statement on line 15 that calculates the average of the two integers entered by the user. The arithmetic expression in this assignment statement includes three operations. First, the two integers are added. Then the integer sum is explicitly converted to a floating point number. Finally, the floating point sum is divided by 2. The explicit conversion (casting) to type Float is necessary because Ada makes no implicit type conversions. The syntax of an explicit type conversion is similar to that of a function call using the type as the name of the function.

You may feel that program Average required more typing than you would like to do. Prefixing the name of each library procedure with its package name (e.g., Ada.Integer_Text_IO) may seem daunting. Of course, most integrated development environments such as the GNAT Programming Studio (GPS) provide smart code completion, making the chore easier. Ada provides another alternative, the *use clause*, which allows us to make use of resources from program units without having to prefix them with the unit name. It is possible that different program units define resources with the same name. For example, both Ada.Text_IO and Ada.Integer_Text_IO include a subprogram called Put. The compiler uses the signature of the subprogram call to determine which Put to call. You will see an error message if the compiler is not able to resolve a name. A shorter version of our Average program that illustrates the use clause follows. We have also used positional parameter association to shorten the parameter lists.

```ada
with Ada.Text_IO;            use Ada.Text_IO;
with Ada.Integer_Text_IO ;   use Ada.Integer_Text_IO ;
with Ada.Float_Text_IO ;     use Ada.Float_Text_IO ;
procedure Average is   -- Shorter version with "use clauses"
   -- Display the average of two integers entered by the user
   A : Integer ;    -- The first integer
   B : Integer ;    -- The second integer
   M : Float ;      -- The average of the two integers
begin
   Put_Line ("Enter two integers .");
   Get (A),
   Get (B);
   New_Line;

   M := Float (A + B) / 2.0;

   Put ("The Average of your two numbers is ");
   Put (M, 1, 2, 0);
   New_Line;
end Average;
```

Throughout the remainder of this book we will make use of prefixing and named parameter association when it makes the code clearer for the reader.

One final note before leaving this simple program. Ada is case insensitive. Thus, the three identifiers – Total, total, and tOtAl – are equivalent. It is considered bad practice to use different casings for the same identifier. A commonly used switch for the GNAT compiler requests that warnings be given for uses of different casings.

2.1 Control Structures

Ada provides two statements for making decisions on the basis of some condition: the if statement and the case statement. Section 5.3 of the ARM (2012)

provides the details of the if statement and section 5.4 provides the details of the
case statement. Ada provides a loop statement with several different iteration
schemes. These schemes are described in detail in section 5.5 of the ARM. In
this section we will provide examples of each control structure.

2.1.1 *If Statements*

Following are some examples of various forms of the if statement.

```
if A < 0 then                  if A = B then
    A := -A;                       F := 3;
    D := 1;                    elsif A > B then
end if;                            F := 4;
                               else
if A in 1 .. 12 then               F := 5;
    B := 17;                   end if;
end if;


if A > B then                  if A >= B and A >= C then
    E := 1;                        G := 6;
    F := A;                    elsif B > A and B > C then
else                               G := 7;
    E := 2;                    elsif C > A and C > B then
    F := B;                        G := 8;
end if;                        end if;
```

Ada provides the following equality, relational, logical, and membership
operators commonly used in the Boolean expressions of if statements.

Equality Operators		Logical Operators	
=	equal	not	logical negation
/=	not equal	and	logical conjunction
Relational Operators		or	logical disjunction
		xor	exclusive or
<	less than	and then	short circuit and
<=	less than or equal to	or else	short circuit or
>	greater than	**Membership Operators**	
>=	greater than or equal to	in	not in

Boolean expressions that include both **and** and **or** operators must include
parentheses to indicate the desired order of evaluation. Section 4.5 of the ARM
(2012) gives a complete listing and description of all of Ada's operators and
the six precedence levels.

2.1.2 *Case Statement*

The case statement selects one of many alternatives on the basis of the value of
an expression with a discrete result. An example of a case statement follows.

```
Success := True;
case Ch is
   when 'a' .. 'z' =>
      H := 1;
   when 'A' .. 'Z' =>
      H := 2;
   when '0' .. '9' =>
      H := 3;
   when '.' | '!' | '?' =>
      H := 4;
   when others =>
      H := 5;
      Success := False;
end case;
```

The case selector may be any expression that has a discrete result. In our
example, the expression is the character variable Ch. Variable Ch is of the
language-defined type Character, a type whose 256 values correspond to the
8-bit Latin-1 values. Ada also provides 16-bit and 32-bit character types, which
are described in section 3.5.2 of the ARM (2012).

Our example contains five case alternatives. The determination of which
alternative is executed is based on the value of the case selector. Each alternative
is associated with a set of discrete choices. In our example, these choices are
given by ranges (indicated by starting and ending values separated by two
dots), specific choices (separated by vertical bars), and **others**, which handles
any selector values not given in previous choice sets. The **others** alternative
must be given last. Ada requires that there be an alternative for every value in
the domain of the discrete case selector. The **others** alternative is frequently
used to meet this requirement.

2.1.3 *Conditional Expressions*

Conditional expressions are not control structures in the classical sense. They
are expressions that yield a value from the evaluation of one or a number of
dependent expressions defined within the conditional expression. Conditional
expressions can be used in places such as declarations and subprogram parameter lists where conditional statements are not allowed. Conditional expressions

can also reduce duplication of code snippets. Ada has two conditional expressions: the *if expression* and the *case expression*.

If Expressions

If expressions are syntactically similar to if statements but yield a value rather than alter the flow of control in the program. Because they yield a single value, if expressions are more limited than if statements. Following are three examples of if statements and, to their right, equivalent assignment statements using if expressions.

```
if  A > B then    C := ( if  A > B then D + 5 else F / 2);
    C := D + 5;
else
    C := F / 2;
end if ;
```

```
if  A > B then    C := ( if  A > B then D + 5 elsif A = B then 2 * A else F / 2);
    C := D + 5;
elsif  A = B then
    C := 2 * A;
else
    C := F / 2;
end if ;
```

```
if  X >= 0.0 then    Y := Sqrt ( if  X >= 0.0 then X else −2.0 * X);
    Y := Sqrt (X);
else
    Y := Sqrt (−2.0 * X);
end if ;
```

Notice that the if expressions are enclosed in parentheses and do not include **end if**. You may nest if expressions within if expressions. The expressions such as D + 5, F / 2, and 2 * A within the if expression are called *dependent expressions*. In the last example, the if expression determines whether X or −2X is passed to the square root function.

If the type of the expression is Boolean, you may leave off the final else part of the if expression. The omitted else part is taken to be True by default. Thus, the following two if expressions are equivalent:

(**if** C − D = 0 **then** E > 2 **else** True)   (**if** C − D = 0 **then** E > 2).

Boolean if expressions are commonly used in preconditions, postconditions, and loop invariants. Here, for example, is a precondition that states that if A is less than zero then B must also be less than zero. However, if A is not less than zero, the precondition is satisfied (True).

```
Pre => (if A < 0 then B < 0);
```

This if expression implements the implication $A < 0 \rightarrow B < 0$. We look more at implications in Chapter 5 in our discussion of the basics of mathematical logic.

Case Expressions

Case expressions return a value from a number of possible dependent expressions. As you might expect, case expressions are syntactically similar to case statements. The following case expression assigns the Scrabble letter value for the uppercase letter in the variable Letter[1].

```
Value := (case Letter is
           when 'A' | 'E' | 'I' | 'L' | 'U' |
                'N' | 'O' | 'R' | 'S' | 'T'    => 1,
           when 'D' | 'G'                      => 2,
           when 'B' | 'C' | 'M' | 'P'          => 3,
           when 'F' | 'H' | 'V' | 'W' | 'Y'    => 4,
           when 'K'                            => 5,
           when 'J' | 'X'                      => 8,
           when 'Q' | 'Z'                      => 10);
```

In this example the dependent expressions are all simple integer literals. Case expressions with Boolean dependent expressions are commonly used in preconditions, postconditions, and loop invariants. While we may leave off the final else part of an if expression, a case expression must have a dependent expression for every possible value the case selector (Letter in our example) may take. The compiler would complain if we had omitted any of the twenty-six uppercase characters.

2.1.4 *Loop Statements*

Ada's loop statement executes a sequence of statements repeatedly, zero or more times. The simplest form of the loop statement is the infinite loop. Although it may at first seem odd to have a loop syntax for an infinite loop, such loops are common in embedded software where the system runs from the time the device is powered up to when it is switched off. Following is an example of such a loop in an embedded temperature controller. It obtains the current temperature from an analog-to-digital converter (ADC) and adjusts the output of a gas valve via a digital-to-analog converter (DAC).

```
loop
   ADC.Read (Temperature);           -- Read the temperature from the ADC
   Calculate_Valve (Current_Temp => Temperature,  -- Calculate the new
                    New_Setting  => Valve_Setting); -- gas valve setting
   DAC.Write (Valve_Setting);        -- Change the gas valve setting
end loop;
```

We use an exit statement within a loop to terminate the execution of that loop when some condition is met. The exit statement may go anywhere in the sequence of statements making up the loop body. A loop that reads and sums integer values until it encounters a negative sentinel value follows. The negative value is not added to the sum.

```
Sum := 0;
loop
   Ada.Integer_Text_IO.Get (Value);
   exit when Value < 0;
   Sum := Sum + Value;
end loop;
```

There are two iteration schemes that may be used with the loop statement. The *while* iteration scheme is used to create a pretest loop. The loop body is executed while the condition is true. The loop terminates when the condition is false. The following loop uses a while iteration scheme to calculate an approximation of the square root of X using Newton's method.

```
Approx := X / 2.0;
while abs (X - Approx ** 2) > Tolerance loop
   Approx := 0.5 * (Approx + X / Approx);
end loop;
```

This program fragment uses two operators not found in some programming languages. The operator **abs** returns the absolute value of its operand, and ** is used to raise a number to an integer power.

The *for* iteration scheme is used to create deterministic counting loops. A simple example of this scheme is as follows.

```
for Count in Integer range 5 .. 8 loop
   Ada.Integer_Text_IO.Put (Count);
end loop;
```

As you can probably guess, this loop displays the four integers 5, 6, 7, and 8. Let us look at the details underlying the for iteration scheme. The variable Count in this example is called the *loop parameter*. The loop parameter is not defined in a declarative part like normal variables. Count is defined only for the body of this loop. The range 5 .. 8 defines a discrete subtype with four values. The body of the loop is executed once for each value in this discrete subtype. The values are assigned to the loop parameter in increasing order. Within the body of the loop, the loop parameter is treated as a constant; we cannot modify it. To make our loops more general, we can replace the literals 5 or 8 in our example with any expression that evaluates to an integer type. We will revisit this topic when we discuss types and subtypes later in this chapter.

If we add the reserved word **reverse** to the for loop, the values are assigned to loop parameter in decreasing order. The following for loop displays the four numbers in reverse order.

```
for Count in reverse Integer range 5 .. 8 loop
    Ada.Integer_Text_IO.Put (Count);
end loop;
```

Reversing the order of the values in our example range creates a subtype with a *null range* a subtype with no values. A for loop with a null range iterates zero times. Such a situation often arises when the range is defined by variables. Each of the following for loops displays nothing:

```
A := 9;
B := 2;

for Count in Integer range A .. B loop    -- With a null range, this
    Ada.Integer_Text_IO.Put (Count);      -- loop iterates zero times
end loop;

for Count in reverse Integer range A .. B loop    -- With a null range, this
    Ada.Integer_Text_IO.Put (Count);              -- loop iterates zero times
end loop;
```

2.2 Subprograms

A *subprogram* is a program unit whose execution is invoked by a subprogram call. Ada provides two forms of subprograms: the *procedure* and the *function*. We use a procedure call statement to invoke a procedure. You saw examples of procedure call statements in the program Average at the beginning of this chapter. We invoke a function by using its name in an expression. A function returns a value that is used in the expression that invoked it.

The definition of a subprogram can be given in two parts: a declaration defining its signature and a body containing its executable statements. The specification for package Sorters on page 13 includes the declaration of procedure Selection_Sort . Alternatively, we can skip the subprogram declaration and use the specification at the beginning of the body to define the signature. We will take this second approach in this section and use separate declarations when we discuss packages. Section 6 of the ARM (2012) provides the details on subprograms.

2.2.1 *Procedures*

Let us start with a complete program called Example that illustrates the major features of a procedure.

```
1   with Ada.Text_IO;
2   with Ada.Integer_Text_IO ;
3   procedure Example is
4
5      Limit : constant Integer := 1_000;
6
7      procedure Bounded_Increment
8         (Value    : in out Integer ;   -- A value to increment
9          Bound    : in      Integer ;   -- The maximum that Value may take
10         Changed :     out Boolean)  -- Did Value change?
11      is
12      begin
13         if Value < Bound then
14            Value    := Value + 1;
15            Changed := True;
16         else
17            Changed := False;
18         end if ;
19      end Bounded_Increment;
20
21      Value    : Integer ;
22      Modified : Boolean;
23
24   begin -- procedure Example
25      Ada.Text_IO.Put_Line ("Enter a number.");
26      Ada.Integer_Text_IO . Get (Value);
27      Bounded_Increment (Bound    => Limit / 2,
28                         Value    => Value,
29                         Changed => Modified);
```

```
30    if  Modified then
31         Ada.Text_IO.Put_Line ("Your number was changed to ");
32         Ada.Integer_Text_IO . Put (Item   => Value,
33                                    Width  => 1);
34      end if ;
35   end Example;
```

The first thing you might notice is that our program is itself a procedure. It is called the *main procedure*. Each procedure consists of a declarative part where all of its local resources are defined and a sequence of statements that are executed when the procedure is called. The declarative part of procedure Example contains four declarations: the named constant Limit, the procedure Bounded_Increment, and the two variables Value and Modified. Named constants are assigned values that we may not change. This program also introduces the language-defined type Boolean with possible values True and False.

Execution of our program begins with the executable statements of the main procedure (line 25 of procedure Example). The first statement executed is the call to procedure Put_Line that displays the prompt "Enter a number." The program then obtains a value from the user, calls procedure Bounded_Increment, and finally, based on the actions of the procedure just called, it may display a message.

Parameter Modes

Many programming languages require that programmers assign parameter passing mechanisms such as pass-by-value and pass-by-reference to their parameters. Ada uses a higher level means based on the direction of data flow of the parameter rather than the passing mechanism. Procedure Bounded_Increment illustrates all of the three different modes we can assign to a parameter.

in　　Used to pass data from the caller into the procedure. Within the procedure, an in mode parameter is treated as a constant. The actual parameter may be any expression whose result matches the type of the formal parameter. In our example, parameter Bound has mode in.

out　　Used to pass results out of the procedure back to its caller. You should treat the formal parameter as an uninitialized variable. The actual parameter must be a variable whose type matches that of the formal parameter. In our example, parameter Changed has mode out.

in out　　Used to modify an actual parameter. A value is passed in, used by the procedure, possibly modified by the procedure, and returned to the caller. It is like an out mode parameter that is initialized to the value of the actual parameter. Because a value is returned, the actual parameter must be a variable. In our example, parameter Value has mode in out.

As you might imagine, the SPARK analysis tools make use of these parameter modes to locate errors such as passing an uninitialized variable as an in parameter.

Scope

The scope of an identifier determines where in the program that identifier may be used. We have already seen one example of scope in our discussion of the for loop. The scope of a loop parameter is the body of the loop. You may not reference the loop parameter outside the body of the loop. The scope of every other identifier in an Ada program is based on the notion of *declarative regions*. Each subprogram defines a declarative region. This region is the combination of the subprogram declaration and body. A declarative region is more than the declarative part we defined earlier.

Let us look at the declarative regions defined in program Example on page 28. The declarative region of procedure Example begins after its name (on line 3) and ends with its **end** keyword on line 35. Similarly, the declarative region for procedure Bounded_Increment begins just after its name (on line 7) and ends with its **end** keyword on line 19. Note that Bounded_Increment's declarative region is nested within the declarative region of Example. Also note that Bounded_Increment's declarative region contains the definition of its three parameters.

Where a particular identifier may be used is determined from two rules:

- The scope of an identifier includes all the statements following its definition, within the declarative region containing the definition. This includes all nested declarative regions, except as noted in the next rule.
- The scope of an identifier does not extend to any nested declarative region that contains a locally defined *homograph*.[2] This rule is sometimes called *name precedence*. When homographs exist, the local identifier takes precedence within the procedure.

Based on these rules, the variables Value and Modified may be used by the main procedure Example but not by procedure Bounded_Increment. The constant Limit could be used in both procedure Example and procedure Bounded_Increment. Because Limit is declared within procedure Example's declarative region, Limit is said to be *local* to Example. As Limit is declared in procedure Bounded_Increment's enclosing declarative region, Limit is said to be *global* to Bounded_Increment. The three parameters, Value, Bound, and Changed, are local to procedure Bounded_Increment.

Although global constants are useful, the use of global variables is usually considered a bad practice as they can potentially be modified from anywhere. We use the style of always declaring variables after procedures so that the variables may not be accessed by those procedures. In Chapter 3, we use global variables whose scope is restricted to implement variable packages. We may include a global aspect to indicate that a procedure accesses or does not access global variables. Should a procedure violate its stated global access, the SPARK tools will give an error message.

2.2.2 *Functions*

Functions return a value that is used in the expression that invoked the function. While some programming languages restrict return values to scalars, an Ada function may return a composite value such as an array or record. SPARK restricts all function parameters to mode *in*. This mode restriction encourages programmers to create functions that have no side effects. For the same reason, SPARK functions may use but not modify global variables. Here is an example of a function that is given a real value and acceptable error tolerance. It returns an approximation of the square root of the value.

```
function Sqrt (X : in Float; Tolerance : in Float) return Float is
    Approx : Float;   -- An approximation of the square root of X
begin
    Approx := X / 2.0;
    while abs (X - Approx ** 2) > Tolerance loop
        Approx := 0.5 * (Approx + X / Approx);
    end loop;
    return Approx;
end Sqrt;
```

The signature of this function includes its parameters and the type of the value that it returns. Approx is a local variable that holds our approximation of the square root of X. Execution of the **return** statement completes the execution of the function and returns the result to the caller. You may have multiple return statements in a function. Should you need to calculate a square root in your programs, it would be better to use a function from a library rather than our example code.

Expression Functions

Expression functions allow us to write functions consisting of a single expression without the need to write a function body. The executable code of an expression function is an expression written directly within the specification of the function. Here, for example, is a Boolean expression function that returns

True if the second parameter is twice the first parameter regardless of the sign of either number:

```
function Double ( First     : in  Integer ;
                  Second    : in  Integer ) return Boolean is
  (abs Second = 2 * abs First );
```

Note that the expression implementing function Double is enclosed in parentheses. A common use of expression functions is within assertions such as preconditions, postconditions, and loop invariants. Replacing complex expressions with well-named function calls can make assertions easier to read. Of course, we can also easily reuse the expression in other assertions.

2.3 Data Types

A computer program operates on data stored in memory. Our programs reference this data through symbolic names known as *objects*. An object is declared as either variable or constant. In Ada, every object must be of a specific type. The *data type* establishes the set of possible values that an object of that type may take (its domain) and the set of operations that can be performed with those values. For example, an integer type might have a domain consisting of all of the whole numbers between $-2, 147, 483, 648$ and $+2, 147, 483, 647$. Operations on these numbers typically include the arithmetic operators $(+, -, \times, \div)$, equality operators $(=, \neq)$, and relational operators $(<, >, \leq, \geq)$.

The primary predefined types in Ada are Boolean, Character, Integer, Float, Duration, and String. You are familiar with most of these types from your prior programming experiences. Duration is a real number type used to keep track of time in seconds. As you saw in the examples earlier in this chapter, an Ada variable is declared by writing its name followed by the name of its type. Here are some more examples:

```
Found     : Boolean;
Letter    : Character;
Count     : Integer ;
Distance  : Float ;
```

Constant declarations are similar but require the addition of the word constant and a value:

```
Pay_Taxes : constant Boolean    := True;
Negative  : constant Character  := 'N';
Maximum   : constant Integer    := 1_247_962;
-- Note the use of underscores to
```

```
Origin     : constant Float     := 0.0;
-- improve readability of the literal
File_Name : constant String     := "data.txt";
```

Ada allows us to define our own simple and complex types. Using these types, we can create accurate models of the real world and provide valuable information to the SPARK tools so we can identify errors before the program is executed. Let us look at an example program with an obvious error:

```
with Ada.Float_Text_IO;
procedure Bad_Types is
    Room_Length    : Float;    -- length of room in feet
    Wall_Thickness : Float;    -- thickness of wall in inches
    Total          : Float;    -- in feet
begin
    Ada.Float_Text_IO.Get (Room_Length);
    Ada.Float_Text_IO.Get (Wall_Thickness);
    Total := Room_Length + 2.0 * Wall_Thickness;
    Ada.Float_Text_IO.Put (Item => Total, Fore => 1, Aft => 2, Exp => 0);
end Bad_Types;
```

In this example we have defined three variables, each of which holds a real number. The programmer ignored the comments given with each of these variable declarations and neglected to convert the wall thickness measurement from inches to feet before adding it to the room length measurement. Although the error in this short program is obvious, finding similar errors in large programs requires a great deal of effort in testing and debugging. Ada's type model helps eliminate a wide class of errors from our programs. However, as the example illustrates, we can still have such errors in our Ada programs when we do not take full advantage of the type system to model our values.

SPARK's types are a subset of Ada's types. Ada's access types (pointers) and controlled types are not amenable to formal analysis and therefore not part of SPARK. At the time of this writing, SPARK does not support task types. We expect that to change in the near future. Figure 2.1 shows the relationships among SPARK's various types. The hierarchy in this figure is similar to a class inheritance hierarchy. Type Boolean *is an* enumeration type. An enumeration type *is a* discrete type. The types whose names are in italics in Figure 2.1, such as *Scalar*, are abstract entities used to organize the classification of types. The set of operations available for all Ada types[3] include assignment (:=) and equality testing (= and /=).

Figure 2.1 shows that types are divided into two groups: atomic and composite. A composite type is one whose values may be decomposed into smaller

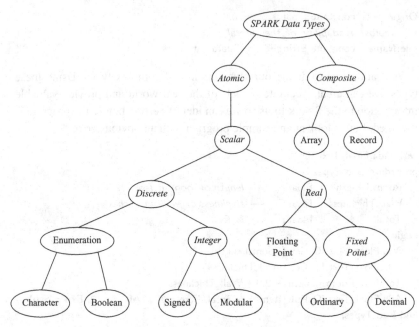

Figure 2.1. The SPARK type hierarchy.

values. A string type is a composite type. A string value is composed of characters. We can access and use the individual characters making up a string. An atomic type is one whose values cannot be decomposed into smaller values. A character type is an atomic type. A character value cannot be decomposed into smaller values. Integers and real numbers are also atomic types.

2.3.1 *Scalar Types*

A scalar type is an atomic type with the additional property of ordering. We can compare scalar values with the relational operators ($<$, $<=$, $>$, and $>=$). Characters, integers, and real numbers are all scalar types.

One of the principles of object-oriented programming is the development of classes that accurately model the objects in the problem. We can apply this same approach to the design of our scalar types. By using scalar types that more accurately reflect the nature of the data in a problem we are solving, we can write better programs. One research study on the nature of costly software faults indicates that poor models of scalar quantities were responsible for nearly 90 percent of the errors in the cases studied (Eisenstadt, 1997; McCormick, 1997). Ada allows programmers to define their own scalar data types that accurately model the scalar values in the problem domain.

Figure 2.1 shows that there are two kinds of scalar types. Real types provide the mechanisms for working with real numbers. A discrete type is a scalar type with the additional property of unique successors and predecessors. We will look at specific real and discrete types in the next sections.

Real Types

The storage and manipulation of real numbers is the substance of the discipline of numerical analysis. The underlying problem with computations involving real numbers is that very few real numbers can be represented exactly in a computer's memory. For example, of the infinite number of real numbers in the interval between 10,000.0 and 10,001.0, only 1,024 are represented exactly in the IEEE 754 single precision representation. The numbers with exact representations are called *model numbers*. The remaining numbers are approximated and represented by the closest model number. The representational error for a particular real number is equal to the difference between it and the model number used to represent it.

Floating Point Types

Here is a revised version of our simple program for adding room dimensions. In place of the language-defined type Float, we have defined two new floating point types: Feet and Inches. Because the variables Room_Length and Wall_Thickness are now different types, the SPARK tools will catch the inappropriate addition of feet and inches we had in our earlier erroneous program.

```
with Ada.Text_IO;
procedure Good_Types is
    -- Declarations of two floating point types
    type Feet   is digits 4 range 0.0 .. 100.0;
    type Inches is digits 3 range 0.0 .. 12.0;

    -- Instantiation of input/output packages for feet and inches
    package Feet_IO is new Ada.Text_IO.Float_IO (Feet);
    package Inch_IO is new Ada.Text_IO.Float_IO (Inches);

    function To_Feet (Item : in Inches) return Feet is
    begin
        return Feet (Item) / 12.0;
    end To_Feet;

    Room_Length    : Feet;
    Wall_Thickness : Inches;
    Total          : Feet;
```

```
begin
   Feet_IO.Get (Room_Length);
   Inch_IO.Get (Wall_Thickness);
   Total := Room_Length + 2.0 * To_Feet (Wall_Thickness);
   Feet_IO.Put (Item => Total, Fore => 1, Aft => 1, Exp => 0);
end Good_Types;
```

The addition of feet and inches requires that we convert a value from one unit to another. We have included a function that makes this conversion. The function To_Feet first does an explicit type conversion (3 inches is converted to 3 feet), which is then divided by 12 to complete the unit conversion.

Our two new floating point types are defined by the type definitions at the beginning of the program. To define a new floating point type, we must specify the minimum number of decimal digits we require in the mantissa in the floating point numbers. This number follows the word **digits** in the type definition. The specification of a range for a floating point type is optional. If the range is omitted, the compiler will create a floating point type with the widest range possible.

We select the minimum number of digits in the mantissa based on the expected precision of our largest value. For our room length, we selected 100 feet as the upper bound of our domain. We estimated that the precision of a measurement of a 100-foot-long room is one-tenth of a foot. Therefore, we need four digits of precision to represent 100.0 – three account for the digits to the left of the decimal point and one for the digit to the right of the decimal point. Should we use a laser range finder with a precision of a thousandth of a foot in place of a tape measure, we would increase the number of digits of precision to six, three on each side of the decimal point. Similarly, we estimated that the precision of a measurement of a 12-inch-thick wall is one-tenth of an inch. So we need a total of three digits of precision for our wall thickness type. The precisions we select are minimums we will accept. The compiler will select the most efficient floating point representation available on the hardware with at least the precision we specify. The most common representations used are those specified by the IEEE 754 standard for floating point representation. We usually consider the precisions specified in our floating point type definitions as documentation on the precision of our actual data.

We cannot use the procedures in the library package Ada.Float_Text_IO to do input and output with values of type Feet and Inches. Ada provides a generic library package that may be instantiated to obtain packages for doing input and output with our own floating point types. You can see the two instantiations for packages Feet_IO and Inch_IO immediately following the definitions of our two floating point types. We talk more about Ada's generic facilities in Sections 2.4.2 and 3.3.3.

Fixed Point Types

As illustrated in Figure 2.1, Ada provides support for two representations of real numbers: fixed point and floating point. Fixed point numbers provide a fixed number of digits before and after the radix point. When we write a real number on paper, we usually use a fixed point format such as

12.75   0.00433   1258.1

In a floating point number, the radix point may "float" to any location. Floating point is the computer realization of scientific notation. A floating point value is implemented as two separate numbers: a mantissa and an exponent. The following are all valid representations of 1,285.1:

$.12581 \times 10^4$ 1.2581×10^3 12.581×10^2
125.81×10^1 1258.1×10^0 $12581. \times 10^{-1}$

Floating point is by far the more commonly used representation for real numbers. In most programming languages, floating point is the only type available for representing real numbers. Floating point types support a much wider range of values than fixed point types. However, fixed point types have two properties that favor their use in certain situations. First, fixed point arithmetic is performed with standard integer machine instructions. Integer instructions are typically faster than floating point instructions. Some inexpensive embedded microprocessors, microcontrollers, and digital signal processors do not support floating point arithmetic. In such cases, fixed point is the only efficient representation available for real numbers.

The second advantage of fixed point is that the maximum representational error is constant throughout the range of the type. The maximum representational error for a floating point type depends on the magnitude of the number. This difference is a result of the distribution of model numbers in each of the representations. The distance between model floating point numbers varies through the range; it depends on the value of the exponent. The distance between model fixed point numbers is constant throughout the range.

Figure 2.2 illustrates the difference in model number distributions. Figure 2.2a shows the model numbers for a very simple floating point representation. There are ten model numbers between 1.0 and 10.0, ten model numbers between 0.1 and 1.0, and ten model numbers between 0.01 and 0.1. Figure 2.2b shows the model numbers for a simple fixed point representation. The distance between model numbers is constant throughout the range. Figure 2.2 shows

a. A simple floating point type   (digits = 1)

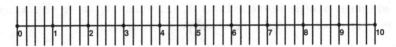

b. A simple fixed point type   (delta = 0.25)

Figure 2.2. Distribution of model numbers.

that the representational error for a floating point number gets larger as the number gets larger, whereas the representational error for a fixed point number is constant throughout its range.

Does the choice of real number representation really make a difference in our applications? "On February 25, 1991, a Patriot missile defense system operating at Dhahran, Saudi Arabia, during Operation Desert Storm failed to track and intercept an incoming Scud [missile]. This Scud subsequently hit an Army barracks, killing 28 Americans" Blair, Obenski, and Bridickas (1992). The Patriot battery failed because of a software problem related to the storage and use of floating point numbers. The system stored time, in tenths of a second, in a floating point variable. Table 2.1, taken from the Government Accounting Office report, shows the magnitude of the error in representing this time as a floating point value. As with all floating point representations, the magnitude of the error increases with the magnitude of the value.

Table 2.1. Magnitude of range gate error when modeling
time as a floating point real number

| Time | | Absolute inaccuracy | Approximate shift in missile range gate |
Hours	Seconds	(Seconds)	(Meters)
0	0.0	0.0	0
1	3600.0	0.0034	7
8	28800.0	0.0275	55
20	72000.0	0.0687	137
48	172800.0	0.1648	330
72	259200.0	0.2472	494
100	360000.0	0.3433	687

Table 2.1 shows that the floating point representation error grows as the number grows. After twenty hours, the time is off enough that the target is outside the range gate and the Patriot missile fails to launch against a threat. After the tragedy, the software was corrected by replacing the floating point time variables with fixed point variables. Let us note that Ada's predefined type Duration is a fixed point type for seconds.

To declare a fixed point type, we specify the maximum distance between model numbers that we are willing to accept. The maximum representational error is half of this distance. We may also specify an optional range for the type. Here are two examples:

```
type Thirds is delta 1.0 / 3.0 range 0.0 .. 100_000.0;
type Volts  is delta 2.0**(−12) range 0.0 .. 5.0;
```

Thirds is a fixed point type with a specified distance of $\frac{1}{3}$ (0.33333...) between model numbers and Volts is a fixed point type with a specified distance of $\frac{1}{4096}$ (0.000244140625) between model numbers. Both of these types are called *ordinary fixed point types*. The actual distance between model numbers in our fixed point type may be smaller than our request. The actual distance between model numbers is the largest power of two that is less than or equal to the value given for delta. So although we specified a delta value of $\frac{1}{3}$ for Thirds, the actual delta used is the power of two, $\frac{1}{4}$ (2^{-2}). The delta we specified for Volts is a power of two so it is used directly. Because the distance between model numbers is some power of two, ordinary fixed point types are sometimes called *binary fixed point types*.

Neither floating point nor ordinary fixed point types are appropriate for currency calculations. Neither is capable of accurate storage of decimal fractions that are so important in commercial applications. Ada's *decimal fixed point types* are the more appropriate choice for such values. Here is an example:

```
type Dollars is delta 0.01 digits 12;
```

For decimal fixed point types, we must specify both a delta that is a power of ten and the number of decimal digits. A range is optional. A value of type Dollars contains twelve decimal digits. Because the distance between model numbers is 0.01, two of these digits are to the right of the decimal point, leaving ten digits for the left side of the decimal point.

We use the generic packages Ada.Text_IO.Fixed_IO and Ada.Text_IO.Decimal_IO to instantiate packages for the input and output of ordinary and decimal fixed point types. You may find the details for the available I/O operations in section A.10.9 of the ARM (2012). Here are the instantiations for our example types:

```
package Thirds_IO is new Ada.Text_IO.Fixed_IO (Thirds);
package Volts_IO is new Ada.Text_IO.Fixed_IO (Volts);
package Dollar_IO is new Ada.Text_IO.Decimal_IO (Dollars);
```

Ada's rules that prevent the mixing of different types are more relaxed for fixed point type multiplication and division. Multiplication and division are allowed between any two fixed point types. The type of the result is determined by the context. So, for example, if we assign the result of multiplying a Volts value and a Thirds value to a Volts variable, the result type of the multiplication would be Volts. Similarly, if we assign the same product to a Thirds variable, the result type of the multiplication would be Thirds. Additionally, a fixed point value may be multiplied or divided by an integer yielding the same fixed point type.

2.3.2 Discrete Types

Recall that a scalar type is an atomic type with the additional property of ordering. A discrete type is a scalar type with the additional property of unique successors and predecessors. The language-defined types Boolean, Character, and Integer are all discrete types. In the next sections we will look at defining our own discrete types.

Enumeration Types

An enumeration type provides a means for defining a type by enumerating (listing) all the values in the domain. The following program illustrates the definition and use of three enumeration types:

```
with Ada.Text_IO;          use Ada.Text_IO;
with Ada.Integer_Text_IO;  use Ada.Integer_Text_IO;
procedure Enum_Example is
   --Declaration of three enumeration types
   type Day_Type is (Monday, Tuesday, Wednesday, Thursday,
                     Friday, Saturday, Sunday);
   type Traffic_Light_Color is (Red, Green, Yellow);
   type Pixel_Color        is (Red, Green, Blue, Cyan,
                               Magenta, Yellow, Black, White);

   package Day_IO is new Ada.Text_IO.Enumeration_IO (Day_Type);

   function Next_Day (Day : in Day_Type) return Day_Type is
   begin
```

```
      if  Day = Day_Type'Last then
          return Day_Type'First;
      else
          return Day_Type'Succ (Day);
      end if;
   end Next_Day;

   Today    : Day_Type;
   Tomorrow : Day_Type;
   Count    : Integer;
begin
   Put_Line ("What day is today?");
   Day_IO.Get (Today);
   Tomorrow := Next_Day (Today);
   Put ("Tomorrow is ");
   Day_IO.Put (Item  => Tomorrow,
               Width => 1,
               Set   => Ada.Text_IO.Lower_Case);
   New_Line;

   if  Today > Tomorrow then
       Put_Line ("Today must be Sunday");
   end if;
   New_Line;

   Put_Line ("The week days are ");
   for  Day in Day_Type range Monday .. Friday loop
       Day_IO.Put (Day);
       New_Line;
   end loop;
   New_Line (2);

   for  Color in  Traffic_Light_Color  loop
       Put_Line ( Traffic_Light_Color 'Image (Color));
   end loop;
   New_Line (2);

   Count := 0;
   for  Color in  Pixel_Color  range Red .. Yellow loop
       Count := Count + 1;
   end loop;
   Put (Item => Count, Width => 1);
end Enum_Example;
```

Each of our three enumeration types is defined by listing literals for all of the values in the domain. These literals are case insensitive. We could also have typed MONDAY or monday for the first value of Day_Type. Notice that Red is both a Pixel_Color literal and a Traffic_Light_Color literal.

We may instantiate packages for the input and output of enumeration values. In our example program, we instantiated the Ada library generic package Enumeration_IO to create the package Day_IO that allows us to get and put day values. You may find the details of the input and output operations available for enumeration values in section A.10.10 of the ARM (2012). Like the defining literals, the input values are not case sensitive. For output, we may select between all uppercase or all lowercase values. The first portion of the main procedure in our example calls procedures get and put in package Day_IO to get a day and display the next day.

Our main subprogram calls the function Next_Day to determine the day that follows the day entered by the user. This function has our first use of attributes. An *attribute* is an operator that yields a characteristic of a type or object. Some attributes require parameters. Here are the most common attributes for scalar types:

'First	Returns the lower bound of the type
'Last	Returns the upper bound of the type
'Image	Returns a string equivalent to the given value
'Value	Returns a value equivalent to the given string

And here are two additional attributes available for discrete types:

'Succ	Returns the successor of the given value
'Pred	Returns the predecessor of the given value

Let us look at the attributes used in program Enum_Example. The expression Day_Type'Last (read "day type *tick* last") in the if statement of our function uses the attribute 'Last to determine the last (largest) value in the domain of the type. As you might expect, the attribute 'First returns the first (smallest) value in the domain of the type. The attribute 'Succ requires a parameter. It returns the successor of the value passed to it. Because there is no successor for the value Sunday in type Day_Type, passing Sunday to the successor attribute function is an error. The purpose of the if statement in function Next_Day is to avoid this error by returning the first day of our type (Monday) for the one case in which the successor function fails. The attribute 'Pred returns the predecessor of a value passed to it. It is an error to use this function to determine the predecessor of the smallest value in the type's domain. You may find descriptions of the attributes available for all scalar types in section 3.5 of the ARM (2012). Additional attributes for all discrete types are described in section 3.5.5. Sections 3.5.8 and 3.5.10 describe attributes available for all floating point and fixed point types.

The next portion of the main subprogram of our example illustrates the use of relational operators with enumeration values. These operators use the order of the literals in each enumeration type definition. Day_Type defines an order of days in which Monday is the smallest day and Sunday is the largest day. The if statement that asks whether Today is greater than Tomorrow is true only when Today is Sunday.

The remainder of our example program illustrates additional variations of the for loop. Our previous for loop examples used only integer loop parameters. A loop parameter may be of any discrete type. Recall that a loop parameter is not declared before the loop. Its type and range are defined by the discrete subtype definition following the reserved word **in**.

The second loop in our example program uses a type name without a range. This loop iterates through all three values of type Traffic_Light_Color displaying each value. We used another approach for displaying the traffic light colors in this loop. The 'Image attribute function returns an uppercase string equivalent to the enumeration parameter. We then used Ada.Text_IO.Put_Line to display this string. The advantage of the 'Image attribute is its simplicity. However, it does not provide the control available for formatting enumeration values available in the put procedures created in instantiations of enumeration I/O packages.

Integer Types

Most programmers use the integer type defined in their language for all variables that hold whole numbers. As we saw earlier in our room length example, using the same type for different quantities may result in logic errors requiring debugging effort. By again using different and appropriate types for our integers, we can have more confidence in our software. Ada provides both signed and unsigned integer types.

Signed Integers. To define a new signed integer type, we need only specify the range. Here are the definitions of three signed integer types and the declaration of a variable of each of those types:

```
type Pome      is range  0 ..  120;
type Citrus    is range −17 ..  30;
type Big_Range is range −20 .. 1_000_000_000_000_000_000;

Apples  : Pome;
Oranges : Citrus ;
Fruit   : Big_Rang;
```

The range of each type is specified by a smallest and largest value, not by some storage unit size such as byte or word. Because they are different types, a comparison of Apples and Oranges is illegal. Of course, should you really want to combine apples and oranges in an expression, you can use explicit type conversions as in

```
Fruit := Big_Range (Apples) + Big_Range (Oranges);
```

Operations available for signed integers include +, −, *, /, **, **abs**, **rem**, and **mod**. The **rem** (remainder on division) and **mod** (mathematical modulo) operators return the same result when both of their operands are positive. Should one of your operands be negative, you should consult the formal definitions of these two similar operators given in section 4.5.5 of the ARM (2012). The attributes 'First, 'Last, 'Succ, 'Pred, and 'Image discussed for enumeration values are also available for signed integers.

To do input and output of our own integer types, we need to instantiate a package from the generic integer I/O package available in the Ada library. Here are the instantiations for the three integer types we defined:

```
package Pome_IO  is new Ada.Text_IO.Integer_IO (Pome);
package Citrus_IO is new Ada.Text_IO.Integer_IO ( Citrus );
package Big_IO    is new Ada.Text_IO.Integer_IO (Big_Range);
```

Modular Integers. Modular integer types are unsigned integer types that use modular arithmetic. The value of a modular integer variable wraps around after reaching an upper limit. To define a modular integer type, we need only specify a modulus. Here are some modular integer type definitions and variable declaration:

```
type Digit  is mod 10;      -- range is from 0 to 9
type Byte   is mod 256;     -- range is from 0 to 255
type Nybble is mod 16;      -- range is from 0 to 15
type Word   is mod 2**32;   -- range is from 0 to 4,294,967,295

Value : Nybble;
```

The following assignment statement illustrates the modular nature of this type:

```
Value := 12 + 8;    -- Value is assigned 4
```

In addition to the usual arithmetic operators, the logical operators **and**, **or**, **xor**, and **not** are available for modular integer types. These operators treat the values as bit patterns. The result of the **not** operator for a modular type is defined as the difference between the high bound of the type and the value of the operand. For a modulus that is a power of two, this corresponds to a bit-wise complement of the binary representation of the value of the operand.

You may recall using the logical operators and bit masks in your assembly language, C, C++, or Java programs to clear, set, and toggle individual bits in a computer's memory. Thus, you might think that Ada's modular types provide the mechanism for Ada programs to manipulate individual bits. Ada provides a much higher level approach to bit manipulation. This topic is beyond the scope of this work. See McCormick, Singhoff, and Hugues (2011) for a full discussion of low level programming with Ada.

Again, we must instantiate packages to do input and output with the types we define. You can find the details on these packages and the get and put procedures in section A.10.8 of the ARM (2012). Here are the instantiations for our four modular types:

```
package Digit_IO  is  new Ada.Text_IO.Modular_IO (Digit);
package Byte_IO   is  new Ada.Text_IO.Modular_IO (Byte);
package Nybble_IO is  new Ada.Text_IO.Modular_IO (Nybble);
package Word_IO   is  new Ada.Text_IO.Modular_IO (Word);
```

2.3.3 *Subtypes*

By defining our own types, we make our programs easier to read and safer from type errors and allow range checking by the SPARK tools. In some cases, values with different constraints are related so closely that using them together in expressions is common and desired. Although explicit type conversion allows us to write such expressions, Ada provides a better solution – the *subtype*. Subtypes allow us to create a set of values that is a subset of the domain of some existing type. Subtypes inherit the operations from their base type. Subtypes are compatible with the type from which they were derived and all other subtypes derived from that type. A subset is defined by specifying an existing type and an optional constraint. Let us look at some examples:

```
subtype Uppercase is  Character range 'A' .. 'Z';
subtype Negative  is  Integer    range Integer'First .. -1;

type    Day_Type is (Monday, Tuesday, Wednesday, Thursday,
                     Friday, Saturday, Sunday);
subtype Weekday is Day_Type range Monday .. Friday;
subtype Weekend is Day_Type range Saturday .. Sunday;

type    Pounds     is digits 6 range 0.0 .. 1.0E+06;
subtype UPS_Weight is Pounds   range 1.0 .. 100.0;
```

```
subtype FedEx_Weight is Pounds  range 0.1 .. 1.0;

subtype Column_Number is Ada.Text_IO.Count;  -- A synonym


Total      : Pounds;
Box        : UPS_Weight;
Envelope : FedEx_Weight;
```

The domain of the subtype Uppercase is a subset of the domain of the language-defined type Character. Objects of subtype Uppercase may be combined with or used in place of objects of type Character. Similarly, the domain of the subtype Negative is a subset of the domain of the language-defined type Integer. The domain of subtypes Weekday and Weekend are both subsets of the programmer-defined type Day_Type. The following assignment statement illustrates the combining of subtypes with the same base type:

```
-- Adding two different subtypes with same base type
Total := Box + Envelope;
```

Subtype definitions may also be used to create synonyms – subtypes with the same domain as their base type. Synonyms are often used to provide a more problem specific name for a type whose name is more general or to eliminate the need to prefix a type name defined in a package. The subtype Column_Number is an example of such a synonym.

There are two commonly used language-defined subtypes defined in Ada. Positive is a subtype of Integer with a range that starts at one. Natural is a subtype of Integer with a range that starts at zero.

2.3.4 *Scalar Types and Proof*

Defining and using our own types and subtypes to accurately model real-world values helps prevent errors in our programs. Selecting appropriate ranges for variables provides an additional benefit when using the SPARK proof tools. Take, for example, the following assignment statement:

```
A := B / C;
```

To prove that the program containing this statement is correct requires the tool to prove that C can never be zero. This proof is much simpler if C is declared to be some type or subtype that does not include zero in its range (for example, subtype Positive). Here is another example whose proof can be simplified by using appropriate ranges:

```
A := (B + C) / 2;
```

Can you see the error lurking in this simple statement? If B and C are both very large numbers, their sum may exceed that of the processor's accumulator. To ensure that this statement is correct, the tool must prove that the sum of the two numbers cannot exceed the maximum accumulator value. By declaring types or subtypes with limited ranges for B and C, the proof tool's job is much easier. Using types and subtypes with appropriate ranges rather than the predefined types Integer and Float will reduce the effort both you and the proof tools expend to verify your program.

2.3.5 *Array Types*

Arrays are composite types whose components have the same type. We access a specific component by giving its location via an index. Defining an array type requires two types: one type or subtype for the component and one type or subtype for the index. The component may be any type. The index may be any discrete type. Here are some examples of array definitions:

```
type Index_Type      is range 1..1000;
type Inventory_Array is array (Index_Type) of Natural;

subtype Lowercase    is Character range 'a' .. 'z';
type    Percent      is range 0..100;
type    Frequency_Array is array (Lowercase) of Percent;

type Day_Type is (Monday, Tuesday, Wednesday, Thursday,
                  Friday, Saturday, Sunday);
type On_Call_Array is array (Day_Type) of Boolean;

Inventory : Inventory_Array;
Control   : Frequency_Array;
Unknown   : Frequency_Array;
On_Call   : On_Call_Array;
```

Variable Inventory is an array of 1,000 natural numbers indexed from 1 to 1,000. Control and Unknown are arrays of 26 percentages indexed from a to z. On_Call is an array of seven Boolean values indexed from Monday to Sunday.

Ada provides a rich set of array operations. Let us start with a selection operation. We use *indexing* to select a particular component in an array. We can use indexing to obtain a value from an array or change a value in an array. Here are some examples using the variables we just defined:

```
Inventory (5)    := 1_234;
Control ('a')    := 2 * Control ('a');
```

```
On_Call (Sunday) := False;

Total_Days := 0;
for Day in Day_Type loop
   if On_Call (Day) then
      Total_Days := Total_Days + 1;
   end if;
end loop;
```

Assignment is another operation available with arrays. As usual, strong typing requires that the source and target of an assignment statement be the same type. The following assignment statement makes the array Unknown a copy of the array Control.

```
Unknown := Control;
```

We can use the equality operators to compare two arrays of the same type. If the array components are discrete values, we can also compare two arrays with any of the relational operators. The relational operators are based on lexicographical order (sometimes called dictionary order) using the order relation of the discrete component type. We frequently use relational operators with arrays of characters (strings). Here is an example that uses two of the array variables we defined earlier:

```
if Control = Unknown then
   Put ("The values in the two arrays are identical");
elsif Control < Unknown then
   Put ("The values in Control come lexicographically before those in Unknown");
end if;
```

Slicing is another selection operation. It allows us to work with sub-arrays. We use slicing to read a portion of an array or write a portion of an array. A range is used to specify the portion of interest. Here are two examples of slicing:

```
-- Copy elements 11-20 into locations 1-10
Inventory (1 .. 10) := Inventory (11 .. 20);

-- Copy elements 2-11 into locations 1-10
Inventory (1 .. 10) := Inventory (2 .. 11);
```

Our second example illustrates slice assignment with overlapping ranges. Such assignments are useful in shuffling the components in an array when inserting or deleting components in an array-based list.

Although indexing and slicing both access components, their results are quite different. The indexing operation accesses a single component. The slicing operation accesses an array. So while the expressions Inventory (5) and Inventory (5..5) are very similar, their result types are very different. Inventory (5) is a natural number, whereas Inventory (5..5) is an array consisting of one natural number.

Our slicing examples also illustrate the sliding feature of array assignment. The index ranges of the source and target of these assignments are different. The ten values in the source array slide into the target array. The range of the indices of the source and target may be different. The two restrictions for array assignment are that the target and source be the same type and that the number of components is the same.

We define multidimensional arrays by defining multiple indices. The following examples illustrate two ways to define an array in which we use two indices to locate a component:

```
type Row_Index is range  1 ..  1000;
type Col_Index is range −5 .. +5;

type Two_D_Array is array (Row_Index, Col_Index) of Float;

type One_Row          is array (Col_Index) of Float;
type Another_2D_Array is array (Row_Index) of One_Row;

Canary : Two_D_Array;      −− A 2−dimensional array variable
Finch  : Another_2D_Array; −− An array of arrays  variable
```

The syntax for indexing a two-dimensional array is different from that for indexing an array of arrays. Here are examples of each kind:

```
−− Assign zero to row 12, column 2 of the 2−D array
Canary (12, 2) := 0.0;

−− Assign zero to the second component of the 12th array
Finch (12)(2)  := 0.0;
```

Slicing is limited to one-dimensional arrays. We cannot slice the array variable Canary. However, we can slice an array in our array of arrays variable Finch.

Constrained and Unconstrained Array Types

All the previous array examples were of constrained arrays. A constrained array type is an array type for which there is an index range constraint. An unconstrained array type definition provides only the type of the index, it does not specify the range of that type. Here is an example:

type Float_Array **is array** (Positive **range** <>) **of** Float;

This statement defines the unconstrained array type Float_Array. The components of this array type are type Float and the index of this array is subtype Positive. We did not specify the range of the positive index. The box symbol, <>, indicates that this is the definition of an unconstrained array type. Because there is no range constraint for this array type, we cannot use an unconstrained array type to declare an array variable because the compiler cannot determine how much memory to allocate to such an array variable.

Illegal   : Float_Array;   -- *This declaration will not compile*

The two important uses of unconstrained array types are (a) as a base for a constrained array subtype and (b) for the type of a formal parameter. Here are examples of constrained array subtypes:

subtype Small_Array **is** Float_Array (1 .. 10);
subtype Large_Array **is** Float_Array (1000 .. 9999);

Small : Small_Array; -- *An array of 10 Float values*
Large : Large_Array; -- *An array of 9,000 Float values*

Because the arrays Small and Large have the same base type, we can combine them in expressions like these:

Large (1001 .. 1010) := Small;   -- *Copy 10 values*
if Small /= Large (2001 .. 2010) **then**   -- *Compare 10 values*
   -- *Copy 21 values*
   Large (2001 .. 2021) := Small & 14.2 & Small;
end if;

The second assignment statement in the preceding example illustrates another array operation, *concatenation*. The & operator may be used to concatenate two arrays, an array and a component, or two components. The result in all cases is an array. In our example, we created a 21 component array by concatenating a copy of array Small with the value 14.2 and a second copy of Small.

Here is an example of a subprogram specification with an unconstrained array parameter:

function Average (Values : **in** Float_Array) **return** Float;

The formal parameter Values will match any actual parameter that is a constrained array subtype of Float_Array. The formal parameter will take on the index constraint of the actual parameter. Here are some calls to function Average using our two previously defined array variables:

```
Avg := Average (Small);                  -- Average of 10 values
Avg := Average (Large);                  -- Average of 9,000 values
Avg := Average (Large (2001..2010));     -- Average of 10 values
Avg := Average (Large & Small);          -- Average of 9,010 values
```

Array Attributes

As you just saw, we can pass different size arrays to function Average. We do not need to pass the size of the array or its starting or ending indices. The function makes use of attributes to obtain the properties of the actual array parameter. Earlier we introduced some of the most commonly used attributes for discrete types. There are attributes for array types as well. The attributes most commonly used with arrays are as follows:

'First	Returns the lower bound of the index range
'Last	Returns the upper bound of the index range
'Length	Returns the number of components in the array
'Range	Returns the index range of the array ('First .. 'Last)

Here is the body of function Average, which uses two of these attributes:

```
function Average (Values : in Float_Array) return Float is
   Sum : Float;
begin
   Sum := 0.0;
   for Index in Values'Range loop
      Sum := Sum + Values (Index);
   end loop;
   return Sum / Float (Values'Length);
end Average;
```

When working with unconstrained array parameters, you should not make any assumptions about the first or last index values. Although many arrays use 1 as a starting index, you should use the attributes rather than make such an assumption.

Section 3.6 of the ARM (2012) provides the details on array types and attributes. There you may also find how to use attributes with multidimensional arrays.

Array Aggregates

An array aggregate is a collection of components enclosed in parentheses. One might think of an array aggregate as an array literal. Aggregates are commonly used to initialize array objects. Here are some examples of using array aggregates to initialize the array variable Small defined earlier:

```
Small := (0.0, 1.0, 2.0, 3.0, 4.0, 5.0, 4.0, 3.0, 2.0, 1.0);  -- by position
Small := (1 .. 10 => 0.0);                                     -- by name
Small := (1 .. 5 => 0.0, 6 .. 10 => 1.0);
Small := (1 | 3 | 5 | 7 | 9 => 0.0, others => 1.0);
Small := (others => A + Sqrt (B));
```

In the first example, the ten components assigned to the array Small are given by position: 0.0 is assigned to Small(1), 1.0 is assigned to Small(2), and so on. In the other examples, we use array indices as names to assign values to specific locations within the array. Similar to the case selector, we can use ranges and individual index values separated by vertical bars to associate locations with values. The others keyword may be used last to associate a value with locations not previously specified. The last example, which calculates a value from the variables A and B, demonstrates that aggregates are not true literals, but simply collections of components.

Array aggregates are available for multidimensional arrays. Let us look at an example. Here is a two-dimensional array of integers with three rows indexed from -1 to 1 and four columns indexed from 1 to 4:

```
type Row_Range  is range −1 .. 1;
type Col_Range  is range 1 .. 4;
type Table_Array is array (Row_Range, Col_Range) of Integer;

Table : Table_Array;   -- 2-dimensional array with 12 elements
```

And here are examples of using aggregates to assign values to Table:

```
-- Assign all elements by position
Table := ((1, 2, 3, 4),
          (5, 6, 7, 8),
          (9, 8, 7, 6));
-- Assign rows by name, columns by position
Table := (−1 => (1, 2, 3, 4),
           0 => (5, 6, 7, 8),
           1 => (9, 8, 7, 6));
-- Assign all elements by name
Table := (−1 => (1 .. 4 => 2),
           0 => (1 .. 3 => 3, 4 => 6),
           1 => (2 => 5, others => 7));
Table := (−1 .. 1 => (1 .. 4 => 0));
Table := (others => (others => 0));
```

Strings

We conclude our discussion of unconstrained arrays with a very brief discussion of Ada's predefined fixed-length string type. Type String is predefined as an unconstrained array of characters with a positive index.

```
—— Type String is defined in Ada.Standard as
type String is array ( Positive range <>) of Character;
```

Here are examples of declarations of a string subtype, a string constant, and several string variables:

```
subtype Name_String is String (1 .. 20);   —— A constrained array type

Currency : constant String := " Dollars";

Name    : Name_String;        —— A string containing 20 characters
Address : String (1 .. 40);   —— A string containing 40 characters
City    : String (3 .. 22);   —— A string containing 20 characters
```

Fixed-length strings are efficient but require more thought in their use than varying-length strings. For example, you may not assign a string of one length to a string of another length. We can make use of array slicing to make assignments to different length strings.

```
Name := Address; —— Illegal Assigning 40 characters to a 20 character  string
Name := "Peter"; —— Illegal Assigning  5 characters to a 20 character  string
Address := Name; —— Illegal Assigning 20 characters to a 40 character  string

City := Name;              —— Legal Both source and target contain 20 characters
Name := Address (1 .. 20); —— Legal Both source and target contain 20 characters
Address := Name & Name;    —— Legal Both source and target contain 40 characters
Address (9 .. 28) := Name; —— Legal Both source and target contain 20 characters
```

In the last statement, only twenty of the forty characters in the variable Address are changed by the assignment.

Should we want to store fewer characters in a fixed-length string than its length, we can make use of additional variables to keep track of the string's "real" length and use that variable to slice the string. Here is an example that demonstrates how we might store five characters in a fixed-length string with a length of twenty.

```
Count := 5;
Name (1 .. Count) := "Peter";
Put (Name (1 .. Count));        —— Display Peter
```

Here is a complete program that uses type String to illustrate constrained array subtypes, slicing, unconstrained array parameters, and array attributes:

```
with Ada.Text_IO;
procedure Palindrome is

    function Is_Palindrome (Item :  in  String) return Boolean is
        Left_Index   : Natural;   -- Two indices mark the beginning and
        Right_Index : Natural;   -- end of the unchecked portion of Item
    begin
        Left_Index   := Item' First ;
        Right_Index := Item'Last;
        loop
            exit  when Left_Index >= Right_Index or else
                        Item (Right_Index) /= Item (Left_Index );
            Left_Index   := Left_Index + 1;
            Right_Index := Right_Index - 1;
        end loop;
        return  Left_Index >= Right_Index;
    end Is_Palindrome;

    Max_Length : constant Positive := 100;
    subtype Line_Type is  String (1 .. Max_Length);

    Line  : Line_Type;   -- Characters entered by user
    Count : Natural;       -- Number of characters entered

begin
    Ada.Text_IO.Put_Line ("Enter a  line ." );
    -- Get_Line reads characters to end of line
    -- Last is the index of the last character read
    Ada.Text_IO.Get_Line (Item => Line,
                            Last => Count);
    -- Slice off garbage before  calling  Is_Palindrome
    if Is_Palindrome (Line (1 .. Count)) then
        Ada.Text_IO.Put_Line (" is a palindrome" );
    else
        Ada.Text_IO.Put_Line (" is not a palindrome" );
    end if;
end Palindrome;
```

The fixed-length string variable Line contains 100 characters. The variable Count keeps track of the index of the last "good" character in Line. The call to procedure Get_Line fills in Line with the characters typed at the keyboard. The

Get_Line procedure reads characters until either the string is filled (100 characters for Line) or it encounters a line terminator. If our user types the word toot and then presses the enter key, the first four characters of Line will be t o o t and the remaining ninety-six characters will be undefined. When we call the function Is_Palindrome, we slice off the garbage passing only the characters entered by the user.

2.3.6 Record Types

Arrays are homogeneous composite types – the components are all of the same type. Records are heterogeneous composite types – the components may be different types. In an array we access a specific component by giving its position in the collection. We access a specific component in a record by giving its name. The following declarations define a simple record type for an inventory system.

```
subtype Part_ID is Integer range 1000 .. 9999;
type     Dollars is delta 0.01 digits 7 range 0.0 .. 10_000.0;

type Part_Rec is
   record
      ID       : Part_ID;
      Price    : Dollars;
      Quantity : Natural;
   end record;

Part       : Part_Rec;
Discount : Dollars;
```

There are three components (fields) defined in type Part_Rec. Each component is identified by a name. The name is used with the variable name to select a particular component in the record. Here are some examples that illustrate component selection:

```
Part.ID         := 1234;
Part.Price      := 1_856.25;
Part.Quantity := 597;
Discount        := 0.15 * Part.Price;
```

Record Aggregates
In the previous example, we used three assignment statements to give the record variable Part a value. We can use a record aggregate to assign a value to a record variable with a single assignment statement. A record aggregate

is a record value written as a collection of component values enclosed with parentheses. The association of values in the aggregate and the record field may be given by position or by name. Here are examples of each:

```
Part := (1234, 1_856.25, 597);  -- Assign values by position

Part := (ID       => 1234,    -- Assign values by name
         Quantity => 597,
         Price    => 1_856.25);
```

When using named association in a record aggregate, we can order the fields as we like.

Discriminants

We often parameterize record types with one or more discriminants. A *discriminant* is a record component on which other components may depend. Whereas ordinary record components can be any constrained type, discriminants are limited to discrete types. The following declarations use a discriminated record to define an array-based list of inventory records. The discriminant, Max_Size, is used to define the index constraint of the array component.

```
type Part_Array is array ( Positive range <>) of Part_Rec;

type Inventory_List  (Max_Size : Positive ) is
   record
      Size  : Natural;
      Items : Part_Array (1.. Max_Size);
   end record;
```

When we use a discriminated record in the declaration of an object, we supply an actual value for the discriminant. The following declaration defines an inventory list that holds a maximum of 1,000 part records:

```
Inventory : Inventory_List (Max_Size => 1000);
```

Inventory is a record with three components: Max_Size, Size, and Items. The last component is an array of part records. Here is some code that accesses the information in this data structure:

```
-- Append a new part to the inventory list
if Inventory . Size = Inventory . Max_Size then
   Put_Line ("The inventory list is full");
else
   Inventory . Size := Inventory . Size + 1;
   Inventory . Items (Inventory . Size) := New_Part;
end if ;
```

2.3.7 *Derived Types*

Subtypes allow us to define subsets of existing types whose values may be combined with any other subtype that shares the same base type. Sometimes we would like to create a new type that is similar to an existing type yet is a distinct type. Here is an example of a definition of a derived type:

```
-- Define a floating point type
type Gallons is digits 6 range 0.0 .. 100.0;
-- Define a new type derived from Gallons
type Imperial_Gallons is new Gallons;
```

Type Imperial_Gallons is a derived type. Gallons is the *parent* of Imperial_Gallons. Derived types are not limited to scalar types. We can derive types from array and record types as well. The domain of the derived type is a copy of the domain of the parent type. Because they are different types, however, values of one type may not be assigned to objects of the other type. We may use explicit type conversions to convert a value of one type to a value of the other type.

The most common use of derived types is in the creation of class hierarchies associated with object-oriented programming. A detailed discussion of classes and inheritance is not in the scope of this book.

2.4 Subprograms, More Options

2.4.1 *Overloading*

We may have two subprograms with the same name as long as their signatures differ. The signature of a subprogram consists of the number, the types, and the order of the parameters. For functions, the type of the returned value is also considered. The formal parameter names and modes are not part of the signature. Here are examples of specifications of three different procedures with the same name:

```
procedure Calc (A : in   Integer ;
                C : out Integer );

procedure Calc (A : in   Integer ;
                C : out Float );

procedure Calc (A : in   Integer ;
                B : in   Integer ;
                C : out Integer );
```

We may also overload operators. Let us look at an example. Here is a record type for the coordinates of a point on a plane and two point variables:

```
type Point is        -- Cartesian coordinates of a point
   record
      X_Coord : Float;
      Y_Coord : Float;
   end record;


P1 : Point;
P2 : Point;
```

The following function, that overloads the $<=$ operator, may be used to determine whether the Left point is the same distance from or closer to the origin than the Right point. Notice that we must enclose the operator symbols in double quotes.

```
function "<=" (Left : in Point; Right : in Point) return Boolean is
-- Returns True when Left is the same distance from
-- or closer to the origin than Right
   Left_Squared  : Float;
   Right_Squared : Float;
begin
   Left_Squared  := Left.X_Coord ** 2 + Left.Y_Coord ** 2;
   Right_Squared := Right.X_Coord ** 2 + Right.Y_Coord ** 2;
   return Left_Squared <= Right_Squared; -- Calls <= for Float numbers
end "<=";
```

Finally, some code that calls function "$<=$". The call may be made as either an infix operator or a normal function call (prefix operator). When the function call syntax is used, the operator must be enclosed in double quotes.

```
-- Function called as an infix operator
if P1 <= P2 then
   Put_Line ("P1 is not further from the origin than P2");
else
   Put_Line ("P1 is further from the origin than P2");
end if;


-- "Normal" function call
if "<=" (P1, P2) then ...
```

2.4.2 *Generic Subprograms*

Ada provides parameterized *generic units* for writing reusable software components. Generic units are templates that can be instantiated to create a unit for a specific application. While the initial effort to create a generic unit may be higher, the long-term savings can be substantial. Not only can we reuse the code in the template, but also we need only test one instance to verify all future instantiations.[4] We have already seen how to use generic packages to create packages for doing input and output with the types we define. Now let us look at writing our own generic units.

Suppose we have written the following function to count the number of times a particular character occurs in a string of characters:

```
function Count (Source   :  in  String;
                Pattern  :  in  Character) return Natural is
-- Returns the number of times Pattern occurs in Source
   Result : Natural := 0;
begin
   for Index in Source'Range loop
      if Source (Index) = Pattern then
         Result := Result + 1;
      end if;
   end loop;
   return Result;
end Count;
```

While this function is specific for counting characters in a string, the same logic could be used for counting occurrences of objects in any array. For each different application we need different types for the parameters Source and Pattern. Rather than write a new counting function for each application, we can write a single generic function and instantiate it as appropriate. We supply the different types for each application through *generic parameters*. We define *generic formal parameters* in the specification of the generic unit and supply *generic actual parameters* when we instantiate the generic unit for a particular application. Ada provides many different kinds of generic formal parameters with specific rules for what actual parameters may be supplied. Table 2.2 shows the commonly used generic formal types with descriptions of what generic actual types are acceptable. See the ARM (2012), Barnes (2014), or Wikibooks (2014) for a complete list.

Let us start with our type for Pattern. This type is also the type of the components in the array we wish to process. There are no restrictions on what

Table 2.2. Some of Ada's generic formal types

Generic formal type	Acceptable generic actual types
type T is range <>;	Any signed integer type.
type T is mod <>;	Any unsigned integer (modular) type.
type T is (<>);	Any discrete type.
type T is digits <>;	Any floating point type.
type T is delta <>;	Any ordinary fixed point type.
type T is delta <> digits <>;	Any decimal fixed point type.
type T is array (Indx) of Cmp;	Any array type with index of type Indx and components of type Cmp. The formal and actual array parameters must both be constrained or both be unconstrained.
type T is private;	Any type for which assignment and equality testing are available (nonlimited).
type T is limited private;	Any type at all.

type the component of an array can be. We do, however, need to compare a component in our array to Pattern so this type must be one for which the equality operator is defined. The generic formal parameter type **private** meets this requirement. Any type that has assignment and equality testing may be supplied as an actual parameter for a private generic formal type – that is every type we have seen at this point.

The generic formal parameter type for the array is a little more complicated. We have three decisions to make:

1. What types should we allow for the index of the array?
2. Should the array type be constrained or unconstrained?
3. What types should we allow for the component of the array?

Our selection for the type of Pattern has already given us the answer to the third question – it can be any type. As an unconstrained array type can be of any length; it is more general than a constrained array type. Indeed, our original example's array type was an unconstrained array of characters indexed by positive numbers. We could choose to use a positive index for our array. However, we can be more general. The only restriction on the index of an array is that it must be a discrete type. The formal generic parameter type (<>) will match any discrete actual type. By now your head is probably spinning with all of this new terminology so let us go right to the code that implements all this text. Here is the specification of a general object counting function:

```
generic
    type Component_Type is private;  -- Any type with assignment and equality testing
    type Index_Type    is (<>);  -- Any discrete type
    type Array_Type    is array (Index_Type range <>) of Component_Type;
function Generic_Count (Source  : in Array_Type;
                        Pattern : in Component_Type) return Natural;
-- Returns the number of times Pattern occurs in Source
```

A generic unit begins with the keyword **generic**, followed by a list of generic formal parameters, followed by the unit specification. Let us review the choice of generic formal parameters in this example. Component_Type is a formal type that will match any actual type that allows assignment and equality testing. Index_Type is a formal type that will match any discrete actual type. Finally, Array_Type is a formal type that will match any actual unconstrained array type that is indexed by the actual type given for Index_Type and has components of the actual type given for Component_Type.

Now let us create some actual counting functions from our generic function. Here are the types for an unconstrained array of percentages indexed by character:

```
type Percent is range 0 .. 100;
type Percent_Array is array (Character range <>) of Percent;
```

Here is the instantiation of a function to count how many times a particular percentage value occurs in an array:

```
function Percent_Count is new Generic_Count
                  (Component_Type => Percent,
                   Index_Type      => Character,
                   Array_Type      => Percent_Array);
```

And here is a call to our newly created function using an array aggregate with ten values for the Source and the literal 5 for the Pattern:

```
The_Count := Percent_Count (Source  => (5, 6, 7, 5, 3, 4, 19, 16, 5, 23),
                            Pattern => 5);
```

Let us look at another instantiation of the generic function. This time, we will look at one that counts the number of times a particular character occurs

in a string – an equivalent of the nongeneric function we gave at the beginning
of this section – and a sample call.

```
function Char_Count is new Generic_Count
                        (Component_Type => Character,
                         Index_Type     => Positive,
                         Array_Type     => String);

The_Count := Char_Count (Source => "How now brown cow",
                         Pattern => 'w');
```

Writing a separate specification for nongeneric subprograms is optional.
Generic subprograms must be written with separate specifications and bodies.
The executable code of Generic_Count is identical to the original function we
wrote for counting character occurrences in a string.

```
function Generic_Count (Source  : in Array_Type;
                        Pattern : in Component_Type) return Natural is
    Result : Natural := 0;
begin
    for Index in Source'Range loop
        if Source (Index) = Pattern then
            Result := Result + 1;
        end if;
    end loop;
    return Result;
end Generic_Count;
```

When writing the body, we have no idea of what actual types will be supplied
for Array_Type and Component_Type. So, what operations can we apply to the
parameters Source and Pattern? All we know about Source is that it is an
unconstrained array indexed by some discrete type. We made use of the array
attribute 'Range and array indexing in this body. We have no idea of the type of
the parameter Pattern. However, we do know that it supports assignment and
equality testing. It is only the latter that we needed to implement the function.

Let us make this counting logic even more general. Perhaps we would like
to know how many values in an array of percentages are greater than ninety.
Or, how many values in an array of Cartesian points are inside a circle of radius
of 1.0 centered on the origin. To accomplish these tasks, we need to replace
the equality test in the if statement with a test for some other property. To
accomplish this task, we make use of generic formal subprograms. As our last

example was of a generic function, this time we will write a generic procedure. Here is its specification:

```
generic
    type Component_Type is limited private;   —— Any type
    type Index_Type     is (<>);              —— Any discrete type
    type Array_Type     is array (Index_Type range <>) of Component_Type;
    with function Selected (From_Source : in  Component_Type;
                            Pattern     : in  Component_Type) return Boolean;
procedure Tally (Source  : in  Array_Type;
                 Pattern : in  Component_Type;
                 Result  : out Natural);
—— Returns the number of items in Source that are selected  for a given Pattern
—— Calls function Selected to determine if an element in Source  qualifies
```

This generic procedure has three generic formal type parameters and one generic formal function parameter. We have changed the type of the generic formal parameter Component_Type to **limited private**. This change allows the component to be of any type, even if it should not have assignment and equality testing operations. The new generic formal parameter Selected is a function that takes two Component_Type parameters and returns a Boolean value. In our application, we can pass any actual function that has the same signature as function Selected. Here, for example, is an instantiation of this generic procedure that tallies the number of percentage values in an array that is greater than some value. The actual function passed for the generic formal function parameter Selected is the > for percents so it returns True when a percent value in the array Source is greater than the percentage in Pattern.

```
—— Instantiate a procedure to determine how many percentages
—— in an array indexed by characters are greater than some value
procedure Tally_Percents is new Tally (Component_Type => Percent,
                                       Index_Type     => Character,
                                       Array_Type     => Percent_Array,
                                       Selected       => ">");
```

Types Percent and Percent_Array are defined on page 61. Here is a sample call of the procedure we instantiated from the generic procedure Tally to count all the values in an array greater than five.

```
—— Determine how many values in My_Percents are greater than 5
Tally_Percents (Source  => My_Percents,
                Pattern => 5,
                Result  => The_Count);
```

Summary

SPARK is a subset of the Ada language. This is a summary of the Ada features in the SPARK subset that are discussed in this chapter.

- Ada provides all of the control structures expected in a high level programming language.
- If expressions and case expressions may be used to select a value from a number of dependent expressions.
- The loop statement and exit statement may be used to implement any iteration scheme.
- The for loop option may be used to implement counting loops.
- The while loop option may be used to implement pre-test loops.
- Ada provides two kinds of subprograms: procedures and functions.
- Parameter passing modes are based on direction of data flow not on the underlying passing mechanism.
- The nested structure of an Ada program provides a powerful mechanism for controlling the scope of identifiers.
- Ada's type model is perhaps the most important feature, giving Ada a significant advantage over other programming languages.
- Programmer-defined scalar types allow us to more accurately model the problem we are solving.
- Ada provides both floating point and fixed point representations for real numbers.
- Ada provides both signed and unsigned (modular) representations for integer numbers.
- Enumeration types allow us to create types by listing all possible values in the domain.
- Attributes provide information about a type or object.
- Subtypes allow us to create a set of values that is a subset of the domain of some existing type.
- We may index our arrays with any discrete data type; we are not limited to integer indices.
- Indexing allows us to access an element of an array.
- Slicing allows us to access a portion of an array; a slice is an array.
- Unconstrained array types allow us to define formal array parameters that match any size actual array parameter.
- Records are heterogeneous composite data types.
- Derived types allow us to create a new and different type from an existing type.

- Subprogram names may be overloaded provided each has a different signature. The signature consists of the number and types of parameters and, for functions, the type returned.
- Generic units allow us to write code that may be reused in other applications.

Exercises

2.1 What is the purpose of the *with clause*?

2.2 Where is the *declarative part* of an Ada program located?

2.3 Define the following terms:
   a. formal parameter   f. local variable
   b. actual parameter   g. global variable
   c. dependent expression   h. data type
   d. loop parameter   i. model number
   e. scope   j. attribute

2.4 What is meant by *parameter association*? Describe how parameters are associated with *named parameter association* and *positional parameter association*.

2.5 What is the purpose of the *use clause*?

2.6 True or False? Ada is case sensitive.

2.7 Write an if statement that checks three integer variables, A, B, and C, and displays one of the three messages: "Two of the values are the same," "All three values are the same," or "All of the values are different."

2.8 Ada has two different operators for *and* (**and** and **and then**) and two different operators for *or* (**or** and **or else**). The latter operator in each case is called the *short circuit* form. Read section 4.5.1 of the ARM and then explain the difference between the normal and short circuit forms of these logical operators.

2.9 Which of the four if statements in the examples given on page 22 could be translated into if expressions?

2.10 Why cannot the case statement example on page 23 be translated into a case expression?

2.11 Write a loop that displays all of the integers between 0 and 100 that are evenly divisible by 3.

2.12 True or False? A for loop with a null range executes exactly one iteration.

2.13 Write a procedure that swaps the contents of its two integer parameters.

2.14 Write a function that returns the larger of its two real parameters.

2.15 What two characteristics does a data type define?

2.16 Suppose we have a type for complex numbers. Why is this type not an atomic type?

2.17 Why is 5.3 not the unique successor of 5.2?

2.18 Errors in quantities can be expressed in absolute terms or relative terms. For each of the following quantities, determine which type of error (absolute or relative) makes more sense, then declare the most appropriate Ada type for that quantity:
    a. Distances in light years to various galaxies in the universe
    b. Altitude in feet of an aircraft
    c. Number of gallons of gasoline in a car's fuel tank
    d. Bank account balance

2.19 Write a Boolean function called Nearly_Equal that returns True if two float numbers are nearly equal. Two numbers are considered nearly equal if the absolute value of their difference is less than 0.001 percent of the smaller number.

2.20 Suppose we have a type for a choice in the game rock-paper-scissors with a domain consisting of the three possible player choices.
    a. Why is this type an atomic type?
    b. Is this type a scalar type? Explain your answer.

2.21 What, if any, are the restrictions on the types we may use for the *components* of an array type? What, if any, are the restrictions on the types we may use for the *index* of an array type?

2.22 Declare an array type whose components are positive whole numbers indexed by Pixel_Color (defined on page 40).

2.23 Given the following unconstrained array type

```
type Int_Array is array (Character range <>) of Integer;
```

complete the following function that returns the value of the largest value in the array:

```
function Max (Items : in Int_Array) return Integer is
```

2.24 Given the following array type that defines an unconstrained array of real numbers:

```
type Float_Array is array ( Positive range <>) of Float;
```

2.25 Why is the following variable declaration illegal? Write a declaration for a string variable suitable for holding a person's name.

```
Name : String;
```

Write an instantiation of the generic procedure Tally given on page 63 that tallies up the number of floating point numbers in an array that are nearly equal to a given number. Make use of the function Nearly_Equal you wrote for Exercise 2.19.

2.26 Given the following array types that define an unconstrained array of Cartesian points (defined on page 58) indexed by Natural integers, an array variable that holds 100 points, and a variable that holds a count of points:

```
type      Point_Array is array (Natural range <>) of Point;
subtype Point_List   is Point_Array (101 .. 200);

My_Points   : Point_List ;
Point_Tally : Natural;
```

a. Write an instantiation of the generic procedure Tally given on page 63 that tallies up the number of points in an array that are not further from the origin than a given point. You may use the function "<=" defined on page 58.

b. Write a call to the procedure you instantiated to tally the number of points in the array My_Points that are on or inside a circle of radius 1.0. Put the result into the variable Point_Tally. You may either declare a variable to hold a pattern point or use a record aggregate in your procedure call.

3

Programming in the Large

DeRemer and Kron (1975) distinguished the activities of writing large programs from that of writing small programs. They considered large programs to be systems built from many small programs (modules), usually written by different people. It is common today to separate the features of a programming language along the same lines. In Chapter 2, we presented the aspects of Ada required to write the most basic programs. In this chapter, we discuss some of Ada's features that support the development of large programs.

To facilitate the construction of large programs, Ada makes use of programming units. An Ada program consists of a main subprogram that uses services provided by library units. A *library unit* is a unit of Ada code that we may compile separately. Library units are often called *compilation units*. We have already made use of many predefined library units in our examples. The *with clause* provides access to a library unit. The *use clause* provides direct visibility to the public declarations within a library unit so we do not have to prefix them with the name of the library unit.

A library unit is a subprogram (a procedure or function), package, or generic unit. The main subprogram is itself a library unit. Subprograms, packages, and generic units that are nested within another programming unit are not library units; they must be compiled with the programming unit in which they are nested. Generally, we use a compiler and linker to create an executable from a collection of library units. Library units also play a role in mixing SPARK and non-SPARK code in a single program – a topic we discuss in Chapter 7. In the following sections, we will introduce you to the package and to generic units.

Encapsulation and information hiding are the cornerstones of programming in the large. Both concepts deal with the handling complexity. There are two aspects of encapsulation: the combining of related resources and the separation of specification from implementation. In object-oriented design and programming, we use encapsulation to combine data and methods into a single entity called a *class*. Encapsulation also allows us to separate what methods a class supplies for manipulating the data without revealing how those methods are implemented.

The *package* is Ada's construct for encapsulation. The package supports abstract data types, separate compilation, and reuse. We write packages in two parts: the package declaration and the package body. The declaration specifies the resources the package can supply to the rest of the program. These resources may include types, subtypes, constants, variables, and subprograms. The package body provides the implementation of the subprograms defined in the package declaration.

Information hiding is related to but different than encapsulation. Encapsulation puts things into a box. Whether that box is opaque or clear determines whether the information is hidden or not.

Information hiding is what we do in the design process when we hide the decisions that are most likely to change. We hide information to protect the other portions of our design from changes to that decision. Modern programming languages provide mechanisms to ensure that details of a design are not accessible to portions of our program that do not need those details.

Information hiding ensures that the users of a class are not affected when we make a change to the implementation of that class. Suppose, for example, our program makes use of a sorted list. If we were to change the implementation of that list from one based on linked lists to one based on arrays, information hiding ensures that this change has no affect on the parts of our program that use a sorted list.

The major Ada construct for information hiding is the *private type*, which is introduced in Section 3.3.2. Private subprograms and private child packages are additional Ada constructs for restricting access to design details.

Although there are many different ways to define and use packages, we can usually place packages into one of four categories: definition packages, utility packages, type packages, and variable packages. This classification scheme is neither strict nor inclusive. In the following sections we will look at an example from each category.

3.1 Definition Packages

A definition package groups together related constants and types. Such packages are useful when the same types must be used in several different programs

or by different programmers working on different parts of one large program.
Here is an example of a definition package:

```
with Ada.Numerics;
package Common_Units is

    type Degrees is digits 18 range 0.0  ..  360.0;
    type Radians is digits 18 range 0.0  ..  2.0 * Ada.Numerics.Pi;

    type Volts is delta 1.0 / 2.0**12 range −45_000.0 .. 45_000.0;
    type Amps  is delta 1.0 / 2.0**16 range −1_000.0 .. 1_000.0;
    type Ohms  is delta 0.125         range  0.0 .. 1.0E8;

    type Light_Years is digits 12 range 0.0  .. 20.0E9;

    subtype Percent is  Integer range 0  ..  100;
end Common_Units;
```

This package defines six types and one subtype. It uses the value of π from
the Ada library definition package Ada.Numerics. Because definition packages
have no subprograms, there is nothing to implement. In fact, the compiler will
give us an error should we try to compile a body for it. Here is a short program
that uses our definition package:

```
with Common_Units; use type Common_Units.Ohms;
with Ada.Text_IO;  use Ada.Text_IO;
procedure Ohms_Law is

    package Ohm_IO is new Fixed_IO (Common_Units.Ohms);
    package Amp_IO is new Fixed_IO (Common_Units.Amps);
    package Volt_IO is new Fixed_IO (Common_Units.Volts);

    A  : Common_Units.Amps;
    R1 : Common_Units.Ohms;
    R2 : Common_Units.Ohms;
    V  : Common_Units.Volts;
begin
    Put_Line ("Enter current and two resistances");
    Amp_IO.Get (A);
    Ohm_IO.Get (R1);
    Ohm_IO.Get (R2);
    V := A * (R1 + R2);
    Put ("The voltage drop over the two resistors  is ");
```

```
Volt_IO.Put (Item => V,
             Fore => 1,
             Aft  => 2,
             Exp  => 0);
  Put_Line (" volts");
end Ohms_Law;
```

This program also illustrates the *use type clause*. When we declare a type, we define its domain and a set of operations. As type Ohms is a fixed point type, the operations include all of the standard arithmetic operators. To add two resistance values, we use the plus operator. However, because this operator is defined in package Common_Units, we must either prefix the plus operator with the package name or include a use clause to access the operator directly. A use clause makes all of the resources in the named package available without prefixing. A use type clause is more specific; it allows us to use operators[1] of the given type without prefixing.

3.2 Utility Packages

A utility package groups together the constants, types, subtypes, and subprograms necessary to provide some particular service. The library package Ada.Numerics.Elementary_Functions is a utility package that includes twenty-nine mathematical functions such as square root, trigonometric functions, and logarithms for Float values. There is also a generic version of this mathematical package that may be instantiated for any floating point type. Here is the declaration of a utility package that provides three operations for control over output displayed on a screen:

```
package Display_Control is

  procedure Bold_On;
  -- Everything sent to the screen after this procedure
  -- is called will be displayed in bold characters

  procedure Blink_On;
  -- Everything sent to the screen after this procedure
  -- is called will be blinking

  procedure Normal;
  -- Everything sent to the screen after this procedure
  -- is called will be displayed normally

end Display_Control;
```

The implementation of these three operations depends on the display hardware. Having placed this dependency in a package body allows us to use the operations without knowledge of that hardware. Here is a body for this package with the implementation for a display that supports ANSI escape sequences. It includes one procedure body for each procedure declared in the package specification.

```
with Ada.Text_IO;
with Ada.Characters.Latin_1;   -- Characters in the
                               -- ISO 8859-1 character set
package body Display_Control is

-- Assumes that the display accepts and processes American
-- National Standards Institute (ANSI) escape sequences.

    -- Code to start an ANSI control string (the Escape
    -- control character and the left bracket character)
    ANSI_Start : constant String :=
                    Ada.Characters.Latin_1.ESC & '[';

    procedure Bold_On is
    begin -- "ESC[1m" turns on Bold
        Ada.Text_IO.Put (ANSI_Start & "1m");
        -- Send any buffered characters to the display
        Ada.Text_IO.Flush;
    end Bold_On;

    procedure Blink_On is
    begin -- "ESC[5m" turns on Blink
        Ada.Text_IO.Put (ANSI_Start & "5m");
        Ada.Text_IO.Flush;
    end Blink_On;

    procedure Normal is
    begin -- "ESC[0m" turns off all attributes
        Ada.Text_IO.Put (ANSI_Start & "0m");
        Ada.Text_IO.Flush;
    end Normal;

end Display_Control;
```

This package body uses resources from two library packages. Although not necessary in this package body, bodies may include additional subprograms.

These helper subprograms are local to the package body; they may not be called from outside.

3.3 Type Packages

We use the type package to create abstract data types (ADTs). An *abstract data type* consists of a set of data values and associated operations that are specified independent of any particular implementation. The abstract data type is a fundamental concept of Ada (Dale and McCormick, 2007; Barnes, 2014; Ben-Ari, 2009). Our example for an abstract data type is a bounded queue. Here is the package declaration for a bounded queue whose elements are integers:

```
package Bounded_Queue_V1 is
-- Version 1, details of the queue type are not hidden

   subtype Element_Type is Integer ;

   type Queue_Array is array ( Positive range <>) of Element_Type;
   type Queue_Type (Max_Size : Positive ) is
      record
         Count : Natural;      -- Number of items
         Front : Positive ;    -- Index of first  item
         Rear  : Positive ;    -- Index of last item
         Items : Queue_Array (1 .. Max_Size);   -- The element array
      end record;

   function Full (Queue : in Queue_Type) return Boolean;

   function Empty (Queue : in Queue_Type) return Boolean;

   function Size (Queue : in Queue_Type) return Natural;

   function First_Element (Queue : in Queue_Type) return Element_Type
      with
         Pre => not Empty (Queue);

   function Last_Element (Queue : in Queue_Type) return Element_Type
      with
         Pre => not Empty (Queue);

   procedure Clear (Queue : in out Queue_Type)
      with
         Post => Empty (Queue) and then Size (Queue) = 0;
```

```
procedure Enqueue (Queue : in out Queue_Type;
                   Item   : in       Element_Type)
    with
       Pre  => not Full (Queue),
       Post => not Empty (Queue) and then
               Size (Queue) = Size (Queue'Old) + 1 and then
               Last_Element (Queue) = Item;

procedure Dequeue (Queue :    in out Queue_Type;
                   Item   :    out Element_Type)
    with
       Pre  => not Empty (Queue),
       Post => Item = First_Element (Queue'Old) and then
               Size (Queue) = Size (Queue'Old) - 1;
```

end Bounded_Queue_V1;

This package defines a queue type as a record with five components (a discriminant and four fields) and eight queue operations. Five of the queue operations include contracts for preconditions and postconditions. We will get to those shortly. But first, let us look at a short program that uses the abstract queue type defined in the package specification.

```
with Bounded_Queue_V1; use Bounded_Queue_V1;
with Ada.Text_IO;      use Ada.Text_IO;
procedure Bounded_Queue_Example_V1 is
-- Uses the first version of the bounded queue package

    My_Queue : Bounded_Queue_V1.Queue_Type (Max_Size => 100);
    Value    : Integer ;

begin
    Clear (My_Queue); -- Initialize queue
    for Count in Integer range 17 .. 52 loop
       Enqueue (Queue => My_Queue, Item => Count);
    end loop;
    for Count in Integer range 1 .. 5 loop
       Dequeue (Queue => My_Queue, Item => Value);
       Put_Line ( Integer 'Image (Value));
    end loop;
    Clear (My_Queue);
    Value := Size (My_Queue);
    Put_Line ("Size of cleared queue is " & Integer 'Image (Value));
end Bounded_Queue_Example_V1;
```

The first declaration in this example program defines a bounded queue with a maximum size of 100. For clarity, we chose to prefix the type Queue_Type in our declaration of the variable My_Queue even though the use clause allows us to omit the package name. After the loop enqueues thirty-six values, the program dequeues five values and displays them. After clearing the queue, it displays the size of the queue.

All that remains is to complete the body of our queue package where we implement the queue operations defined in the package specification. Here is the body of our bounded queue package:

```
package body Bounded_Queue_V1 is

    function Full (Queue : in Queue_Type) return Boolean is
    begin
        return Queue.Count = Queue.Max_Size;
    end Full;

    function Empty (Queue : in Queue_Type) return Boolean is
    begin
        return Queue.Count = 0;
    end Empty;

    function Size (Queue : in Queue_Type) return Natural is
    begin
        return Queue.Count;
    end Size;

    function First_Element (Queue : in Queue_Type) return Element_Type is
    begin
        return Queue.Items (Queue.Front);
    end First_Element;

    function Last_Element (Queue : in Queue_Type) return Element_Type is
    begin
        return Queue.Items (Queue.Rear);
    end Last_Element;

    procedure Clear (Queue : in out Queue_Type) is
    begin
        Queue.Count := 0;
        Queue.Front := 1;
        Queue.Rear  := Queue.Max_Size;
    end Clear;
```

```
procedure Enqueue (Queue : in out Queue_Type;
                   Item   : in       Element_Type) is
begin
   Queue.Rear := Queue.Rear rem Queue.Max_Size + 1;
   Queue.Items (Queue.Rear) := Item;
   Queue.Count := Queue.Count + 1;
end Enqueue;

procedure Dequeue (Queue : in out Queue_Type;
                   Item   :     out Element_Type) is
begin

   Item := Queue.Items (Queue.Front);
   Queue.Front := Queue.Front rem Queue.Max_Size + 1;
   Queue.Count := Queue.Count - 1;
end Dequeue;

end Bounded_Queue_V1;
```

3.3.1 *Introduction to Contracts*

The contracts in our queue package specification (page 73) are given in the form of aspects. An *aspect* describes a property of an entity. Ada 2012 defines nearly seventy different aspects that we may use in our programs. In this chapter, we will look at a few of these standard aspects. An implementation of Ada may provide additional aspects. We will begin our look at SPARK specific aspects in Chapter 4.

The specification of a typical aspect consists of a name, an arrow (=>), and a definition. Take, for example, the postcondition aspect of procedure Clear:

```
procedure Clear (Queue : in out Queue_Type)
   with
      Post => Empty (Queue) and then Size (Queue) = 0;
```

The name Post indicates that this aspect is a postcondition for the procedure. This aspect requires a Boolean definition after the arrow. Our Boolean definition is an expression that includes calls to the queue functions Empty and Size. Postconditions are expected to be true after completion of the operation. In this case, after Clear completes its execution we expect that the queue will be empty and have a size of zero. Of course, there could be an error in the implementation of procedure Clear. We need to verify that Clear does indeed meet its postcondition.

Testing is the obvious way to verify this procedure. We could write a test program that enqueues items into a queue, clears the queue, and finally calls and displays the values returned by functions Empty and Size. Ada 2012 provides a quicker way of testing postconditions. By setting a compiler option, we can have the Ada compiler generate code to check contracts at runtime. Should any postcondition in the program not be true on completion of a subprogram call, the program will halt with a runtime error stating which postcondition was violated.

Executing the postcondition definition at the end of every subprogram call increases the running time of our programs. And, of course, just because our test runs never find a violation of a postcondition does not mean that the subprogram is correct for all possible executions. SPARK provides another approach to verifying postconditions. We can use the GNATprove tool to formally verify the postcondition without executing the code. We will discuss this static verification approach in Chapter 6.

Now let us look at the contract for procedure Enqueue.

```
procedure Enqueue (Queue : in out Queue_Type;
                   Item   : in       Element. Type)
   with
      Pre  => not Full (Queue),
      Post => not Empty (Queue) and then
              Size (Queue) = Size (Queue'Old) + 1 and then
              Last_Element (Queue) = Item;
```

The aspect name Pre indicates a precondition for a subprogram. This Boolean expression should be true each time the subprogram is called. As with postconditions, the Boolean expression may include function calls. In this example, the precondition tells us that the procedure Enqueue should not be called when the queue is full. As with postconditions, setting a compiler option will generate code to check the precondition each time the subprogram is called. Should a precondition in the program not be true for a subprogram call, the program will halt with a runtime error stating which precondition was violated. We may also use the GNATprove tool to statically verify that all subprogram calls in our program meet the given preconditions.

The postcondition for procedure Enqueue states that, after calling the procedure, the queue is not empty, its size has been increased by one, and the item is the last element of the queue. The logic of the size expression illustrates the use of the 'Old attribute to refer to the original value of an **in out** mode parameter. In our example, after calling procedure Enqueue, the size of the resulting queue (Queue) is one greater than the size of the queue before the call (Queue'Old).

As preconditions refer to the state of the parameters before the call, the 'Old
attribute may not be used in them. The precondition **not** Full (Queue) refers to
the queue that is passed in to be modified by the procedure.

We use the 'Result attribute to refer to the result of a function in its postcondition. Here, for example, is a function that returns the square root of a natural
number:

```
function Sqrt (Item :  in  Natural) return Natural
    with
        Post => Sqrt'Result ** 2 <= Item and then
                (Sqrt'Result + 1) ** 2 > Item;
```

The postcondition states that the result of the function is the largest whole
number whose square is less than or equal to the parameter Item.

3.3.2 Information Hiding

The details of the type Queue_Type defined in our queue package specification on
page 73 are public. Programmers using this package may ignore the operations
defined in the package and access the components of the record directly to
manipulate a queue. They may set the fields defining a queue with inconsistent
or invalid states. Should we later change the record defining the queue type,
the parts of the program that accessed the original components would fail.
This approach is at odds with the concept of information hiding. By enforcing
information hiding we can eliminate the possibilities for inconsistency while
ensuring that changes to the implementation details have no affect on other
parts of the program.

Ada uses the *private type* for information hiding. Here is a second version of
our queue package that uses a private type to protect the details that comprise
our queue type:

```
package Bounded_Queue_V2 is
-- Version 2, details of the queue type are hidden

    subtype Element_Type is Integer ;

    type Queue_Type (Max_Size : Positive) is private ;

    function Full (Queue : in Queue_Type) return Boolean;

    function Empty (Queue : in Queue_Type) return Boolean;

    function Size (Queue : in Queue_Type) return Natural;
```

```
function First_Element (Queue : in Queue_Type) return Element_Type
   with
      Pre => not Empty (Queue);

function Last_Element (Queue : in Queue_Type) return Element_Type
   with
      Pre => not Empty (Queue);

procedure Clear (Queue : in out Queue_Type)
   with
      Post => Empty (Queue) and then Size (Queue) = 0;

procedure Enqueue (Queue : in out Queue_Type;
                   Item  : in      Element_Type)
   with
      Pre  => not Full (Queue),
      Post => not Empty (Queue) and then
              Size (Queue) = Size (Queue'Old) + 1 and then
              Last_Element (Queue) = Item;

procedure Dequeue (Queue : in out Queue_Type;
                   Item  :     out Element_Type)
   with
      Pre  => not Empty (Queue),
      Post => Item = First_Element (Queue'Old) and then
              Size (Queue) = Size (Queue'Old) - 1;

private

type Queue_Array is array ( Positive range <>) of Element_Type;
type Queue_Type (Max_Size : Positive) is
   record
      Count : Natural  := 0;      -- Number of items
      Front : Positive := 1;      -- Index of first item
      Rear  : Positive := Max_Size;  -- Index of last item
      Items : Queue_Array (1 .. Max_Size);   -- The element array
   end record;

end Bounded_Queue_V2;
```

The first change to notice in this version is that the definition of Queue_Type has been changed from a record type to **private**. An application programmer may use this type to declare queue variables. As with the public record implementation in our first version, the discriminant Max_Size is used to give a maximum size to each queue object. The operations on a private type object available to a programmer are limited to those defined in the package specification (Full, Empty, Clear, Enqueue, and Dequeue in our example), assignment, and equality testing.

The second change is the division of the specification into two parts by the keyword **private** written just after the definition of procedure Dequeue. Everything above the word **private** may be freely used by an application programmer. This part of the package specification is called the *visible part*. Everything below the word **private** is hidden. This part of the package is called the *private part*. A client programmer using this package may see these details when they read the specification, but they may not reference them in their programs. In our example, the details of the array type used to store the elements of a queue and the record type that actually defines the queue type are *private*. Application programmers may not manipulate the fields of the queue record as they could with our first version. They must call the public operations in the package to manipulate a queue.

The package body for our hidden version that implements the operations is identical to that of the public version. A copy is available on http:// www.cambridge.org/us/academic/subjects/computer-science/programming-languages-and-applied-logic/building-high-integrity-applications-spark. The sample application we gave on page 74 that made use of our queue type may be used with the hidden version simply by changing the imported package name.

3.3.3 *Generic Packages*

Both versions of our queue package define a queue type whose elements are integers. To create a type for a queue of characters, we could copy the integer queue package specification and body, change the type of the element from integer to character, and compile our new files. Ada's generic packages provide a simpler and safer approach. In Chapter 2 we used generic packages from the Ada library to create packages for the input and output of our own scalar types. Now we look at writing such a package. We use generic parameters to supply the information needed by the compiler to customize our package. With our queue, we need only supply the type of the element we wish to store in our queues. Table 2.2 lists the most commonly used generic formal types. As the queue package body makes use of element assignment and the contracts in the queue specification make use of element equality testing, the appropriate generic formal type is **private**. Here is the specification of a generic queue package that can be instantiated for any element type that has assignment and equality testing operations:

generic
    type Element_Type **is private** ;
package Bounded_Queue **is**
$--$ *Final version, generic with hidden details*

    type Queue_Type (Max_Size : Positive) **is private** ;

    function Full (Queue : **in** Queue_Type) **return** Boolean;

    function Empty (Queue : **in** Queue_Type) **return** Boolean;

    function Size (Queue : **in** Queue_Type) **return** Natural;

    function First_Element (Queue : **in** Queue_Type) **return** Element_Type
        with
            Pre $=>$ **not** Empty (Queue);

    function Last_Element (Queue : **in** Queue_Type) **return** Element_Type
        with
            Pre $=>$ **not** Empty (Queue);

    procedure Clear (Queue : **in out** Queue_Type)
        with
            Post $=>$ Empty (Queue) **and then** Size (Queue) $= 0$;

    procedure Enqueue (Queue : **in out** Queue_Type;
                    Item   : **in**   Element_Type)
        with
            Pre $=>$ **not** Full (Queue),
            Post $=>$ **not** Empty (Queue) **and then**
                    Size (Queue) $=$ Size (Queue'Old) $+ 1$ **and then**
                    Last_Element (Queue) $=$ Item;

    procedure Dequeue (Queue : **in out** Queue_Type;
                    Item   :   **out** Element_Type)
        with
            Pre $=>$ **not** Empty (Queue),
            Post $=>$ Item $=$ First_Element (Queue'Old) **and then**
                    Size (Queue) $=$ Size (Queue'Old) $- 1$;

private

    type Queue_Array **is array** (Positive **range** $<>$) **of** Element_Type;

```
type Queue_Type (Max_Size : Positive) is
  record
      Count : Natural   := 0;     -- Number of items
      Front : Positive  := 1;     -- Index of first  item
      Rear  : Positive  := Max_Size;  -- Index of last  item
      Items : Queue_Array (1 .. Max_Size);  -- The element array
  end record;
```

```
end Bounded_Queue;
```

The reserved word **private** is used for two different purposes in this package. It is used in the definition of the generic formal parameter Element_Type to specify that the actual parameter can be any type that has assignment and equality testing. The generic package body may only use those operations with values of this type. The second use of **private** in our generic package specification is in the definition of Queue_Type. As before, this type restricts the operations that can be used in an application to those defined in the package. In both situations, private restricts access to details. In a generic formal parameter, it restricts the writer of the package body. In a type declaration, it restricts the application using the type. The third time the word **private** appears in this package (eleven lines up from the bottom on a line by itself) relates to the second usage. As we discussed in the previous section, the details of our private Queue_Type are given below this line. Everything above this line is public and accessible to other program units.

When we instantiate a queue package from this generic package, we supply an actual parameter that is the type of the desired queue component. Here is a version of our queue application revised to use the generic queue package to instantiate a queue type with character components:

```
with Bounded_Queue;
with Ada.Text_IO;   use Ada.Text_IO;
procedure Bounded_Queue_Example is
    -- Uses the generic version  of the bounded queue package

    -- Instantiate a queue package with  character elements
    package Char_Queue is new Bounded_Queue (Element_Type => Character);
    use Char_Queue;

    My_Queue : Char_Queue.Queue_Type (Max_Size => 100);
    Value    : Character;

begin
    Clear (My_Queue); -- Initialize  queue
```

```
for Char in Character range ' f '  ..  ' p ' loop
   Enqueue (Queue => My_Queue, Item => Char);
end loop;
for Count in Integer range 1  ..  5 loop
   Dequeue (Queue => My_Queue, Item => Value);
   Put (Value);
   New_Line;
end loop;
Clear (My_Queue);
Put_Line (" Size of cleared queue is " & Integer ' Image (Size (My_Queue)));
end Bounded_Queue_Example;
```

3.4 Variable Packages

A variable package is used to encapsulate a single object. This concept is sometimes called a *singleton* or *singleton class*. As an example, we look at some packages that might be used in a simulation of the game of Bingo. Players of this game manage a number of different Bingo cards. As there are many cards involved, we would use a type package with appropriate operations to model them. When the game is played, numbers are randomly drawn from a single source. We can use a variable package to model this source. We begin with a definition package that describes the numbers used in Bingo.

```
package Bingo_Numbers is

-- This package defines BINGO numbers and their associated letters

   -- The range of numbers on a Bingo Card
   type Bingo_Number is range 0  ..  75;

   -- 0 can't be called , it  is  only  for  the Free Play square
   subtype Callable_Number is  Bingo_Number range 1 .. 75;

   -- Associations between Bingo numbers and letters
   subtype B_Range is Bingo_Number range 1  ..  15;
   subtype I_Range is Bingo_Number range 16 .. 30;
   subtype N_Range is Bingo_Number range 31 .. 45;
   subtype G_Range is Bingo_Number range 46 .. 60;
   subtype O_Range is Bingo_Number range 61 .. 75;

   -- The 5 Bingo letters
   type Bingo_Letter is  (B, I, N, G, O);

end Bingo_Numbers;
```

Here is the specification of a variable package that models the basket from which Bingo numbers are drawn:

```
with Bingo_Numbers; use Bingo_Numbers;
package Bingo_Basket is

    function Empty return Boolean;

    procedure Load    -- Load all the Bingo numbers into the basket
        with
            Post => not Empty;

    procedure Draw (Letter : out Bingo_Letter;
                    Number : out Callable_Number)
    -- Draw a random number from the basket
        with
            Pre => not Empty;

end Bingo_Basket;
```

Notice that there is no type for a Bingo basket and no basket parameter for any of the operations. The package body hides a single basket. All three operations act on this hidden basket object. Here is that body:

```
with Ada.Numerics.Discrete_Random;
package body Bingo_Basket is

    type Number_Array is array (Callable_Number) of Callable_Number;
    The_Basket : Number_Array; -- A sequence of numbers in the basket
    The_Count : Bingo_Number; -- The count of numbers in the basket

    package Random_Bingo is new Ada.Numerics.Discrete_Random
                            (Result_Subtype => Callable_Number);
    use Random_Bingo;
    -- The following object holds the state of a random Bingo number generator
    Bingo_Gen : Random_Bingo.Generator;

    procedure Swap (X : in out Callable_Number;
                    Y : in out Callable_Number) is
        Temp : Callable_Number;
    begin
        Temp := X; X := Y;  Y := Temp;
    end Swap;
```

```
function Empty return Boolean is (The_Count = 0);
-- Example of an expression function

procedure Load is
    Random_Index : Callable_Number;
begin
    -- Put all numbers into the basket (in order)
    for Number in Callable_Number loop
        The_Basket (Number) := Number;
    end loop;
    -- Randomize the array of numbers
    Reset (Bingo_Gen);   -- Seed random generator from clock
    for Index in Callable_Number loop
        Random_Index := Random (Bingo_Gen);
        Swap (X => The_Basket (Index),
              Y => The_Basket (Random_Index));
    end loop;
    The_Count := Callable_Number'Last;   -- all numbers now in the basket
end Load;

procedure Draw (Letter : out Bingo_Letter;
                Number : out Callable_Number) is
begin
    Number := The_Basket (The_Count);
    The_Count := The_Count - 1;

    -- Determine the letter using the subtypes in Bingo_Definitions
    case Number is
        when B_Range => Letter := B;
        when I_Range => Letter := I;
        when N_Range => Letter := N;
        when G_Range => Letter := G;
        when O_Range => Letter := O;
    end case;
end Draw;
end Bingo_Basket;
```

The variable The_Basket, an array containing all of the Bingo numbers, is global to all of the operations in this package body. The global variable The_Count keeps track of how many numbers in this array have not yet been drawn. Function Empty returns True when The_Count is zero. Together, these two variables maintain the state of the bingo basket. The variable Bingo_Gen is a random Bingo number generator used globally by the Load operation. Procedure

Swap was not defined in the package specification. It is not a basket operation but a local subprogram called by procedure Load.

3.4.1 *Package Initialization*

A program using our Bingo_Basket package should call the Load operation to initialize the global package variable The_Basket before drawing numbers from it. This explicit initialization is appropriate for this particular variable package as we will likely use this package to play multiple Bingo games. However, some situations require that initialization occur only once. For example, consider the following package that implements a serial number generator:

```
package Serial_Numbers is
    type Serial_Number is range 1000 .. Integer'Last;
    procedure Get_Next (Number : out Serial_Number);
end Serial_Numbers;
```

Calls to procedure Get_Next return the next available serial number. Because we do not want to repeat numbers, we have not included an operation to initialize the sequence. Instead, we set the initial serial number in the package body:

```
package body Serial_Numbers is

    Next_Number : Serial_Number := Serial_Number'First;

    procedure Get_Next (Number : out Serial_Number) is
    begin
        Number := Next_Number;
        Next_Number := Next_Number + 1;
    end Get_Next;

end Serial_Numbers;
```

The declaration of the global package variable Next_Number includes an assignment of an initial value. This value is assigned to the variable during elaboration of this package body. *Elaboration* is the runtime processing of declarations. Elaboration brings the item being declared into existence and then, if the declaration includes an initial value, assigns that value to the item.

When a variable package encapsulates a nontrivial data structure, initializing that data structure may require more than can be accomplished with assignments of initial values to its variables. We may, for example, need a loop to create an initial linked list. Package bodies may include an optional sequence of statements that are executed when the body is elaborated. This initialization code is placed between a **begin** and the **end** of the package. Here is how we might use package initialization code to give Next_Number its initial value:

```
package body Serial_Numbers2 is

    Next_Number : Serial_Number;

    procedure Get_Next (Number : out Serial_Number) is
    begin
        Number := Next_Number;
        Next_Number := Next_Number + 1;
    end Get_Next;

begin -- package initialization code
    Next_Number := Serial_Number'First;
end Serial_Numbers2;
```

There are no restrictions on what may be included in package initialization code. We can call subprograms defined there or in any package. It is, however, wise to keep this initialization code simple to minimize the possibility of an exception being raised. Although package initialization code is primarily used to initialize the state of a variable package (by initializing its global variables), there are no rules against using it in any package that has a body.

When does elaboration occur? Each time we call a subprogram, all of its local declarations are elaborated prior to the execution of the code after the word **begin**. In this case, storage for the local variables is allocated on the stack and any initial values are assigned.

Each package specification and body is elaborated once after the program is loaded. The order in which packages are elaborated must follow the basic rule that a unit must be elaborated before another unit can use a resource within it. For most projects, the Ada compiler can determine a legal elaboration order. However, using packages with mutual dependencies may make it difficult or impossible for the compiler to determine an elaboration order. Ada provides pragmas that we may use to give the compiler hints on a correct order. In some cases, however, it may be necessary to remove mutual dependencies by restructuring the design of the program. Section 3.6 provides additional discussion and examples of elaboration.

3.5 Child Packages

Ada provides a hierarchical naming scheme for library units. A package named Apple may have a child package with the name Apple.McIntosh. Apple is the parent of McIntosh. This naming scheme overcomes problems with uniqueness of names just as a hierarchical file system allows us to distinguish between two files with the same name by keeping them in two different directories. We have seen examples of this hierarchy of package names in the Ada library. Ada is the parent package of all predefined units in the library. Text_IO is a child of Ada containing resources for the input and output of text.

In addition to providing a hierarchy for organizing names, child units provide important information hiding properties. We have seen how private types are used to hide the details of an abstract data type. In our bounded queue type package examples, the record and array defining the implementation are not accessible to program units that use our queue type. These clients must use the operations, such as Enqueue, that we defined in the public portion of the package specification to manipulate queue objects. However, the details of the private type are available in the package body where the operations are implemented. These private details are also available to the private part and body of a child package. This access allows a group of units to share private information while keeping that information hidden from external clients.[2]

This sharing allows us to easily extend an abstract data type. In fact, child packages are the key construct for object-oriented programming features such as inheritance and dynamic dispatching that are beyond the scope of this book. Let us look at an example. Here is the specification of a simple stack type package:

```
package Stacks is
-- Implements a simple stack of integers (with no safety features)
    type Stack_Type (Max_Size : Positive ) is private ;

    procedure Clear (Stack : out Stack_Type);
    function Empty (Stack : in Stack_Type) return Boolean;
    procedure Push (Item  : in     Integer ;
                    Stack : in out Stack_Type);
    procedure Pop (Item :     out Integer ;
                   Stack : in out Stack_Type);
private
    type Stack_Array is array ( Positive range <>) of Integer;
    type Stack_Type (Max_Size : Positive ) is
        record
            Top  : Natural := 0;  -- Initialize all stacks to empty
            Items : Stack_Array (1 .. Max_Size);
        end record;
end Stacks;
```

And here is a child package specification with a new operation for our stack type:

```
package Stacks.More is
    function Peek (Stack : in Stack_Type) return Integer ;
    -- Returns a copy of the top element on the Stack
end Stacks.More;
```

We certainly could have added function Peek to our original stack package. However, that change to the original package would require us to recompile all clients that used it. And, of course, we wanted to illustrate a use of child packages. To that end, here is the body of our child package:

```
package body Stacks.More is
    function Peek (Stack : in Stack_Type) return Integer is
    begin
        return Stack.Items (Stack.Top);
    end Peek;
end Stacks.More;
```

You can see that this body makes use of the details of the stack type given in the private part of the stack package specification.

3.5.1 *Private Children*

Package Stacks.More is an example of a *public child package*. Public child packages allow extension and continued privacy of their private types to provide additional resources for clients.

When developing a subsystem, there are times that we would like to decompose it into pieces without giving clients of that subsystem direct access to those pieces. Ada's *private child package* provides the mechanism for hiding these pieces. The use of resources from a private child package is restricted to the hierarchy of packages rooted at its parent.

To illustrate this role of private child packages, consider a flight management system (FMS). An FMS is a component of the cockpit software that automates a wide variety of in-flight tasks. A primary function of an FMS is in-flight management of the flight plan. Here is an outline of a package that supplies clients with operations on flight plans:

```
package FMS is
    type Flight_Plan is private ;
    . . .
    -- Many operations on flight plans
    . . .
```

```
private
   -- Hidden details of the  flight  plan type
   type Flight_Plan is  ....
end FMS;
```

Navigational databases and position determination are two of the many components making up an FMS. The client of our flight management subsystem has no need to access these two components directly. They are accessed by operations in the FMS that are called by the clients. Therefore, we place these two subsystems into private child packages. Here are the outlines of these two private children:

```
private  package FMS.Navigation_Database is
   . . .
end FMS.Navigation_Database;

private  package FMS.Positioning is
   . . .
end FMS.Positioning;
```

The body of package FMS will with these private packages to use their resources. Client units cannot with these packages.

Let us look at one more level of this FMS design. Position information is obtained through multiple subsystems including the global positioning system, inertial reference systems (IRS), and VHF omnidirectional radio range (VOR). As these three subsystems are components of the positioning system, we make them private child packages of that system.

```
private  package FMS.Positioning.GPS is
   . . .
end FMS.Positioning.GPS;

private  package FMS.Positioning.IRS is
   . . .
end FMS.Positioning.IRS;

private  package FMS.Positioning.VOR is
   . . .
end FMS.Positioning.VOR;
```

In this book we make use of private child packages in the development of hierarchical state abstractions (Sections 4.3.3 and 7.3.3), isolating non-SPARK code from legacy Ada software (Section 8.2), and partitioning unproved SPARK code (Section 9.3.5).

3.5.2 *Visibility and the Child Hierarchy*

Each of the packages in our hierarchy may have both visible and private parts
and a body. These parts and bodies may access parts of other packages in the
hierarchy by default or by withing them. Of course, we can with any public
unit outside the hierarchy. Here are the visibility rules:

* A child specification never needs to *with* its parent; a specification may *with* a
  sibling except that a public child specification may not *with* a private sibling;
  a specification may not *with* its own child.
* A body never needs to *with* its parent.
* The entities of a parent are accessible by simple name within its descendants
  (children, grandchildren, etc.); **use** clauses are not required.
* A **with** clause given in the specification of a parent also applies to its body
  and its descendants.
* A private child is never visible outside the tree rooted at its parent. And
  within that tree, it is not visible to the visible parts of public siblings.
* The private part and body of any child can access the private parts of its
  ancestors (parent, grandparent, etc.).
* The visible part of a private child can access the private parts of its ancestors.
* A **with** clause for a child automatically implies **with** clauses for all its ancestors.
* A **use** clause for a unit makes the resources in its descendants accessible by
  simple name. Those descendants must be *withed*.
* A **private with** clause allows the private part but not the visible part of a
  package to access resources in the named package. A public child may
  private with a private sibling.

Figure 3.1 illustrates the direct visibility between children and parent packages. This visibility is automatic; it does not require any **with** or **use** context
clauses. The arrows show that every private part of a specification has direct
visibility of the visible part of that specification. Every body has access to
everything in its specification and the specification of its parent. Both the visible part and the private part of a private child have direct access to everything
in their parent's specification. The access of a public child is more limited. The
visible part of a public child can only access resources in its parent's visible
part. However, the private part of a public child has direct access to everything
in its parent' specification.

Figure 3.2 shows options for obtaining access to other related units via
with clauses placed at the beginning of a package specification or body. In all
cases, a **with** clause provides access to only the resources in the visible part of

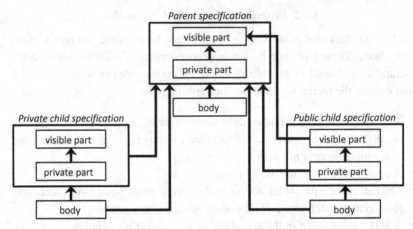

Figure 3.1. Direct visibility with child packages.

the package being withed. The body of a parent package may with any of its descendants. The body of any descendant in the hierarchy, whether private or public, can with any other package in the hierarchy. But as shown in Figure 3.1, no with is needed to access ancestor packages. Whereas the specification of a private child package can with any package in the hierarchy, the specification of a public child may only with other public children.

There are two special forms of the **with** clause. Including a **private with** clause at the beginning of a package's specification allows access to the named package from only the private part of that specification. The dotted arrow in Figure 3.2 representing a **private with** clause shows that resources in a private

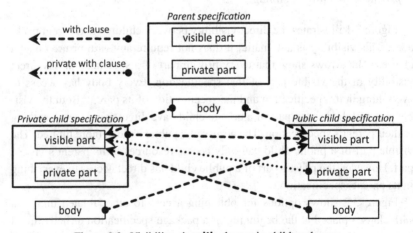

Figure 3.2. Visibility via **with** clauses in child packages.

child's visible part may be used in the private part of a public child. In later chapters, we make use of **private with** clauses to exempt private parts from our SPARK analyses. A **limited with** provides a mechanism for mutually dependent units. We have not used any **limited with** clauses in this book.

Both public and private children can themselves have children of both kinds. A private child of a public child begins a new hierarchy of visibility beginning at its public parent. A private child of a private child also begins a new hierarchy of visibility beginning at its private parent. A public child of a private child extends the specification of the private child. This public child is visible to the bodies of its public uncles (packages sharing the same grandparent as the new public child) and to all parts of its private uncles.

Child packages provide a very flexible mechanism for implementing complex architectures. As usual, it is important to keep the relations between modules as understandable as possible.

3.6 Elaboration

We conclude this chapter with another look at elaboration, a concept introduced in Section 3.4.1. Elaboration is the runtime processing of a declaration, declarative part, or program unit body. This processing occurs during the execution of a program and consists of activities such as allocating space and providing initial values to objects. As shown in Section 3.4.1, the elaboration of a package body may include the execution of the sequence of statements at the end of the body.

Here is a simple example of elaboration in a procedure:

```
procedure Elaboration_Demo (Size  :  in  Positive ;
                            Count :  out Natural)  is
  Line  : String (1 .. Size) := (others => ' ');
  Guess : Float := (1.0 + Ada.Numerics.Elementary_Functions.Sqrt (5.0)) / 2.0;
begin
   . . . .
end Elaboration_Demo;
```

When procedure Elaboration_Demo is called, its declarations are elaborated before the execution of the statements between its **begin** and **end**. Space for the array variable Line with Size components is allocated on the system stack and all its components are initialized to blank. Similarly, space is allocated for Guess and it is initialized to $\frac{1+\sqrt{5}}{2}$, the Golden Ratio.

Subprogram calls are possible during elaboration as demonstrated by the call to the square root function in the initialization of Guess. Such calls allow any arbitrary part of the program to be executed as part of elaboration.

Elaboration can be more complicated with packages as the order in which packages are elaborated is important. Take, for example, the following two skeleton package specifications and bodies:

```
with Pack_B;
package Pack_A is
    Var_1 : Integer  :=  2 * Pack_B.Var_3 / 3;
    . . . .
end Pack_A;
-----------------------
package body Pack_A is
    Var_2 :  Integer := 5 * Pack_B.Var_3 / 6;
    . . . .
end Pack_A;


-----------------------------------------------

package Pack_B is
    Var_3 :  Integer   := 17;
    . . . .
end Pack_B;
-----------------
with Pack_A;
package body Pack_B is
    Var_4 :  Integer  := 3 * Pack_A.Var_1 / 4;
    . . . .
end Pack_B;
```

During the elaboration of the specification of Pack_A, the value of Pack_B. Var_3 is used in the initialization of Var_1. So it is important that the elaboration of the specification of Pack_B be completed before the elaboration of the specification of Pack_A. Similarly, the elaboration of the specification of Pack_B must be completed before the elaboration of the body of Pack_A. Finally, the body of Pack_B uses the value of Pack_A.Var_1 in the initialization of Var_4. So the specification of Pack_A must be elaborated before the body of Pack_B.

The determination of legal orders of elaboration in a program with many packages is a problem that must be solved prior to linking the object code of the packages into an executable file.[3] The GNAT Ada compiler uses a tool called GNATbind that, among other tasks, checks that an acceptable order of elaboration exists for the program and generates a main program incorporating a valid elaboration order.

A program with circular elaboration dependencies has no valid order of elaboration. In such cases, GNATbind issues an error message. It is then up to the programmer to reorganize the packages into a set that does have a valid order of elaboration or provide the binder with additional information so it can find a valid order. Decomposing a package into child packages is one way to remove circular elaboration dependencies.

Appendix C of the *GNAT User's Guide* (GNAT, 2015b) provides an excellent discussion of the elaboration process, elaboration problems, and solutions. These solutions include a number of pragmas that a programmer may use to give additional information to the binder that might allow it to determine a valid order that it could not determine on its own.

Summary

- A library unit is a separately compiled program unit.
- In Ada, library units may be subprograms, packages, or generic units.
- The with clause provides access to the public declarations in a library unit.
- The use clause provides direct visibility of the public declarations in a library unit so we do not have to prefix them with the library unit name.
- Packages provide the logical structure to large software applications.
- Packages are the primary means in Ada for abstraction, encapsulation, and information hiding.
- A package consists of a specification and a body that implements the specification.
- We define a definition package as a package that groups together related constants and types.
- As there are no operations to implement, a definition package has no body.
- We define a utility package as a package that groups together related constants, types, and subprograms that provide some service.
- The type package is used to create abstract data types.
- Private types are used to encapsulate the details of an abstract data type.
- We use aspects to specify preconditions and postconditions for operations in a package.
- We may use an optional compiler switch to generate code to check each precondition and postcondition when our program executes.
- Generic packages are templates that may be instantiated for a specific purpose.
- Generic formal parameters provide the mechanism for customizing generic packages.
- A variable package is used to create singletons – hidden single objects.

- A package may contain initialization code that is executed when the package is elaborated.
- Initialization code is commonly used to initialize the state of a variable package that encapsulates a nontrivial data structure.
- Public and private child packages allow us to decompose subsystems in a structured manner.
- Public children enable the decomposition of the view of a subsystem to the user of the subsystem.
- Private children enable the decomposition of the implementation of a subsystem.
- Private with clauses allow access to the named package's visible part from only the private part of that specification.
- Elaboration is the runtime processing of a declaration, declarative part, or program unit body.

Exercises

3.1 What are the purposes of the *with clause* and *use clause*?

3.2 Define the following terms (some require knowledge from sources outside of this book).

a.	Encapsulation	g.	Aspect
b.	Information hiding	h.	Attribute
c.	Definition package	i.	Precondition
d.	Utility package	j.	Postcondition
e.	Abstract data type	k.	Variable package
f.	Type package	l.	Elaboration

3.3 Look at the specification of the package Ada.Text_IO in section A.10.1 of the Ada Reference Manual. Explain how this package could be classified as a utility package. Explain how this package could be classified as a type package.

3.4 Obtain a copy of the specification and body of the Bounded_Queue_V2 from the http://www.cambridge.org/us/academic/subjects/computer-science/ programming-languages-and-applied-logic/building-high-integrity- applications-spark. Also obtain a copy of the sample application Bounded_Queue_Example_V1.

  a. Make the necessary changes in names so the application will use this second version of the queue package. Build and run the application.

  b. Corrupt the implementation of the dequeue procedure by incrementing the length of the queue rather than decrementing it. Build and run the application. Was the error detected or were the results simply incorrect?

c. Look up the appropriate switch for the compile command that adds code to check the contracts at runtime. Build and run the application with this switch. Was the error detected or were the results simply incorrect?

3.5 Ada uses the reserved word **private** to restrict access to details. Who has complete access (application programmer or package programmer) to the details of a private type? Who has complete access to the details of a private generic parameter?

3.6 Using version 2 of our queue package as a guide, write a type package for a stack whose components are characters. Include appropriate preconditions and postconditions. Write, build, and run a simple test program that uses your stack package.

3.7 Convert the character stack package you wrote in Exercise 3.6 into a generic package that may be instantiated for any component type that supports assignment. Modify your test program, build, and run it.

3.8 Why can we not use the 'Old attribute in preconditions?

3.9 Why does the square root function, Sqrt, defined on page 78 not require a precondition stating that Item is not negative?

3.10 Write the specification of a generic type package for a mathematical set with operations Union, Intersection, Is_Member, Add_Value, Remove_Value, and Make_Empty. Encapsulate the set in a private type. Use an array of Booleans indexed by the set component type to implement the set type. Select an appropriate generic formal parameter type for the set component type. (Hint: What restrictions must we place on the kind of elements we might use in this simple array implementation?) Check the syntax of your package specification.

3.11 Write the body of the set package from the Exercise 3.10. A set is made empty by setting all components in the array to False. An element is added to or removed from a set by setting its component to True or False. The Union operation may be implemented by **or**'ing the corresponding Boolean components in the two arrays to create a resulting array of Booleans. Similarly, the Intersection may be implemented by **and**'ing the corresponding components.

3.12 Write a simple application that uses the generic set package developed in Exercises 3.10 and 3.11. Instantiate a set package whose components are the twenty-six uppercase letters of the alphabet. Write a procedure that displays the letters in a set. (Hint: Write a loop that goes through all twenty-six letters and displays those that are members of the set.) Include code to construct sets and perform operations on them.

3.13 What is *elaboration?* When does elaboration occur for a subprogram?

3.14 Procedure Load in the package body of Bingo_Basket resets the random number generator each time it is called. We need only reset the generator once. Use package initialization to make this change to the body of Bingo_Basket. Also set the initial basket to empty.

3.15 What is the major use of public children in the decomposition of a system? Of private children?

3.16 What restriction does a private with clause impose that is not imposed by a with clause?

4

Dependency Contracts

In this chapter we describe SPARK's features for describing data dependencies and information flow dependencies in our programs. This analysis offers two major services. First, it verifies that no uninitialized data is ever used. Second, it verifies that all results computed by the program participate in some way in the program's eventual output – that is, all computations are *effective*.

The value of the first service is fairly obvious. Uninitialized data has an indeterminate value. If it is used, the effect will likely be a runtime exception or, worse, the program may simply compute the wrong output. The value of the second service is less clear. A program that produces results that are not used is at best needlessly inefficient. However, ineffective computations may also be a symptom of a larger problem. Perhaps the programmer forgot to implement or incompletely implemented some necessary logic. The flow analysis done by the SPARK tools helps prevent the programmer from shipping a program that is in reality only partially complete.

It is important to realize, however, that flow analysis by itself will not show your programs to be free from the possibility of runtime errors. Flow analysis is only the first step toward building robust software. It can reveal a significant number of faults, but to create highly robust systems, it is necessary to use proof techniques as described in Chapter 6.

As described in Chapter 1, there are three layers of analysis to consider in increasing order of rigor:

1. Show that the program is legal Ada that abides by the restrictions of SPARK where appropriate. The most straightforward way to verify this is by compiling the code with a SPARK-enabled compiler such as GNAT.
2. Show that the program has no data dependency or flow dependency errors. Verify this by running the SPARK tools to "examine" each source file.

3. Show that the program is free from runtime errors and that it honors all its contracts, invariants, and other assertions. Verify this by running the SPARK tools to "prove" each source file.

We recommend making these three steps explicit in your work. Move on to the next step only when all errors from the previous step have been remedied. This chapter discusses the second step.

4.1 Data Dependency Contracts

The *data dependency contract* describes what global data a subprogram depends on and whether that data is read, written, or both. The data dependency contract appears as a Global aspect on a subprogram's declaration.

The use of global data is normally discouraged. This is primarily because it is difficult for programmers to reason about the behavior of a program when it makes frequent, undisciplined use of such data. Normally, one expects a subprogram to only read its **in** parameters and modify its **out** parameters. Reads and writes the subprogram makes to global data is not obvious from the call site and is easy to ignore. For example, if a call Process(X, Y) reads a global variable Z, it is easy to forget to initialize Z before the call is made.

SPARK's data dependency contracts allow the programmer to explicitly specify what global data each subprogram uses in a manner that is similar to the way subprogram parameters are specified. Thus, global data read and written is clearly defined as part of each subprogram's declaration. The SPARK tools use this information to ensure all global data is initialized before it is needed and all results written to global data are used. The flow analysis done by the SPARK tools verifies that the body of a subprogram manipulates both parameters and global data as described by the parameter list and the data dependency contract.

As an example, consider the following abbreviated package specification for a package that performs raster graphics drawing:

```
pragma SPARK_Mode (On);
package Raster_Graphics is

    Workspace_Size : constant := 100;
    type Coordinate_Type is new Integer range 1 .. Workspace_Size;
    type Point is
        record
            X, Y : Coordinate_Type;
        end record;
```

```
type Line_Algorithm_Type is (Bresenham, Xiaolin_Wu);
type Status_Type is (Success, Line_Too_Short, Algorithm_Not_Implemented);

Status          : Status_Type;
Line_Algorithm  : Line_Algorithm_Type;
Line_Count      : Natural;

procedure Draw_Line (A, B : in Point)
   with
   Global => (Input => Line_Algorithm,
              Output => Status,
              In_Out => Line_Count);
```

end Raster_Graphics;

The first line of this package specification, **pragma** SPARK_Mode (On), informs the SPARK tools that this unit follows all the rules of the SPARK language. We say that this unit is "in SPARK." We can write programs in which certain units are written in SPARK while other units are written in full Ada or another programming language. We discuss mixing SPARK, full Ada, and C in Chapter 7. We can also use an aspect to state that a unit is in SPARK as follows:

```
package Raster_Graphics
   with Spark_Mode => On
is
```

In this book we use both the pragma and the aspect to state that a unit is in SPARK. We talk more about SPARK mode in Section 7.1.1.

Now let us look at the details of the package specification Raster_Graphics. The package draws on a square workspace of size 100 pixels. It first introduces Coordinate_Type to distinguish other integer values from values used to represent coordinates on the drawing space. The package then defines a record type Point for representing specific two-dimensional positions.

The procedure Draw_Line draws a line between two points A and B. The data dependency contract, as given by the Global aspect, specifies three global variables used by the procedure. Three modes can be used in data dependency contracts to indicate the direction of data flow just as subprogram parameters can use three modes for that purpose. In this case the desired line drawing algorithm is read, a status value representing the success or failure of the procedure is written, and a counter of the total number of lines ever drawn is updated. Each mode can only appear once but can be associated with an arbitrary list of variables enclosed in parentheses.

Global variables used by a subprogram behave similarly to parameters where the actual argument is fixed. However, it is not necessary in the data dependency contract to specify the types of the global variables. To be used in the contract, the variables must be visible at that point in the program. Thus, their types are available from their declarations elsewhere. In the preceding example, the global variables are declared inside the specification of package Raster_Graphics.

One important rule is that the variables mentioned in the data dependency contract have to be entire objects. For example, it is not permitted to use a single array element or record component. The variable must be the entire array or record even if the subprogram accesses only one component of the composite entity.

SPARK also requires that functions only read from global data. Thus, the modes Output and In_Out are illegal for functions. This is consistent with SPARK's restriction that functions have only **in** parameters. It is necessary to ensure that the unspecified evaluation order of subexpressions remains deterministic.

Consider, for example, an assignment statement such as

X := F(A) + F(B);

If F were allowed to output to a global variable, the final result stored in that variable would depend on the order in which the operands to + are evaluated. However, that order is unspecified by the language. To ensure the program always produces well-defined, predictable results, outputs cannot be allowed to depend on such unspecified ordering. The concern is eliminated by forbidding functions from having side effects such as writing to global data. This problem does not arise in the case of procedures because each procedure is called in its own statement, and the order in which statements execute is specified.

Procedure Draw_Line described earlier has two ordinary parameters and makes use of three global variables. One might wonder why some or all of those global variables were not declared as parameters instead. Doing so would be considered better style in the eyes of many developers.

There are, however, at least two cases in which the use of global data is reasonable. Perhaps the most important use of global data is to hold the internal state of a variable package. We used this approach with the Bingo basket package in Section 3.4. We discuss the SPARK aspects for managing internal state in Section 4.3.

Global data is also useful when a nested subprogram accesses the local variables or parameters of an enclosing subprogram. To demonstrate this, consider the following abbreviated body of package Raster_Graphics. For now we will continue to let Draw_Line access three global variables, although, in a more reasonable application, some or all of those global variables might be passed into Draw_Line as parameters.

```
pragma SPARK_Mode(On);
package body Raster_Graphics is

   procedure Draw_Line(A, B : in Point) is

      Min_Distance : constant Coordinate_Type := 2;

      -- Verify that A, B are far enough apart.
      -- Write error code to Status if not.
      procedure Check_Distance
        with
          Global => (Input => (A, B),
                     Output => Status)
      is
         Delta_X : Coordinate_Type := abs (A.X - B.X);
         Delta_Y : Coordinate_Type := abs (A.Y - B.Y);
      begin
         if Delta_X**2 + Delta_Y**2 < Min_Distance**2 then
            Status := Line_Too_Short;
         else
            Status := Success;
         end if;
      end Check_Distance;

   begin
      Check_Distance;
      if Status = Success then
         case Line_Algorithm is
            when Bresenham =>
               -- Algorithm implementation not shown...
               Line_Count := Line_Count + 1;

            when Xiaolin_Wu =>
               Status := Algorithm_Not_Implemented;
         end case;
      end if;
   end Draw_Line;

end Raster_Graphics;
```

We assume, for purposes of illustration, that Draw_Line requires the end points of the line to be sufficiently far apart. Perhaps it is required for very short lines to be represented as large dots, or perhaps the underlying drawing hardware does not work reliably for short lines. In any case Draw_Line needs to check the distance between the points it is given and uses a helper subprogram Check_Distance to do so.

However, from Check_Distance's point of view the parameters of the enclosing procedure, as well as the local variables of the enclosing procedure that are declared above Check_Distance (if any), are global variables. The flow analysis done by the SPARK tools thus requires any global variables that are used to be mentioned in Check_Distance's data dependency contract.

Notice that Check_Distance also writes to the global variable Status. It must specify this in its data dependency contract despite the fact that the enclosing procedure has already done so. The body of each subprogram, even nested subprograms, is analyzed on its own so all information moving into and out of each subprogram must be declared. Flow analysis will ensure that the modes are all consistent. For example, if Check_Distance's data dependency contract was

```
procedure Check_Distance
  with
    Global  => (In_Out => (A, B),
                Output => Status) ...
```

flow analysis would object because A and B are **in** parameters of the enclosing subprogram and thus may not be modified. The constant Min_Distance in the body of package Raster_Graphics is handled differently. Because it is a constant that is initialized with a static expression,[1] it can be used by any of the subprograms for which it is visible without being mentioned in the data dependency contract of those subprograms.

Finally, notice that Draw_Line increments Line_Count. Flow analysis verifies that the mode on that global variable is consistent with this usage. Also, the SPARK tools will understand that, because the global variable has an input mode, it must be initialized in some way before Draw_Line can be called.

4.2 Flow Dependency Contracts

An important part of the flow analysis done by the SPARK tools is to track which values are used in the computation of which results. Techniques for doing flow analysis inside a subprogram are well known and described in detail in, for example, textbooks on compiler design (Aho et al., 2007). However, to accomplish the larger goal of ensuring no information is misused in the overall program, it is necessary to extend flow analysis across subprograms, including across subprograms in different packages.

Ada promotes the construction of large software systems as collections of loosely coupled packages. These packages are developed independently, often in parallel, and only integrated into the final program after they have been separately tested and analyzed. SPARK would be useless for realistic programs if it did not support this style of development.

SPARK allows programwide flow analysis to be carried out on packages independently by requiring the programmer to declare the way information moves into and out of a subprogram as part of that subprogram's declaration. These *flow dependency contracts* are used when analyzing code that calls the subprogram and checked when analyzing the implementation of the subprogram.

As an example, consider a procedure that searches a string for the first occurrence of a given character starting at a given position. It returns a status value of true if the character is found along with its location in the string. The declaration of this procedure might look like the following:

```
procedure Search (Text      : in   String;
                  Letter    : in   Character;
                  Start     : in   Positive ;
                  Found     : out  Boolean;
                  Position  : out  Positive )
   with
      Global  => null,
      Depends => (Found     => (Text, Letter,  Start ),
                  Position  => (Text, Letter,  Start ));
```

The flow dependency contract, expressed using the Depends aspect, describes how each output of the procedure depends on the inputs. In this case the value produced for Found depends on the text being searched, the letter being searched for, and the starting position of the search. The value produced for Position depends on the same three inputs.

Based on the intended behavior, or *semantics*, of Search, it is intuitively clear that the dependencies expressed above are correct. For example, Found clearly depends on Start. If Letter appears only in the first position of the text, the search will succeed if Start is the beginning of the string but fail if Start is in the middle of the string. Similarly, Found clearly depends on the letter being searched for and on the text being searched.

Notice that we can meaningfully declare the flow dependency contract for procedure Search without having to implement it – or even look at its implementation. Thus, the flow dependency contracts can be written in a package specification before the body is written. They represent a formal way of expressing a certain aspect of each subprogram's semantic behavior.

As an aside, we note that Search does not make use of any global data. This can be stated explicitly by adding

```
Global  => null
```

to the aspect specification on Search. However, not specifying data (or flow) dependency contracts explicitly is not necessarily an error. We describe in more detail the effect of leaving off the contracts in Section 4.5.

Let us look at an example that illustrates flow analysis through multiple procedures. Consider another procedure that is intended to take strings in the form "NAME=NUMBER" and return the specified number if the name matches a given name. The declaration of this procedure, with its flow dependency contract, is as follows:

```
procedure Get_Value (Text  :  in       String;
                     Name :  in       String;
                     Value :  in out  Integer )
   with
      Global   => null,
      Depends => (Value => (Text, Name, Value));
```

Here, the intention is for Value to be initialized to a default before Get_Value is called. If the given string is malformed or if it does not include Name as a prefix, Value is unchanged.

The body of Get_Value is as follows:

```
procedure Get_Value (Text   :  in       String;
                     Name :  in       String;
                     Value :  in out  Integer )  is

   Equals_Found     :  Boolean;
   Equals_Position  :  Positive ;
begin
   if  Text'Length > 0 then
      Search (Text      => Text,
              Letter    => '=',
              Start     => Text'First,
              Found     => Equals_Found,
              Position  => Equals_Position);
```

```
if Equals_Found then
    if Name = Text (Text'First .. Equals_Position - 1) then
        Value := Integer'Value (Text ( Equals_Position + 1 .. Text'Last ));
    end if ;
  end if ;
 end if ;
end Get_Value;
```

The assignment to the parameter Value requires the conversion of a string of digits, such as "4932", to an integer. We use the 'Value attribute to accomplish this conversion.

Notice that Get_Value makes use of the procedure Search specified on page 105. When doing the flow analysis of Get_Value, the SPARK tools will know, from the flow dependency contract on the declaration of Search, that Equals_Found depends on Text. Furthermore, because Equals_Found is used in the controlling expression of an if statement, any values written inside that statement also depend, indirectly, on Text. Finally, because Name is used in the controlling expression of the if statement enclosing the assignment to Value, it follows that Value depends on Name. Notice also that Value depends on its own input because, if Equals_Found is false, the procedure returns with Value unchanged.

Our simple "by inspection" analysis has shown that the flow dependency contract is obeyed. However, if the procedure was incomplete, it is possible that some part of the flow dependency contract would be violated and flow analysis would produce diagnostics as appropriate. Flow analysis helps the programmer avoid shipping an incomplete program.

Continuing this example, suppose that later a change is made to Search that changes the way information flows through that procedure. The flow dependency contract on Search would have to be updated to reflect this change. Thus, Get_Value would need to be reanalyzed, and it is possible it might then contain flow errors as a result of the change to Search. In this way, changing the body of Search has the potential of causing a cascade of changes to the callers of Search, to the callers of those callers, and so forth.

This cascade might sound unappealing, but it is no different than what might happen if a parameter was removed from Search's parameter list or if the type of a parameter was changed. In that case, the callers of Search would have to be edited appropriately along with, potentially, the callers of those callers, and so forth. The flow dependency contract is part of the subprogram's interface just as is the parameter list. It serves to expose more information about the subprogram's behavior than can be done by the parameter list alone. The flow analysis done by the SPARK tools checks the consistency of this additional information just as a traditional Ada compiler checks the consistency of each call's arguments.

There are many implementations of Search that will satisfy the parameter types and modes. A large number of those implementations have nothing to do with searching a string for a particular character, despite whatever suggestive names are used. The flow dependency contract rules out some of those implementations as flow errors leaving behind a smaller set of implementations that conform to both the parameter types and modes and the flow dependency contract.

However, it is still easy to see that many incorrect implementations of Search exist that satisfy the flow dependency contract. To further tighten the possibilities, the programmer can use pre- and postconditions to describe more precisely the relationship between the subprogram's outputs and its inputs. We introduced the Pre and Post aspects with the bounded queue package in Section 3.3. We cover these aspects in more detail in Section 6.2.

One important point, however, is that flow dependency contracts must be complete. If you use the Depends aspect at all, you must fully describe all flows into and out of the subprogram, including flows involving global data described by the data dependency contract. In contrast, as you will see, pre- and postconditions are often incomplete. They may not describe every aspect of the relationship between inputs and outputs. In this respect effective use of pre- and postconditions depends significantly on your skill with them and on the proof technology being used. However, flow contracts are more reliable in the sense that your program will simply not pass SPARK examination until it is completely free of flow errors.

4.2.1 *Flow Dependency Contract Abbreviations*

In general, a flow dependency contract consists of an association between each output of a subprogram and a list of the inputs on which that output depends. Writing these associations can be tedious and repetitive so SPARK provides two important abbreviations that make writing flow dependency contracts easier.

First, it is common for multiple outputs to depend on the same inputs. An especially common case, although not universal, is when each output depends on all inputs. The procedure Search shown previously is like this. The syntax of flow dependency contracts allows the programmer to associate a list of outputs with a list of inputs. Thus, a contract such as

```
with
   Depends => (Found => (Text, Letter, Start),
               Position => (Text, Letter, Start))
```

can be abbreviated as

with
    Depends => ((Found, Position) => (Text, Letter, Start))

The understanding is that each output mentioned in an output list depends on all of the inputs mentioned in the associated input list.

For the case of **in out** parameters or global variables that are In_Out, it is common for the output value of the parameter or variable to depend on its own input value. The parameter Value in the previously shown procedure Get_Value is like this. In that case, the symbol =>+ can be used to indicate that each output on the left side depends on itself as well as on all inputs on the right side. For example, the contract

with
    Depends => (Value => (Text, Name, Value))

can be abbreviated as

with
    Depends => (Value =>+ (Text, Name))

In the important case where an **in out** parameter or In_Out global variable depends on only itself, a flow dependency contract such as Value => Value can be abbreviated to Value =>+ **null**. The abbreviated form can be read as, "Value depends on itself and nothing else."

Sometimes an output depends on no inputs whatsoever. This occurs when a subprogram writes a value from "out of the blue" to initialize an output. For example,

procedure Initialize (Value : **out** Integer)
    with
        Depends => (Value => **null**);

The flow dependency contract Value => **null** can be read as, "Value depends on nothing." It means the subprogram sets the value without reference to any input.

Finally, it is also possible to give a flow dependency contract that uses **null** on the output side of a dependency as shown in the following example:

procedure Update (Value : **in out** Integer ;
                Adjust : **in**   Integer)
    with
        Depends => (Value =>+ **null**,
                null   => Adjust);

Here, Value depends only on itself, and nothing depends on Adjust. Thus, Adjust is not used in the computation of any results. Such a flow dependency contract is unusual, but it explicitly documents that a particular value is not (yet) being used.

4.3 Managing State

For our purposes, the *state of a package* consists of the values of all global variables defined inside the package together with the state of any packages nested within the package. By placing these entities within the private part of the package specification or the package body, the state of a package is hidden from its clients. When a subprogram in a package is called, the caller is not directly aware of any global variables or nested packages the subprogram uses or modifies. Restricting the visibility of data as much as feasible is an important principle of software engineering. This hiding allows the representation of that data to be changed at a later time with minimal impact on the rest of the program. If clients of a package only interact with the package's internal state by way of a small set of public subprograms, the precise design of that state is not significant to the clients.

As an example consider a package that encapsulates a datebook. The package might provide subprograms for adding events to the datebook, removing events from the datebook, and enumerating the events currently stored in the datebook. The specification of such a package could be, in part as follows:

```
with Dates;
package Datebook is
    type Status_Type is (Success, Description_Too_Long, Insufficient_Space );

    procedure Add_Event (Description :  in   String;
                         Date        :  in   Dates.Datetime;
                         Status      :  out  Status_Type);
end Datebook;
```

Here we assume the package Dates provides a type Dates.Datetime that represents a combined date and time.

Each event that is entered into the datebook has a short description and an associated date and time when the event occurs. For purposes of this example, the duration of the event and other information about the event is ignored. The procedure Add_Event, one of several procedures the package might contain, adds information about an event to the datebook and returns a status indication, by way of an out parameter, to report the success or failure of that operation.

Everything seems fine, but where, exactly, is the datebook to which events are being added? In this case the datebook is presumably implemented in the form of global data inside the body of package Datebook. It is the package's state.

It might be implemented as a simple array of records where each record stores information about a single event, or it might be implemented in some more elaborate way. Perhaps the package maintains indexes to speed up datebook queries. Perhaps the package packs event descriptions into some auxiliary data structure to save space. None of this matters to the users of the package.

However, the fact that the package contains internal state that is accessed and modified by the public subprograms is important to flow analysis. For example, Add_Event updates the internal state by adding a new event record to the datebook. Because the new state depends on the existing state, Add_Event must effectively read the existing state. This implies that the internal state of the package must already be initialized in some way before Add_Event can be called.

To talk about the internal state in SPARK aspects, it is necessary to give that internal state a name. It is not necessary to declare the internal state fully. In fact, doing so would expose the information hidden by the package. The clients are not interested in the details of how the internal state is organized. They are only interested in the fact that it exists and in how it is read and updated by the public subprograms. Thus, all that is needed is for the internal state to be abstracted into a single name called a *state abstraction*.

The following example shows a SPARK version of the Datebook specification. Here a state abstraction named State is introduced to represent the internal state of the package:

```
with Dates;
package Datebook
  with
    Abstract_State => State
is
    type Status_Type is (Success, Description_Too_Long, Insufficient_Space );

    procedure Add_Event (Description :  in    String ;
                         Date        :  in    Dates.Datetime;
                         Status      :  out   Status_Type)
      with
        Global  => (In_Out => State),
        Depends => (State   =>+ (Description, Date),
                    Status  => (Description , State ));
end Datebook;
```

The name State in this example is a name chosen by the programmer to identify the internal state of the package. Because we wish to keep the nature of this internal state as hidden as possible, we cannot easily give it a more descriptive name. As you will see in Section 4.3.2, it is sometimes desirable to break the abstract state into two or more components. In that case, we would give the components names that distinguish them clearly.

We have enhanced the declaration of Add_Event with descriptions of the effects it has on the package's internal state. Notice that State is treated as a kind of global variable. In fact, that is exactly what it is. The state abstraction represents the global data inside the package. The details of this hidden data are not needed by the clients of the package. They need only be aware that the package has a state and that the subprograms they call use and/or change that state.

The data and flow dependency contracts on Add_Event indicate that the status depends on the state of the datebook and on the incoming description. Add_Event can fail if the datebook is already full or if the description is overly large.

If the only public subprogram in the package is Add_Event as shown in the preceding example, the flow analysis done by the SPARK tools will complain that the internal state of the package has no way of being initialized. Procedure Add_Event requires that State has a value before it is called. How does State get its initial value?

One approach would be to provide an initialization procedure. It might be declared as follows:

```
procedure Initialize
  with
    Global  => (Output => State),
    Depends => (State => null);
```

This procedure takes no parameters because it initializes global data inside the package. The data and flow dependency contracts say this by declaring that the procedure gives the state abstraction a value from "nothing." With this procedure it is now possible to call Add_Event correctly by first calling Initialize. Flow analysis will ensure that this happens.

In some cases the global data inside a package can be initialized without the help of an explicit procedure call. As we saw in Section 3.4.1, the internal state of a variable package can be initialized with suitable static expressions or with initialization code executed when the package body is elaborated. In such cases the package initializes itself. The aspect declaration on the package can be changed to reflect this behavior as the following example shows:

```
with Dates;
package Datebook
  with
    Abstract_State => State,
    Initializes    => State
```

is

    type Status_Type **is** (Success, Description_Too_Long, Insufficient_Space);

    −− *No Initialize procedure needed*
    procedure Add_Event (Description : **in** String ;
                              Date   : **in**   Dates.Datetime;
                              Status   : **out** Status_Type)
        with
          Global => (In_Out => State),
          Depends => (State   =>+ (Description, Date),
                     Status => (Description , State));
end Datebook;

If during program development the internal state becomes complicated enough to require a special initialization procedure, one can be added and the Initializes aspect removed. Flow analysis will ensure that the new procedure will get called as needed.

The package Datebook presented so far is a kind of variable package as discussed in Section 3.4. It allows a single datebook variable to be manipulated. Before looking at the body of package Datebook, it is useful to consider an alternative implementation as a type package, as described in Section 3.3. The following version, named Datebooks (note the plural), provides a Datebook private type and has no internal state. Instead, the components of the private type hold the state of each Datebook object.

with Dates;
package Datebooks **is**
    type Datebook **is private** ;

    type Status_Type **is** (Success, Description_Too_Long, Insufficient_Space);

    procedure Add_Event (Book   : **in out** Datebook;
                            Description : **in**   String ;
                            Date   : **in**   Dates.Datetime;
                            Status   :   **out** Status_Type)
        with
          Depends => (Book =>+ (Description, Date),
                    Status => (Description , Book))
private

    −− *Provide a full definition for the private type Datebook*

    Maximum_Description_Length : **constant** := 128;
    subtype Description_Index_Type **is**

```
      Positive range 1 .. Maximum_Description_Length;
   subtype Description_Count_Type is
      Natural range 0 .. Maximum_Description_Length;
   subtype Description_Type is String ( Description_Index_Type );

   -- Each Event_Record handles exactly one datebook entry.
   type Event_Record is
      record
         Description_Text  : Description_Type;
         Description_Size  : Description_Count_Type;
         Date              : Dates.Datetime;
         Is_Used           : Boolean;
      end record;

   subtype Event_Index_Type is
      Positive range 1 .. Maximum_Number_Of_Events;
   type Datebook is
      array (Event_Index_Type) of Event_Record;

end Datebooks;
```

In this version the caller must create a Datebook object and explicitly pass it to
the various subprograms in the package. Accordingly, those subprograms, such
as Add_Event, must now be given an additional parameter. The subprograms
no longer have a data dependency contract, but the flow dependency contract
appropriate for the new parameter mimics the flow dependency contract used
with the state abstraction in the original version of the package.

This version has some advantages over the previous version. First, it allows
clients to create and manipulate many different Datebook objects. Second, package Datebooks has no internal state, which presents advantages in multi-tasking
environments. However, the original version was easier to use because clients
did not need to create their own datebooks. The most appropriate approach
depends on the application's needs.

The private section, shown in full earlier, seems complicated. However, the
original Datebook package needs similar declarations in the package body to
fully define the internal state of that package. This is described in more detail
in the next section.

4.3.1 *Refinement*

When a state abstraction is used, the body of the package must explicitly declare
which global variables and nested package state, if any, compose the abstract

state. Such entities are called the *constituents* of the state abstraction, and the process of breaking a state abstraction into its constituents is called *refinement*. In simple cases, a state abstraction might be refined to a single package global variable, thus, having a single constituent. In more complex cases, the state abstraction will be refined to multiple package global variables.

For example, suppose the Datebook package is implemented by way of an array of records in which each record contains information about one event, similar to the way the Datebooks package works. The array would thus be the single constituent of the state abstraction. The package body might look, in part, as follows:

```
package body Datebook
  with
    Refined_State  => (State => Event_Array)
is
    −− Provide an appropriate type  definition .
    Maximum_Description_Length : constant := 128;
    subtype Description_Index_Type is
        Positive range 1 .. Maximum_Description_Length;
    subtype Description_Count_Type is
        Natural range 0 .. Maximum_Description_Length;
    subtype Description_Type is  String ( Description_Index_Type );

    −− Each Event_Record handles exactly one datebook entry.
    type Event_Record is
      record
          Description_Text  : Description_Type ;
          Description_Size  : Description_Count_Type;
          Date              : Dates.Datetime;
          Is_Used           : Boolean;
      end record;

    subtype Event_Index_Type is
        Positive range 1 .. Maximum_Number_Of_Events;
    type Event_Array_Type is
        array (Event_Index_Type) of Event_Record;

    Event_Array : Event_Array_Type;

    −− Body of add event operation
    procedure Add_Event . . .
end Datebook;
```

The Refined_State aspect on the package body specifies which global variables inside the package form the constituents of the abstract state previously declared. In our example, the abstract state State is refined to the single global variable Event_Array. It is an error to have an abstract state in a package specification without also refining it in the package body.

In addition, the data and flow dependency contracts in the package specification must be refined in the package body to explicitly specify the effects those subprograms have on the refined state. These refined contracts appear inside the package body as they reference information that is internal to the package. The body of procedure Add_Event might be

```
procedure Add_Event (Description :  in   String;
                     Date        :  in   Dates.Datetime;
                     Status      :  out  Status_Type)
   with
       Refined_Global  => (In_Out => Event_Array),
       Refined_Depends => (Event_Array =>+ (Description, Date),
                           Status      => (Description, Event_Array))
   is
       Found     : Boolean;     -- Is there an available slot?
       Available : Event_Index_Type := Event_Index_Type' First ; -- Location
   begin
       -- If the given description won't fit there is no point continuing.
       if Description 'Length > Maximum_Description_Length then
           Status := Description_Too_Long;
       else
           -- Search for a free slot in the event array.
           Found := False;
           for Index in Event_Index_Type loop
               if not Event_Array (Index).Is_Used then
                   Available := Index;
                   Found := True;
                   exit ; -- We found a available slot in the array
               end if ;
           end loop;

       if not Found then
           -- If there is no free slot return an error.
           Status :=  Insufficient_Space ;
       else
           -- Otherwise fill in the free slot with the incoming information.
           -- Need to pad the description with blanks.
```

```
        Event_Array ( Available ). Description_Text := Description &
           (1 .. Maximum_Description_Length − Description'Length => ' ');
        Event_Array ( Available ). Description_Size := Description 'Length;
        Event_Array ( Available ). Date    := Date;
        Event_Array ( Available ). Is_Used := True;
        Status := Success;
     end if ;
   end if ;
end Add_Event;
```

Notice that the Refined_Global and Refined_Depends aspects are expressed in terms of the actual package global variable rather than in terms of the state abstraction as was done in the package specification.

The example so far shows a one-to-one correspondence between a state abstraction and a single constituent variable. A more elaborate implementation of the Datebook package might include an index that allows events to be looked up quickly on the basis of a commonly used field. In that case the state abstraction might be refined to two package global variables as follows:

```
package body Datebook
  with
     Refined_State => (State => (Event_Array, Event_Index))
is
     type Event_Array_Type is . . .
     type Event_Index_Type is . . .

     Event_Array : Event_Array_Type;
     Event_Index : Event_Index_Type;
end Datebook;
```

Similarly, the refined data and flow dependency contracts on the subprograms must be updated to describe the effects those subprograms have on the individual constituents. It is likely that Add_Event will modify both the datebook itself and its index. For example,

```
package body Datebook
  with
     Refined_State => (State => (Event_Array, Event_Index))
is

   . . .

     procedure Add_Event (Description : in   String ;
                          Date        : in   Dates.Datetime;
                          Status      : out  Status_Type)
```

```
   with
      Refined_Global  => (In_Out => (Event_Array, Event_Index)),
      Refined_Depends => (Event_Array =>+ (Description, Date),
                          Event_Index =>+ (Description, Date),
                          Status      => (Description, Event_Array) )
   is
      -- Local variables of Add_Event omitted
   begin
      -- Body of Add_Event omitted
   end Add_Event;

end Datebook;
```

Notice that in this case Status does not depend on the Event_Index. Presumably, the success or failure of Add_Event is not affected by the index. In the package specification, Status depends on the overall state abstraction State as it depends on one of that abstraction's constituents, namely the Event_Array.

The important point is that the new version of the Datebook package has changed the internal organization of the datebook without changing the specification of the package. Not only do clients of this package not need to be recompiled, but flow analysis of those clients does not need to be redone. Of course, the analysis of package Datebook's body does need to be redone, causing the SPARK tools to consider the new refined contracts in light of the changes in the implementation.

4.3.2 *Multiple State Abstractions*

In the formulation of the Datebook package so far, a single state abstraction is used to abstract two constituents: the datebook itself and its index. This maximizes the amount of information hidden from the package's clients. Suppose, now, that one wanted to add a public subprogram to compact the index. The specification must be changed to include this subprogram and to declare how it interacts with the state abstraction provided by the package. We give this package the name Indexed_Datebook to inform its users of its different nature as compared to the previously described Datebook package. Because the index is now public information, it is appropriate to reflect that information in the package's name:

```
with Dates;
package Indexed_Datebook
   with
      SPARK_Mode    => On,
      Abstract_State => State
```

is

    type Status_Type **is** (Success, Description_Too_Long, Insufficient_Space);

    procedure Initialize
      with
        Global => (Output => State),
        Depends => (State => **null**);

    procedure Compact_Index
      with
        Global => (In_Out => State),
        Depends => (State =>+ **null**);

    procedure Add_Event (Description : **in**   String ;
                    Date   : **in**   Dates.Datetime;
                    Status   : **out** Status_Type)
      with
        Global => (In_Out => State),
        Depends => (State   =>+ (Description, Date),
                 Status => (Description , State));

end Indexed_Datebook;

Because Compact_Index only updates the internal state, it need not take parameters. The flow dependency contract shows that the new state depends only on the old state. Because the data dependency contract declares that the state has mode In_Out, flow analysis will require that the initialization procedure for the package be called before Compact_Index can be used.

However, using a single state abstraction can sometimes cause unnecessary and undesirable coupling between the subprograms in a package. For example, suppose the event index can be initialized directly by the package and does not need the help of an initialization procedure. In that case, it should be possible to call Compact_Index without first calling Initialize . Perhaps some programs may find it convenient to do so.

These ideas can be expressed by using multiple state abstractions. The following version of the specification shows this. The name State has been dropped in favor of two more descriptive names.

with Dates;
package Indexed_Datebook_V2
  with
    SPARK_Mode => On,
    Abstract_State => (Book, Index),
    Initializes   => Index

```
is

  type Status_Type is (Success,  Description_Too_Long,   Insufficient_Space );

  procedure  Initialize
    with
      Global   => (Output => (Book, Index)),
      Depends => ((Book, Index) => null);

  procedure Compact_Index
    with
      Global   => (In_Out => Index),
      Depends => (Index =>+ null);

  procedure Add_Event (Description : in   String;
                       Date        : in   Dates.Datetime;
                       Status      : out  Status_Type)
    with
      Global   => (In_Out => (Book, Index)),
      Depends => (Book  =>+ (Description, Date),
                  Index =>+ (Description, Date),
                  Status => ( Description , Book));

end Indexed_Datebook_V2;
```

In addition to declaring two state abstractions, the package declares that one of those abstractions is automatically initialized. The data and flow dependency contracts on procedure Compact_Index indicate that it only needs the Index abstraction to be initialized before it can be used. Flow analysis will now allow Compact_Index to be called before Initialize is called.

The body of package Indexed_Datebook needs to also show how each state abstraction is refined. For example,

```
package body Datebook
  with
    Refined_State  => (Book => Event_Array,
                       Index => Event_Index)
is
    . . .
end Datebook;
```

The refined aspects on the subprogram bodies remain as before because they were written in terms of the constituents anyway. Flow analysis will verify, of course, that the refined contracts on the bodies are consistent with the contracts in the declarations of the subprograms.

This approach reduces the *false coupling* between subprograms as a result of an overly abstracted view of the package's internal state. However, the price that is paid is more exposure of the package's internal structure to clients.

Suppose after making this change it was decided that the index was unnecessary and it was removed. The data and flow dependency contracts in the specification would need to be updated to reflect this change, necessitating a reanalysis of all clients along with possible modifications to the contracts of those clients. One might be tempted to replace the procedure Compact_Index with a version that does nothing so as to avoid removing the procedure outright (and breaking client code that calls it). However, the SPARK contracts for the new procedure would indicate that it has no effect and flow analysis would produce a warning because of this. Thus, the introduction of multiple state abstractions in a single package should be done cautiously as it is a form of information exposure; undoing such a change later might be more difficult than one desires.

4.3.3 *Hierarchical State Abstractions*

Complex state information may be simplified by the use of state hierarchies implemented by a hierarchy of packages. A general state at the top level may be refined into concrete state variables and abstract states contained in lower level packages. This refinement into abstract states can continue until all have been refined into concrete state variables. Let us look at an example:

```
package Hierarchical_State_Demo
    with SPARK_Mode   => On,
         Abstract_State => Top_State,
         Initializes    => Top_State
is
    procedure Do_Something (Value   : in out Natural;
                            Success :     out Boolean)
        with Global  => (In_Out => Top_State),
             Depends => (Value    =>+ Top_State,
                         Success  => (Value, Top_State),
                         Top_State =>+ Value);
end Hierarchical_State_Demo;
```

In the body of package Hierarchical_State_Demo, we refine the state Top_State into the concrete state variable Count and the abstract state State (defined in the nested package A_Pack):

```
package body Hierarchical_State_Demo -- Nested implementation
    with SPARK_Mode => On,
         Refined_State => (Top_State => (Count, A_Pack.State))
```

```
is
   package A_Pack
      with Abstract_State => State,
           Initializes    => State
   is
      procedure A_Proc (Test : in out Natural)
         with Global   => (In_Out => State),
              Depends => (Test  =>+ State,
                          State =>+ Test);
   end A_Pack;
```

```
   package body A_Pack
      with Refined_State => (State => Total)
   is
      Total : Natural := 0;

      procedure A_Proc (Test : in out Natural)
         with Refined_Global  => (In_Out => Total),
              Refined_Depends => ((Test =>+ Total,
                                   Total =>+ Test)) is
      begin
         . . . .
      end A_Proc;
   end A_Pack;
```

```
   Count : Natural := 0;

   procedure Do_Something (Value   : in out Natural;
                           Success :     out Boolean)
      with Refined_Global  => (In_Out => (Count, A_Pack.State)),
           Refined_Depends => (Value         =>+ (Count, A_Pack.State),
                               Success       =>
(Value, Count, A_Pack.State),
                               Count         =>+ null,
                               A_Pack.State =>+ (Count, Value)) is
   begin
      . . . .
   end Do_Something;
end Hierarchical_State_Demo;
```

The Refined_Globals and Refined_Depends of procedure Do_Something also refer
to the abstract state State. Notice that the Initializes => Top_State in the top
level package specification is fulfilled by assignment of an initial value to Count
and the Initializes => State aspect in the specification of the nested package

A_Pack. The body of package A_Pack refines the abstract state State into the concrete variable Total, which is used in the Refined_Global and Refined_Depends aspects of procedure A_Proc.

We could easily extend the logic illustrated by this example with additional abstract states in packages nested within the body of Hierarchical_State_ Demo (to widen our hierarchy) or with packages nested within the body of package A_Pack (to deepen our hierarchy). The obvious problem with these extensions is that the package body Hierarchical_State_Demo grows larger with each additional state abstraction.

A seemingly obvious answer to this problem is to put the nested package into an independent library unit and use a **with** clause to gain access to it. Here is a version of Hierarchical_State_Demo that does just that:

```
with Hierarchical_State_Demo . A_Pack;
package body Hierarchical_State_Demo  —— Child package implementation
   with SPARK_Mode => On,
        Refined_State => (Top_State => (Count, A_Pack.State))
is
   Count : Natural := 0;

   procedure Do_Something (Value  :  in out Natural;
                           Success :     out Boolean)
     with Refined_Global  => (In_Out => (Count, A_Pack.State)),
          Refined_Depends => (Value         =>+ (Count, A_Pack.State),
                              Success       => (Value, Count, A_Pack.State),
                              Count         =>+ null,
                              A_Pack.State  =>+ (Count, Value)) is
   begin

      . . . .

   end Do_Something;
end Hierarchical_State_Demo;
```

Removing the nested package A_Pack has made this body much shorter. We made A_Pack a child of Hierarchical_State_Demo to align our package hierarchy with our abstract state hierarchy.

However, we run into difficulty when we attempt to examine the independent child package containing our new abstract state. SPARK requires that all refined states be hidden from clients – in our example, the clients of Hierarchical_State_Demo. This was not a problem when the package with the abstract state used in the refinement was nested in the body. But as an ordinary child package, it is accessible to all.

The solution is to make A_Pack a private child package. That way its resources are only accessible to its parent, Hierarchical_State_Demo, and its parent's descendants. Here is the specification for the private child package A_Pack:

```
private package Hierarchical_State_Demo.A_Pack
   with SPARK_Mode => On,
        Abstract_State => (State with Part_Of => Top_State),
        Initializes    => State
is
   procedure A_Proc (Test : in out Natural)
      with Global  => (In_Out => State),
           Depends => (Test   =>+ State,
                       State  =>+ Test);
end Hierarchical_State_Demo.A_Pack;
```

This private child package specification contains the option Part_Of. When refining to an abstract state defined in a private child package, this option must be included with that abstract state. The Part_Of option denotes the encapsulating state abstraction of which the declaration is a constituent. In our example, State is a constituent of Top_State. The reasons for requiring the Part_Of option when the abstract state is not "local" are given in section 7.2.6 of the SPARK *2014 Reference Manual* (SPARK Team, 2014a).

The body of package A_Pack requires no modification from the original given on page 121. Complete code for both the nested and private child versions of Hierarchical_State_Demo are available on our http://www.cambridge.org/us/academic/subjects/computer-science/programming-languages-and-applied-logic/building-high-integrity-applications-spark.

4.4 Default Initialization

One of the purposes of flow analysis is to ensure that no ineffective computations take place. However, Ada allows you to define default initializers for types that require it, a feature that ensures all objects of that type are initialized. If you attempt to re-initialize such an object to a nondefault value, you might wonder if that causes the default initialization to be ineffective.

To illustrate, consider the following declarations that introduce a type for arrays of ten integers:

```
subtype Array_Index_Type is  Positive range 1 .. 10;
type    Integer_Array     is array (Array_Index_Type) of Integer ;
```

Now consider a simple function that adds the elements of such an array. In this example, we only consider flow issues, so concerns about overflow during the computations can be set aside for now.

```ada
function Add_Elements (A : Integer_Array) return Integer is
   Sum : Integer := 0;   -- Ineffective   initialization
begin
   Sum := 0;
   for Index in A'Range loop
      Sum := Sum + A (Index);
   end loop;
   return Sum;
end Add_Elements;
```

This function contains a redundant initialization of Sum, first when the variable is declared and then again later at the top of the function's body. Flow analysis flags the initialization as a flow issue saying that it has "no effect" as the value initialized is overwritten without being used.

This is fine, but now consider the case when Ada's facilities for specifying a default initial value for a type are used. You might introduce a special kind of integer to use as accumulators.

```ada
type Accumulator is new Integer
   with Default_Value => 0;
```

The use of the Default_Value aspect means that each time an object of type Accumulator is declared, it will automatically be given the value zero. This ensures accumulators are always initialized to a reasonable value. Now consider a second, somewhat different, implementation of Add_Elements:

```ada
function Add_Elements2 (A : Integer_Array) return Integer is
   Sum : Accumulator;
begin
   -- Sum is automatically  initialized .
   -- Yet assignment below does not cause a flow issue .
   Sum := 1;  -- Start with a bias value.
   for Index in A'Range loop
      Sum := Sum + Accumulator (A (Index)); -- note type conversion
   end loop;
   return Integer (Sum);
end Add_Elements2;
```

In this version, Sum is automatically initialized to its default value of zero. Ordinarily this would be a nice convenience for a function like this. However, Add_Elements2 wishes to bias the accumulated sum by one and thus re-initializes Sum to 1 in the body of the function. Significantly, this does not cause flow analysis to flag the default initialization as ineffective. The tools understand that it is reasonable to override the default initialization in some circumstances and, thus, does not consider doing so a flow problem.

Because Accumulator is a new type distinct from Integer, it is now necessary to do some type conversions in Add_Elements2. You might wonder why not define Accumulator as a subtype of Integer. Alas, Ada does not allow the Default_Value aspect to be applied to a subtype.

As another example, consider the following record definition that wraps a pair of integers. Here default values are specified for both components.

```
type Pair_With_Default is
   record
      X :  Integer := 0;
      Y :  Integer := 0;
   end record;
```

Now consider a function Adjust_Pair that takes a Pair_With_Default and moves it on the (x, y) plane:

```
function Adjust_Pair (P :  Pair_With_Default) return Pair_With_Default is
   Offset  :  Pair_With_Default;
begin
   -- Offset is automatically  initialized .
   -- Yet assignment below does not cause a flow issue.
   Offset . Y := 1;
   return  (P.X + Offset.X, P.Y + Offset.Y);
end Adjust_Pair ;
```

As with the previous example, Offset is default initialized. Yet the assignment to Offset . Y is not a flow issue because the re-initialization of a default initialized value is considered reasonable and correct. Furthermore, the use of Offset . X in the return expression is not a flow issue because, of course, Offset has a default initializer for its X component.

You might wonder what happens if the record had default initializers for only some of its components:

```
type Pair_With_YDefault is
   record
      X :  Integer ;
      Y :  Integer := 0;
   end record;
```

Although such a type declaration is legal in full Ada, it is not allowed in SPARK. Either all components must have default initializers or none of them can.

Variable packages can also be, in effect, default initialized when they are elaborated. Consider again the Datebook example, shown here with a procedure that clears the datebook of all events. For brevity, the other subprograms in the package are not shown.

```
with Dates;
package Datebook
  with
    Abstract_State  => State,
    Initializes     => State
is
  procedure Clear
    with
      Global   => (Output => State),
      Depends => (State => null);
end Datebook;
```

The Datebook package models a single object represented by the state abstraction State. The Initializes aspect asserts that the package initializes the state when it is elaborated. However, the Clear procedure also initializes the state as evidenced from its flow dependency contract, State => null. If a nervous programmer calls Clear before using the package, the programmer would then be re-initializing a default initialized "variable." Following the principle described earlier, flow analysis will not flag this as a flow issue.

In general, re-initialization may bring the entity being re-initialized to a new starting state. In the preceding example of Adjust_Pair Offset . Y is set to a starting value of 1 as per the needs of the enclosing subprogram. Similarly, a complex package might have several "clearing" procedures that clear the internal state in different ways.

Of course re-initialization entails some overhead. When a value is re-initialized, the time spent doing the default initialization was wasted. This is an argument against defining default initializations for all entities everywhere. Instead, the programmer may wish to explicitly initialize an object when, if, and how the programmer desires. However, default initialization is useful for certain types and certain packages; the SPARK tools allow re-initialization in those cases when it makes sense.

4.5 Synthesis of Dependency Contracts

Conceptually, SPARK requires every subprogram to have both data and flow dependency contracts. However, it is not necessary to explicitly include these contracts in all cases; the SPARK tools can synthesize them using rules discussed in this section.

You can write SPARK code without tediously providing data and flow dependency contracts everywhere provided you are content with the synthesized contracts. This means you can "convert" existing Ada code to SPARK by just adding an appropriate SPARK_Mode aspect to an existing compilation unit as we describe in Section 7.1.1, and, of course, removing any non-SPARK constructs the unit might be using. It is not necessary to annotate all subprograms with dependency contracts before starting to work with the SPARK tools. Applying SPARK to existing Ada in this way is called *retrospective analysis*.

Earlier we emphasized that the data and flow dependency contracts are part of the specification of a subprogram. Like the parameter list, the dependency contracts should, ideally, be written as part of your design process before you have implemented the subprogram. Applying SPARK to your code base as you design and implement is called *constructive analysis*.

Yet even in the constructive case, relying on synthesized contracts is sometimes reasonable. This is particularly true for subprograms that are nested inside other subprograms or that are used only in the context of a particular package. The internal subprograms exist to service the enclosing subprogram or package and are really part of the implementation of the enclosing entity and not design elements in themselves.

The precise rules for how contracts are synthesized are detailed, but the effect is largely intuitive:

1. If a Global aspect exists but a Depends aspect does not the flow dependency contract is synthesized by assuming each output depends on all inputs. For small subprograms such as the Search procedure on page 105, this is often exactly correct. In any case the resulting flow dependency is conservative in the sense that it might define more dependencies than actually exist. This has the potential to increase the number of false positives in the callers but does not, for example, allow any errors such as the accidental use of uninitialized values[2]. If false positives prove to be problematic, you can always add more precise flow dependency contracts explicitly.

2. If a Depends aspect exists but a Global aspect does not the data dependency contract is synthesized by examining the flow dependency contract and constructing the data dependencies from the flows. For example, suppose a subprogram is declared as follows:

```
procedure Do_Something(X : in Integer; Y : out Integer)
  with
    Depends => (Y => (X, A, B), B => (X, A), C => X);
```

This contract mentions A, B, and C, which must be visible as global variables at this point in the program. The flows specified require that A be an input, C be an output, and B be both an input and an output. The synthesized data dependency contract is thus

with

Global => (Input => A, In_Out => B, Output => C)

3. If neither a Global aspect nor a Depends aspect exists, the SPARK tools analyze the body of the subprogram to synthesize the data dependency contract and then use that to synthesize the flow dependency contract as described earlier.

In some cases, however, the body of the subprogram is not available, not analyzed, or imported from another language. One important example of this is when processing the specification of a library package with no source code for the body. In that case the SPARK tools assume the subprogram makes use of no global data at all, but a warning is produced to alert the programmer of this (possibly incorrect) assumption. The synthesized flow dependency contract then only considers the subprogram's parameters and, as usual, assumes each output depends on all inputs.

Functions are handled in largely the same way as procedures. The synthesized data dependency contract takes the function result as the only output of the function. It is possible to specify flows to the output of a function F by using F'Result explicitly in the flow dependency contract. However, writing explicit flow dependency contracts for functions is uncommon as the generated contracts are often exactly correct.

There are two other important issues to keep in mind with respect to dependency contract use and synthesis. First, it is permitted to declare more dependencies than actually exist. The SPARK tools will detect the inconsistency, but it is not considered an error. The diagonstic message is justifiable using pragma Annotate,[3] allowing you to "pre-declare" dependencies that you anticipate future versions of your code may need. Callers will thus be forced to consider such dependencies even if they are not currently active. For example, callers might be required to initialize certain global variables before calling your subprogram if you have declared those variables as Input data dependencies, even if your subprogram does not currently use them.

It is also important to understand that synthesized dependency contracts are not checked in the body of the subprogram to which they apply. The synthesized contracts are too aggressive in many cases, for example, declaring more flows than actually exist, resulting in many false positives. However, the synthesized dependency contracts are used in the analysis of calling code. The aggressive contracts might increase the number of false positives in callers as well, yet practice shows the burden of these false positives is usually minimal. In cases where it matters, false positives can be avoided by making the dependency contracts explicit.

In the future, the SPARK tools will also be able to synthesize Abstract_State, Refined_State, Refined_Global, and Refined_Depends aspects. However, at the time of this writing, support for synthesizing these aspects is largely missing. For example, if you include Abstract_State in a package, you must explicitly provide the corresponding refined dependency contracts. On the other hand, at the time of this writing, the SPARK tools are able to synthesize dependency contracts of a subprogram in terms of the abstract state of packages being referenced by that subprogram.

Summary

- The development of SPARK programs can be split into three stages: verifying that the program is in the SPARK subset, verifying that the program has no flow errors, and verifying that the program is free from runtime errors and that all executable contracts are obeyed.
- The data dependency contract using the Global aspect specifies what global variables a subprogram uses and the modes on those variables. The three modes for global variables are equivalent to those for parameters.
- The data dependency contract treats global variables like additional parameters to the subprogram where the argument used at every call site is the same.
- The global variables used in data dependency contracts must be entire variables; they cannot be components of some larger variable.
- Functions can only input from global variables.
- Using global variables should be avoided or at least minimized. They are reasonable, however, when accessing local variables and parameters of an enclosing subprogram or when accessing the global state of a package from inside that package.
- Global constants initialized with a static expression do not need to be mentioned in the data dependency contract.
- When analyzing a subprogram with a data dependency contract, the SPARK tools verify that the modes declared on the global variables are consistent with the way those variables are actually used.
- The flow dependency contract using the Depends aspect specifies for each output of a subprogram which inputs the output depends on.
- Flow dependency contracts on a subprogram can, and ideally should, be specified before that subprogram is written; they form part of the subprogram's interface.

- Flow analysis verifies that no uninitialized data is used and that all computations are effective.
- Flow dependency contracts constrain the set of legal implementations beyond that required by the parameters alone.
- Flow dependency contracts are complete in the sense that flow analysis will fail unless all data flow information is fully in place. In contrast, pre- and postconditions are only as strong as the programmer makes them.
- It is possible to declare that an output of a subprogram depends on no inputs (and is thus being initialized by the subprogram) using **null** on the input side of the dependency.
- SPARK allows compilation units to be separately analyzed. Dependency contracts on called subprograms participate in the analysis of the calling subprogram.
- A state abstraction is a name representing global state inside a package (either global variables or the state of internally nested packages).
- Once declared, a state abstraction can be used as a kind of global variable for the purposes of data dependency and flow dependency contracts on the public subprograms of the package.
- An Initializes aspect can be used to specify that a package initializes its internal state without the help of a specific initialization procedure.
- Each state abstraction must be refined in the package body into its constituent global variables or nested package state.
- When refining state abstraction in a package body, the data dependency and flow dependency contracts on the public subprograms must also be refined in the body. They must be refined in terms of the state abstraction's constituents.
- A package can define multiple state abstractions to reduce false couplings between subprograms at the cost of exposing more details of the package's internal structure.
- When an entity (variable or variable package) is default initialized, it is not a flow error to re-initialize it. The default initialization is not marked as ineffective.
- The SPARK tools can synthesize data and flow dependency contracts for subprograms that are not explicitly marked as having them.
- If a subprogram has a Global aspect but no Depends aspect, the synthesized flow dependency contract takes each output as depending on all inputs.
- If a subprogram has a Depends aspect but no Global aspect, the synthesized data dependency contract is generated from the inputs and outputs listed in the flow dependency contract.
- If a subprogram has neither a Global aspect nor a Depends aspect, the synthesized data dependency contract is deduced from the body of the subprogram,

if available, and the synthesized flow dependency contract is computed from the data dependency contract as usual.

- The synthesized contracts are conservative. They may include flows that do not exist causing false positives.
- Without access to a subprogram's body, if no contracts exist, the SPARK tools cannot synthesize a data dependency contract and instead assume the subprogram does not use global data. A warning is issued to this effect.
- Dependencies are not checked in the body of subprograms that have synthesized contracts. This is done to avoid excessive numbers of false positive messages.
- The ability to synthesize contracts allows retrospective analysis where SPARK is used on existing code written without SPARK in mind. It also allows you to not bother writing dependency contracts on, for example, internal subprograms.

Exercises

4.1 Which of the following data dependency contracts are definitely illegal and why?

    a.   **function** F(X : Integer) **return** Integer
              with
                 Global => (Input => (Y, Z));

    b.   **function** F(X : Integer) **return** Integer
              with
                 Global => (Input => Y, In_Out => Z);

    c.   **procedure** P(X : **in out** Integer)
              with
                 Global => Dates.Compilation_Date;

    d.   **procedure** P(X : **in out** Integer)
              with
                 Global => (Input => Y, In_Out => (X, Z));

4.2 What is an "ineffective" computation?

4.3 Which of the following flow dependency contracts are definitely illegal and why?

    a.   **procedure** P(X : **in** Integer; Y : **in out** Integer)
              with
                 Depends => (Y => X);

b.
```
procedure P(X : in Integer ; Y : in out Integer )
   with
      Depends => (Y =>+ X);
```

c.
```
procedure P(X : in Integer ; Y : in out Integer )
   with
      Global  => (Output => (Count, Timestamp)),
      Depends => (Y =>+ X, Count => (X, Y));
```

d.
```
procedure P(X : in Integer ; Y : in out Integer )
   with
      Global  => (Output => (Count, Timestamp)),
      Depends => (Y =>+ X,
                  Count => (X, Y),
                  Timestamp => Count);
```

e.
```
procedure P(X : in Integer ; Y : in out Integer )
   with
      Global  => (Output => Timestamp, In_Out => Count),
      Depends -> (Y =>+ X,
                  Count => (X, Y),
                  Timestamp => X);
```

f.
```
procedure P(X : in Integer ; Y : in out Integer )
   with
      Global  => (Output => Timestamp, In_Out => Count),
      Depends => (Y =>+ X,
                  Count =>+ (X, Y),
                  Timestamp => X);
```

4.4 Modify the specifications of versions 1 and 2 of the bounded queue package in Chapter 3, pages 73 and 78, to include appropriate data dependency and flow dependency contracts.

4.5 Modify the specification and body of the Bingo basket package in Chapter 3, page 84, to include appropriate data dependency and flow dependency contracts. This package encapsulates the state of a Bingo basket.

4.6 Modify the specification and body of the serial number package in Chapter 3, page 86, to include appropriate data dependency and flow dependency contracts.

4.7 State abstractions expose, to a certain degree, the internal structure of a package and thus seem to partially break information hiding. Is this a problem? Discuss.

4.8 What does it mean to say an object is default initialized? Default initialization is never considered ineffective even if the object is later re-initialized. Why not?

4.9 Consider the following simple package with a global variable and a swap procedure that exchanges its parameter with the global variable:

```
package Example is
    G : Integer ;


    procedure Swap(X : in out Integer )
        with Global => (In_Out => G);
    end Example;
```

What flow dependency contract is synthesized for Swap? Is it accurate?

4.10 When a contract is synthesized, it is not checked in the body of the subprogram to which the contract applies. Consider the following subprogram with a flow dependency contract:

```
procedure P(X : in out Integer )
    with Depends => (X =>+ A, A => B);
```

a. What data dependency contract is synthesized?
b. If P's body, in fact, makes use of another global variable C, will the inconsistency be detected? Be careful!

4.11 When a contract is synthesized, it is not checked in the body of the subprogram to which the contract applies. Consider the following subprogram with a data dependency contract:

```
procedure P(X : in out Integer )
    with Global => (Input => A, Output => B);
```

a. What flow dependency contract is synthesized?
b. If P's body does not actually have one of the flow dependencies in the synthesized contract, will the inconsistency be detected?

4.12 We recommend explicitly declaring data and flow dependency contracts on the public subprograms of a package. Why?

4.13 When is it reasonable to rely on synthesized data and flow dependency contracts?

4.14 What is the difference between *constructive analysis* and *retrospective analysis*?

5

Mathematical Background

In this chapter we present some background in mathematical logic in the context of software analysis. This material may be review for some readers, but we encourage all to at least skim this chapter to gain understanding of our notation, terminology, and use in writing SPARK programs. You may wish to consult a discrete mathematics textbook such as those by Epp (2010), Gersting (2014), or Rosen (2011) for a complete treatment of these topics.

5.1 Propositional Logic

A *proposition* is a meaningful declarative sentence that is either true or false. Propositions are also called *logical statements* or just *statements*. A statement cannot be true at one point in time and false at another time. Here, for example, are two simple propositions, one true and one false:

Sodium Azide is a poison.
New York City is the capital of New York state.

Not all statements that can be uttered in a natural language are unambiguously true or false. When a person makes a statement such as, "I like Italian food," there are usually many subtle qualifications to the meaning at play. The speaker might really mean, "I usually like Italian food," or, "I've had Italian food that I liked." The true meaning is either evident from the context of the conversation or can be explored in greater depth by asking clarifying questions. In any case, the speaker almost certainly does not mean he or she definitely likes all Italian food in the world. The original statement is neither completely true nor completely false.

Even mathematical expressions may be ambiguous. We cannot tell whether the expression $x \geq 17$ is true or false as we do not know the value of x. We can

Table 5.1. Connectives of propositional logic

Symbol	Formal name	Informal name
¬	Negation	not
∧	Conjunction	and
∨	Disjunction	or
→	Implication	conditional
↔	Equivalence	biconditional

turn this expression into a proposition by giving x a value. In Section 5.4, we will show how to use quantifiers to give values to such variables.

Whereas literature, poetry, and humor depend on the emotional impact of ambiguous statements rife with subtle meanings, high-integrity systems must be constructed in more absolute terms. The pilot of an aircraft wants to know that if a certain control is activated, the landing gear will definitely respond. Thus, we are interested in statements with clear truth values.

We use symbols such as s_1, s_2, s_3, ... to represent statements. For example, s_1 might represent "The Chicago Cubs won the world series this year," s_2 might represent "The winner of the world series is the best baseball team," and s_3 might represent "The players of the best baseball team have the highest average salary." We can combine these statements using operators called *propositional connectives*. The names and symbols used for these operators are given in Table 5.1 in decreasing order of precedence. As usual, parentheses can be used to clarify or override the normal precedence.

All of the connectives listed in Table 5.1 are infix binary operators except for ¬, which is a prefix unary operator. The truth values for these connectives are given in the Table 5.2.

The first two propositional logic connectives in Table 5.2 behave according to their informal descriptions: $\neg s_1$ means "not s_1" and returns true whenever s_1 is false and vice versa, and $s_1 \wedge s_2$ means "s_1 and s_2." It returns true only when both s_1 and s_2 are both true. You are certainly familiar with operators in

Table 5.2. Truth tables for propositional connectives

x	y	$\neg x$	$x \wedge y$	$x \vee y$	$x \rightarrow y$	$x \leftrightarrow y$
F	F	T	F	F	T	T
F	T	T	F	T	T	F
T	F	F	F	T	F	F
T	T	F	T	T	T	T

various programming languages that carry out negation and conjunction. Here are two assignment statements that illustrate their use in SPARK with Boolean variables A, B, and C:

```
A := not B;
A := B and C;
```

The other connectives require some additional explanation: ∨, the or connective, is *inclusive* in the sense that it returns true when either one or both of its operands are true. In common speaking, the word or is sometimes used in an *exclusive* sense ("You can have cookies or candy [but not both]"). In propositional logic this *exclusive or* function can be simulated with a more complex formula:

$$(s_1 \vee s_2) \wedge \neg(s_1 \wedge s_2)$$

Informally, this reads, "You can have (cookies or candy) and not (cookies and candy)." Notice that even though people do not normally speak with parentheses, it is often necessary to add some clarification to the informal expression to avoid ambiguity. Without the parentheses the listener might wonder if the speaker meant, "You can have (cookies or (candy and not cookies)) and candy." In real life, ambiguities of this nature are often resolved using contextual information, which humans are exceptionally good at processing, but misunderstandings do sometimes occur regardless. SPARK provides operators for inclusive and exclusive or:

```
A := B or C;    -- Inclusive or
A := B xor C;   -- Exclusive or
```

The implication connective, →, captures the meaning of conditional expressions. Let s_1 be the statement, "You work hard in this course," and s_2 be "You will get a good grade." For now we will suppose these statements have well-defined truth values. In that case, the formula $s_1 \rightarrow s_2$ informally translates to "If you work hard in this course, then you will get a good grade." This formula is often read "s_1 implies s_2."

Table 5.2 shows that the only time the conditional expression is false is when the first statement, called the *antecedent*, is true and the second statement, called the *consequent*, is false. In that world, you did work hard and yet you got a poor grade anyway – the conditional expression was not true. In all other cases, however, the conditional expression is considered true. Sometimes this can lead to surprising results. For example, the following statement is true: "If the moon is made of green cheese, then you will win the lottery this year." Because the antecedent is false, it does not matter what the truth value of the consequent

Table 5.3. Logical connectives associated with common
English phrases

English phrase	Proposition
A and B, A but B, A also B, A in addition B, A moreover B	$A \wedge B$
A or B	$A \vee B$
if A, then B, A only if B, A implies B, A, therefore B, B follows from A, A is a sufficient condition for B, B is a necessary condition for A	$A \rightarrow B$
A if and only if B, A is a necessary and sufficient condition for B	$A \leftrightarrow B$

might be. In effect, the conditional expression does not apply in that case. Conditional expressions with false antecedents are said to be *vacuously true*.

In SPARK, conditional expressions may be written as if expressions. For example, the value of a determined by the logical statement $b \rightarrow c$ may be written in SPARK as

    A := (if B then C);

Recall from Section 2.1.3 that an if expression without an else clause evaluates to true when the condition is false, just as in the definition of implication. This vacuously true behavior is essential when we prove SPARK verification conditions.

The biconditional connective expresses the idea that the truth value of its operands are always the same. If $s_1 \leftrightarrow s_2$ is true, then s_1 and s_2 have identical truth values in all cases. The phrase "if and only if," as often used in mathematical texts, is translated to the biconditional connective. "P if and only if Q" means $P \leftrightarrow Q$. This property is used to express the concept of *logical equivalence* that we discuss in Section 5.2. SPARK does not have a construct to directly implement the biconditional. Instead, we must make use of a logically equivalent expression described in Section 5.2.

One of the tasks of developing software is the translation of English language expressions into formal expressions. This translation is particularly important when working with logical connectives. Table 5.3 gives a number of common English phrases and their equivalent logical expressions.

It is important to remember that English, like any natural language, is often ambiguous and nuanced. Furthermore, people often speak inaccurately. Use Table 5.3 only as a guide.

Table 5.4. Truth table for $\neg s_1 \wedge (s_2 \to (s_3 \vee (s_1 \leftrightarrow s_3)))$

Three inputs					$s_3 \vee$	$s_2 \to$	$\neg s_1 \wedge (s_2 \to$
s_1	s_2	s_3	$\neg s_1$	$s_1 \leftrightarrow s_3$	$(s_1 \leftrightarrow s_3)$	$(s_3 \vee (s_1 \leftrightarrow s_3))$	$(s_3 \vee (s_1 \leftrightarrow s_3)))$
F	F	F	T	T	T	T	T
F	F	T	T	F	T	T	T
F	T	F	T	T	T	T	T
F	T	T	T	F	T	T	T
T	F	F	F	F	F	T	F
T	F	T	F	T	T	T	F
T	T	F	F	F	F	F	F
T	T	T	F	T	T	T	F

We used Table 5.2 to define the five propositional connectives. Truth tables are also used to show all the possible values of a complex statement. For example, the possible values of the complex statement s_4 defined as

$$s_4 = \neg s_1 \wedge (s_2 \to (s_3 \vee (s_1 \leftrightarrow s_3)))$$

are given in Table 5.4. This table contains a row for each combination of the three primitive statements (s_1, s_2, s_3) that define s_4. The number of rows in a truth table for a complex statement is 2^n when n is the number of different primitive statements in the definition of the complex statement. The three primitive statements defining s_4 are written as the first three columns of Table 5.4. The eight rows contain all the possible combinations of values of these three inputs. The remaining five columns in the table correspond to the five logical connectives used in the definition of s_4 and are in the order that the connectives would be evaluated from the three inputs.

Certain formulae have the property of being true regardless of the truth values of their constituent statements. These expressions are said to be *tautologies*. A simple example of a tautology is $s_1 \vee \neg s_1$. If s_1 is true, then $s_1 \vee \neg s_1$ is true. And if s_1 is false, $s_1 \vee \neg s_1$ is still true. Although tautologies might at first glance appear to be uninteresting, they play a very important role in validating arguments, as we will see in Section 5.3.

5.2 Logical Equivalence

Look at the fourth column (labeled $\neg s_1$) and the last column of Table 5.4. The values in these two columns are identical. We say that $\neg s_1$ and $\neg s_1 \wedge (s_2 \to (s_3 \vee (s_1 \leftrightarrow s_3)))$ are *logical equivalents*. The symbol $\Leftrightarrow$ is used to indicate the

Table 5.5. Logical equivalences

Name	*or* form	*and* form
Commutative	$A \vee B \Leftrightarrow B \vee A$	$A \wedge B \Leftrightarrow B \wedge A$
Associative	$(A \vee B) \vee C \Leftrightarrow A \vee (B \vee C)$	$(A \wedge B) \wedge C \Leftrightarrow A \wedge (B \wedge C)$
Distributive	$A \vee (B \wedge C) \Leftrightarrow (A \vee B) \wedge (A \vee C)$	$A \wedge (B \vee C) \Leftrightarrow (A \wedge B) \vee (A \wedge C)$
De Morgan	$\neg(A \vee B) \Leftrightarrow \neg A \wedge \neg B$	$\neg(A \wedge B) \Leftrightarrow \neg A \vee \neg B$
Absorption	$A \vee (A \wedge B) \Leftrightarrow A$	$A \wedge (A \vee B) \Leftrightarrow A$
Idempotent	$A \vee A \Leftrightarrow A$	$A \wedge A \Leftrightarrow A$
Identity	$A \vee False \Leftrightarrow A$	$A \wedge True \Leftrightarrow A$
Universal bound	$A \vee True \Leftrightarrow True$	$A \wedge False \Leftrightarrow False$
Complement	$A \vee \neg A \Leftrightarrow True$	$A \wedge \neg A \Leftrightarrow False$
Double negation		$\neg(\neg A) \Leftrightarrow A$
Conditional as disjunction		$A \rightarrow B \Leftrightarrow \neg A \vee B$
Biconditional as conjunction		$A \leftrightarrow B \Leftrightarrow (A \rightarrow B) \wedge (B \rightarrow A)$

logical equivalence of two statements as shown here:

$$\neg s_1 \quad \Leftrightarrow \quad \neg s_1 \wedge (s_2 \rightarrow (s_3 \vee (s_1 \leftrightarrow s_3)))$$

We can substitute the value of one statement for the value of the other statement. Another way to look at this particular equivalence is that the statement $\neg s_1 \wedge (s_2 \rightarrow (s_3 \vee (s_1 \leftrightarrow s_3)))$ can be simplified to $\neg s_1$.

Simplification of statements, like the simplification of algebraic expressions, can be accomplished by applying certain rules. The rules we use for simplifying statements are called *logical equivalences*. Table 5.5 summarizes the most commonly used logical equivalences. Each of the logical equivalences in Table 5.5 could be proven by constructing a truth table.

Let us look at some examples to show how these logical equivalences can be used to simplify statements. The name after each line is that of the logical equivalence we used to obtain the line from the previous line. In the first example, we use logical equivalences to reduce the number of logical connectives from four to two. In the second example, we simplify a complex statement to a single primitive statement with no connectives.

$$\neg(p \wedge \neg q) \vee q$$

$(\neg p \vee \neg(\neg q)) \vee q$	De Morgan
$(\neg p \vee q) \vee q$	Double negation
$\neg p \vee (q \vee q)$	Association
$\neg p \vee q$	Idempotent

$$\neg(q \to q) \vee (p \wedge q)$$

$$\neg(\neg q \vee p) \vee (p \wedge q) \qquad \text{Conditional as disjunction}$$

$$(\neg(\neg q) \wedge \neg p) \vee (p \wedge q) \qquad \text{De Morgan}$$

$$(q \wedge \neg p) \vee (p \wedge q) \qquad \text{Double negation}$$

$$(q \wedge \neg p) \vee (q \wedge p) \qquad \text{Commutative}$$

$$q \wedge (\neg p \vee p) \qquad \text{Distributive}$$

$$q \wedge True \qquad \text{Compliment}$$

$$q \qquad \text{Identity}$$

5.3 Arguments and Inference

An argument is an attempt to convince someone of something. In formal logic, an *argument* is expressed by a set of statements called *premises* that together support the truth of another statement called a *conclusion*. Here is an example of an argument with two premises followed by a conclusion:

If Horace swallowed Sodium Azide, then Horace was poisoned.
Horace swallowed Sodium Azide.
Therefore, Horace was poisoned.

All arguments can be expressed in the following form:

$$(p_1 \wedge p_2 \wedge p_3 \wedge p_4 \wedge p_5 \wedge p_6 \ldots \wedge p_n) \to c$$

where the p's are the premises and c is the conclusion. Informally, this statement says that if all of the premises are true, then the conclusion is true. As premises in a poorly constructed argument can have no relationship to the conclusion, having true premises is not sufficient to show that the conclusion is true. We need to be concerned with the form of the argument. An argument is said to be *valid* if this implication is a tautology. Only when an argument is valid is the conclusion a logical consequence of its premises.

Consider the poisoning argument given at the beginning of this section. If we use s_1 to represent "Horace swallowed Sodium Azide" and s_2 to represent "Horace was poisoned," we can write the argument formally as

$$((s_1 \to s_2) \wedge s_1) \to s_2$$

One way to demonstrate that this statement is a tautology, and therefore a valid argument, is to construct a truth table as we have done in Table 5.6. There you can see that no matter what the values of the inputs s_1 and s_2, the value of the argument, $((s_1 \to s_2) \wedge s_1) \to s_2$, is true. Note that there is only one row

Table 5.6. Truth table for $((s_1 \rightarrow s_2) \wedge s_1) \rightarrow s_1$

s_1	s_2	$s_1 \rightarrow s_2$	$(s_1 \rightarrow s_2) \wedge s_1$	$((s_1 \rightarrow s_2) \wedge s_1) \rightarrow s_1$
F	F	T	F	T
F	T	T	F	T
T	F	F	F	T
T	T	T	T	T

in this truth table where both of the two premises, $s_1 \rightarrow s_2$ and s_1, are true. Because of the nature of implication, when a premise is false, the argument is vacuously true. Thus, to show that an argument is valid, we need only fill in the rows of the truth table in which the premises are all true.

Whereas truth tables provide one method of validating arguments, they are cumbersome when there are large numbers of inputs and premises. Another approach is to construct a formal proof of the validity of an argument. We do this by applying derivation rules called *rules of inference* or *inference rules*. We use these rules to derive new valid statements that follow from previous statements. Inference rules are like "mini-arguments" that are known to be valid. Our poison argument is an example of one of the most common inference rules called modus ponens. It may expressed as follows:

$$\frac{s_1 \rightarrow s_2 \qquad s_1}{s_2}$$

Informally this notation means that the conclusion below the line follows from the hypotheses spaced out above the line. More precisely, this notation means that if one forms a conditional expression with the conjunction of the hypotheses as the antecedent and the conclusion as the consequent, that conditional expression is a tautology.

Many useful rules of inference exist. Here are the most commonly used ones:

Modus ponens	Modus tolens	Conjunction	Simplification
$\dfrac{A \rightarrow B \qquad A}{B}$	$\dfrac{A \rightarrow B \qquad \neg B}{\neg A}$	$\dfrac{A \qquad B}{A \wedge B}$	$\dfrac{A \wedge B}{A \qquad B}$

Addition	Hypothetical syllogism	Disjunctive syllogism
$\dfrac{A}{A \vee B}$	$\dfrac{A \rightarrow B \qquad B \rightarrow C}{A \rightarrow C}$	$\dfrac{A \vee B \qquad \neg A}{B}$

Contrapositive	Disjunction elimination	Resolution
$\dfrac{A \rightarrow B}{\neg B \rightarrow \neg A}$	$\dfrac{A \vee B \qquad A \rightarrow C \qquad B \rightarrow C}{C}$	$\dfrac{A \vee B \qquad \neg A \vee C}{B \vee C}$

The simplification rule contains two conclusions. This is a shorthand for two different rules with the same premises and two different conclusions.

Here are two example proofs using rules of inference to demonstrate an argument is valid (the statement defining the argument is a tautology). To accomplish the proof, we start with the premises and use various inference rules and logical equivalences to transform them to the conclusion. The right column of each proof describes how the particular statement on the line was derived from prior lines.

$\neg(s_1 \lor \neg s_2) \land (s_2 \to s_3) \to (\neg s_1 \land s_3)$ – The argument to validate

1.	$\neg(s_1 \lor \neg s_2)$	Premise
2.	$s_2 \to s_3$	Premise
3.	$\neg s_1 \land \neg(\neg s_2)$	De Morgan applied to line 1
4.	$\neg s_1 \land s_2$	Double negation applied to line 3
5.	$\neg s_1$	Simplification applied to line 4
6.	s_2	Simplification applied to line 4 (again)
7.	s_3	Modus ponens applied to lines 2 and 6
8.	$\therefore (\neg s_1 \land s_3)$	Conjunction applied to lines 5 and 7

$(s_1 \to s_3) \land (s_3 \to \neg s_2) \land s_2 \to \neg s_1$ – The argument to validate

1.	$s_1 \to s_3$	Premise
2.	$s_3 \to \neg s_2$	Premise
3.	s_2	Premise
4.	$s_1 \to \neg s_2$	Hypothetical syllogism applied to lines 1 and 2
5.	$\neg(\neg s_2)$	Double negative applied to line 3
6.	$\therefore \neg s_1$	Modus tollens applied to lines 4 and 5

This approach to proving argument validity has a direct counterpart in SPARK. GNATprove can generate arguments[1] called *verification conditions* (VCs) for each subprogram. It uses our preconditions as premises and our postconditions as conclusions. If we can prove these VCs, we have shown that our postconditions always follow from our preconditions. Fortunately, we do not have to manually perform the proofs like we did in the preceding examples. GNATprove makes use of automated theorem provers to accomplish the task.

However, we sometimes need to help out the prover with additional assertions. We will look at the details of program proof in Chapter 6.

What do you think of the following argument?

> If the moon is made of green cheese, then NASA can feed the world.
> The moon is made of green cheese.
> Therefore, NASA can feed the world.

This argument is valid by modus ponens. As we know, however, the second premise is false. That makes the argument statement $(p_1 \land p_2) \rightarrow c$ vacuously true. Argument validity is just about argument form or syntax. Most useful arguments have premises that are true. An argument that is valid and has true premises is said to be a *sound argument*. This principle applies to program proof. GNATprove will check that the preconditions we write for our subprograms are always true.

5.4 Predicate Logic

The statements studied so far are fixed statements. However, the interesting logical structure of many useful statements is lost when expressed in such simple terms. For example, a statement such as "all students work hard" might be a legitimate statement but expressing it as such does not convey the significant fact that it is a statement about an entire set of entities.

To express such statements more directly, we need to first parameterize them. Instead of treating a statement as a bare fact s_1, we can give it multiple parameters $s_1(x_1, x_2, \ldots, x_n)$. We call such parameterized statements *predicates*. The values of x_i are taken from a set U called the *universe of discourse* and can be any set that is convenient.

For example, let U be the set of all humans alive on Earth today. Let the predicate $s(x)$ be true if $x \in U$ is a student.[2] Let the predicate $w(x)$ be true if $x \in U$ works hard. Once appropriate arguments are given to a predicate, we will take the resulting statement to be either true or false. For now, we require that all arguments come from the same set U and thus are, in effect, the same type.

If Alice $\in U$, then a statement such as s(Alice) is true if Alice is a student and false otherwise. The statement s(Alice) $\rightarrow w$(Alice) means informally "if Alice is a student then Alice works hard." This statement is a statement about Alice specifically. It might be true or it might be false. In any case, the truth of a similar statement about Bob $\in U$, s(Bob) $\rightarrow w$(Bob), might be entirely different.

What can we say about an expression $M = s(x) \rightarrow w(x)$? A *variable* x stands for an as yet unspecified element of U. Without a particular value for x, M is not a statement – it has no truth value. We say that the variable x is *unbound* in M.

To make M into a proper statement, we need to *bind* the variable x. There are two binders that interest us the *universal quantifier*, symbolized with ∀, and the *existential quantifier*, symbolized with ∃.

The statement $\forall x \, (s(x) \rightarrow w(x))$ reads informally as, "for all x, if x is a student, then x works hard." More precisely, we mean $\forall x \in U \, (s(x) \rightarrow w(x))$, but the universe of discourse is usually evident from context and not normally mentioned explicitly in the formulae. It is important to note that x ranges over the whole set U. Recall that when the antecedent of an implication is false, the implication is vacuously true. So $s(x) \rightarrow w(x)$ is automatically true for any x that is not a student.

SPARK uses the syntax **for all** and the arrow delimiter, $=>$, to implement the universal quantifier. The expression on the right side of the assignment statement

A := (**for all** X **in** Integer => (**if** X **rem** 10 = 0 **then** X **rem** 2 = 0));

implements the quantified predicate $\forall x \in \mathbb{Z} \, (d(x) \rightarrow e(x))$, where $\mathbb{Z}$ (our universe of discourse) is the set of all integers, $d(x)$ is the predicate "x is evenly divisible by 10," and $e(x)$ is the predicate "x is even." This expression states that any integer that is evenly divided by 10 is even. As you might imagine, true is assigned to variable A.

At the beginning of this section we talked about the statement, "all students work hard," and we now have a formal encoding of that statement using the universal quantifier that exposes the fact that it is a statement about an entire set of entities. We could bury the quantification inside a simple statement by just setting $s_1 = \forall x \, (s(x) \rightarrow w(x))$ and then talk about s_1. There is nothing wrong with this, and at times it is entirely appropriate. However, many interesting proofs will require the more detailed view of the predicate's internal, universally quantified structure.

Now let us look at the use of the existential quantifier to bind statement variables. Consider the informal statement, "some students work hard." This means that there is at least one student who works hard or, equivalently, there exists a student who works hard. This statement can be encoded using the existential quantifier as $s_2 = \exists x \, (s(x) \wedge w(x))$. The truth of s_2 implies that there is at least one entity in U that is both a student and who works hard. The precise number of such entities that satisfy the predicate is not specified; it could even be all of them. Notice that $\exists x \, (s(x) \rightarrow w(x))$ is something entirely different.

To understand it we can use the conditional as a disjunction equivalent (from Table 5.5) on the expression covered by the quantifier to obtain $\exists x\,(\neg s(x) \vee w(x))$. If there is even one entity in U that is not a student, this statement is true. It is clear this has nothing to do with saying that some students work hard.

SPARK uses the syntax **for some** and the arrow delimiter, $=>$, to implement the existential quantifier. The expression on the right side of the assignment statement (that calls the Boolean function Is_Prime)

A := (**for some** X **in** Natural $=>$ (X **rem** 2 $=$ 0 **and then** Is_Prime (X)));

implements the quantified predicate $\exists x \in \mathbb{N}\,(e(x) \wedge p(x))$, where $\mathbb{N}$ (our universe of discourse) is the set of all natural numbers, $e(x)$ is the predicate "x is even," and $p(x)$ is the predicate "x is a prime number." This expression states that some natural number is both even and prime. As 2 is a prime number, true is assigned to variable A.

Our examples illustrate a common association between quantifiers and logical connectives. The universal quantifier, $\forall$, is most commonly associated with the implication operator, $\rightarrow$. The existential quantifier, $\exists$, is most commonly associated with the conjunction operator, $\wedge$.

We can simplify quantified expressions by narrowing the domain of the bound variable. For example, our statement, "all students work hard," may be written as either

$$\forall x \in U\,(s(x) \rightarrow w(x)) \quad \text{or} \quad \forall x \in S\,(w(x)),$$

where U is the set of all humans alive on earth today and S is the set of all students (a subset of U). Similarly our statement, "some students work hard," may be written as either

$$\exists x \in U\,(s(x) \wedge w(x)) \quad \text{or} \quad \exists x \in S\,(w(x)).$$

We frequently use types or subtypes to narrow domains when writing quantifiers in SPARK. For example, the subtype declaration

subtype Digit **is** Integer **range** $-9\,$..$\,9$;

limits the value of the bound variable X in the following quantified expression:

A := (**for all** X **in** Digit $=>$ X $**$ 2 $<$ 100);

How can we determine whether a quantified predicate is true or false? To show that a universally quantified predicate is false, we simply need to find one value of the bound variable that results in the predicate being false. For example, to show that the statement $\forall x\,(s(x) \rightarrow w(x))$ is false, we need to find one student who does not work hard. It takes more effort to show that a universally quantified predicate is true. We need to go through the entire universe

Table 5.7. Quantifiers associated with common English phrases

English phrase	Quantifier
for all, all, every, each, any	use ∀
there exists, some, one, at least one	use ∃

of discourse to see that there are no values that make our predicate false. In your discrete math class, you probably studied how direct proofs can be used in place of this brute force approach.

With the existential quantifier, we need find only one value that makes the predicate true to say the entire statement is true. To show that it is false, we must go through all of the values in the domain to make sure that none of them satisfy the predicate.

As with logical connectives we need to be able to translate English phrases into logical quantifiers. Our examples should give you some insight into the correspondences. Table 5.7 shows the most common English phrases for our two quantifiers. However, as with Table 5.3, care still needs to be used when translating English statements into formal logical statements.

All of our predicates to this point have had a single parameter. We may have multiple parameter predicates. For example, let the predicate $c(x, y)$ stand for "person x likes cuisine y," where "likes" means that they would be willing to go with a group of friends to a restaurant that specializes in that cuisine. This predicate involves two universal sets of discourse: U, the set of all humans alive today, and F, the set of all possible food cuisines. Table 5.8 gives examples of the use of this two-parameter predicate.

Predicates with multiple parameters are usually used in statements with multiple quantifiers. Table 5.9 provides some examples. Here we use the predicate $c(x, y)$ defined for the previous table and the predicate $l(x, y)$ defined as "person x loves person y." For the second half of the table, the universe of discourse is implied to be U, the set of all people alive today.

Table 5.8. Examples using the predicate $c(x, y)$, "person x likes cuisine y"

Predicate	English translations
c (Bob, Thai)	Bob likes Thai food.
$\forall p \in U\ (c(p, \text{Chinese}))$	Everybody likes Chinese food.
$\forall f \in F\ (c(\text{Mildred}, f))$	Mildred likes all cuisines.
$\exists f \in F\ (\neg c(\text{Horace}, f))$	Horace does not like some cuisine.
$\exists p \in U\ (c(p, \text{Mexican}))$	Somebody likes Mexican food.

Table 5.9. Examples using multiple quantifiers with the predicates
$c(x, y)$, "person x likes cuisine y," and $l(x, y)$, "person x loves person y"

Predicate	English translations
$\forall p \in U \ (\forall f \in F \ (c(p, f)))$	Everybody likes all cuisines.
$\forall p \in U \ (\exists f \in F \ (c(p, f)))$	Everybody likes some cuisine.
$\exists p \in U \ (\forall f \in F \ (c(p, f)))$	Somebody likes all cuisines.
$\exists p \in U \ (\exists f \in F \ (c(p, f)))$	Somebody likes some cuisine.
$\forall p \ (l(p, Raymond))$	Everybody loves Raymond.
$\exists p \ (\forall q \ (\neg l(p, q)))$	Somebody loves no one.
$\exists p \ (\forall q \ (\neg l(q, p)))$	There is somebody that no one loves.
$\forall p \ (\exists q \ (l(p, q)))$	Everybody loves somebody.
$\exists p \ (\forall q \ (l(p, q)))$	Somebody loves everybody.
$\forall p \ (\forall q \ (l(p, q) \rightarrow p = q))$	Everybody loves only themselves.

It takes practice to translate quantified statements into English and even more practice to translate English into quantified statements. Each of the three discrete mathematics textbooks referenced at the beginning of this chapter provides a wealth of further examples.

Let us look at some realistic examples of the use of the existential and universal quantifiers in a SPARK program. Here is the specification for a search procedure that determines the location of the first occurrence of a value in an array of values:

```
type Array_Type is array ( Positive range <>) of Integer;

procedure Find_First ( List     : in   Array_Type;
                       Value    : in   Integer ;
                       Position : out  Positive )
   with
      Depends => (Position => (List, Value)),
      Pre     => (for some Index in List ' Range => List (Index) = Value),
      Post    => (Position in List ' Range and then
                  List ( Position ) = Value and then
                  (for all Index in List ' First .. Position − 1 =>
                   List (Index) /= Value));
```

The precondition states that there is at least one occurrence of Value in the array List, $\exists Index \ (List(Index) = Value)$. The predicate variable Index has a domain (universe of discourse) of the range of the array List's index.

The postcondition is a conjunction of three parts. The first part states that the result Position is a legal subscript for the array List. The second part states that Position is the location of Value in List. The third part uses a universal quantifier with a limited domain to state that all the locations before Position do not contain Value.

Here is another search procedure that has a slightly different specification. This time, the value we are looking for may or may not be in the array. Also, the array does not contain any duplicate values. The answers consist of a Boolean telling whether or not the value was found and, if it was found, a position giving its location in the array.

```
procedure Find_Only  ( List      :  in  Array_Type;
                        Value     :  in  Integer ;
                        Found     :  out Boolean;
                        Position  :  out Positive )
    with
    Depends => ((Found, Position) => (List, Value)),
    Pre     => (List'Length > 0 and then
                List 'Last < Positive 'Last and then
                ( for all  J  in  List 'Range =>
                  ( for all  K  in  List 'Range =>
                    ( if  List (J) = List (K) then J = K)))),
    Post    => (Position in  List 'Range and then
                ((Found and then List ( Position ) = Value)
                        or else
                (not Found and then Position = List 'Last and then
                ( for all  J  in  List 'Range => List (J) /= Value))));
```

We have three preconditions. The first states that there is at least one element in the array. The second states that the upper bound of the array is less than the largest Positive value. These first two preconditions ensure that there is no overflow in any of the arithmetic expressions required in the body. The third precondition states that the array has no duplicate values. This check requires two universal quantifiers. The way to state that there are no duplicates is to compare all pairs of values in the array. If we find an equality in this comparison, the two indexes must be the same. We used the same logic in the last example in Table 5.9. In formal terms this last postcondition may be expressed as

$$\forall j \, (\forall k \, ((\mathit{Value}(j) = \mathit{Value}(k)) \rightarrow (j = k))).$$

The postcondition is more complicated. The first part states that the location returned is a legal subscript of the array. The second part states that either we found the value in the array at the returned location or we did not find the value in the array. In the case we did not find the value in the array, the location returned is the largest index of the array.

Summary

- A proposition is a meaningful declarative sentence that is either true or false.
- *Logical statement* and *statement* are synonyms of proposition.
- Statements may be represented by symbols such as s_1, s_2, A, and P.
- Statements may be combined using the logical connectives ¬ (negation), ∧ (conjunction), ∨ (disjunction), → (implication), or ↔ (equivalence).
- In the implication $a \rightarrow b$, a is called the *antecedent*, and b is called the *consequent*.
- An implication with a false antecedent is vacuously true.
- *Truth tables* are used to define logical connectives and to show the possible values of a complex statement.
- A *tautology* is a statement that is always true irregardless of the truth values of any primitive statements defining it.
- Two propositions are *logically equivalent* when they have the same values for all "inputs".
- *Logical equivalences* are used to simplify logical statements.
- A *formal argument* is a set of statements called *premises* that together support the truth of another statement called the *conclusion*.
- Arguments are expressed in the form $(p_1 \land p_2 \land p_3 \land p_4 \land p_5 \land p_6 \dots \land p_n) \rightarrow c$.
- A *valid argument* is one whose implication form is a tautology.
- A truth table can be used to show that an argument is valid.
- *Rules of inference* are valid arguments that may be used to show that other arguments are valid.
- SPARK uses arguments called *verification conditions* to demonstrate that the postconditions of a subprogram may be derived from its preconditions.
- A *sound argument* is a valid argument whose premises are all true.
- A *predicate* is a parameterized statement. We must supply specific values for a predicate's parameters to determine its truthfulness.
- An *unbound variable* is a variable without a value that is used in a predicate. We cannot determine the truthfulness of a predicate with unbound variables.
- We may use the *universal quantifier*, ∀, or the *existential quantifier*, ∃, to bind a variable in a predicate.

• Converting English language sentences into propositions with quantified predicates and logical connectors is an important skill for software engineers who write SPARK preconditions and postconditions.

Exercises

5.1 Define the following terms.

a. proposition

b. statement

c. propositional connective

d. conjunction

e. disjunction

f. exclusive or

g. implication

h. antecedent

i. consequent

j. vacuously true

k. logical equivalence

l. tautology

5.2 Complete the following truth table to prove the logical equivalence conditional as disjunction, $x \rightarrow y \Leftrightarrow \neg x \vee y$.

x	y	$x \rightarrow y$	$\neg x$	$\neg x \vee y$
F	F			
F	T			
T	F			
T	T			

5.3 Complete the following truth table to prove the absorption logical equivalence, $x \wedge (x \vee y) \Leftrightarrow x$.

x	y	$x \vee y$	$x \wedge (x \vee y)$
F	F		
F	T		
T	F		
T	T		

5.4 Given that p is true, q is false, and r is true, what are the truth values of the following propositions?

a. $\neg(p \wedge q) \vee r$

b. $(p \wedge q) \vee r$

c. $p \wedge (q \vee r)$

d. $\neg p \vee \neg(\neg q \wedge r)$

e. $q \rightarrow (p \vee q)$

f. $(p \vee q) \rightarrow r$

g. $r \rightarrow (\neg p \wedge \neg q)$

h. $q \vee (\neg p \rightarrow r)$

5.5 Translate the statement definition $a = b \leftrightarrow c$ into a SPARK assignment statement using the Boolean variables A, B, and C. You will need to use a logical equivalence from Table 5.5.

5.6 Use the logical equivalences from Table 5.5 to simplify the following propositions. State the name of each equivalence you use as in the examples on page 140.

a. $p \wedge \neg(p \wedge q)$
b. $(p \rightarrow q) \wedge p$
c. $(p \vee q) \wedge (p \vee \neg q)$
d. $p \vee (q \wedge \neg p)$
e. $p \wedge \neg(p \wedge \neg q)$
f. $\neg(p \wedge q) \wedge (p \vee \neg q)$

5.7 Let P be the statement "Roses are red," Q be the statement "Violets are blue," and R be the statement "Sugar is sweet." Translate the following English sentences into formal statements.

a. Roses are red and violets are blue.
b. Roses are red, but sugar is not sweet.
c. It is not true that roses are red and violets are blue.
d. Roses are red, but sugar is sweet.
e. Roses are red only if violets are blue.
f. Roses being red is a sufficient condition for violets being blue.
g. Roses being red is a necessary condition for violets being blue.
h. Roses being red follows from violets being blue.
i. If roses are red and violets are blue, then sugar is sweet.
j. Whenever roses are red, violets are blue and sugar is sweet.
k. Roses are red, and if sugar is sour, then violets are not blue.

5.8 Define the following terms.

a. argument
b. premise
c. conclusion
d. valid argument
e. sound argument
f. inference rule

5.9 Use inference rules and logical equivalences to show that the following arguments are valid. Label each step as we did on page 143.

a. $(A \rightarrow B) \wedge (C \vee \neg B) \wedge A \rightarrow C$
b. $A \wedge (\neg B \rightarrow \neg A) \rightarrow B$
c. $\neg(A \vee \neg B) \wedge (B \rightarrow C) \rightarrow (\neg A \wedge C)$
d. $\neg A \wedge (A \vee B) \rightarrow B$
e. $(\neg A \rightarrow \neg B) \wedge B \wedge (A \rightarrow C) \rightarrow C$

5.10 Given the predicates

$c(x)$ is x is a car,
$m(x)$ is x is a motorcycle, and
$f(x)$ is x is fast,

translate each of the following English sentences into formal statements. The universe of discourse is all things in the world. Recall that $\forall$ is usually associated with → and that ∃ is usually associated with ∧. We have given an answer for the first one.

a. All cars are fast.   *answer* $\forall x(C(x) \rightarrow F(x))$

b. Some motorcycles are fast.

c. All cars are fast but no motorcycle is fast.

d. Only motorcycles are fast.

e. No car is fast.

f. If every car is fast, then every motorcycle is fast.

g. Some motorcycles are not fast.

h. If no car is fast, then some motorcycles are not fast.

5.11 Given the predicates

$bx)$ is x is a bee,

$f(x)$ is a flower,

$s(x)$ is x stings, and

$p(x, y)$ is x pollinates y.

translate each of the following English sentences into formal statements. The universe of discourse is all things in the world. Recall that ∀ is usually associated with → and that ∃ is usually associated with ∧. We have given an answer for the second one.

a. All bees sting.

b. Some flowers sting.   *answer* $\exists x \, (F(x) \wedge S(x))$

c. Only bees sting.

d. Some bees pollinate all flowers.

e. All bees pollinate some flowers.

5.12 The predicate $e(x)$ is "x is an even integer." Use only this predicate and quantifiers to translate the following English sentences into formal statements. The universe of discourse is all integers.

a. Some integers are even.

b. All integers are even.

c. Some integers are odd.

d. Some integers are both even and odd.

e. The sum of an even integer and 12 is an even integer.

f. The sum of any two even integers is an even integer.

5.13 The following function is given an array of percentages and a specific percentage. It returns the number of percentages in the array that are less than the given specific percentage. As you can see from the code, it accomplishes this task by searching for the first value in the array that is greater than or equal to the specific percentage. For this algorithm to work, the values in the array must be in ascending order. Complete the precondition that states this requirement.

```
type Percent        is delta 0.25 range 0.0 .. 100.0;
type Percent_Array is array ( Integer range <>) of Percent;

function Num_Below (List      : in Percent_Array;
                            Value : in Percent) return Natural
-- Returns the number of values in List that are less than Value
    with
        Pre => (

is
    Result : Natural;
    Index  : Integer ;
begin
    Result := 0;
    Index  := List ' First ;
    loop
        exit when Index > List'Last or else List (Index) >= Value;
        Result := Result + 1;
        Index  := Index + 1;
    end loop;
    return Result ;
end Num_Below;
```

5.14 Add a second precondition to the function in Exercise 5.13 that states that List contains at least one value.

6

Proof

In this chapter we describe how you can use SPARK to prove certain correctness properties of your programs. When you ask to "prove" your code, the SPARK tools will by default endeavor to prove that it will never raise any of the predefined language exceptions that we describe in Section 6.1. If you additionally include pre- and postconditions, loop invariants, or other kinds of *assertions*, the tools will also attempt to prove that those assertions will never fail.

It is important to understand that proofs created by the SPARK tools are entirely static. This means if they succeed, the thing being proved will be true for every possible execution of your program regardless of the inputs provided. This is the critical property of proof that sets it apart from testing.

However, Ada assertions are also executable under the control of the assertion policy in force at the time a unit is compiled. Assertions for which proofs could not be completed can be checked when the program is run, for example during testing, to help provide a certain level of confidence about the unproved assertions. Testing can thus be used to complement the proof techniques described here to obtain greater overall reliability. We discuss this further in Section 8.4.

6.1 Runtime Errors

A *logical error* is an error in the logic of the program itself that may cause the program to fail as it is executing. It is an error that, in principle, arises entirely because of programmer oversight. In contrast, an *external error* is an error caused by a problem in the execution environment of the program, such as being unable to open a file because it does not exist. If a program is correct, it should not contain any logical errors. However, external errors are outside of a program's control and may occur regardless of how well constructed the

155

program might be. A properly designed program should be able to cope with any external errors that might arise. However, the handling of external errors is outside the scope of this book and is a matter for software analysis, design, and testing (see Black, 2007).

We distinguish a *runtime error* as a special kind of logical error that is detected by Ada-mandated checks during program execution. Examples of runtime errors include the attempt to access an array with an out of bounds index, arithmetic overflow, or division by zero. Other kinds of logical errors include calling a subprogram without satisfying its precondition, but those errors are not checked by the Ada language itself. However, you can include custom assertions to check for such errors. We describe how to do so in Section 6.2.

For programs written in an unsafe language such as C, runtime errors often produce "undefined behavior," referred to as *erroneous execution* in the Ada community, that commonly result in a crash. Such errors are often caused by exploitable faults and indicate potential security problems as well. In contrast, Ada raises an exception when a runtime error occurs. A careful programmer will provide exception handlers[1] to deal with runtime errors in some sensible way by, for example, reporting the error or even attempting to recover from it.

Unfortunately, in a high-integrity system after-the-fact handling of runtime errors is not acceptable. If a program does something illogical, such as divide by zero, that means whatever the programmer intended to happen did not actually happen. An exception handler can make a guess about how to proceed from that point, but it is only a guess. Because the error should never have occurred in the first place, the exception handler cannot know with certainty how to respond. For example, retrying the failed operation may cause the same illogical computation to be attempted again, potentially resulting in an infinite loop of ineffective error handling actions.

In a high-integrity context, it is important that runtime errors never occur. The ability SPARK gives you to construct a mathematical proof that a program has no runtime errors justifies SPARK's lack of support for exception handling. A program proved free of runtime errors will never raise an exception and thus has no need for exception handling. In Section 7.1 we discuss the issues arising when calling full Ada libraries from SPARK and how to deal with the exceptions those libraries might produce.

As a side effect, it may also be possible to create more efficient programs with SPARK than with full Ada, both in terms of space and time. If the program has been proved exception-free, it can be compiled with all runtime checks disabled. This allows the compiler to create a faster and more compact executable than might otherwise be the case. Finally, it may be possible to enjoy additional

savings by using a reduced Ada runtime system without exception handling
support. We discuss how and when to suppress runtime checks in Section 6.8.

Proving that a program is free of runtime errors is the first level of proof
to pursue in SPARK programming. It is important to understand, however, that
showing freedom of runtime errors does not show that the program is "correct"
in the intuitive sense. SPARK also allows one to prove higher level correctness
properties. The techniques for doing so are discussed in the later sections of
this chapter. Those techniques extend the methods described here. Proving
freedom from runtime errors is the basis from which more complex proofs are
constructed.

6.1.1 *Predefined Exceptions*

The SPARK language allows the programmer to explicitly raise an exception,
but the SPARK tools attempt to prove that the **raise** statement will never actually
execute. This feature allows you to, for example, declare a Not_Implemented
exception and raise it in subprograms that are unfinished. The SPARK tools will
not able to prove such a subprogram as long as there is a way for the exception
to be raised, serving as a reminder that more work needs to be done[2].

The only exceptions that could conceivably arise in a pure SPARK program
are those that are predefined in the Ada language and raised automatically by the
Ada compiler when language-mandated checks fail. There are four predefined
exceptions. They are potentially raised for a wide variety of reasons. In this
section we describe these four predefined exceptions and outline how SPARK
manages them.

Program_Error

The Program_Error exception arises in full Ada for a variety of program organi-
zational problems that cannot always be detected by the compiler. The complete
list of situations where Program_Error might be raised is long, but as one example, the exception will be raised if the execution of a function ends without
returning a value. To see how that might happen, consider the following function that searches an array of integers and returns the index associated with the
first occurrence of zero in the array.

```
subtype Index_Type is Natural range 0 .. 1023;
type Integer_Array is array(Index_Type) of Integer ;

function Search_For_Zero (Values : in Integer_Array ) return Index_Type is
begin
    for Index in Index_Type loop
```

```
      if  Values (Index)  = 0 then
          return  Index;
      end  if ;
   end loop;
end Search_For_Zero;
```

The function ends as soon as the search is successful by returning from inside the loop. What happens if the array does not contain a zero value? In full Ada the function "falls off" the end and Program_Error is raised. This function is not necessarily wrong. If it is only used on arrays that contain at least one zero value, it will behave as intended. However, this function as written entails the possibility that an exception will be raised and that is not acceptable in a high-integrity application.

The preceding function is not legal SPARK because it can be shown statically to raise an exception – Program_Error in this case – under certain circumstances. One way to fix the problem would be to add a return statement to the path that currently falls off the end. The programmer would need to decide what value should be returned if a zero does not appear in the array.

An alternative approach would be to add a precondition to the function that ensures it is always called with an array containing at least one zero value. It is also necessary to add an explicit **raise** statement at the end of the function. The modifications are shown as follows:

```
subtype Index_Type is Natural range 0 .. 1023;
type Integer_Array  is  array(Index_Type) of Integer ;

function Search_For_Zero (Values :  in  Integer_Array ) return Index_Type
   with Pre =>  (for some Index in Index_Type => Values(Index) = 0)
is
begin
   for Index in Index_Type loop
      if Values (Index) = 0 then
         return Index;
      end if ;
   end loop;
   raise Program_Error;
end Search_For_Zero;
```

The SPARK tools will attempt to prove that the explicit **raise** can never execute, and the precondition allows that proof to be successful. The SPARK tools will also attempt to prove that the precondition is satisfied at every call site. We discuss preconditions in Section 6.2.1.

The explicit **raise** also prevents the flow of control from falling off the end of the function and triggering the automatically generated exception. The SPARK tools do not see this as an error but instead regard the explicit **raise** as a signal that you want the tools to prove the raise statement will never execute.

You can also use an explicit **raise** of Program_Error as a way of documenting arbitrary "impossible" events in your program. The SPARK tools will then try to prove that those events are, indeed, impossible, as you believe. Consider, for example, a simple package for managing a street light. The specification might look as follows:

```
pragma SPARK_Mode (On);
package Lights is
   type Color_Type is (Red, Yellow, Green);

   function Next_Color (Current_Color : in Color_Type) return Color_Type;

end Lights;
```

Function Next_Color takes a color and returns the next color to be used in a specific sequence. An enumeration type defines the three possible color values. The body of this package is shown as follows:

```
pragma SPARK_Mode(On);
package body Lights is

   function Next_Color (Current_Color : in Color_Type) return Color_Type is
      Result : Color_Type;
   begin
      case Current_Color is
         when Red =>
            Result := Green;
         when Yellow =>
            Result := Red;
         when Green =>
            Result := Yellow;
      end case;
      return Result;
   end Next_Color;

end Lights;
```

Function Next_Color uses a **case** statement to handle each of the possible colors. Ada's full coverage rules for case statements, described in Section 2.1.2, ensure that every color is considered. Suppose now that a new color is added to the set of possible colors so the definition of Color_Type becomes

```
type Color_Type is (Red, Yellow, Green, Pink);
```

The Ada compiler will require a case for Pink be added to the case statement in Next_Color. Suppose, however, that you believe the logic of your program is such that Next_Color will never be called with a Pink value. To satisfy the compiler you might include an empty case such as

```
when Pink =>
   null ;
```

This executes the special *null statement* in that case, which does nothing. However, if calling Next_Color with a Pink value is a logical error, this approach just hides the error and is thus highly undesirable.

Another strategy would be to explicitly raise Program_Error as a way of announcing the error in terms that cannot be easily swept under the rug:

```
when Pink =>
   raise Program_Error;
```

Now the SPARK tools will attempt to prove this case can never happen, thus verifying what you believe to be true about your program. However, with Next_Color written as we have shown so far, that proof would fail. Using a precondition makes the proof trivial:

```
function Next_Color (Current_Color : in Color_Type) return Color_Type
   with Pre => Current_Color /= Pink;
```

Of course, now the SPARK tools will try to prove that this precondition is satisfied at each call site.

Tasking_Error

Ada has extensive support for writing programs built from multiple, interacting tasks. Certain error conditions can arise in connection with these tasking features, and in that case Tasking_Error is raised. The version of SPARK 2014 available at the time of this writing does not support any of Ada's tasking features and, thus, avoids Tasking_Error entirely.[3] However, we note that because SPARK allows you to build programs from a mixture of SPARK and full Ada, as we discuss in Section 7.1, it is possible to use the SPARK tools to analyze the sequential portions of a larger concurrent program.

Storage_Error

In an Ada program, Storage_Error is raised if a program runs out of memory. There are two primary ways that can happen. First, the program might run out of heap space while objects are dynamically allocated. Second, the program might run out of stack space to hold local variables while subprograms are called.

SPARK avoids Storage_Error from heap exhaustion by disallowing heap allocated memory. Unfortunately, avoiding stack overflow is more difficult, and SPARK by itself cannot guarantee that a program will not raise Storage_Error.

However, an analysis can be done to ensure a program will not run out of stack space. The approach requires two steps. First, it is necessary to forbid all forms of recursion, both direct where a subprogram calls itself and indirect where two (or more) subprograms call each other. It is very difficult to put a static bound on the amount of stack space required by a recursive program because the number of recursive invocations is, in general, only discovered dynamically. The SPARK tools do not detect recursion, but additional tools such as AdaCore's GNATcheck can do so.

If a program is not recursive, and if it does not make any indirect calls (SPARK forbids such calls), it is possible to build a tree representing the subprogram calls it might make. Such a tree is referred to as a *call tree*. For example, if procedure A calls procedures B1 and B2, then the tree would have B1 and B2 as children of A.

With a complete call tree in hand, one must then compute the stack space required on each path from the tree's overall root, representing the main procedure, to each leaf. Some of these paths may not be possible executions and could potentially be ruled out by a static analysis. Some of these paths may contain dynamically sized local variables, and an upper bound on the size of those variables would need to be statically determined. Although the SPARK tools do not do this analysis, GNATstack from AdaCore or StackAnalyzer from AbsInt are two tools available at the time of this writing that do.

Alternatively, stack usage can be dynamically analyzed during testing. It may then be possible to obtain a worst case upper bound on the required stack size via reasoning about the test cases. However the bound is obtained, stack overflow can be avoided by providing the program with stack space that equals or exceeds that bound.

Technically, the Ada standard allows the compiler to raise Storage_Error during the execution of potentially any construct at all. Indeed some compilers do make implicit use of additional storage in a manner that is not visible to the programmer. Thus, completely ruling out Storage_Error also requires tools that are aware of the compiler's implementation strategies.

Constraint_Error

We have seen how SPARK manages Program_Error, Tasking_Error, and Storage_Error, making it possible to write programs that will not raise those exceptions.

The last exception predefined by Ada is Constraint_Error. This exception is raised whenever a constraint is violated, such as when (a) a value is assigned to a variable that violates the range constraint of that variable's type; (b) an array element is accessed with an index that is out of bounds for that array; or (c) overflow occurs during arithmetic operations.

Certain sources of Constraint_Error in full Ada cannot arise in SPARK because of limitations in the SPARK language. For example, Ada raises Constraint_Error if an attempt is made to dereference a null access value (pointer). That is not possible in SPARK because SPARK forbids access values. However, many sources of Constraint_Error are possible in SPARK. Guaranteeing that Constraint_Error cannot arise requires constructing proofs based on the structure of the code being analyzed.

6.1.2 *Verification Conditions*

At each point in your program where a language-mandated check must occur, the SPARK tools generate a *verification condition*, also called a *proof obligation* in some literature. Each verification condition is a logical implication as described in Section 5.3. The hypotheses of the verification condition are taken from the the code leading to that program point with every possible path to the program point being considered. The conclusion of the verification condition is, in essence, that the exception will not be raised. That is, the conclusion states the condition that would cause the exception is false. If the verification condition is proved, then the hypotheses imply the exception will never occur.

In a typical program, a large number of verification conditions are generated, some with complex hypotheses. The SPARK tools make use of automatic theorem provers to discharge the verification conditions without human intervention. At least that is the idea. Usually, it is necessary to help the tools by organizing the program in a particular way or by providing additional information to the tools. We discuss these techniques in the context of several examples in the following sections of this chapter. Once we have discharged all of the verification conditions, we have great confidence that our program contains no runtime errors.

6.2 Contracts

Some of the most significant additions to Ada 2012 relative to earlier versions of the language are the facilities supporting *contract based programming*. This is a style of programming in which the semantics of subprograms and the

Table 6.1. Ada/SPARK assertions

Aspect/Pragma	Supported in SPARK	SPARK only	Cross reference
Assert	Yes	No	Section 6.3.1
Assert_And_Cut	Yes	Yes	Section 6.3.2
Assume	Yes	Yes	Section 6.3.3
Contract_Cases	Yes	Yes	Section 6.2.6
Dynamic_Predicate	No	No	Section 6.2.5
Initial_Condition	Yes	Yes	Section 6.2.2
Loop_Invariant	Yes	Yes	Section 6.4
Loop_Variant	Yes	Yes	Section 6.5
Post	Yes	No	Section 6.2.2
Pre	Yes	No	Section 6.2.1
Refined_Post	Yes	Yes	Section 6.2.3
Static_Predicate	Yes	No	Section 6.2.5
Type_Invariant	No	No	Section 6.2.4

properties of types are formally specified in the program itself by way of assertions written by the software designer. We use the term *assertion* to refer to a specific condition encoded into the program and reserve the term *contracts* to refer to the abstract concept of using assertions to formalize a program's behavior.

In Ada, assertions created during program design are executable. During runtime they can be checked to ensure that the behaviors specified by the designers are being realized. The SPARK tools go beyond this dynamic checking and endeavor to statically prove that none of the assertions will ever fail.

Table 6.1 shows all the assertion forms available to an Ada/SPARK programmer with references to where we discuss each form in more detail. At the time of this writing not all assertion forms that exist in Ada are yet supported by SPARK. Unsupported assertions are indicated as such in the table. Furthermore, SPARK adds some assertion forms that are not part of standard Ada. Those that are SPARK specific are also indicated in the table.

Whenever a program unit is compiled, some *assertion policy* is in effect. The Ada standard defines only two such policies, Check and Ignore, although compilers are allowed to provide additional policies.

If the assertion policy is Check, then any assertion that fails (evaluates to false) causes an Assertion_Error exception from the Ada.Assertions package to be raised. It is important to understand that this check occurs at runtime and recovery must be done at runtime, for example, by way of a suitable exception handler. In this respect, assertions are similar to the runtime errors described in Section 6.1. However, unlike runtime errors, it is up to the programmers to explicitly include assertions in their programs. Furthermore, assertions can be used to check whatever conditions the programmers deem appropriate.

An assertion policy of Ignore causes the compiler to remove the assertion checks so they will not be tested at runtime. In that case, failures of the assertions are not detected, probably causing other, less well-behaved failures. One of the main goals of SPARK is to allow proof that all assertions never fail.[4] In that case, the program can be compiled with an assertion policy of Ignore without being concerned about unexpected failures. In addition to increasing the reliability of the program, SPARK can improve its performance because the assertions consume resources, such as processor time, to check.

In the following subsections we describe how to specify assertions and give some hints about their use. Our approach is to show examples of increasing complexity and realism to give a feeling for how SPARK assertions work in practice.

6.2.1 *Preconditions*

Ada allows subprograms to be decorated with preconditions. A *precondition* is a logical expression (an expression with Boolean type) that must hold (evaluate to True) whenever the subprogram is called. Preconditions are specified using the Pre aspect. Because the expression used to define the precondition is arbitrary, it can be used to encode conditions of any complexity.

As an example, consider a package, Shapes, that does some geometric computations on two-dimensional shapes. All coordinates used by the package are in Cartesian form and constrained to a workspace in the range of -100 to 100 pixels in each dimension. An abbreviated specification of the package follows:

```
pragma SPARK_Mode(On);
package Shapes is

    subtype Coordinate_Type is  Integer range −100 .. +100;
    subtype Radius_Type      is  Coordinate_Type range 0 ..  10;

    type Circle is
        record
            Center_X : Coordinate_Type;
            Center_Y : Coordinate_Type;
            Radius   : Radius_Type;
        end record;
```

```
—— Return True if X, Y are inside  circle  C.
function  Inside_Circle  (X, Y :  in  Coordinate_Type;
                          C    :  in  Circle )  return Boolean
     with
        Pre => C.Center_X + C.Radius in Coordinate_Type and
               C.Center_X − C.Radius in Coordinate_Type and
               C.Center_Y + C.Radius in Coordinate_Type and
               C.Center_Y − C.Radius in Coordinate_Type;
end Shapes;
```

Here, a circle is described by the coordinates of its center and a radius. The function Inside_Circle takes a pair of X, Y coordinates and a circle and returns true if the given coordinates are inside the given circle.

The precondition given on Inside_Circle enforces the rule that the circle must be entirely contained in the workspace. We do not want to consider circles that overlap the allowed range of coordinates such as a circle with a center near the boundaries of Coordinate_Type and with a large radius.

Because the precondition is part of the subprogram's declaration, it is known to all users of the subprogram and becomes part of the subprogram's interface. It is the caller's responsibility to ensure that the precondition is satisfied. If it is not (and if the assertion policy is Check), then an exception will be raised at runtime. However, the SPARK tools will generate a verification condition at each location where Inside_Circle is called that, if proved, shows the precondition is satisfied at each of those places.

Notice that ordinary Ada subtype constraints are a kind of precondition. Consider, for example, a function Fibonacci that computes Fibonacci numbers.[5] If it is declared as

```
function Fibonacci (N :  in  Natural)  return  Natural;
```

it will raise Constraint_Error even for fairly small values of N. This is because the Fibonacci sequence grows very rapidly and causes an arithmetic overflow to occur inside the function if N is even moderately large. In particular, for systems using 32 bits for type Integer, the largest Fibonacci number that can be calculated is for $N = 46$. One could express this constraint by adding a precondition:

```
function Fibonacci (N :  in  Natural)  return  Natural
   with
      Pre => N <= 46;
```

However, it is more appropriate to use Ada's facilities for creating scalar subtypes instead of a precondition.

```
subtype Fibonacci_Argument_Type is Natural range 0 .. 46;

function Fibonacci (N : in Fibonacci_Argument_Type) return Natural;
```

Now an attempt to use a value out of range will cause Constraint_Error rather than Assertion_Error as a failed precondition would do, but the SPARK tools will attempt to prove that the error cannot occur in either case.

Using subtypes when possible is best because, being simpler, they are easier for the compiler to manage and optimize. They will also continue being checked even if the assertion policy is Ignore. However, Ada's scalar subtypes are relatively limited because they can only express certain restricted kinds of constraints such as range constraints. In contrast, preconditions are entirely general and can be used to express conditions of arbitrary complexity. In the example of Inside_Circle , scalar subtypes cannot capture the desired condition. A small circle right at the edge of the coordinate system might still be acceptable. Trying, for example, to constrain the type used to represent the coordinates of the circle's center is not a solution. The acceptability of a circle depends on the interaction between the values of its components.

In Section 5.4 we introduced Ada's syntax for quantified expressions using **for all** or **for some**. Preconditions, and assertions in general, can often make good use of quantified expressions particularly when arrays are involved. In fact, it is primarily their use in assertions that motivated the addition of quantified expressions to the Ada language.

As an example, consider a procedure that implements the binary search algorithm. This algorithm takes an array and a data item and efficiently checks to see if the array contains the data item. However, the algorithm requires that it be given an array in sorted order. The following specification of package Searchers contains the declaration of a procedure Binary_Search[6] along with a precondition:

```
package Searchers
  with SPARK_Mode => On
is
    subtype Index_Type is Positive range 1 .. 100;
    type Array_Type is array (Index_Type) of Integer ;

    procedure Binary_Search (Search_Item : in   Integer ;
                             Items       : in   Array_Type;
                             Found       : out  Boolean;
                             Result      : out  Index_Type)
        with
            Pre =>
```

```
              ( for  all  J  in  Items' Range  =>
                   ( for  all  K  in  J + 1 ..  Items' Last  =>  Items(J) <= Items(K)));
end Searchers ;
```

The precondition uses two nested for-all quantified expressions to assert that each item of the array comes before (or is the same as) all the items that follow it. The SPARK tools will, as usual, create a verification condition at each place where Binary_Search is called to prove that the precondition is satisfied.

It bears repeating that assertions in Ada are executable. With that in mind, notice that the precondition given for Binary_Search runs in $O(n^2)$ time. In contrast, the binary search algorithm itself runs in only $O(\log n)$ time.

An alternative way of expressing that the array is sorted is

```
Pre => (for  all  J  in  Items' First  ..  Items' Last − 1 =>
           Items (J) <= Items (J+1))
```

This has the advantage of running in only $O(n)$ time, and it might also be considered clearer. However, it is still asymptotically slower than the algorithm to which it is attached. Because assertions can use quantified expressions over large arrays, and even call recursive functions, they can consume large amounts of space and time. Expressive assertions thus have the potential to render unusable a program that would otherwise have acceptable performance characteristics. We discuss this issue further in Section 6.8.

6.2.2 *Postconditions*

A *postcondition* is a condition that is asserted to be true when a subprogram completes its actions and returns control to the caller. It describes the effects of the subprogram. Postconditions are, thus, formal statements derived from the functional requirements that our program must meet.

Postconditions are introduced with the Post aspect. As an example, consider the Searchers package again. A version of that package follows, where the Binary_Search procedure has been given a postcondition:

```
package Searchers2
  with SPARK_Mode => On
is
    subtype Index_Type is Positive range 1 .. 100;
    type Array_Type is array (Index_Type) of Integer ;

    procedure Binary_Search (Search_Item :  in    Integer ;
                             Items        :  in    Array_Type;
                             Found        :  out Boolean;
                             Result       :  out Index_Type)
```

```
with
  Pre =>
    ( for all J in Items'Range =>
      ( for all K in J + 1 .. Items'Last => Items(J) <= Items(K))),
  Post =>
    ( if Found then Search_Item = Items (Result)
                else ( for all J in Items'Range => Search_Item /= Items(J)));

end Searchers2 ;
```

The postcondition says that if the procedure reports it has found the search item, then that item exists at the reported position in the array. The else clause says that if the procedure does not find the search item, the item does not exist at any location in the array.

Preconditions and postconditions have a dual relationship. A precondition is an obligation on the caller to show, either by runtime testing or proof, that the condition is true before calling a subprogram. Inside the subprogram the precondition can be used in the hypotheses of verification conditions, being taken as a given in the context of the subprogram's body.

Postconditions, on the other hand, are obligations on the subprogram itself to show that the condition is true when the subprogram returns. The calling context can use the postcondition in the hypotheses of verification conditions that appear past the point of the call.

Callers are interested in weak preconditions that are easy to prove but strong postconditions that provide a lot of information they can use after the call. In contrast, implementers want strong preconditions that provide a lot of information in the subprograms being implemented but weak postconditions that are easy to prove. Both sides of the call want to make as few promises as possible but get as many promises as they can.

Of course in real programs, just as in real life, a balance must be struck. Postconditions describe what it means for a subprogram to be correct and thus would ideally be written as part of the subprogram's design. The more specific (stronger) a postcondition is, the more information about the subprogram's behavior it captures. Preconditions often need to be provided to support the postcondition.

For example, in the case of Binary_Search, the implementation has no chance of proving the postcondition unless it "knows" the array is already sorted. The algorithm depends on that. Thus, the precondition is necessary if the postcondition is to be proved.

The Binary_Search procedure has only in and out parameters. In the case of in out parameters (or In_Out global items), it is sometimes necessary to reference the original value of the parameter (or global item) in the postcondition. As an example, consider a procedure that finds the smallest prime factor of a natural number and returns both the factor and the original number after the factor has been divided out:

```
procedure Smallest_Factor (N      :  in out  Positive ;
                           Factor :     out  Positive )
       with
         Post  =>  Is_Prime(Factor) and
                   (N = N'Old / Factor) and
                   (N'Old rem Factor = 0);
```

Here we make use of a function Is_Prime that returns true if and only if its argument is a prime number.

The procedure changes the value of N. However, we can reference its original value in the postcondition using the 'Old attribute. This implies that the compiler must maintain a copy of the value of N before the procedure is called so it can use that copy when the postcondition is evaluated. Here, N is just an integer so keeping a copy of it is not expensive. Yet this is another example of how assertions can potentially consume significant resources; consider the case when the parameter is a large data structure.

In general, we can talk about the *prestate* of a subprogram as the state of the entire program just before the subprogram begins executing. Similarly, we can talk about the *poststate* of a subprogram as the state of the entire program after the subprogram returns. In these terms, the 'Old attribute can be said to make a copy of a part of the prestate for use in the evaluation of the postcondition.

Care is needed when using 'Old with arrays. Consider the following four expressions. Here, A is an array and Index is a variable of the array's index subtype.

- A'Old(Index) accesses the original array element at the position given by the current Index. Here *original* means part of the prestate, and *current* means the value when the postcondition is executing – that is, part of the poststate.
- A(Index'Old) accesses the current array element at the position given by the original Index.
- A'Old(Index'Old) accesses the original array element at the position given by the original Index. Both the original array (in its entirety) and the original Index are saved when the subprogram is entered.
- A(Index)'Old is largely the same as A'Old(Index'Old). In particular, it refers to the original value of the expression A(Index). However, only the original value of A(Index), not the entire array, is saved when the subprogram is entered.

The last case illustrates a general rule. The prefix of 'Old can be an arbitrary expression, the value of which is saved when the subprogram is entered. For example, (X + Y)'Old in a postcondition causes the original value of the expression X + Y to be saved and used when evaluating the postcondition. Each usage of 'Old in a postcondition implies the creation of a separate saved value. We also note that because the expression used as a prefix to 'Old is copied, it cannot have a limited type.[7]

The postcondition of Smallest_Factor shown earlier does not fully describe the intended behavior of the procedure. It only says that Factor is some prime factor of the original value of N, but not necessarily the smallest one. Although the postcondition is not as strong as it could be, it still conveys useful information into the calling context. Proving that the postcondition will always be satisfied is a partial proof of the correctness of the procedure. The remaining properties could be explored with testing. We describe the interplay between proof and testing in more detail in Section 8.4.

The postcondition can be strengthened as follows:

```
procedure Smallest_Factor (N       : in out Positive ;
                           Factor : out Positive )
   with
      Post => (N = N'Old / Factor) and
              (N'Old rem Factor = 0) and
              (for all J in 2 .. Factor − 1 => N'Old rem J /= 0);
```

The additional quantified expression says there are no other factors of the original N that are smaller than Factor. It is no longer necessary to directly assert that Factor is prime because it is a mathematical fact that the smallest factor of a number will always be prime. Notice that now the postcondition relys on a mathematical property that is proved outside the scope of the program. This is an example of the interplay between design and implementation. Although SPARK allows you to formalize the construction of your software, it is not by itself a complete formal design methodology.

Function results are normally anonymous, so to reference them in a postcondition for a function, it is necessary to use the 'Result attribute. Consider a function version of Smallest_Factor that returns the smallest factor of a natural number:

```
function Smallest_Factor (N : in Positive ) return Positive
   with
      Post => (N rem Smallest_Factor'Result = 0) and
              (for all J in 2 .. Smallest_Factor'Result − 1 => N rem J /= 0);
```

It is not necessary to use 'Old here because in this case N is an **in** parameter that the function cannot change.

Package Initial Conditions

As we describe in Section 3.4.1, when a package is elaborated, certain initialization activities can occur. Global variables in the package specification or body that have initialization expressions are given their initial values. Also, the package body can have a sequence of statements used to perform more complex package-wide initializations. The Initial_Condition aspect can be used on a package specification to assert a condition that is true after the package has been fully elaborated. Conceptually the aspect is like a kind of package-wide postcondition.

Typically, Initial_Condition makes sense in cases where a variable package has an abstract state that it initializes, as described in Section 4.3. The initial condition can then capture information about the result of that initialization. The SPARK tools generate a verification condition to show that the package's elaboration does indeed initialize the internal state as specified.

As an example, consider again the Datebook package discussed in Section 4.3. Here we show an abbreviated specification that includes a function returning the number of events in the datebook. For brevity, the other subprograms in the package are not shown.

```
with Dates;
package Datebook
   with
      Abstract_State   => State,
      Initializes      => State,
      Initial_Condition => Number_Of_Events = 0
is
   function Number_Of_Events return Natural
      with
         Global => (Input => State);
end Datebook;
```

If the Initial_Condition aspect is used, it must appear after the Abstract_State and Initializes aspects, if they are present. It can also only use visible variables and subprograms. In the preceding example, the package initial condition asserts that after elaboration, the number of events in the datebook is zero. This is an intuitive expectation, now formally specified and checked by the SPARK tools.

Notice that function Number_Of_Events is declared after it is used in the Initial_Condition aspect of package Datebook. This order violates the scope rules defined on page 30. Our Datebook example shows one of the few places where Ada allows use of as yet undeclared entities – assertions can reference names that are declared later in the same declarative part. We will make frequent use of this exception to Ada's scope rules.

6.2.3 *Private Information*

Consider the type package Shapes on page 164. In many applications it would be more appropriate to keep the representation of circles hidden by making type Circle private. However, by moving the details of Circle into the private section, we find another problem – the precondition for function Inside_Circle no longer compiles. The precondition of a public subprogram cannot make use of hidden (private) information.

To work around this issue, we can introduce a public function, In_Bounds, that tests if a Circle is entirely inside the workspace. The following package Shapes2 shows these changes:

```
pragma SPARK_Mode(On);
package Shapes2 is
    subtype Coordinate_Type is Integer range −100 .. +100;
    subtype Radius_Type is Coordinate_Type range 0 .. 10;
    type Circle is private;

    −− Return True if X, Y are inside circle C.
    function Inside_Circle (X, Y : in Coordinate_Type;
                            C    : in Circle ) return Boolean
        with Pre => In_Bounds (C);

    −− Return True if C is entirely in the workspace.
    function In_Bounds (C : in Circle ) return Boolean;

private
    type Circle is
        record
            Center_X : Coordinate_Type;
            Center_Y : Coordinate_Type;
            Radius   : Radius_Type;
        end record;
end Shapes2;
```

The precondition on Inside_Circle has been rewritten to make use of the new function. The body of function In_Bounds is written in the package body and has access to the package's private information. Thus, it can make use of the representation of type Circle as necessary. Defining functions for use in assertion expressions can also improve the readability of such expressions as they become complex, and it simplifies the sharing of elaborate conditions between multiple assertions. Notice that as mentioned in the previous section, we are using In_Bounds in an assertion before it has been declared.

The function In_Bounds is a perfectly ordinary function. It can be called by clients of the package like any other public function. In fact, it offers a useful service that might be of interest to package clients. It is also possible to create functions that can only be used in assertion expressions. We discuss these *ghost functions* in more detail in Section 9.1.1.

As you might expect, postconditions on subprograms in the visible part of a package are also forbidden from using private information. We can introduce functions to specify the effect of a subprogram in abstract terms just as we did with the precondition of the Inside_Circle function. For example, the Shapes2 package does not provide a way to create initialized Circle objects. We can remedy this problem by adding a suitable constructor function to the package:

```
function Make_Circle (X, Y :  in  Coordinate_Type;
                      R   :  in  Radius_Type) return  Circle
   with
      Post => In_Bounds (Make_Circle'Result);
```

Here we assume Make_Circle forces the resulting circle to be in bounds by adjusting the radius if necessary without indicating an error. How desirable such behavior is in practice will depend on the design of the overall application.

The SPARK tools can reason that Circle objects returned from Make_Circle will be acceptable to Inside_Circle without knowing anything about what In_Bounds does. The tools can treat the function abstractly. This relies on In_Bounds having no side effects, a requirement of all functions in SPARK, nor reading any global variables as specified in its data dependency contract (synthesized in this case).

Subprograms in a package body have full access to the information in the private part of the package specification. Helper subprograms inside the body of package Shapes2 may need to see the effects of Make_Circle in terms of the private structure of type Circle. Just knowing that the circle objects returned by Make_Circle are "in bounds" is not enough. Internal subprograms may need to know something about the relationship between the circle's center coordinates and radius. Internal subprograms are allowed to have that knowledge, but how can they be given it?

SPARK allows you to refine a postcondition in the body of a package to express it in terms of the private information available in the body. An implementation of Make_Circle that refines the postcondition in the specification using the Refined_Post aspect follows:

```
function Make_Circle (X, Y  : in Coordinate_Type;
                      Radius : in Radius_Type) return Circle
   with Refined_Post =>
     (Make_Circle' Result . Center_X + Make_Circle'Result . Radius
        in Coordinate_Type and
      Make_Circle' Result . Center_X - Make_Circle'Result . Radius
        in Coordinate_Type and
      Make_Circle' Result . Center_Y + Make_Circle'Result . Radius
        in Coordinate_Type and
      Make_Circle' Result . Center_Y - Make_Circle'Result . Radius
        in Coordinate_Type)
is
   R : Radius_Type := Radius;
begin
   if  R >= Coordinate_Type'Last - X then
      R := Coordinate_Type'Last - X;
   end if ;
   if  R >= X - Coordinate_Type'First then
      R := X - Coordinate_Type'First;
   end if ;
   if  R >= Coordinate_Type'Last - Y then
      R := Coordinate_Type'Last - Y;
   end if ;
   if  R >= Y - Coordinate_Type'First then
      R := Y - Coordinate_Type'First;
   end if ;
   return  (X, Y, R);
end Make_Circle;
```

The effect of Make_Circle is described in internal terms. The SPARK tools will generate verification conditions to show that the body of the subprogram honors the refined postcondition. In addition, the tools will generate a verification condition that shows the precondition (if any), together with the refined postcondition, implies the publicly visible postcondition. This allows the refined postcondition to be stronger than the public postcondition (it can say more), but not weaker.

Callers of Make_Circle inside the package body will use the refined postcondition as it is written in terms of the private information of interest to them. The general rule is that if the refined aspects are visible, they are used. This includes the Refined_Global and Refined_Depends aspects mentioned in Section 4.3.1.

Of course, the refined postcondition cannot be used by clients of the package to help prove verification conditions in the calling context. This is a necessary restriction because the refined postcondition is written in private terms to which the clients have no access. In effect, the public postcondition sanitizes the refined postcondition to make it appropriate for clients. If the private information changes, the refined postcondition might have to be updated, but the public postcondition captures essential design information and need not (should not) be changed.

If a refined postcondition is not used, the public postcondition takes its place and represents the only information known about the effect of the subprogram, even to internal callers. If the public postcondition is not used, it is taken to be true, which is easily proved from any refined postcondition that might exist.

In the earlier implementation of Make_Circle, the SPARK tools cannot prove that the public postcondition follows from the refined postcondition. This is because the public postcondition is written in terms of function In_Bounds, and the effect In_Bounds has on the private components of Circle is not known to the SPARK tools. We need to add a refined postcondition to In_Bounds:

```
function In_Bounds (C : in Circle) return Boolean
   with
      Refined_Post => In_Bounds'Result =
      (C.Center_X + C.Radius in Coordinate_Type and
       C.Center_X − C.Radius in Coordinate_Type and
       C.Center_Y + C.Radius in Coordinate_Type and
       C.Center_Y − C.Radius in Coordinate_Type)
is
begin
   return
      (C.Center_X + C.Radius in Coordinate_Type and
       C.Center_X − C.Radius in Coordinate_Type and
       C.Center_Y + C.Radius in Coordinate_Type and
       C.Center_Y − C.Radius in Coordinate_Type);
end In_Bounds;
```

The refined postcondition asserts that the value returned by In_Bounds is the same as that given by its implementation. Of course this is extremely redundant. SPARK has a special rule that helps in cases like this. When an expression function is used (see Section 2.2.2), the body of the expression function automatically serves as its postcondition. In effect, a postcondition is generated that asserts the expression function returns the same value as its implementation. Such a postcondition is trivially proved, yet this behavior means expression functions can be thought of as fragments of logic that have been factored out of the assertions. In effect, expression functions are pure specification. Thus, we can more easily write In_Bounds like this:

```
function In_Bounds (C : in Circle) return Boolean is
  (C.Center_X + C.Radius in Coordinate_Type and
   C.Center_X − C.Radius in Coordinate_Type and
   C.Center_Y + C.Radius in Coordinate_Type and
   C.Center_Y − C.Radius in Coordinate_Type);
```

Expression functions are often fairly short and make excellent candidates for being inline expanded.[8] A common idiom is to declare the function in the visible part of the package using the Inline aspect and implement it as an expression function in the private part of the package specification. Here the specification of Shapes3 illustrates this approach:

```
pragma SPARK_Mode(On);
package Shapes3 is
    subtype Coordinate_Type is Integer range −100 .. +100;
    subtype Radius_Type is Coordinate_Type range 0 .. 10;
    type Circle is private;

    −− Create a circle object.
    function Make_Circle (X, Y   : in Coordinate_Type;
                          Radius : in Radius_Type) return Circle
       with
          Post => In_Bounds (Make_Circle'Result);

    −− Return True if X, Y are inside circle C.
    function  Inside_Circle  (X, Y : in Coordinate_Type;
                              C    : in Circle) return Boolean
       with Pre => In_Bounds (C);

    −− Return True if C is entirely in the workspace.
    function In_Bounds (C : in Circle) return Boolean
       with Inline => True;

private
    type Circle is
       record
          Center_X : Coordinate_Type;
          Center_Y : Coordinate_Type;
```

```
    Radius    : Radius_Type;
  end record;

function In_Bounds (C :  Circle ) return Boolean is
  (C.Center_X + C.Radius in Coordinate_Type and
   C.Center_X - C.Radius in Coordinate_Type and
   C.Center_Y + C.Radius in Coordinate_Type and
   C.Center_Y - C.Radius in Coordinate_Type);
end Shapes3;
```

The SPARK tools can now prove that Make_Circle satisfies its public post-condition because it "knows" what In_Bounds does. Furthermore, the refined postcondition is no longer needed on Make_Circle in this case because In_Bounds captures all the necessary information in a way that is also usable to internal subprograms. Thus we have come full circle and can remove the Refined_Post aspect on Make_Circle as well.

The moral of this story is, try to implement functions used in public assertions as expression functions in the private section of a package's specification or in the package's body.

We finish this section by noting that private information may also include the internal state of a package such as any global data that it contains. Much of the previous discussion applies equally to the case when a public assertion needs to access such internal state. However, in that case the implementation of any functions used in the assertion would need to be in the package body where the package's internal state can be accessed; being in the private part of the specification would not be enough.

6.2.4 *Type Invariants*[9]

So far we have discussed assertions that are attached to subprograms and that describe conditions associated with calling subprograms or with the values returned by subprograms. However, Ada also allows you to attach assertions to the types themselves. Such assertions describe properties of all objects of those types. In this section we describe type invariants and give some hints about how SPARK may support them in the future.

In package Shapes3 in the previous section, a precondition was used to ensure that Circle objects are sensible before passing them to function Inside_ Circle . If the package provided many subprograms, each would presumably need similar preconditions for all Circle parameters.

Alternatively, one could apply postconditions on all subprograms to check that the Circle objects returned by them are sensible. This was done with the

Make_Circle function. Because the Circle type is private, it is not necessary to do both. Circles can only be changed by the subprograms in the package. If all subprograms that return circles return only valid circles, the subprograms that accept circles can just assume they are valid.

In any case, the assertion we are trying to apply – that all circles are entirely inside the workspace – is really a restriction on the type Circle and not a restriction associated with the procedures that manipulate circles. Ada provides a way to express this idea more directly using a *type invariant*. The following specification of package Shapes4 illustrates the approach:

```
pragma SPARK_Mode(On);
package Shapes4 is
    subtype Coordinate_Type is Integer range −100 .. +100;
    subtype Radius_Type is Coordinate_Type range 0 .. 10;
    type Circle is private
        with
            Type_Invariant => In_Bounds (Circle);

    −− Create a circle object.
    function Make_Circle (X, Y   : in Coordinate_Type;
                          Radius : in Radius_Type) return Circle ;

    −− Return True if X, Y are inside circle C.
    function  Inside_Circle  (X, Y : in Coordinate_Type;
                              C    : in Circle ) return Boolean;

    −− Return True if C is entirely in the workspace.
    function In_Bounds (C : in Circle ) return Boolean
        with Inline ;

private
    type Circle is
        record
            Center_X : Coordinate_Type;
            Center_Y : Coordinate_Type;
            Radius   : Radius_Type;
        end record;

    function In_Bounds (C : in Circle ) return Boolean is
        (C.Center_X + C.Radius in Coordinate_Type and
         C.Center_X − C.Radius in Coordinate_Type and
         C.Center_Y + C.Radius in Coordinate_Type and
         C.Center_Y − C.Radius in Coordinate_Type);
end Shapes4;
```

The only change relative to the earlier Shapes3 package is that the condition on the circle being in the workspace has been moved from being a precondition of Inside_Circle and a postcondition of Make_Circle to being an invariant of the Circle private type. Notice that in the expression used for the type invariant the name of the type itself, Circle, is used as a stand-in for the object of that type being checked.

Type invariants can only be applied to private types. The condition they assert is only enforced at the "boundary" of the package that implements the type. Inside that package, objects may go through intermediate states where the invariant is temporarily false. However, the invariant is checked whenever a public subprogram returns to ensure that objects seen by the clients of the package are always in a proper state. In this respect, type invariants are somewhat like postconditions that are automatically applied to all public subprograms. Because SPARK does not currently support type invariants, their effect could be simulated, in large measure, by tediously defining appropriate postconditions.

Package Shapes4 as currently defined provides no default initialization for a Circle object. Merely declaring a Circle may cause the type invariant to fail as type invariants are also checked after default initialization and the initial values of the components of a Circle are indeterminate.

Sensible default initialization can be specified by simply adding appropriate initializers to the components of the record defining Circle:

```
type Circle is
   record
      Center_X : Coordinate_Type := 0.0;
      Center_Y : Coordinate_Type := 0.0;
      Radius   : Radius_Type := 0.0;
   end record;
```

A default initialized Circle will now obey its invariant.

Once SPARK supports type invariants, it will generate verification conditions at each place where an invariant check is needed that, if proved, will show that the check cannot fail.

6.2.5 *Subtype Predicates*

In addition to type invariants, Ada also allows assertions to be applied to nonprivate types in the form of *subtype predicates*. In some ways, subtype predicates are similar to constraints, such as range constraints, that limit the allowed values of a subtype. They are checked in similar places. However, it is natural to describe subtype predicates as assertions because, like other kinds of assertions, they are conditions of arbitrary complexity provided by the programmer and are under the control of the the assertion policy.

Dynamic Predicates[10]

A type can be considered a set of values (a domain) and a set of operations that can be applied to those values. Ada's **subtype** declaration creates a subtype by specifying a subset of the domain of the base type. Consider, for example,

```
subtype Pixel_Coordinate_Type is Natural range 0 .. 1023;
```

Instead of being the entire set of values associated with Natural, Pixel_Coordinate_Type is associated with a subset of those values in the range from 0 to 1023.

While this facility is useful, it is also quite limited. To define a more complex subset requires a more general method of specification. Dynamic predicates allow you to define which values are in the subset by using an arbitrary condition, for example,

```
subtype Even_Type is Natural
   with Dynamic_Predicate => Even_Type mod 2 = 0;
```

As with the Type_Invariant aspect, when the name of the type appears in the condition, it is interpreted as a stand-in for the value being tested. If the condition is true the value is in the subtype being defined. In this example Even_Type has values that are even natural numbers.

As another example consider the following:

```
subtype Prime_Type is Natural
   with Dynamic_Predicate => Is_Prime (Prime_Type);
```

Here the values of Prime_Type are the natural numbers for which function Is_Prime returns true – presumably prime numbers.

The precise locations where dynamic predicates are checked is given in section 3.2.4 of the *Ada Reference Manual* (2012), but intuitively they are checked in the same places where the simpler constraints are checked: during assignment to an object, when passing values as parameters to subprograms, and so forth. For example, if E is of type Even_Type, an expression such as

```
E := (A + B) / 2;
```

raises Assertion_Error when the expression (A + B) / 2 results in an odd number. Notice that although the dynamic predicate is like a kind of user-defined constraint, the Constraint_Error exception is not used if the predicate fails. The checking of dynamic predicates is controlled by the assertion policy just as with other kinds of assertions.

When SPARK does support dynamic predicates, it will likely still impose some restrictions on their use as compared to full Ada. For example, consider the following type definition:

```
type Lower_Half is
   record
      X : Natural;
      Y : Natural;
   end record
with Dynamic_Predicate => Lower_Half.X > Lower_Half.Y;
```

Instances of the Lower_Half type represent points in the first quadrant that are below the line $y = x$. However, in full Ada the dynamic predicate is not checked when individual components are modified. Thus, if Point were a variable of type Lower_Half, the program could set Point.X := 0 without causing Assertion_Error to be raised. It is likely SPARK will close that loophole by forbidding dynamic predicates that depend on the components of a composite type such as in this example.

Dynamic predicates that depend on global variables, for example, by calling a function F that reads such a variable, also create problems. Consider, for example, the following dynamic predicate:

```
subtype Example_Type is Natural
   with Dynamic_Predicate => F (Example_Type);
                     -- function F reads some global variable
```

Because the global variable might change during the life of the program, a value of type Example_Type might sometimes be valid (in the subtype) and sometimes not, even if the value itself does not change. It is likely SPARK will forbid examples such as this as well.

Static Predicates

Dynamic predicates are very general, but there is a price to be paid for their generality. It is not reasonable (or normally even possible) for the compiler to compute the membership of a subtype defined with a dynamic predicate. As a result, subtypes defined with dynamic predicates cannot be used in certain areas where subtypes are allowed.

As an example, consider the following case statement in which the selector, N, has type Natural:

```
case N is
   when Even_Type => ...
   when Prime_Type => ...
end;
```

Ada's full coverage rules require that every possible value of N be accounted for in the various **when** clauses. In this example that is not the case since because there are natural numbers that are neither even nor prime. However, the compiler cannot be expected to know this without understanding the detailed semantics of the predicates used to define the subtypes. Those predicates might involve calling functions of significant complexity, such as is the case for Prime_Type in this example. Thus, the example is ruled out because it uses subtypes defined with dynamic predicates.

Ada defines a more restricted form of subtype predicate, called a *static predicate*, that does support many (although not all) of the usual features of subtypes while still allowing some degree of customization. Furthermore, at the time of this writing, SPARK supports static predicates.

The precise rules for the kinds of predicate specifications that can be used as static predicates is given in section 3.2.4 of the *Ada Reference Manual* (2012). However, as one example, we show a static predicate using a membership test to specify a non-contiguous range of values. Consider a package for managing a game of Scrabble. The specification of the package might be, in part, shown as follows:

```
pragma SPARK_Mode(On);
package Scrabble is

    subtype Scrabble_Letter is Character range 'A' .. 'Z';

    subtype Scrabble_Value is Positive
        with Static_Predicate => Scrabble_Value in 1 .. 5 | 8 | 10;

    type Scrabble_Word is array( Positive range <>) of Scrabble_Letter;

    subtype Scrabble_Score is Natural range 0 .. 100;
    function Raw_Score (Word : in Scrabble_Word) return Scrabble_Score
        with Pre => (Word'Length <= 10);

end Scrabble;
```

Here a subtype Scrabble_Letter is used to constrain Character to just the uppercase letters used by the game. The subtype Scrabble_Value is defined with a static predicate to only contain the values that are actually used on the various letters. The type Scrabble_Word is an unconstrained array of letters intended to hold a single word. The function Raw_Score adds together the value of the letters in the given word and returns it as a value in the range from 0 to 100. The precondition on Raw_Score ensures that words of no longer than ten characters are used. This is the justification for limiting the return value to 100 (the maximum value of a letter is 10). Notice that in this case the postcondition is stated using a subtype.

The type Scrabble_Word cannot easily be made into a fixed size of an array of ten Scrabble_Letter because there is no character, such as a space, in Scrabble_Letter to use as padding needed for short words. You might be tempted to define Scrabble_Letter using a static predicate like this:

```
subtype Scrabble_Letter is Character
  with Static_Predicate => Scrabble_Letter in 'A' .. 'Z' | ' ';
```

However, the body of the package uses Scrabble_Letter as an index subtype for an array, and subtypes with predicates can never be used in that situation. Here is the body of package Scrabble:

```
pragma SPARK_Mode(On);

package body Scrabble is

   type Scrabble_Value_Lookup is array ( Scrabble_Letter ) of Scrabble_Value;
   Lookup_Table : constant Scrabble_Value_Lookup :=
     ('A' => 1, 'B' => 3, 'C' => 3, 'D' => 2,
      'E' => 1, 'F' => 4, 'G' => 2, 'H' => 4,
      'I' => 1, 'J' => 8, 'K' => 5, 'L' => 1,
      'M' => 3, 'N' => 1, 'O' => 1, 'P' => 3,
      'Q' => 10, 'R' => 1, 'S' => 1, 'T' => 1,
      'U' => 1, 'V' => 4, 'W' => 4, 'X' => 8,
      'Y' => 4, 'Z' => 10);

   function Raw_Score (Word : in Scrabble_Word) return Scrabble_Score is
      Total_Score : Scrabble_Score := 0;
   begin
      for Letter_Index in Word'Range loop
         pragma Loop_Invariant ( Total_Score <= 10*(Letter_Index - Word'First));
         Total_Score := Total_Score + Lookup_Table (Word (Letter_Index));
      end loop;
      return Total_Score;
   end Raw_Score;

end Scrabble;
```

A lookup table is defined to translate Scrabble letters into their corresponding values. It is declared as a constant with a static expression as an initializer so that even though it is read by function Raw_Score, it is not necessary to declare it as global input.

The SPARK tools are able to work with the subtype defined with a static predicate and prove this function obeys its postcondition. The Loop_Invariant pragma is used to help the tools handle the loop. Loop invariants are discussed in detail in Section 6.4.

6.2.6 *Contract Cases*

It is common for preconditions to divide the input space of a subprogram into several equivalence classes (disjoint subdomains) where each class has its own postconditions. Although we can use Pre and Post aspects to handle contracts of arbitrary complexity, SPARK provides the Contract_Cases aspect to simplify writing contracts for subprograms that divide their input space into a substantial number of different equivalence classes.

As a simple example, consider a function Sign that takes an arbitrary integer and returns -1 if the integer is negative, 0 if the integer is zero, and $+1$ if the integer is positive. Such a function might be declared and contract specified as follows:

```
subtype Sign_Type is Integer range −1 .. 1;

function Sign (X : in Integer) return Sign_Type
   with
      Contract_Cases =>
         (X < 0 => Sign'Result = −1,
          X = 0 => Sign'Result = 0,
          X > 0 => Sign'Result = 1);
```

This example shows three contract cases. Each case consists of a Boolean condition intended to be checked when the subprogram is called followed by a Boolean consequent that is checked when the subprogram returns. In effect, each contract case is like a mini-precondition followed by a corresponding postcondition.

When the subprogram is called, all of the conditions are checked and exactly one must be true. When the subprogram returns the consequent associated with the condition that was true is checked. At runtime Assertion_Error is raised if

- none of the conditions are true at the time of the call,
- more than one of the conditions are true at the time of the call, or
- the consequent associated with the true condition is false when the subprogram returns.

The SPARK tools generate verification conditions to prove

- the conditions cover the entire input domain of the subprogram (and thus it will always be the case that one of them will be true),
- the conditions are mutually exclusive, and
- the subprogram always returns with the consequent true for each corresponding precondition.

In other words, the tools generate verification conditions to show that Assertion_Error will never be raised.

It is important that the contract cases divide the entire input domain into disjoint subdomains. To illustrate, consider a function In_Unit_Square as an extension of our Sign function. In_Unit_Square returns +1 if the given X, Y coordinates are inside a square centered on the origin with a side length of two. Otherwise the function returns 0 for points in the first and third quadrants and −1 for points in the second and fourth quadrants. The following specification of this function using Contract_Cases must ensure that each case is disjoint.

```
function In_Unit_Square (X, Y : in Integer) return Sign_Type
   with
      Contract_Cases =>
         (X >= 0 and Y >= 0 and not (X <= 1 and Y <= 1) =>
              In_Unit_Square ' Result = 0,
          X < 0 and Y >= 0 and not (X >= −1 and Y <= 1) =>
              In_Unit_Square ' Result = −1,
          X < 0 and Y < 0 and not (X >= −1 and Y >= −1) =>
              In_Unit_Square ' Result = 0,
          X >= 0 and Y < 0 and not (X <= 1 and Y >= −1) =>
              In_Unit_Square ' Result = −1,
          others  −> In_Unit_Square'Result = 1);
```

Here we use **others** to specify a case not handled by the other cases (the case where the given point is on the square). If **others** appears, it must be last. Because **others** is always true, it is trivial to show that at least one of the previous cases will always be available. Showing that the four cases, one for each quadrant, are really disjoint is less obvious, but the SPARK tools will take care of that.

The implementation of In_Unit_Circle could follow the structure of the contract cases, but it need not. Here is an implementation based on an **if** ... **elsif** ... chain:

```
function In_Unit_Square (X, Y : in Integer) return Sign_Type is
begin
   if X in −1 .. 1 and Y in −1 .. 1 then
```

```
      -- In the square.
      return 1;
   elsif  X >= 0 and Y >= 0 then
      -- First quadrant.
      return 0;
   elsif  X < 0 and Y >= 0 then
      -- Second quadrant.
      return −1;
   elsif  X < 0 and Y < 0 then
      -- Third quadrant.
      return 0;
   else
      -- Fourth quadrant.
      return −1;
   end if;
end In_Unit_Square;
```

This implementation takes advantage of the fact that the first succeeding condition stops the comparisons. The conditions in the implementation are not mutually exclusive, but they do not need to be. The SPARK tools will generate verification conditions to show that this implementation does meet the contract cases provided in the specification. However, this example shows that as the number of parameters (and input global items) to the subprogram increases, the dimensionality of the space that must be partitioned over the contract cases increases as well.

Also notice that the consequent of a contract case is evaluated after the subprogram returns, and so it is permitted to use the 'Result and 'Old attributes there as in postconditions.

Finally we note that it is permitted to use the normal Pre and Post aspects with Contract_Cases. The semantics are largely intuitive: the pre- and postconditions must be obeyed in addition to the contract cases. See the SPARK 2014 Reference Manual (SPARK Team, 2014a) for the full details.

6.2.7 Runtime Errors in Assertions

Because assertions are executable, the possibility exists that a runtime error could occur while the assertions are being evaluated. Thus, executing an assertion might raise an exception other than Assertion_Error because of problems in the assertion itself. The SPARK tools will generate verification conditions for the assertions to prove that they, along with the rest of the program, are free of runtime errors.

If the assertion is possibly false or outright illogical, it is appropriate for the tools to object to it. However, there are situations in which an assertion is mathematically true and yet causes runtime errors when evaluated. There is only one way that can happen: arithmetic overflow. If the assertion contains other kinds of runtime errors such as division by zero or accessing an array out of bounds, the assertion does not make sense anyway.

As an example, consider the following silly procedure with a precondition that expresses a true fact about the parameters:

```
procedure Silly (X      : in   Positive ;
                 Y       : in   Positive ;
                 Result : out  Positive )
   with
      Pre => ((X + Y) / 2 in Positive)
is
begin
   if  X > 10 then
      Result := 1;
   else
      Result := Y / 2 + 1;
   end if ;
end Silly ;
```

The precondition asserts that the average of the two Positive parameters is in the range of Positive and then does some pointless computations that nevertheless are completely free of runtime error and obey the synthesized flow dependency contract. There is nothing wrong with this procedure, yet the evaluation of the precondition may raise Constraint_Error because X + Y might overflow the base type of Positive. The SPARK tools will generate an unprovable verification condition attempting to check that overflow will not occur.

One way to work around this is to write the assertions carefully so that they too will be free of runtime error. However, you may feel frustrated by this, particularly if you plan to deploy your program with assertion checking disabled, as we discuss in Section 6.8. The assertions are, after all, intended to be statements about the design of your system. Why can they not be evaluated in the pure mathematical world where concerns about machine limitations do not exist?

In fact, the GNAT compiler and SPARK tools provide some options for controlling the way overflow is handled. Three different overflow modes are provided:

- STRICT: Overflow is handled as according to the Ada standard. Arithmetic computations are done in a subtype's base type.
- MINIMIZED: Computations are done in an oversized integer type selected by the compiler such as Long_Long_Integer (which is 64 bits for the GNAT compiler). This will not prevent all possibilities of overflow, but it will prevent many common cases and remains reasonably efficient.
- ELIMINATED: Computations are done in an extended integer type with unbounded size. No overflow is possible although, conceivably, Storage_Error might be raised.

The overflow mode can be selected separately for both general computations in the normal part of your program and for computations done in assertions. By default the tools use STRICT for both. In cases where you plan to deploy with assertions disabled, you might consider changing the overflow mode on assertions to ELIMINATED. This reduces the number of verification conditions that must be proved in the assertions themselves, and the performance penalty of doing computations with extended integers will not be paid if the assertions are not actually executed anyway. See the GNAT and SPARK user's guides for more information about overflow mode handling. We show a more practical example of these issues in Section 6.7.

Keep in mind that the expressions in assertions are general and could call functions that are not in SPARK. Such functions might raise any exception at all. Assertions might also raise Storage_Error if they involve unbounded recursion. For example, if the postcondition on some function F called F itself, the postcondition of the second call would be checked as part of evaluating the postcondition of the first call, and so forth. This is not necessarily an error; if the postcondition is written properly, it will have a base case that does not entail calling F.

For example, consider the following specification of a function Fibonacci to compute Fibonacci numbers:

```
function Fibonacci(N : Natural) return Natural
   with
      Contract_Cases =>
         (N = 0 => Fibonacci'Result = 0,
          N = 1 => Fibonacci'Result = 1,
          others => Fibonacci'Result = Fibonacci(N − 1) + Fibonacci(N − 2));
```

We leave it as an exercise to the reader to consider what happens if the Fibonacci function is implemented recursively as well. It probably goes without saying that recursive assertions are best avoided.

6.3 Assert and Assume

The assertions we have seen so far are contractual in that they form part of the design of your system and should, ideally, be written when the package specifications are written. In this section we look at assertions that can be used in the body of a subprogram to make statements about a computation in progress. In essence these assertions are implementation details that, in a perfect world, would be unnecessary. However, because theorem proving is an evolving technology, it is sometimes necessary for you to assist the tools by providing "stepping stones" that allow an overall proof to be built from several simpler proofs. In the language of mathematics the assertions we cover in this section allow you to state, in effect, lemmas and corollaries to simplify proving more complex statements.

All three of the assertions in this section are provided as pragmas rather than aspects. This is because, unlike the previous assertions, they behave more like executable statements rather than as information associated with a declaration. The Assert pragma is part of Ada, but the other two – Assert_And_Cut and Assume – are specific to SPARK.

6.3.1 *Assert*

The Assert pragma allows you to specify an arbitrary condition that you believe to be true. The pragma can appear any place in a subprogram where a declaration or an executable statement can appear. Each assertion carries a proof obligation to show that the specified condition is always true at that point. You can use Assert as a kind of check on your thinking. Suppose in the middle of some complex subprogram you find yourself saying something like, "X should be greater than one here." You can express this idea in the program itself like this:

```
pragma Assert (X > 1);
```

When we humans reason about programs, we make many such statements in our minds. We then use these statements to reason about other constructs appearing later in the program. For example, we might say, "Because X was greater than one a few lines before, thus-and-such an assignment statement

will always assign an in-bounds value." For each Assert pragma the SPARK
tools generate a verification condition to check it. Likewise, the tools will use
the asserted condition in the hypotheses of following verification conditions.
Thus for both humans and SPARK, assertions can help clarify what is happening
in the program and simplify the process of deriving conclusions about what the
code does.

To illustrate some of the issues, we present a somewhat contrived example
of a subprogram that calculates a student's semester bill at a hypothetical state
university. The specification of package Students provides the necessary type
and subprogram declarations.

```
with Dates;
package Students
    with SPARK_Mode => On
is
    type    Gender_Type    is (Male, Female, Unspecified );
    type    Meal_Plan_Type is (None, On_Demand, Basic, Full);
    type    Student_ID     is range 0 ..  999_999;
    subtype Valid_Student_ID is Student_ID range 1 ..  Student_ID'Last;

    type GPA_Type is delta 0.01 range 0.00 ..  4.00;
    type Money_Type is delta 0.01 digits 7 range −99_999.99 .. +99_999.99;

    type Student_Record is  private ;

    −− Adjusts the tuition based on student  characteristics .
    function Compute_Bill (Student :  in Student_Record;
                           Base_Tuition :  in Money_Type) return Money_Type
        with
            Pre => (Base_Tuition in 0.00 ..  20_000.00);

private

    type Student_Record is
        record
            Birth_Date    : Dates.Date;
            ID            : Student_ID;   −− An ID of zero means not a real student.
            Gender        : Gender_Type;
            GPA           : GPA_Type;
            Part_Time     : Boolean;
            In_State      : Boolean;      −− True if the student is a state  resident .
            Resident      : Boolean;      −− True if the student  resides on campus.
            Meal_Plan     : Meal_Plan_Type;
```

```
       Self_Insured  : Boolean;        -- True if the student has insurance.
       end record;

end Students;
```

The function Compute_Bill takes a suitably defined student record and a base tuition value for in-state students. It returns the final bill computed as a possibly adjusted tuition, plus fees and insurance premiums, minus any grants received by the student. Notice that Compute_Bill includes a precondition that puts a limit on the size of the Base_Tuition. An alternative approach would be to define a subtype of Money_Type that encodes the constraint on base tuition values.

Similarly, Compute_Bill returns a value of type Money_Type suggesting that negative bills might be possible. If that is not intended, one could either define a suitable subtype of Money_Type or, perhaps, use a postcondition.

The following listing shows an implementation of package Students that passes SPARK examination:

```
package body Students
    with SPARK_Mode => On
is
    function Compute_Bill (Student : in Student_Record;
                           Base_Tuition : in Money_Type) return Money_Type is
        Tuition    : Money_Type;
        Fees       : Money_Type;
        Grants     : Money_Type := 0.00;
        Insurance  : Money_Type := 0.00;
    begin
        Tuition := Base_Tuition;

        if not Student. In_State then
            -- Out of state tuition is 50% higher.
            Tuition := Tuition + Tuition/2;
        end if;

        -- Compute health insurance premium.
        if not Student. Self_Insured then
            Insurance := 1_000.00;
        end if;

        -- Compute base fees depending on full-time/part-time status.
        if Student.Part_Time then
            Fees := 100.00;
        else
```

```
      Fees := 500.00;
    end if ;


    -- Room and board.
    if  Student.Resident then
      Fees := Fees + 4_000.00;  -- Room.
      case Student.Meal_Plan is
        when None       => null;
        when On_Demand => Fees := Fees + 100.00;
        when Basic      => Fees := Fees + 1_000.00;
        when Full       => Fees := Fees + 3_000.00;
      end case;
    else
        -- Nonresident students getting a meal plan pay a premium.
      case Student.Meal_Plan is
        when None       => null;
        when On_Demand => Fees := Fees + 200.00;
        when Basic      => Fees := Fees + 1_500.00;
        when Full       => Fees := Fees + 4_500.00;
      end case;
    end if ;

    -- University policy : give high achieving students a break.
    if  Student.GPA >= 3.00 then
      Grants := Grants + 250.00;

        -- Special directive from the state for very high achieving women.
      if  Student.GPA >= 3.75 and Student.Gender = Female then
        Grants := Grants + 250.00;
      end if ;
    end if ;

    return (( Tuition  + Fees) - Grants) + Insurance;
  end Compute_Bill;

end Students;
```

This implementation considers a number of conditions such as the different cost of meal plans for resident and nonresident students, different base fees for full-time and part-time students, and special grants given to high achieving students.

At the time of this writing, the SPARK tools have trouble proving that the final computation of the bill given by ((Tuition + Fees) − Grants) + Insurance is in range of Money_Type. A careful study of the procedure shows that even if Tuition, Fees, Grants, and Insurance are all at their extreme values, the overall bill should still be in range. Doing this review is tedious because of the many paths through the subprogram that need to be considered. Also, the overall bill is computed by way of both additions and subtractions so one needs to consider all combinations of both upper and lower bounds on the computed values to be sure the final result remains in range in every case.

Ideally, the SPARK tools would do all this work. However, if the tools are having problems, you can provide hints in the form of Assert pragmas. For example, you might add the following assertions just before the **return** statement:

```
pragma Assert (Tuition    in    0.00 ..  30_000.00);
pragma Assert (Insurance in    0.00 ..   1_000.00);
pragma Assert (Fees       in 100.00 ..   7_500.00);
pragma Assert (Grants     in    0.00 ..     500.00);
```

Armed with this knowledge the SPARK tools easily prove that the overall bill is in range. The tools are also able to prove the assertions themselves, provided a suitably large timeout value is used (see Section 9.3), thus proving the entire function free of runtime errors.

It is important to understand that the assertions are only hints to the SPARK tools. A future version of the tools, or perhaps a different back-end prover, might be able to prove the entire function without the help of the assertions. In this sense, the assertions are not contractual; they are not part of the subprogram's specification.

This example illustrates three important concepts:

- What assertions are needed, if any, depends on the capabilities of the SPARK tools and the theorem provers they use. Because the tools are always evolving, you may discover that assertions needed in the past are not needed in the future.
- The Assert pragma can be used to track down problems in the proving process. We discuss this more in Section 9.3.
- Even if the SPARK tools do not need the assertions to complete the proofs, they can still add valuable documentation to your program. Unlike ordinary comments, information documented in Assert pragmas is checkable by the tools or alternatively during runtime.

6.3.2 *Assert and Cut*

In the last section we made the statement, "The SPARK tools will use the asserted condition in the hypotheses of following verification conditions." But what, exactly, do we mean by "following verification conditions"? We must first define this concept more precisely before the use and purpose of the Assert_And_Cut pragma will make sense.

At each place in the program where a check is needed, the SPARK tools generate a verification condition concluding that the check will succeed. The hypotheses used are gathered from statements encountered on the execution path from the beginning of the subprogram to the point of the check. If there is more than one path to the check, the tools must consider all of those paths. This is necessary to show that no matter how execution arrives at a particular point, the condition being checked will succeed. Consider the following simplified version of Compute_Bill:

```
function Compute_Bill (Student : in Student_Record;
                       Base_Tuition : in Money_Type) return Money_Type is
    Fees : Money_Type;
begin
    if Student.Part_Time then
        Fees := 100.00;
    else
        Fees := 500.00;
    end if ;
    return Base_Tuition + Fees;
end Compute_Bill;
```

The SPARK tools will wish to show that Base_Tuition + Fees does not go out of range of Money_Type in the **return** statement. However, in the example there are two paths by which the final statement can be reached depending on the outcome of the conditional. Both of those paths must be considered.

The SPARK tools provide two basic strategies. Using the *one proof per check* strategy, the tools generate a single verification condition that simultaneously considers all the paths to the point of the check. Using the *one proof per path* strategy, the tools generate separate verification conditions for each path. There is also a progressive mode in which the tools first attempt a single proof for the check but, failing that, will attempt to prove individual paths.

The information known when attempting a proof depends on the path taken to reach the check. In the previous example, if the **then** branch of the conditional is taken, the prover knows that Student.Part_Time is true and Fees has the value 100.00. Conversely, if the **else** branch is taken, the prover knows that Student.Part_Time is false and Fees has the value 500.00. This knowledge is added to the hypotheses of the verification condition checking Base_Tuition + Fees.

In the case where one verification condition is generated for each path, the verification conditions are relatively simple but there are more of them. Also, failure to prove a verification condition yields specific information about which path is causing the problem. On the other hand, where one verification condition is generated for each check that includes information from all paths leading to that check, the verification conditions are fewer but more complicated. Also, if the proof fails, teasing out specific information about the failure is harder.

It is important to understand that every check after the conditional will have two paths leading to it because of the two paths produced by the conditional. This includes following conditional statements. In general, as the control flow complexity of a subprogram increases, the number of paths tends to increase exponentially. Consider the following example, also a simplified version of Compute_Bill:

```
function Compute_Bill (Student : in Student_Record;
                       Base_Tuition : in Money_Type) return Money_Type is
     Fees    : Money_Type;
     Grants  : Money_Type := 0.00;
begin
     if Student.Part_Time then
        Fees := 100.00;
     else
        Fees := 500.00;
     end if;

     if Student.GPA >= 3.00 then
        Grants := Grants + 250.00;

        -- Special directive from the state for very high achieving women.
        if Student.GPA >= 3.75 and Student.Gender = Female then
           Grants := Grants + 250.00;
        end if;
     end if;
     return (Base_Tuition + Fees) - Grants;
end Compute_Bill;
```

There are two paths through the first conditional statement. Each of those two paths split when Student.GPA >= 3.00 is tested. The paths that enter the second conditional split again on the innermost **if** statement. Overall, there are six ways to reach the **return** statement and, thus, six different collections of hypotheses that need to be considered when proving (Base_Tuition + Fees) − Grants is in range.

In the version of Compute_Bill shown earlier, there are several control structures in sequence, each multiplying the number of paths, until the total number of ways to reach the final **return** statement, and the Assert pragmas just before it, is quite large. Regardless of the proof strategy used, this increases the computational burden of proving the subprogram.

One approach to dealing with this problem is to factor large subprograms into several smaller ones. The idea is to lift out relatively independent blocks of code from the large subprogram and transform those blocks into (probably local) helper subprograms. Because the SPARK tools do their analysis on a per-subprogram basis, the number of paths in the helper subprograms do not multiply each other. Instead, the effect of the helper subprograms, and whatever paths they contain internally, is summarized by their contracts.

Another approach, that we introduce here, is to add one or more *cut points* to the subprogram. A cut point is a place in the subprogram where all incoming paths terminate and from which a single new path is outgoing. All information gathered by the SPARK tools on the incoming paths is forgotten.

The Assert_And_Cut pragma works like the Assert pragma in that it creates a proof obligation and provides information that the SPARK tools can use on the outgoing paths. However, unlike Assert, the Assert_And_Cut pragma introduces a cut point. Only a single path leaves Assert_And_Cut. Furthermore, the only information known to the SPARK tools immediately after Assert_And_Cut is that which is specifically stated in the pragma.

As an example, here is a version of the Students package body using Assert_And_Cut in function Compute_Bill:

```
package body Students3
    with SPARK_Mode => On
is
    function Compute_Bill (Student : in Student_Record;
                                Base_Tuition : in Money_Type) return Money_Type is
        Tuition    : Money_Type;
        Fees       : Money_Type;
        Grants     : Money_Type := 0.00;
        Insurance  : Money_Type := 0.00;
    begin
        Tuition := Base_Tuition;

        if not Student.In_State then
            -- Out of state tuition is 50% higher.
            Tuition := Tuition + Tuition / 2;
        end if;

        pragma Assert_And_Cut (Tuition in 0.00 .. 30_000.00);
```

```
-- Compute health insurance premium.
if not Student. Self_Insured then
   Insurance := 1_000.00;
end if ;


pragma Assert_And_Cut ((Tuition    in 0.00  ..  30_000.00) and
                       (Insurance in 0.00  ..   1_000.00));


-- Compute base fees depending on full-time/part-time status.
if Student.Part_Time then
   Fees := 100.00;
else
   Fees := 500.00;
end if ;


-- Room and board.
if Student.Resident then
   Fees := Fees + 4_000.00;  -- Room.
   case Student.Meal_Plan is
      when None      => null;
      when On_Demand => Fees := Fees + 100.00;
      when Basic     => Fees := Fees + 1_000.00;
      when Full      => Fees := Fees + 3_000.00;
   end case;
else
   -- Nonresident students getting a meal plan pay a premium.
   case Student.Meal_Plan is
      when None      => null;
      when On_Demand => Fees := Fees + 200.00;
      when Basic     => Fees := Fees + 1_500.00;
      when Full      => Fees := Fees + 4_500.00;
   end case;
end if ;


pragma Assert_And_Cut ((Tuition    in   0.00  ..  30_000.00) and
                       (Insurance in   0.00  ..   1_000.00) and
                       (Fees      in 100.00  ..   7_500.00));


-- University policy : give high achieving students a break.
if Student.GPA >= 3.00 then
   Grants := Grants + 250.00;
```

```
        -- Special directive from the state for very high achieving women.
        if  Student.GPA >= 3.75 and Student.Gender = Female then
            Grants := Grants + 250.00;
        end if;
      end if;

      pragma Assert_And_Cut ((Tuition    in    0.00  ..  30_000.00) and
                             (Insurance  in    0.00  ..   1_000.00) and
                             (Fees       in  100.00  ..   7_500.00) and
                             (Grants     in    0.00  ..     500.00));

      return (( Tuition + Fees) - Grants) + Insurance;
    end Compute_Bill;

end Students3;
```

Here each intermediate result of interest is stated with Assert_And_Cut as soon as it is computed. The multiple paths generated by the preceding control structures are thus blocked, and the number of paths do not multiply as one goes down the function. This keeps the verification conditions simple or small in number depending on the proof strategy being used and speeds up the proving process. However, notice how it is necessary for each Assert_And_Cut to reassert any information that needs to be carried forward.

6.3.3 *Assume*

The Assume pragma is very similar to the Assert pragma in many respects.

1. Assume contains a boolean expression that is evaluated if the assertion policy is set to Check. If that expression returns false the Assertion_Error exception is raised.
2. The SPARK tools use the asserted condition in the hypotheses of verification conditions that follow the Assume.

However, unlike Assert, the Assume pragma does not create a proof obligation. Instead, the SPARK tools just take the assumed condition as a given. Thus, it is important for you to ensure that the assumed condition is true. However, because Assume is executable, like all assertions, a false assumption may be detected during testing by way of the exception raised when it is evaluated. This means the safety of the assumption depends entirely on code review and testing rather than on proof.

In general, you should use Assume only under special circumstances and only with great care. To illustrate the potential danger, consider the effect of an assumption that is blatantly false:

pragma Assume (0 = 1); −− *Assume nothing is something.*

Verification conditions following this assume will contain a false hypothesis. When conjoined with the other hypotheses, the result is a false antecedent. Because a verification condition is just an implication, a false antecendent allows the verification condition to be proved no matter what the consequent might be. You can prove anything from a contradiction. Thus, the preceding Assume allows all following verification conditions to be proved.

Of course this is a silly example. It would fail in testing immediately (provided the program was compiled with an assertion policy of Check). Also, it seems clear nobody would purposely write such an assumption. However, some contradictory assumptions may be less clear. For example, consider the following Assume, where A is an array:

pragma Assume ((**for all** J **in** A'Range => A(J) > 0) **and** (A(A'First) = −1));

Again, all verification conditions after this contradictory assumption would be provable − even verification conditions that had nothing to do with the array A.

Contradictory assumptions might evade detection during code review if they contain complicated conditions, but such an assumption would fail at runtime and so should be easily detectable during testing. The real danger is with assumptions that might only be false sometimes, as in this example:

pragma Assume (C > 0);
A := B / C;

Using the assumption, the SPARK tools successfully prove that B / C does not entail division by zero. Yet what if the assumption is wrong? If the Assume is changed to an Assert, the tools will try to prove that C > 0 is true in all cases. The Assume does not carry that requirement.

So what is the purpose of Assume? The pragma allows you to inject information into your program that you know to be true for reasons unrelated to the program's logic. Without this information the SPARK tools may require you to add error handling or do other processing that in the larger view of your system you know to be unnecessary. In effect, Assume allows you to encode information about the external world that the tools need to know but otherwise would not.

As an example, consider an embedded system using a 64-bit counter as a kind of clock. The following procedure Tick is called each millisecond to update the clock value and do other housekeeping:

```
pragma SPARK_Mode(On);
package body TickTock
    with Refined_State => (TickTock_State => Clock_Value)
is
    type Clock_Type is range 0 .. 2 ** 63 - 1;
    Clock_Value : Clock_Type := 0;

    procedure Tick
        with
            Refined_Global   => (In_Out => Clock_Value),
            Refined_Depends => (Clock_Value =>+ null)
    is
    begin
        Clock_Value := Clock_Value + 1;
        -- Other housekeeping...
    end Tick;

end TickTock;
```

In this simple program, the SPARK tools cannot prove the incrementing of Clock_Value will stay in range. However, if the system initializes at boot time and increments Clock_Value only once every millisecond, it would take more than 290 million years to reach its maximum value.

You could push the proofs through by adding error handling:

```
if Clock_Value = Clock_Type'Last then
    Restart_System;
else
    Clock_Value := Clock_Value + 1;
end if;
```

In the event that the system is still running when the next supercontinent forms, it now has the sense to reboot and re-initialize itself. More importantly, the SPARK tools are now convinced that Clock_Value + 1 is safe. However, adding error handling like this for a condition that will never arise in any realistic scenario is more obscure than useful.

Instead, this is an appropriate place to use Assume:

```
pragma Assume (Clock_Value < Clock_Type'Last);
Clock_Value := Clock_Value + 1;
```

Now the SPARK tools discharge the verification condition associated with incrementing Clock_Value without complaint. Furthermore, the assumption made to do so is documented in the code in an easy-to-find manner. The assumption will potentially even be checked at runtime. In effect, information about the external environment in which the program runs, namely that it will be rebooted at least every 290 million years, is being made known to the tools so they can account for that information in the proofs.

The preceding example seems compelling, but even here caution is necessary. Perhaps at a later time Clock_Type is changed to be

type Clock_Type **is range** 0 .. 2 ** 31 − 1;   −− *32 bits*.

Now Clock_Value will reach its maximum value after only 24.8 days. It is very possible the system might run that long causing Assertion_Error when the assumption fails or Constraint_Error when Clock_Value overflows if assertion checking is off. The SPARK tools will not detect this problem because it is masked by the assumption. Of course after making such a change, all assumptions should be reviewed. Fortunately, the Assume pragmas stand out in the program making it easy to locate them.

We make use of the Assume pragma in Section 9.2 when using transitivity in the proof of the selection sort introduced in Chapter 1.

6.4 Loop Invariants

Loops are a problem. Each execution of a loop is a separate path through the subprogram being analyzed. Yet, in general, the number of times a loop executes is only discovered dynamically. As a result there are potentially an unknown number of paths around a loop and leading away from that loop.

Imagine unwinding a loop so that there are as many sequential executions of its body as there are loop passes. Constructs after the loop might be reachable after one unwinding or after two unwindings, or after any number of unwindings. Verification conditions generated for checks after the loop need to account for each of these potentially infinite number of possibilities. The same applies for constructs in the loop body itself that are repeatedly visited during the loop's execution. In this section we look at the Loop_Invariant pragma provided by SPARK for managing loops. We describe the Loop_Variant pragma used for proving loop termination in Section 6.5.

Using the Loop_Invariant pragma the programmer can assert a Boolean condition that must be true at a particular point in the loop whenever that point is reached. The SPARK tools generate verification conditions considering every path that can reach the loop invariant. If these verification conditions can be discharged, the invariant will always be true. Like all assertions, loop invariants are also executable, depending on the assertion policy, and will raise Assertion_Error if they fail.

One special feature of the Loop_Invariant pragma is that it is a cut point as we described in Section 6.3.2. All paths that reach the invariant are considered terminated at that point. Only one path leaves the invariant. This behavior is essential to control the otherwise unbounded number of paths a program with a loop might contain.

The invariant splits the loop into three parts: the path that enters the loop for the first time and terminates on the invariant, the path that goes from the invariant around the loop and terminates on the invariant again, and finally, the path that goes from the invariant and leaves the loop. Of course each of these parts may entail multiple paths if there are other control structures before, after, or inside the loop. However, this approach fixes the number of paths to something the SPARK tools can know rather than having that number depend on the number of times the loop executes.

A consequence of the invariant being a cut point is that it must appear immediately inside the loop. That means it cannot be nested inside some other control structure such as an **if** statement within the loop. An invariant that was only executed conditionally would not cut the loop nor would it limit the number of paths the SPARK tools need to consider. Loop invariants are so essential that the SPARK tools will automatically generate one for each loop where you do not provide one. The generated invariant only asserts True. It is, thus, trivial to prove but not useful in following proofs.

You might suppose that a loop invariant, even the trivial one generated by the SPARK tools if needed, would block information gathered before the loop from reaching past the loop. This would be an expected consequence of the invariant being a cut point. However, the SPARK tools have special handling that allow them to convey information gathered before the loop about objects not modified in the loop past the cut point and to verification conditions beyond the loop. This simplifies the writing of loop invariants because it is not necessary to reassert information in the invariant about objects the loop does not modify.

Like the Assert and Assume pragmas, Loop_Invariant is not really contractual. It is needed to assist the SPARK tools in proving verification conditions in the face of a potentially unknown number of loop iterations. As the tools evolve, they may become better at generating loop invariants without assistance. You may find that you need to explicitly state fewer of them in the future than in the past.

As an example, consider a package that provides a buffer type as a kind of array of characters together with some subprograms for operating on buffers. A part of the specification of such a Buffers package might look like

```
package Buffers is

   Maximum_Buffer_Size : constant := 1024;
   subtype Buffer_Count_Type is Natural  range 0 .. Maximum_Buffer_Size;
   subtype Buffer_Index_Type is Positive range 1 .. Maximum_Buffer_Size;
   type    Buffer_Type       is array (Buffer_Index_Type) of Character;

   -- Returns the number of occurrences of Ch in Buffer.
   function Count_Character (Buffer : in Buffer_Type;
                             Ch     : in Character) return Buffer_Count_Type;
end Buffers;
```

Here is the body of function Count_Character:

```
   function Count_Character (Buffer : in Buffer_Type;
                             Ch : in Character) return Buffer_Count_Type is
      Count : Buffer_Count_Type := 0;
   begin
      for Index in Buffer_Index_Type loop
         pragma Loop_Invariant (Count < Index);

         if Buffer (Index) = Ch then
            Count := Count + 1;
         end if;
      end loop;
      return Count;
   end Count_Character;
```

The SPARK tools are interested in showing, among other things, that the value of Count will not go out of range despite it being incremented inside the loop. This is a reasonable concern. If the loop runs an excessive number of times, Count could be incremented too often. Yet in this case, the function is fine. The value of Count is initialized to zero and it is incremented at most the number of times the loop runs, which is 1,024 passes. Thus, even if the inner conditional is true for every pass, Count would only be 1,024 and still in range at the end of the loop.

To convey this information to the tools, we add a Loop_Invariant pragma to the loop asserting that whenever that point is reached, the value of Count is always less than the loop parameter. The tools can easily show this is true. On entry to the loop, Count is zero and Index is one. Each time around the loop Index is always incremented and Count is only sometimes incremented, depending on the path. Either way Count remains less than Index if it was so on the previous iteration. Finally, the tools use the information in the loop invariant to readily show that Count + 1 will never go out of the allowed range of Buffer_Count_Type.

As a second example, consider a procedure for copying an ordinary string value into a buffer. The declaration of that procedure might look like

```
procedure Copy_Into (Buffer  :  out Buffer_Type;
                      Source :  in   String)
·    with
     Depends => (Buffer => Source);
```

If the source string is too long, this procedure is intended to truncate that string and only copy the characters that will fit into the buffer. If the source string is too short, the buffer is to be padded with spaces. Here is an implementation of this procedure:

```
procedure Copy_Into (Buffer  :  out Buffer_Type;
                      Source :  in   String) is
    Characters_To_Copy : Buffer_Count_Type := Maximum_Buffer_Size;
begin
    Buffer := (others => ' ');   -- initialize  to  all  blanks
    if Source'Length < Characters_To_Copy then
       Characters_To_Copy := Source'Length;
    end if ;
    for Index in Buffer_Count_Type range 1 .. Characters_To_Copy loop
       pragma Loop_Invariant
          (Characters_To_Copy <= Source'Length and
           Characters_To_Copy = Characters_To_Copy'Loop_Entry);

       Buffer (Index) := Source (Source' First + (Index − 1));
    end loop;
end Copy_Into;
```

After determining how many characters actually need to be copied, a loop is used to do the copying one character at a time. The loop invariant asserts that the value of Characters_To_Copy does not change as the loop executes. It accomplishes this using the 'Loop_Entry attribute allowing you to refer to a value a variable has when the loop is first entered. The 'Loop_Entry attribute is, thus, similar to the 'Old attribute in that its use requires the compiler to maintain a copy of the variable's earlier value.

The current generation of the SPARK tools does not actually need the loop invariant we wrote in procedure Copy_Into. This relaxation is a result of the special handling afforded to values, such as Characters_To_Copy that do not change inside the loop; it is not actually necessary to reassert information about them at the cut point created by the invariant. However, an earlier generation of the SPARK tools did require the invariant because the technology was less mature at that time. This illustrates the point that the number and nature of the non-contractual assertions required in your programs may change as the tools evolve. However, contractual assertions such as pre- and postconditions embody design information and are to a certain extent tool independent.

Finding an appropriate loop invariant requires a certain amount of practice and skill. You need to find a condition that describes the work of the loop in a nontrivial way, is easy for the tools to prove, and provides useful information for later verification conditions to use.

As a more complex example, consider a procedure that converts an IP version 4 (IPv4) address into a dotted decimal string suitable for display to humans.[11] This procedure is part of package Network.Addresses from the Thumper project that we describe in Section 8.5. Here the specification of the package is shown, in part. In this code the type Network.Octet is an 8-bit modular type holding values in the range of 0 to 255.

```
package Network.Addresses is

    type IPv4 is private ;

    subtype Address_String_Index_Type is Positive range 1 .. 15;
    subtype Address_String_Type is String ( Address_String_Index_Type );
    subtype Address_Length_Type is Natural range 7 .. 15;

    procedure To_IPv4_String (Address          : in  IPv4;
                              Text             : out Address_String_Type;
                              Character_Count : out Address_Length_Type)
        with
            Global  => null,
            Depends => ((Text, Character_Count) => Address);

private
    subtype IPv4_Address_Index_Type is Integer range 1 .. 4;
    type IPv4 is array (IPv4_Address_Index_Type) of Network.Octet;

end Network.Addresses;
```

This package takes advantage of the fact that the text form IP addresses require at most fifteen characters. It thus defines a suitable subtype to express this limitation. However, because some IP addresses are shorter than fifteen characters, the procedure To_IPv4_String also outputs a count of the number of characters that were actually required. The procedure pads the output string with spaces in that case. Here is one attempt at implementing this procedure:

```
subtype Digit_Type is Character range '0' .. '9';
subtype Value_Type is Network.Octet range 0 .. 9;
type    Value_To_Digit_Type is array(Value_Type) of Digit_Type;

Digit_Lookup_Table : constant Value_To_Digit_Type :=
   Value_To_Digit_Type'( '0', '1', '2', '3', '4', '5', '6', '7', '8', '9');

procedure To_IPv4_String (Address         : in  IPv4;
                          Text            : out Address_String_Type;
                          Character_Count : out Address_Length_Type) is

   subtype Skip_Type is Positive range 1 .. 4;

   Index    : Address_String_Index_Type;
   Count    : Natural;
   Skip     : Skip_Type;
   Value    : Network.Octet;
   Digit_2  : Digit_Type;
   Digit_1  : Digit_Type;
   Digit_0  : Digit_Type;
begin
   Text  := Address_String_Type'(others => ' ');
   Count := 0;

   -- For each octet...
   for J in IPv4_Address_Index_Type loop

      -- Compute starting position in output string .
      Index := Text' First + Count;

      -- Compute the digit characters for this octet.
      Value   := Address (J);
      Digit_2 := Digit_Lookup_Table(Value / 100);
      Value   := Value rem 100;
      Digit_1 := Digit_Lookup_Table(Value /  10);
      Value   := Value rem 10;
      Digit_0 := Digit_Lookup_Table(Value);
```

```
   -- Output the digits appropriately .
   if  Digit_2  /= '0'  then
      Text (Index + 0) := Digit_2;
      Text (Index + 1) := Digit_1;
      Text (Index + 2) := Digit_0;
      Skip := 3;
   elsif  Digit_1  /= '0'  then
      Text (Index + 0) := Digit_1;
      Text (Index + 1) := Digit_0;
      Skip := 2;
   else
      Text (Index + 0) := Digit_0;
      Skip := 1;
   end if;


   -- Place the dot unless this is the last octet.
   if  J  /= IPv4_Address_Index_Type'Last then
      Text (Index + Skip) := '.';
      Skip := Skip + 1;
   end if;


   -- Update Count.
   Count := Count + Skip;
 end loop;

 Character_Count := Count;
end To_IPv4_String;
```

This procedure works by looping over each byte in the IP address and filling in appropriate text in the output string as it works. The amount of space in the output string used by each pass of the loop depends on the value of the address component being processed. Sometimes only one digit is needed, but sometimes up to three digits are required. The value of Skip records how much space was used in the current loop pass; that value is used to update the running total of the number of characters consumed so far.

The subprogram contains no flow errors, but the SPARK tools have difficulty proving that the various accesses of the array Text are in bounds. The tools do not "understand" that the loop will execute a limited number of times and never run Count and, hence, Index up to an excessive value.

To help the proofs succeed, we must add a loop invariant that explains to the SPARK tools that Count is suitably bounded. We must find a condition that is both within the tools' ability to prove and yet also adds enough information to let the tools complete the proofs they are stuck on. To find an appropriate invariant, start by asking the question, How do we, as humans, know this code works? Answering this question gives us insight about what we must tell the SPARK tools. Furthermore, if the procedure is in fact faulty, attempting to explain to ourselves why it works will likely reveal the fault. This is the essence of how SPARK transforms incorrect programs into reliable ones.

If we study the procedure, we can see that each loop pass adds at most four characters to the output string (up to three digit characters and a dot). Thus, as a first attempt we add the following loop invariant immediately inside the for loop:

```
pragma Loop_Invariant (Count <= 4*(J−1));
```

This increases the number of verification conditions to be proved as the loop invariant adds additional proof obligations. However, this invariant does allow the tools to verify that the accesses to the Text array are all in bounds – a significant step forward. The only two remaining objections are to the statement

```
Count := Count + Skip;
```

at the end of the loop and to the final assignment to Character_Count before the procedure returns.

One problem is that the last loop pass is special but we do not convey any information about that to the tool. In particular, the dot character is not output in the last pass so only three characters at most are added to the output string. This is important because the size of the output string is exactly fifteen characters and not sixteen as would be required if four characters were output with every pass. To express this concept, we add the following assertion to the end of the loop immediately before the statement Count := Count + Skip:

```
pragma Assert ( if  J < IPv4_Address_Index_Type'Last
               then Skip <= 4
               else Skip <= 3);
```

This informs the tools that the skip distance is at most three during the last loop iteration and allows the tools to discharge the verification condition associated with updating Count.

The remaining issue is on the statement

```
Character_Count := Count;
```

The problem here is that Character_Count has type Address_Length_Type, which is constrained to the range 7 .. 15. The assertions so far only put an upper bound on the number of characters written, and the tools are having trouble showing that at least seven characters are output. To address this, we change the loop invariant to

pragma Loop_Invariant (Count $>=$ 2*(J−1) **and** Count $<=$ 4*(J−1));

Now the tools are able to discharge all verification conditions in the subprogram, proving that it is free of any possibility of runtime error.

It might seem as if this process would have been easier if the types had not been so precisely defined. For example, if Address_Length_Type had a lower bound of one instead of seven, perhaps the final step would not have been necessary. However, loosening type definitions for the sake of making certain proofs easier is almost never the right approach. In fact, loosely specified types typically make proofs more difficult, if not in one place then in another. The tools might be able to use the tight constraint on Address_Length_Type to its advantage when proving verification conditions elsewhere related to IP addresses. Always strive to tighten type definitions; avoid loosening them. Embed as much information as you can into the program.

This example also illustrates the interplay between human reasoning and the SPARK tools. After convincing ourselves of the correctness of the code, we could have just, perhaps, recorded our reasoning in a comment and not bothered with finding suitable SPARK assertions. However, SPARK serves to check our work, which is valuable because humans are very error prone when trying to mentally manage the mass of details required while reasoning about programs. Also, the SPARK assertions are a form of machine readable documentation that can be checked automatically by other programmers less familiar with the code. If a change is made to the procedure, the SPARK tools will alert the programmer making the change to any potential runtime issues introduced.

As an example, consider the following code from the To_IPv4_String procedure:

```
-- Compute the digit characters for this octet.
Value   := Address (J);
Digit_2 := Digit_Lookup_Table (Value / 100);
Value   := Value rem 100;
Digit_1 := Digit_Lookup_Table (Value /  10);
Value   := Value rem 10;
Digit_0 := Digit_Lookup_Table (Value);
```

It is necessary that the values used to index the lookup table are all in the range 0 .. 9. No doubt the programmer considered that when writing the code initially. The SPARK tools also proved this without comment so the programmer did not need to spend time reviewing the code for that error. The tools can thus take care of many "simple" proofs and only require human assistance for the more difficult cases. However, ultimately it is the human and not the tools that generated the "proofs" for the code, even if just mentally. The tools simply serve to check the human's work.

As a final example, consider this implementation of procedure Binary_Search that we specified on page 167:

```
package body Searchers2
   with SPARK_Mode => On
is

   procedure Binary_Search (Search_Item : in   Integer ;
                            Items        : in   Array_Type;
                            Found        : out  Boolean;
                            Result       : out  Index_Type) is

      Low_Index  : Index_Type := Items' First ;
      Mid_Index  : Index_Type;
      High_Index : Index_Type := Items' Last;
   begin
      Found  := False ;
      Result := Items' First ;    -- Initialize Result to "not found" case.

      -- If the item is out of range, it is not found.
      if  Search_Item < Items(Low_Index) or Items(High_Index) < Search_Item then
         return ;
      end if ;


      loop
         Mid_Index := (Low_Index + High_Index) / 2;
         if  Search_Item = Items(Mid_Index) then
            Found  := True;
            Result := Mid_Index;
            return ;
         end if ;

         exit  when Low_Index = High_Index;

         pragma Loop_Invariant
            (Search_Item in Items(Low_Index) .. Items(High_Index ));

         if  Items(Mid_Index) < Search_Item then
            Low_Index := Mid_Index;
```

```
        else
            High_Index := Mid_Index;
        end if ;

    end loop;
end Binary_Search;

end Searchers2;
```

The implementation is non-recursive and relatively straightforward. To complete the proof, an appropriate loop invariant must be given. As usual finding the right loop invariant is the trickiest part of the problem. At the point where the invariant is given the search item has not yet been found and, if it exists in the array at all, it resides between position Low_Index and High_Index inclusive.

With the invariant shown, the preceding implementation of Binary_Search is proved. It will never exhibit any runtime error and it honors its strong postcondition.

Unfortunately, the preceding implementation contains a serious fault. Under certain circumstances the loop runs infinitely without ever making any progress. Consider the case where Low_Index and High_Index are adjacent and the array elements under consideration are the natural numbers 10 and 20. Suppose the search item is 20. The implementation computes a Mid_Index equal to Low_Index in this case. Because the item in the array at that position (10) is less than the search item (20), the implementation sets Low_Index to the value of Mid_Index, which does not change anything. The procedure loops forever.

Although the tools have proved the procedure honors its postcondition, that is only applicable if the procedure returns at all. We have not yet proved that the procedure actually terminates in every case. We discuss how to do that in Section 6.5.

6.5 Loop Variants

In the previous section we saw that it is possible for the SPARK tools to prove even strong postconditions about a subprogram and yet for there to still be serious faults in that subprogram. This unexpected effect occurs because the proof of a postcondition does not consider the possibility of nontermination. The subprogram may simply execute forever without returning. In general, nontermination can occur if the subprogram contains unbounded recursion or if it contains loop statements. In this section we look at how we can prove that a subprogram has no infinite loops.

Many loops in SPARK subprograms obviously terminate and do not need any special handling. For example, a **for** loop runs its loop parameter over a range that is computed when the loop is first encountered. The rules of Ada prevent the loop parameter from being changed in the loop, so it can only advance across the specified range of values. Such loops are guaranteed to terminate once the loop parameter has exhausted its range. However, **while** loops and loops constructed without an iteration scheme (a bare **loop** statement) may run for an indeterminate number of passes. Proving that such loops terminate is often desirable and even necessary as part of a full proof of the enclosing subprogram's correctness.

Proving loop termination can be done with the help of the Loop_Variant pragma. The semantics of Loop_Variant are more complex than for the other assertions we have seen so far. Loop_Variant allows you to define an expression that either always increases (or always decreases) as the loop executes. If the value of the expression has a suitable upper (or lower) bound, then the loop must end because the value of the expression cannot increase (or decrease) infinitely without crossing the bound. The expression is not allowed to stay the same between loop iterations. The expression must "make progress" monotonically toward a bound. Otherwise, the loop might execute forever. For example, the Loop_Variant pragma

```
pragma Loop_Variant (Increases => A - B + C);
```

asserts that the expression $A - B + C$ increases with each iteration of the loop.

The Loop_Variant pragma allows you to specify several expressions. Each expression is prefixed with a change direction of either Increases or Decreases. Here is an example using the integer variables, X, Y, and Z:

```
pragma Loop_Variant (Increases => X, Decreases => Y - Z);
```

This assertion states that during each loop iteration, either the value of X increases or the value of the expression $Y - Z$ decreases. When there are multiple expressions in the pragma, any particular expression may stay the same during a particular iteration as long as one of the other expressions moves in the specified direction.

The order of the expressions in pragma Loop_Variant is significant. In each iteration, expressions are checked in textual order until either a change is found or all expressions have been checked. The assertion is true if the last expression checked moved in the specified direction and false otherwise. Any expressions after the one that moved are ignored. So in our example, if X increases, what happens to Y − Z is not considered.

The expressions in a Loop_Variant pragma must have a discrete type. The domain of any discrete type consists of a *finite* set of ordered values. Therefore, the values of a discrete type are automatically bounded both above and below. In our examples, the expressions have type Integer and so are bounded by Integer ' First and Integer ' Last. It is not necessary for you to specify any other bounds.

Of course the loop may not run the expressions all the way to their bounds. That is not important. It is only necessary for the bound to exist and for the loop to increase (or decrease) the value of the expressions monotonically. That is sufficient to prove that the loop must eventually terminate.

Like all assertions, loop variants are executable under the control of the assertion policy. If they fail, Assertion_Error is raised as usual. Also, like all assertions, the SPARK tools will create a verification condition to prove that the variant never fails. Discharging that verification condition proves that the loop terminates.

In the Binary_Search example in Section 6.4, the procedure made use of a bare **loop** statement with an **exit** statement that ends the loop under certain conditions. Unlike **for** loops, a loop of this form may conceivably execute forever. It is thus appropriate in this case to use Loop_Variant to prove that will not happen.

To find an appropriate loop variant start by asking, What expression describes the progress the loop is making? In the case of Binary_Search one possibility is that High_Index and Low_Index always get closer together:

```
pragma Loop_Variant (Decreases => High_Index   Low_Index);
```

If each iteration of the loop reduces the distance between the two indicies, eventually the loop will end.

The subprogram exits the loop when the difference between the indicies is zero. However, you might wonder what would happen if High_Index − Low_Index skipped over zero and became negative.

The type of the loop variant expression in this case is Integer (the base type of Index_Type). In theory the smallest possible value of High_Index − Low_Index is -99. This could occur if the two index values were at their appropriate extremes. If the loop were truly infinite and yet the loop variant succeeded, then High_Index − Low_Index would decrease forever. Eventually, Constraint_ Error would be raised when one of the two indices goes out of bounds or, if not that, when the subtraction overflows the range of Integer. If the code proves free of runtime error, neither of these cases can occur; the program cannot have both an infinite loop and a satisfied loop variant at the same time.

Unfortunately, the implementation of Binary_Search in Section 6.4 does contain a possible infinite loop, and as you would expect, the loop variant fails to prove. To fix the subprogram, it is necessary to correct the error in such a way as to maintain the proofs of freedom from runtime error, the postcondition, and some suitable loop variant. An implementation that does so follows:

```
package body Searchers3
   with SPARK_Mode => On
is
   procedure Binary_Search (Search_Item :  in   Integer ;
                            Items       :  in   Array_Type;
                            Found       :  out  Boolean;
                            Result      :  out  Index_Type) is
      Low_Index  : Index_Type := Items' First ;
      Mid_Index  : Index_Type;
      High_Index : Index_Type := Items' Last ;
   begin
      Found  := False ;
      Result := Items' First ;   -- Initialize Result to "not found" case.

      -- If the item is out of range, it is not found.
      if  Search_Item < Items(Low_Index) or Items(High_Index) < Search_Item then
         return ;
      end if ;

      loop
         Mid_Index := (Low_Index + High_Index) / 2;
         if  Search_Item = Items(Mid_Index) then
            Found  := True;
            Result := Mid_Index;
            return ;
         end if ;

         exit when Low_Index = High_Index;

         pragma Loop_Invariant (not Found);
         pragma Loop_Invariant (Mid_Index in Low_Index .. High_Index - 1);
         pragma Loop_Invariant (Items(Low_Index) <= Search_Item);
```

```
pragma Loop_Invariant (Search_Item <= Items(High_Index));
pragma Loop_Variant (Decreases => High_Index - Low_Index);

if Items(Mid_Index) < Search_Item then
  if Search_Item < Items(Mid_Index + 1) then
    return;
  end if;
  Low_Index := Mid_Index + 1;
else
  High_Index := Mid_Index;
end if;

  end loop;
end Binary_Search;

end Searchers3;
```

The key idea is to assign Mid_Index + 1 to Low_Index to force Low_Index to advance in the case of a two-element subsequence as described previously. However, this now requires an extra test in case the extra advance skips past the search item's value in the array. These changes caused the SPARK tools to have trouble proving the postcondition in the case of the resulting early return. Adding not Found to the loop invariant clarified for the tools which part of the postcondition was relevant.

Finally, it was necessary to assert a loop invariant that described the relationship between Low_Index, Mid_Index, and High_Index so the effect of the assignments at the bottom of the loop could be tracked. With these changes the SPARK tools are able to prove that the subprogram works and never loops infinitely.

We should note that technically the SPARK tools only allow a single loop invariant in each loop, but as a convenience, it is permitted, as was done in the previous example, to use several Loop_Invariant pragmas in a row. The effect is to create an overall invariant that is the conjunction of the individually listed invariants.

Finally, it bears mentioning that technically proving a particular loop variant does not by itself prove a subprogram returns. A subprogram might contain multiple loops on various paths; proving that one loop terminates leaves open the possibility that a different loop might run infinitely. To ensure that a subprogram always returns, it is necessary to prove that all loops contained in the subprogram that can be feasibly reached terminate. In practice this is not normally an issue, but the SPARK tools by themselves do not provide any direct checking of this requirement.

6.6 Discriminants

Ada provides a way to parameterize record types using discriminants. The basics of this topic were briefly described in Section 2.3.6. In this section we provide a more detailed example of the use of discriminants and show how they interact with SPARK proofs.

A discriminated type is a kind of indefinite type similar in some respects to an unconstrained array type. To declare an object, it is necessary to provide a specific value for the discriminant. The value provided can be dynamically computed, giving you flexibility. However, different objects with different discriminants are still of the same type and thus can be, for example, passed to a single subprogram that accepts that type. In Section 6.7 we show an example of using SPARK with an alternative method of parameterizing types, namely, generics.

As a concrete example of using discriminated types, consider the problem of doing integer computations on very large values. The integer types built into your Ada compiler may support 64-bit computations and conceivably even larger sizes, but they will be limited by whatever is natural for your hardware. However, some applications have a need to do computations on extremely large integers with, for example, 1,024 bits or even more. Many cryptographic algorithms such as RSA or elliptic curve-based cryptosystems need to manipulate such *extended precision* integers.

It is natural to design a package supporting an extended precision integer type. In this example, we will call that type Very_Long. Following the common Ada convention of making the name of a type package plural, we will call the package that defines our type Very_Longs.

Unfortunately, different applications have different needs regarding the size of the numbers they must manipulate. We could design Very_Long to expand (and contract) dynamically as needed, but the natural way of doing this would entail the use of memory allocators, a feature not supported by SPARK. Alternatively, we could set a fixed size for Very_Long, picking a size large enough to support any conceivable application. However, this may still not be enough for some exceptional applications and will waste space and time in the majority of cases where a very large size is not needed.

The type Very_Long is thus a prime candidate for being discriminated with a value that gives the size of the integer. Different objects could thus have different sizes as needed and yet all be of the same type.

For cryptographic applications modeling signed integers, using the usual mathematical operations is not normally needed. Instead, unsigned, modular integers tend to be more useful where addition and subtraction "wrap around" inside a value with a fixed number of bits without overflow. These are the kinds of integers we show in our example. The full specification of package Very_Longs with line numbers for reference is as follows:

```
1   pragma SPARK_Mode(On);
2
3   package Very_Longs is
4
5      -- Here "Digit" means a base 256 digit.
6      Maximum_Length : constant := 2**16;
7      type     Digit_Count_Type is new Natural range 0 .. Maximum_Length;
8      subtype Digit_Index_Type is Digit_Count_Type range 1 .. Digit_Count_Type'Last;
9      type     Very_Long (Length : Digit_Index_Type) is private;
10
11     -- Constructors.
12     function Make_From_Natural (Number : in Natural;
13                                        Length : in Digit_Index_Type) return Very_Long
14        with Post => Make_From_Natural'Result.Length = Length;
15
16     procedure Make_From_Hex_String (Number : in String;
17                                       Result  : out Very_Long;
18                                       Valid   : out Boolean)
19        with
20           Depends => ((Result, Valid) => (Number, Result)),
21           Pre => Number'Length = 2*Result.Length;
22
23     -- Relational operators. Only Very_Longs of equal size can be compared.
24     function "<" (L, R : in Very_Long) return Boolean
25        with Pre => L.Length = R.Length;
26
27     function "<=" (L, R : in Very_Long) return Boolean
28        with Pre => L.Length = R.Length;
29
30     function ">" (L, R : in Very_Long) return Boolean
31        with Pre => L.Length = R.Length;
32
33     function ">=" (L, R : in Very_Long) return Boolean
34        with Pre => L.Length = R.Length;
35
36     -- Returns True if Number is zero.
37     function Is_Zero (Number : in Very_Long) return Boolean;
38
39     -- Returns the number of significant digits in Number.
```

```
40   function Number_Of_Digits(Number : in Very_Long) return Digit_Count_Type;
41
42      -- Modular addition (modulo 256**Length).
43      function ModAdd (L, R : in Very_Long) return Very_Long
44         with
45            Pre  => L.Length = R.Length,
46            Post => ModAdd'Result.Length = L.Length;
47
48      -- Modular subtraction (modulo 256**Length).
49      function ModSubtract (L, R : in Very_Long) return Very_Long
50         with
51            Pre  => L.Length = R.Length,
52            Post => ModSubtract'Result.Length = L.Length;
53
54      -- Modular multiplication (modulo 256**Length).
55      function ModMultiply (L, R : in Very_Long) return Very_Long
56         with
57            Pre  => L.Length = R.Length,
58            Post => ModMultiply'Result.Length = L.Length;
59
60      -- Ordinary multiplication .
61      function "*" (L, R : in Very_Long) return Very_Long
62        with Post => "*"'Result.Length = L.Length + R.Length;
63
64      -- Division returns quotient and remainder.
65      procedure Divide (Dividend  : in  Very_Long;
66                        Divisor   : in  Very_Long;
67                        Quotient  : out Very_Long;
68                        Remainder : out Very_Long)
69         with
70            Depends => (Quotient =>+ (Dividend, Divisor),
71                        Remainder =>+ (Dividend, Divisor)),
72            Pre => (Number_Of_Digits (Divisor) > 1)    and
73                   ( Divisor .Length  = Remainder.Length) and
74                   (Dividend.Length = Quotient.Length ) and
75                   (Dividend.Length = 2*Divisor.Length);
76
77   private
78      type Octet is  mod 2**8;
79      type Double_Octet is  mod 2**16;
80
81      type Digits_Array_Type  is  array (Digit_Index_Type range <>) of Octet;
82
```

```
83    —— The bytes are stored in  little  endian order.
84        type Very_Long (Length : Digit_Index_Type) is
85          record
86                Long_Digits : Digits_Array_Type (1 .. Length);
87          end record;
88
89        function Is_Zero (Number : in Very_Long) return Boolean is
90          (for all J in Number.Long_Digits'Range => Number.Long_Digits (J) = 0);
91
92    end Very_Longs;
```

The package starts by declaring three types. We regard a Very_Long as being expressed in the base 256, where each *extended digit* is an 8-bit value in the range of 0–255. In our discussion of this example, and in the code itself, we use the word *digit* to mean a base 256 extended digit.

Lines 6 and 7 introduce a type used for counting digits in a Very_Long. The maximum number of digits we choose to support is the somewhat arbitrary number 2^{16}. Yet each Very_Long is the length it needs to be; they do not all need to have 2^{16} digits. However, imposing a reasonable bound simplifies many of the proofs. If Digit_Count_Type did not apply any constraints on Natural, the code would be forced to deal with integers having potentially billions of digits. Certain computations on lengths would tend to overflow in this general case. Limiting the range of Digit_Count_Type allows those computations to complete successfully without intricate handling.

Although the limit of 2^{16} digits may seem arbitrary, it is no more arbitrary than a limit of $2^{31} - 1$ that would be typical of Natural'Last on a 32-bit system. If some arbitrary limit must be specified, why not choose one that gives enough "headroom" for doing simple calculations on lengths without overflowing? We note that if this code is compiled for a 16-bit system where Natural'Last is only $2^{15} - 1$, the code will either fail to compile outright or, at worst, fail to prove. Either way the potential problem will be caught during development.

Line 8 introduces a subtype used to index digits in a Very_Long. The indexing discipline assigns the least significant digit the index 1. Although it might seem more natural to start the indexing at zero, that turns out to be unworkable as a result of certain limitations on discriminants we describe shortly.

Line 9 introduces the discriminated Very_Long type itself as private. The discriminant specifies the number of digits in the value. For example, a 1024-bit integer would be $1024/8 = 128$ digits in length. Although the details of Very_Long are hidden from the user, the discriminant is not and, instead, behaves much like a public component of the type. As a result it can be used in pre- and postconditions on the public subprograms.

Notice also that these declarations use the Ada type system to enforce the restriction that zero length Very_Long objects are not allowed. The discriminant cannot take the value zero; every object must be at least one digit in length. Of course, all the digits of a Very_Long could be zero so the length of a Very_Long and the number of significant digits it contains are two separate matters.

There are two constructor subprograms provided on lines 12–21. They allow Very_Long objects to be created from ordinary natural numbers and also from strings of hexadecimal digits. The later subprogram is useful for initializing extremely large values. Because arbitrary strings may contain characters that are not hexadecimal digits, the subprogram returns a Valid parameter set to false if invalid characters are found. Checking this requires error handling at runtime. An alternative strategy would be to strengthen the precondition as follows:

```
Pre => Number'Length = 2 * Result.Length and
    (for all  J  in  Number'Range => Is_Hex_Digit (J))
```

This assumes a function Is_Hex_Digit with the obvious meaning is available.

Although the second approach increases the burden of proof on all callers of the constructor, it allows the error detection code inside the procedure to be removed. It also allows the Valid parameter to be removed along with all the error handling code associated with checking it. Finally, it would allow the procedure to be converted into a function that, in turn, would allow it to be used in a declarative part to initialize a Very_Long as shown in the following example:

```
Some_Number : Very_Long := Make_From_Hex_String ("FFFFFFFF");
```

This example shows an interesting cascade effect arising from moving checks from the dynamic domain of program execution to the static domain of program verification. Furthermore, it could be argued that the modification described here is superior because callers are not likely to intentionally give Make_From_Hex_String an invalid string. The original design suffers from the problem that the flow analysis done by the SPARK tools will require Valid to be checked even in the case when the programmer knows the given string is fine.

Also notice that the precondition of Make_From_Hex_String uses the expression 2*Result.Length. This is an example of a computation that would have been problematic if Digit_Index_Type had the full range of Natural. For example, 2*Natural'Last would (likely) overflow. This is also an example of how the expressions in the assertions themselves are subject to checking by SPARK, as we discussed in Section 6.2.7.

One could allow the full range of Natural in this case by rewriting the precondition as

```
Pre => Number'Length mod 2 = 0 and
       Number'Length / 2 = Result.Length
```

The first condition ensures that the length of the given string is even. Such rewritings are commonly possible, but they can be obscure. It is often easier and better to just constrain the types involved to "reasonable" ranges.

Before leaving Make_From_Hex_String, we point out that the flow dependency contract uses Result as input:

```
Depends => ((Result, Valid) => (Number, Result))
```

This might seem surprising given that Result is an **out** parameter. However, similar to the bounds on parameters of unconstrained array types, the actual parameter used in the call has a specific value of the discriminant set by the caller. The value written to, for example, Result depends on this discriminant. If Result's length is large, the value written to it will be different than if Result's length is small, Thus the dependency as shown is correct.

Returning now to the listing of Very_Long's specification, lines 24–34 declare several relational operators. Private types can already be compared for equality, but it is natural to also have the other relational operators for a numeric type such as Very_Long. Notice that the preconditions require that both numbers being compared be the same size. Although it is mathematically logical to compare numbers with different sizes, the expected application domain (cryptography) does not normally require that. Furthermore, the restriction simplifies the implementation. Notice here that the precondition is being used to describe a relationship between the parameters; something Ada's type system cannot do by itself.

Line 37 declares a convenience function Is_Zero to test if a Very_Long is zero. This function was originally motivated for use in later assertions, but it also has usefulness to clients of the package.

Line 40 declares another convenience function Number_Of_Digits that returns the number of significant digits in a Very_Long. This is different than the Very_Long's length as leading zeros are not significant. In fact, if all the digits of the Very_Long are zero, then the Number_Of_Digits returns zero.

Lines 43–62 declare three arithmetic operators for Very_Long. Unlike the case with the relational operators, most of these functions are given names rather than overloaded operator symbols. This is because they do modular calculations in which the resulting carry is ignored without error. It is best to reserve the operator symbols for functions that follow the usual mathematical behavior. The one exception is the second multiplication operator that does produce an extended result without overflow or loss of information.

The pre- and postconditions on the arithmetic operators assert that they only work on values that are the same size and produce values with specific sizes based on their inputs. The "$*$" operator function produces an extended result large enough to hold the largest possible value it might produce. Notice that leading zero bits are not stripped by any of the subprograms, for example, $01_{16} \times 01_{16} = 0001_{16}$ – that is, two 8-bit values multiplied by "$*$" always produces a 16-bit value.

A division procedure is declared on lines 65–75. Unlike the normal "$/$" operator, Divide returns both the quotient and the remainder. The precondition asserts several important relationships on the sizes of the numbers involved. In summary, it requires that a $2n$-bit dividend be divided by an n-bit divisor to yield a $2n$-bit quotient and an n-bit remainder.

The division algorithm used (Knuth, 1998) requires that the number of significant digits in the divisor be strictly greater than one.[12] This requirement is stated with the precondition

    Number_Of_Digits (Divisor) > 1

using the previously declared convenience function.

Because the pre- and postconditions on the various arithmetic operations all make statements about the sizes of the numbers involved, using them together works smoothly. The outputs of one operation are verified by SPARK to be compatible with the inputs of the next operation. The implementations of the operations can be simplified (possibly giving improved performance) by taking advantage of the restrictions without concern that a misbehaving program might not follow them.

The postconditions on the arithmetic operations do not attempt to capture the actual mathematical result of each operation. Doing so is beyond the scope of this example, and this illustrates that postconditions are, in general, only partial statements of subprogram behavior. Although the SPARK tools will attempt to prove the postconditions as stated are always satisfied, more complete verification of these subprograms will, at the moment, require testing.

The private section of the specification is on lines 78–91. Here, the full view of the private type is provided. The size of the Long_Digits component holding the digits themselves is specified by the discriminant.

It might seem more natural to define the Digit_Index_Type as ranging from zero to Digit_Count_Type'Last $-$ 1. This would allow the least significant digit to be at index zero in the Long_Digits array. However, doing so would require the full view of Very_Long to look like

```
type Very_Long (Length : Digit_Index_Type) is
   record
      Long_Digits : Digits_Array_Type(0 .. Length − 1); −− illegal
   end record;
```

Unfortunately, this is illegal in Ada because the value of the discriminant cannot be used as part of an expression inside the record.

The body of package Very_Longs is too long to display fully here but may be found on http://www.cambridge.org/us/academic/subjects/ computer-science/programming-languages-and-applied-logic/ building-high-integrity-applications-spark. However, it is instructive to look at Number_Of_Digits. That function is too complicated to easily implement as an expression function. Instead it must be implemented as an ordinary function in the package body as the following shows:

```
function Number_Of_Digits (Number : in Very_Long) return Digit_Count_Type
   with
      Refined_Post =>
         (Number_Of_Digits'Result <= Number.Length) and
         ( if Number_Of_Digits'Result > 0 then
            Number.Long_Digits(Number_Of_Digits'Result) /= 0) and
         (for all J in (Number_Of_Digits'Result + 1) .. Number.Long_Digits'Last
            => Number.Long_Digits (J) = 0)
is
   Digit_Count : Digit_Count_Type := 0;
begin
   if not Is_Zero (Number) then
      for Index in Number.Long_Digits'Range loop
         if Number.Long_Digits (Index) /= 0 then
            Digit_Count := Index;
         end if ;

         pragma Loop_Invariant
            (( if Digit_Count > 0 then
               (Number.Long_Digits (Digit_Count) /= 0 and
                  Digit_Count in 1 .. Index)) and
            ( if Index > Digit_Count then
               (for all J in Digit_Count + 1 .. Index =>
                  Number.Long_Digits (J) = 0)));
      end loop;
   end if ;
   return Digit_Count;
end Number_Of_Digits;
```

For SPARK to have any hope of proving the body of Divide free of runtime error, it will need to know how Number_Of_Digits works in terms of the full view of Very_Long. This is because Number_Of_Digits is used in the precondition of Divide to express an important restriction ensuring Divide will not raise an exception. Thus, as described in Section 6.2.3, it is necessary to give Number_Of_Digits a refined postcondition that can be used during the analysis of Divide.

6.7 Generics

As described in Sections 2.4.2 and 3.3.3, Ada supports generic subprograms and generic packages that can be instantiated by the programmer in different ways. In this section we describe how generics are handled by SPARK and, in particular, some of the issues surrounding the proof of generic code.

The central idea with generics and SPARK is that each instantiation of a generic must be proved separately. It is not possible to prove the generic code itself because the specific details of the types and values used to instantiate the generic will affect the proofs. Although in principle it might be possible to prove certain aspects of the generic code once and for all, the SPARK tools currently do not attempt to do this.

Instead, the tools do flow analysis and generate verification conditions at the point where a generic is instantiated. Each instantiation is processed separately. It is possible for all proofs to succeed for one instantiation and yet not for others. In fact, it is possible for one instantiation to be "in SPARK" and others to be outside of the SPARK language entirely – another reason the SPARK tools do not analyze the generic code directly.

We do not normally give a SPARK_Mode to a generic unit. The mode is determined by the mode at the location of the instantiation of the generic unit. However, if the body of the generic unit contains non-SPARK code, that body should be explicitly marked with SPARK_Mode (Off). We do not want the SPARK tools to analyze that body at any instantiation of that generic unit.

As an example, consider the following abbreviated specification of a generic variable package that implements a doubly linked list. The objects in the list are of a type given by the generic parameter Element_Type.

```
generic
    type Element_Type is private ;
    Max_Size : Natural;
    Default_Element : Element_Type;
package Double_List
    with
        Abstract_State    => Internal_List ,
        Initializes       => Internal_List ,
```

```
    Initial_Condition  => Size = 0
is
   type Status_Type is (Success,  Invalid_Step ,
                              Bad_Iterator ,  Insufficient_Space );
   type Iterator  is private ;

   procedure Clear
     with
       Global   => (Output => Internal_List),
       Depends => (Internal_List => null),
       Post     => Size = 0;

   procedure Insert_Before ( It      : in  Iterator ;
                             Item    : in  Element_Type;
                             Status : out Status_Type)
     with
       Global   => (In_Out => Internal_List),
       Depends => (Internal_List => + (It, Item),
                   Status  -> Internal_List );

   function Back return Iterator
     with
       Global  => null;

   function Size return Natural
     with
       Global  => (Input => Internal_List );

private
   -- Position zero is a sentinel node.
   type Iterator  is new Natural range 0 .. Max_Size;
end Double_List ;
```

The traditional way to implement a dynamic list is to use the heap to store nodes in the list. However, if any instantiations are to be analyzed by SPARK, that approach is not possible because SPARK does not support memory allocators or access types. Instead, this package stores the list in a fixed size structure making it more properly called a *bounded* doubly linked list. Although the list can change size dynamically, the region of memory reserved for it cannot. The maximum number of list elements allowed is given as the generic parameter Max_Size.

The package defines a private Iterator type. Objects of that type are used to "point" into the list. An iterator can point at any element in the list and also at a special end-of-list element, also called a *sentinel* element, that conceptually exists just past the last valid element. The Back function returns an iterator to the sentinel; it is valid to call Back even for an empty list.

A more complete package would also include subprograms for moving iterators forward and backward over the list and for reading and writing list items through iterators. The generic parameter Default_Element is intended to be returned when one attempts to (incorrectly) read the list's sentinel. The generic package cannot know what value would be appropriate to return in that case so it relies on the instantiation to provide such a value.

The package specification has SPARK data and flow dependency contracts and a declaration of the abstract state held by the package. Here is the body of this abbreviated package:

```
package body Double_List
    with
        Refined_State => ( Internal_List => (Memory, Count, Free_List, Free))
is
    subtype Index_Type is Iterator ;

    type List_Node is
        record
            Value    : Element_Type;
            Next     : Index_Type;
            Previous : Index_Type;
        end record;

    type Node_Array is array (Index_Type) of List_Node;
    type Free_Array is array (Index_Type) of Index_Type;

    Memory    : Node_Array;   -- Holds the list nodes.
    Count     : Index_Type;   -- Number of items on the list.
    Free_List : Free_Array;   -- Maps available nodes.
    Free      : Index_Type;   -- Points at the head of the free  list .

    procedure Clear
        with
            Refined_Global  => (Output => (Memory, Count, Free_List, Free)),
            Refined_Depends => ((Memory, Count, Free_List, Free) => null)
    is
    begin
        -- Make sure the entire array has some appropriate  initial  value.
        Memory := (others => (Default_Element, 0, 0));
        Count := 0;
```

```
      -- Prepare the free  list .
      Free_List  := (others => 0);
      Free := 1;
      for Index in Index_Type range 1 .. Index_Type'Last − 1 loop
         Free_List (Index) := Index + 1;
      end loop;
   end Clear;


procedure Insert_Before ( It       : in  Iterator ;
                          Item    : in  Element_Type;
                          Status : out Status_Type)
      with
         Refined_Global   => (Input => Free_List,
                              In_Out => (Memory, Count, Free)),
         Refined_Depends => (Memory =>+ (Count, It, Item, Free),
                             (Count, Status) => Count,
                             Free           =>+ (Count, Free_List))
   is
      New_Pointer : Index_Type;
   begin
      if Count = Index_Type(Max_Size) then
         Status :=  Insufficient_Space ;
      else
         Status := Success;

         -- Get an item from the free  list .
         New_Pointer := Free;
         Free :=  Free_List (Free );

         -- Fill in the  fields  and  link  the new item into the  list .
         Memory(New_Pointer) := (Item, It, Memory(It).Previous );
         Memory(Memory(It).Previous).Next := New_Pointer;
         Memory(It).Previous := New_Pointer;

         -- Adjust count.
         Count := Count + 1;
      end if ;
   end Insert_Before ;


function Back return Iterator  is
   begin
      return 0;
   end Back;
```

```
    function Size return Natural is (Natural(Count))
       with Refined_Global => (Input => Count);

begin
   -- Clear the list at package elaboration time.
   Clear ;
end Double_List;
```

A List_Node type is defined containing a value of the list's Element_Type along with two "pointers" to the next and previous nodes in the list. Here, the pointers are implemented as indices into a suitably dimensioned array of list nodes. Each list node has a corresponding component in the Free_List array indicating if the node is available or not. The free list itself is a singly linked list with the head given by Free. The list node at position zero is the sentinel node.

The package body also has SPARK aspects as usual, including a refinement of the package's abstract state and refined data and flow dependency contracts. Although not used in this example, the body may contain other SPARK assertions such as loop invariants needed to prove instantiations of this generic unit.

Despite the SPARK aspects, the SPARK tools do not directly analyze the generic code. Instead, the aspects are used when SPARK analyzes each instantiation. Consider a simple package that provides higher level subprograms around a particular instantiation of a list of integers. For the sake of an example, this package is shown with a single procedure Append_Range that appends a given range of integers onto the list.

```
pragma SPARK_Mode(On);
package List_Handler -- To demonstrate instantiation of generic package.
   with
       Abstract_State => List,
       Initializes    => List
is
   procedure Append_Range (Lower, Upper : in Integer)
       with
          Global  => (In_Out => List),
          Depends => (List =>+ (Lower, Upper));
end List_Handler ;
```

The package is given a SPARK specification by way of the SPARK_Mode pragma. It declares as abstract state the list it is managing. Here is the body of this package:

```
pragma SPARK_Mode(On);
with Double_List ;   -- The generic doubly linked list package
pragma Elaborate_All( Double_List );
```

```
package body List_Handler
  with
     Refined_State => (List => Integer_List. Internal_List )
is
  package Integer_List is new Double_List (Element_Type   => Integer,
                                           Max_Size       => 128,
                                           Default_Element => 0);
  use type Integer_List .Status_Type;

  procedure Append_Range(Lower, Upper : in Integer)
    with
       Refined_Global   => (In_Out => Integer_List. Internal_List ),
       Refined_Depends => (Integer_List. Internal_List  =>+ (Lower, Upper))
  is
     Current :  Integer := Lower;
     Status  :  Integer_List .Status_Type;
  begin
     while Current <= Upper loop
       Integer_List , Insert_Before ( It      => Integer_List .Back,
                                      Item   => Current,
                                      Status => Status);
       exit when Status /= Integer_List .Success or Current = Upper;
       Current := Current + 1;
     end loop;
  end Append_Range;
end List_Handler ;
```

Notice the refined state clause at the beginning of this package body. The abstract state List is refined to the abstract state Internal_List of the instantiated package Integer_List . In effect, the instantiation is a kind of global variable inside package List_Handler.

The **pragma** Elaborate_All(Double_List) that appears at the top of List_Handler's body controls elaborate order. As we described in Section 3.6, dependencies between packages sometimes require special measures be taken to control the order in which they are elaborated to ensure no unelaborated units are used. Because the instantiation of Double_List occurs as a global variable in the body of a library level package, the SPARK tools require that Double_List's body, and transitively the bodies of all packages it depends on, be elaborated first. This is the effect of Elaborate_All . This ensures the elaboration of the instantiation succeeds because all library units required by it will be elaborated by then.

As the SPARK tools do flow analysis and generate verification conditions for the body of package List_Handler, they also do flow analysis and generate verification conditions for the particular instantiation of Double_List being used. If the proofs all succeed, as they do for this example, that only implies the proofs for the Integer_List instantiation succeeded. Other instantiations may have failing proofs and, conceivably, may even have serious errors that the Integer_List instantiation does not.

For example, Integer_List is an instantiation of Double_List with a Max_Size of 128 elements. Because the type of Max_Size is Natural, it is possible to instantiate Double_List with a Max_Size of zero. Conceivably that boundary case may contain runtime problems that the non-zero sized case may not contain. If so, the analysis done by the tools will fail for the problematic instantiation while still passing other, better behaved instantiations.

Some instantiations might not even be SPARK. Consider an instantiation such as

```
type Integer_Access is access Integer ;
package Integer_Pointer_List is
        new Double_List (Element_Type    => Integer_Access,
                         Max_Size        => 128,
                         Default_Element => null);
```

This instantiation creates a list variable that holds integer access values. However, because access types are not allowed in SPARK, this instantiation can not appear in code where SPARK_Mode is on. It is not SPARK.

Double_List is a generic *variable* package. When we instantiate an actual package from it, that instance implements a single list variable. Because it is generic, it can be instantiated multiple times in a program. Thus, our generic variable package supports the creation of multiple list variables. However, the SPARK tools will repeat the proofs for each instantiation. Also, the "variables" created in this way cannot readily be copied or compared as they have, in effect, different types.

An alternative design would be to revise Double_List into a type package that is generic only in the list's element type. One could use a discriminant on the list type to specify the maximum size of each list object at declaration time. This approach has the advantage of allowing list objects to be assigned and compared provided they had the same size (and the SPARK tools would statically prove that was so). It would also mean the tools would only need to prove the Double_List code once for each element type and not once for each list variable. We leave the details of this alternative design as an exercise for the reader.

Ada also allows individual subprograms to be generic. As an example of this, consider the following specification of a package Generic_Searchers that contains a generic procedure that does a binary search of a sorted array. This is a generic version of the Binary_Search procedure described in Section 6.2.1.

```
pragma SPARK_Mode(On);
package Generic_Searchers is

    generic
        type Element_Type is private ;
        type Index_Type    is range <>;
        type Array_Type    is array (Index_Type) of Element_Type;
        with function  " <" (L, R : Element_Type) return Boolean is <>;
    procedure Binary_Search (Search_Item :  in   Element_Type;
                             Items        :  in   Array_Type;
                             Found        :  out  Boolean;
                             Result       :  out  Index_Type)
    with
    Pre  => (for all  J  in  Items' Range =>
                ( for  all  K in J + 1 ..  Items' Last  => Items (J) < Items (K))),
    Post => (if Found then
                    Search_Item = Items (Result)
                else
                    ( for  all  J  in  Items' Range => Items (J) /= Search_Item));

end Generic_Searchers ;
```

The generic Binary_Search procedure is parameterized by an array type along with suitable types for the array indices and elements. Recall that declaring Element_Type as private in this context means that any type can be used as long as it can be copied and provides equality comparison operators. The binary search algorithm makes use of equality comparison of Element_Type objects.

The declaration of Index_Type as

```
type Index_Type is range <>;
```

means that Index_Type can be any signed integral type (or subtype). In contrast, if Index_Type had been declared as

```
type Index_Type is (<>);
```

this would allow any discrete type to be used to index the array including enumeration types. However, the binary search algorithm does computations on index values to find the midpoint between two locations in the array, and those operations are more difficult with enumeration types.

Notice that the declaration of the generic array type parameter requires instantiation with only fully constrained arrays. That is, each instantiation of Binary_Search only works with arrays of a particular size. One could generalize the procedure by allowing it to work with unconstrained array types by changing the declaration of the Array_Type parameter to

type Array_Type **is array** (Index_Type **range** <>) **of** Element_Type;

In that case, each instantiation could work with variable sized arrays of the given type. Although it is more general, this approach has other implications that we will discuss shortly.

Because the binary search algorithm requires that Element_Type have an ordering, the last generic parameter declares a function "<" that can be used to determine if one value comes before another. The generic code does not understand anything about this function other than what is declared in the generic parameter list. However, when the SPARK tools analyze an instantiation, the tools will know at that time precisely which function is actually being used.

For example, consider an instantiation of Binary_Search as follows:

subtype Index_Type **is** Positive **range** 1 .. 10;
type Natural_Array_Type **is array** (Index_Type) **of** Natural;

procedure Natural_Search **is**
    new Searchers.Binary_Search (Element_Type => Natural,
                               Index_Type   => Index_Type,
                               Array_Type
=> Natural_Array_Type);

Here, procedure Natural_Search does a binary search over arrays of exactly ten natural numbers. Because the "<" operator for type Natural is directly visible at the point of instantiation, the compiler will automatically provide it for the "<" generic parameter (this is the meaning of the "box" symbol, <>, at the end of the generic parameter declaration).

When the SPARK tools analyze the instantiation, they understand that "<" is the ordinary less than operation on natural numbers and make use of that information in the proofs. This is helpful because the tools have some built-in knowledge of the properties of fundamental arithmetic operators including relational operators. However, consider a different instantiation using the extended precision integers presented in Section 6.6:

subtype Index_Type **is** Positive **range** 1 .. 10;
subtype Big_Integer **is** Very_Longs.Very_Long (Length => 256/8);
type Big_Array_Type **is array** (Index_Type) **of** Big_Integer

```
procedure Big_Search is
         new Searchers.Binary_Search (Element_Type => Big_Integer,
                                      Index_Type   => Index_Type,
                                      Array_Type   => Big_Array_Type,
                                      "<"          => Very_Longs."<");
```

In this case the elements of the array are 256-bit integers. Notice that because the " $<$ " operator of the Very_Long type is not directly visible, it must be explicitly named as a generic argument in the instantiation.

Unlike the earlier case, the SPARK tools have no built-in knowledge of the behavior of " $<$ " for the Very_Long type. All they know about the operator is what they learn from the contract on the operator function provided by the package. That contract does not completely specify all the relevant properties of Very_Longs." $<$ ", and thus the tools may have more difficulties with the proofs for this instantiation. The necessary properties can be provided to the SPARK tools using an *external axiomatization*, an advanced technique we discuss very briefly in Section 9.4. However, this example shows the value of analyzing each instantiation separately. The tools are able to take advantage of whatever specific information is available for each instantiation. If the tools attempted to prove the generic once and for all, they would not be able to use specialized information to simplify the proofs when appropriate.

Let us now turn our attention to the pre- and postconditions on Binary_Search, repeated here as a convenience.

```
Pre =>
  (for all J in Items' Range =>
    (for all K in J + 1 .. Items' Last => Items (J) < Items (K))),
Post =>
  (if Found then
      Search_Item = Items(Result)
   else
      (for all J in Items' Range => Items (J) /= Search_Item));
```

The precondition is similar to the one given for the nongeneric version of the procedure described in Section 6.2.1. In particular, it asserts that the input array is sorted and also, in this case, that every element in the array is unique. Be aware, however, that such a conclusion relies on the "expected" properties of " $<$ ". While there is nothing in the generic code itself that guarantees " $<$ " behaves as expected, the SPARK tools will use whatever interpretation is justified at the point of instantiation as described previously.

It might seem more natural and more general to use " $<=$ " in the precondition as was done in the nongeneric example. Unfortunately, no " $<=$ " operator is available for Element_Type so such a modification does not compile. As stated previously, because assertions are executable, they must obey the same semantics and name resolution rules as ordinary Ada code. This could be worked around in several ways. You could add a "<=" function to the generic parameter list. Alternatively, you could write out the logic in the precondition itself using

```
Items (K) < Items (J) or Items (K) = Items (J)
```

This works because Element_Type is not a limited type and thus is guaranteed to have an "=" operator.

One could consider using the simpler precondition also mentioned in Section 6.2.1:

```
Pre => (for all J in Items' First  ..  Items' Last − 1 =>
            Items (J) <= Items (J+1))
```

However, it is potentially problematic. Consider the case in which the array contains only one element. In that situation Items' First = Items' Last. The computation Items' Last − 1 might overflow causing a Constraint_Error exception when the precondition is evaluated. Specifically consider an instantiation of Binary_Search as follows:

```
subtype Index_Type2 is Integer range Integer ' First  ..  Integer ' First ;
type Natural_Array_Type2 is array (Index_Type2) of Natural;

procedure Natural_Search2 is
            new Searchers.Binary_Search (Element_Type => Natural,
                                         Index_Type    => Index_Type2,
                                         Array_Type    => Natural_Array_Type2);
```

The Natural_Search2 procedure only searches single element arrays that are indexed by the first (most negative) integer value supported. When the precondition is evaluated, the expression Integer ' First − 1 is computed. This computation likely causes an exception as a result of overflow. The SPARK tools will detect this problem when they generate and attempt to prove the verification conditions associated with the assertion as described in Section 6.2.7. Unfortunately, the preceding instantiation of Natural_Search2 will include an unprovable verification condition associated with the precondition.

Notice that the original precondition suffers from a similar problem because of the computation of J + 1. You can work around this in a couple of ways. One is to change the overflow checking mode used by the tools. Another approach is to make the precondition expression more complex to, for example, only apply the quantified expression in the case when the array has at least two elements (a single element array is already sorted). Alternatively, in this case, you could ignore the issue. Because the tools analyze each instantiation separately, an instantiation that does not have the problem will be successfully proved without incident. In this case, it would be rather silly to instantiate Binary_Search to search arrays of size one, so the failing instantiation would likely never be attempted anyway.

In the meantime, Ada's type system will prevent you from accidentally sending an array of size one to an instantiation expecting some other size. However, notice that more caution is needed if you create a generic procedure expecting an unconstrained array type.

6.8 Suppression of Checks

Once you have successfully completed all the proofs in a program unit, such as a package body, you may wish to suppress the checks ordinarily inserted by the Ada compiler. The SPARK tools will have shown that none of those checks can ever fail, so why suffer their overhead? This allows you to create a program that is both correct and efficient.

One demonstration of this effect is in the SPARK implementation of SPARK-Skein (Chapman, Botcazou, and Wallenburg, 2011), a secure hash algorithm.[13] The SPARK implementation was proved free of runtime errors and, in fact, helped discover a fault in the original reference implementation of the algorithm in C. Yet the SPARK implementation yielded performance, with all checks suppressed, essentially identical to the C implementation.

There are actually two classes of checks to consider, and they are handled differently. The first, which we will simply call "runtime checks," are added by the compiler automatically in accordance with the Ada language. If these checks fail, one of the predefined exceptions, usually Constraint_Error , is raised.

The other kind of checks are the assertions added by the programmer in the form of pre- and postconditions, Assert pragmas, loop invariants, and so forth. These differ from the runtime checks in that they do not exist at all unless the programmer writes them. Furthermore, the compiler is not obligated to execute the assertions by default; it depends on the implementation-defined default assertion policy. Finally, a failed assertion raises the Assertion_Error exception instead of one of the four previously discussed language-defined exceptions.

The methods for suppressing checks and the issues associated with doing so are somewhat different depending on the kind of check being suppressed. In the two sections that follow we describe these issues in more detail.

6.8.1 *Runtime Checks*

Runtime checks are inserted automatically by the compiler to test for situations where one of the predefined exceptions discussed in Section 6.1 should be raised. The Ada standard allows compilers to "optimize away" any runtime checks the compiler can determine will never fail. Because some compilers may analyze the code more deeply than others, there is no easy way to know precisely which runtime checks the compiler removes and which are left behind.

The analysis done by the SPARK tools can be seen as a deepening of the analysis already done by the compiler. The tools fully analyze all runtime checks of certain kinds; if the proofs succeed, none of those runtime checks are necessary. It is thus reasonable to direct the compiler to remove all runtime checks covered by SPARK in fully proved units.

One approach to removing runtime checks in a unit is to use pragma Suppress as follows to remove all checks:

```
package body Example is
   pragma Suppress (All_Checks);

   -- etc.
end Example;
```

However, this needs to be done with care. Certain runtime checks covered by All_Checks, in particular related to memory exhaustion, are not ruled out by SPARK alone. It is theoretically possible to prove a unit free of runtime errors and yet still experience a stack overflow in that unit during execution. With all runtime checks suppressed, such an event would cause the program to execute "erroneously" or, in other words, in an undefined manner instead of raising Storage_Error as usual. This is highly undesirable in a high-integrity context.

It should be mentioned, however, that the Ada standard does not require compilers to remove runtime checks that are mentioned in pragma Suppress. The pragma only grants permission to do so. For example, the GNAT compiler will still check for stack overflow if asked, despite the use of pragma Suppress (All_Checks) in the source code. See the *GNAT Reference Manual* (2015a) for more information.

As a result, the use of pragma Suppress may have less effect on the behavior and performance of your program than you might think, both because the compiler may insert some runtime checks anyway and because the compiler may be optimizing away some runtime checks already. As always, when dealing with performance issues, you should carefully benchmark your program before and after making changes to ensure you are actually having a useful effect.

In any case, to suppress All_Checks safely, you may need to ensure code with runtime checks suppressed will not experience any memory problems, perhaps by using additional tools as described in Section 6.1. You should also review your compiler's documentation to understand what runtime checks, if any, are retained despite the use of pragma Suppress.

A potentially safer, if more tedious, way to suppress runtime checks is to explicitly suppress only the checks that are definitely covered by SPARK's analysis. This requires using multiple Suppress pragmas, one for each check. However, any checks you do not mention or are not aware of will still be checked. Although, this might cause some unnecessary checks to remain, it is safe. The example package body that follows shows this approach.

```
package body Example is
   -- See section 11.5 in the Ada Reference Manual.
   pragma Suppress (Discriminant_Check);
   pragma Suppress (Division_Check);
   pragma Suppress (Index_Check);
   pragma Suppress (Length_Check);
   pragma Suppress (Overflow_Check);
   pragma Suppress (Range_Check);
   pragma Suppress (Tag_Check);
   pragma Suppress (Elaboration_Check);

   -- etc.
end Example;
```

Certain checks mentioned in the *Ada Reference Manual* (2012) are not listed because they pertain to features that are not legal in a SPARK unit. In particular, the checks related to access types are not suppressed. If a future version of SPARK supports analysis of those things, the previous list of Suppress pragmas would be incomplete, but that would only mean some unnecessary checks might remain. The program would not become erroneous.

6.8.2 *Assertions*

Suppressing unnecessary assertions is potentially far more important than suppressing unnecessary runtime checks. This is because assertions can be very expensive to evaluate and can even change the asymptotic running time of the subprograms to which they are attached. We noted this effect, for example, when discussing the Binary_Search example in Section 6.2.1. Consequently, assertions have the potential to slow down programs by a huge factor, making them thousands or even millions of times slower in some cases. For programs that rely on highly efficient algorithms, removing unnecessary assertions could make the difference between meeting performance goals and total unusability.

For this reason some compilers, such as GNAT, do not execute assertions by default. Instead they are only executed by explicitly setting the assertion policy to Check. This can be done for all assertions in the program using a compiler command line option or by setting the configuration pragma Assertion_Policy to the desired policy. Once the SPARK tools have proved that all assertions will never fail, you can disable them by explicitly setting the policy to Ignore, or in the case of GNAT, simply fall back to the default behavior. It is of course necessary to recompile the program if you change the assertion policy for the change to take effect.

Of particular interest are assertions that you might wish to ignore inside a package body but still enforce at the interface to the package. Suppose, for example, that you have successfully discharaged all verification conditions in a certain package body. That means, among other things, that the preconditions on internal subprograms are satisfied at every call site in that body. If you compile the body with the assertion policy set to Ignore, you will remove the overhead associated with those precondition checks. However, you might still want to have preconditions on the public subprograms checked, at least until you have shown that every call site in the entire program necessarily satisfies them. To do this, you can set the assertion policy on the specification where the public subprograms are declared to Check.

The rule is that the assertion policy used for a particular assertion is that which is in force at the point the assertion is defined. Thus, even though the compiler inserts pre- and postcondition checks into the body of the subprograms to which they apply, it is the assertion policy in effect in the specification that affects the pre- and postconditions of public subprograms.

For example, consider the function Search_For_Zero discussed on page 157. A utility package containing this function might have a specification, in part, as follows:

```
package Utility is
   pragma Assertion_Policy (Check);

   subtype Index_Type is Natural range 0 .. 1023;
   type Integer_Array is array (Index_Type) of Integer;
```

```
function Search_For_Zero (Values : in Integer_Array ) return Index_Type
  with
    Pre => (for some Index in Index_Type => Values (Index) = 0),
    Post => Values (Search_For_Zero'Result) = 0;

end Utility ;
```

Here the assertion policy is explicitly set to Check causing the precondition (and postcondition) to be checked at runtime whenever the function is called. However, the body of this package could include

```
pragma Assertion_Policy ( Ignore );
```

This removes all assertion checking inside the body itself. Notice, however, that all calls to Search_For_Zero will have the precondition (and postcondition) checked even if those calls come from inside the package.

The checking of the postcondition in this case is somewhat unfortunate because discharging all verification conditions in the body will have shown the postcondition is always satisfied. However, with the GNAT compiler, it is possible to use the Assertion_Policy pragma to selectively control each kind of assertion individually. See the *GNAT Reference Manual* (2015a) for more information. For example, the specification could be written as follows.

```
package Utility is
  pragma Assertion_Policy (Pre => Check, Post => Ignore);

  subtype Index_Type is Natural range 0 .. 1023;
  type Integer_Array is array(Index_Type) of Integer ;

  function Search_For_Zero (Values : in Integer_Array ) return Index_Type
    with
      Pre => (for some Index in Index_Type => Values (Index) = 0),
      Post => Values (Search_For_Zero'Result) = 0;

end Utility ;
```

Care is required whenever explicitly setting the assertion policy to Ignore. For example, if a change is made to the body of preceding package Utility and not all verification conditions are discharged after the change, you could easily end up with the case in which a postcondition is not satisfied and not checked. However, the SPARK tools always generate verification conditions and attempt to discharge them regardless of the assertion policy setting. Thus, static verification is unaffected by the Assertion_Policy pragma.

Summary

- A logical error is an error in the program's logic as a result of programmer oversight. A runtime error is a special kind of logical error that is detected by Ada-mandated runtime checks.
- An assertion is a programmer-defined check. All assertions are executable under the control of the assertion policy in force when a unit is compiled. A policy of Check enables assertions. A policy of Ignore disables them. If an assertion fails during execution, Assertion_Error is raised.
- The SPARK tools attempt to prove that a program is free of runtime errors and, in addition, all programmer supplied assertions will always be satisfied.
- SPARK eliminates Program_Error and Tasking_Error by prohibiting the features that might raise them.
- SPARK does not eliminate the possibility of Storage_Error, but it simplifies the analysis required to eliminate it.
- SPARK eliminates Constraint_Error as part of proving freedom of runtime errors.
- At each point where a check is required, either as mandated by the Ada standard or as added by the programmer in the form of an assertion, the SPARK tools generate a verification condition that, if proved, shows the check will never fail.
- A precondition is an assertion attached to a subprogram that must hold whenever the subprogram is called. It can be used to constrain the inputs to a subprogram beyond the constraints imposed by the type system. In particular, preconditions can describe required relationships between inputs.
- A postcondition is an assertion attached to a subprogram that must hold whenever the subprogram returns. It describes the effect of the subprogram and is part of the subprogram's functional specification.
- In a postcondition, you can use the 'Old attribute to reference the value of an input when the subprogram is first entered. You can use the 'Result attribute to reference the return value of a function.
- The Initial_Condition aspect can be used on a package to specify the state the package has after elaboration. It serves as a kind of package-wide post-condition and is most useful for packages that have internal state.
- Assertions in the visible part of a package cannot directly reference information in the private section of a package. It is thus sometimes necessary to define and use public functions in such assertions.

- The Refined_Post aspect can be used in the body of a package to describe a subprogram's postcondition in internal terms. SPARK attempts to prove that the public postcondition, if any, follows from the subprogram's precondition and refined postcondition.
- Expression functions are automatically given a refined postcondition that asserts they return the value of the expression used to define them. As a result, expression functions can be thought of as pure specification.
- It is common to define functions in public assertions as inline expression functions in the private section of a package specification.
- A type invariant is an assertion attached to private type that must hold whenever a subprogram manipulating an object of that type returns. They can be approximately thought of as postconditions that are automatically applied to all subprograms manipulating the type.
- Type invariants are currently not supported by SPARK. However, they are part of Ada and can still be used. The SPARK tools will simply not (yet) attempt to prove they never fail.
- Subtype predicates allow you to specify complex constraints on a subtypes. They can be used to specify types more precisely. SPARK currently does not support dynamic predicates but does support static predicates.
- Contract_Cases gives you a way of specifying a collection of pre- and postconditions in a convenient, easy-to-maintain way. It is most applicable when the input domain of a subprogram can be partitioned into disjoint subdomains. SPARK proves that all the cases are mutually exclusive and that they cover the entire input domain.
- Because assertions are executable, there is a possibility they might cause a runtime error when evaluated. The SPARK tools also generate verification conditions to show this will not happen.
- Runtime errors in the assertions can be avoided by adjusting the overflow mode of the GNAT compiler.
- The Assert pragma allows you to inject arbitrary checks into the body of a subprogram. The SPARK tools attempt to prove every Assert is always true, and it uses the asserted information to help with following proofs. The Assert pragma lets you give "hints" to the tools to simplify later proofs.
- The Assert_And_Cut pragma is like the Assert pragma except that it also introduces a cut point. All paths that reach the Assert_And_Cut are terminated. Only a single path leaves the Assert_And_Cut. This is useful for reducing the total number of paths in a subprogram to simplify verification conditions and speed up processing.
- The Assume pragma introduces information for the SPARK tools to use but does not carry any proof obligations itself. It can be used to encode

information external to the program that the tools nevertheless need to complete reasonable proofs.

- The Assume pragma should be used carefully. If the assumption is false, the SPARK tools may end up proving false things. However, Assume is executed as usual so testing may uncover false assumptions.
- A loop invariant is an assertion added to the body of the loop that asserts a condition that is true for every loop iteration. It serves as a cut point and thus prevents the loop from creating a potentially infinite number of paths.
- Despite being a cut point, the SPARK tools give special handling to values that are not changed inside the loop. Information about those values do not need to be reasserted by the loop invariant.
- Choosing loop invariants can be tricky. You need to find a condition that is readily proved on loop entry and for each iteration of the loop and that also provides enough information to prove other verification conditions inside and beyond the loop.
- If the SPARK tools successfully prove a subprogram's postcondition, it only means the postcondition is honored if the subprogram actually returns.
- The Loop_Variant pragma allows you to specify one or more expressions that always increase or always decrease as a loop executes. The expressions must have a discrete type so if the loop variant is true it implies the loop must terminate eventually.
- It is appropriate to use Loop_Variant in **while** loops or in loops constructed with a bare **loop** reserved word.
- SPARK handles discriminated types similarly to the way it handles unconstrained array types. The tools generate verification conditions related to the discriminants as appropriate, and the discriminants can be used in assertions in a natural way.
- The SPARK tools do not analyze generic code directly but instead analyze each instantiation of a generic separately. Some instantiations might prove fully, whereas others might not even be legal SPARK.
- When the SPARK tools analyze a generic instantiation, they use information about the actual generic parameters involved. Some instantiations might be difficult to prove because of the limited information available about the types and operations used.
- In fully proved code, it may be desirable to suppress runtime checks and assertion checks to improve the efficiency of the program. Assertion checks, especially, may warrant suppression because assertions have the potential of slowing down execution asymptotically.

Exercises

6.1 Alice is interested in using a package Bob created. Which of them wants the public subprograms in that package to have strong preconditions? Which of them wants strong postconditions?

6.2 Suppose there is a function File_Exists that takes a string and returns True if a file of the given name is available to your program. Now consider a procedure that reads a configuration file declared as follows:

```
procedure Read_Configuration (String : in File_Name)
   with Pre => File_Exists (File_Name);
```

This is an suspicious use of contracts. Why?

6.3 What is a *cut point* and under what circumstances would it be appropriate to consider introducing one into your code? How would you add a cut point to your code?

6.4 Suppose you wanted to create a subprogram that accepted only even nonnegative integers. You could either use a precondition as follows,

```
procedure Example (X : Natural)
   with Pre => (X mod 2 = 0);
```

or you could use a subtype predicate as follows,

```
subtype Even is Natural
   with Dynamic_Predicate => Even mod 2 = 0;

procedure Example (X : Even);
```

Discuss the relative merits of these two approaches with respect to SPARK programming. Is your answer different if the subtype could be defined using a static predicate instead?

6.5 Type invariants are not supported by SPARK at the time of this writing. However, to a large degree this can be worked around. How?

6.6 Explain how contract cases can be considered a combination of preconditions and postconditions. Is the Contract_Cases aspect strictly necessary, or is it always possible to express contract cases using pre- and postconditions?

6.7 Write a procedure that increments every counter in an array of counters. Prove your procedure free of runtime errors. You will need a precondition to assert that all the counters are not yet at their maximal values. You may also need a suitable loop invariant.

6.8 If one says informally that condition C_1 is "stronger" than condition C_2 (where a condition is a boolean expression), what is the intended formal relationship between C_1 and C_2?

6.9 Consider the specification of package Buffers on page 203. Add the following subprograms to that package. For each subprogram write a suitable postcondition, implement the subprogram, and prove your implementation correct with respect to your postcondition.

a. Add a procedure Reverse_Buffer with a declaration as follows:

procedure Reverse_Buffer (Buffer : **in out** Buffer_Type);

The procedure reverses the contents of Buffer. For example, reversing the string "Hello" results in "olleH".

b. Add a procedure Rotate_Right with a declaration as follows:

procedure Rotate_Right (Buffer   : **in out** Buffer_Type;
                                          Distance : **in**   Buffer_Count_Type);

The procedure moves the contents of Buffer toward higher index values (to the right) by an amount Distance. Any elements that "fall off the end" are brought back to the beginning. For example, rotating the string "Hello" to the right by three results in "lloHe".

c. Add a function Search with a declaration as follows:

function Search (Haystack : Buffer_Type;
                                Needle   : String) **return** Buffer_Count_Type;

The function returns the index in Haystack where Needle first appears or zero if Needle does not appear. It is permitted for Needle to be longer than Haystack in which case it can never be found.

d. Add a procedure Count_And_Erase_Character with a declaration as follows:

procedure Count_And_Erase_Character
              (Buffer : **in out** Buffer_Type;
                Ch   : **in**   Character;
                Count : **out**   Buffer_Count_Type)

The procedure returns in Count the number of times Ch occurs in Buffer. It also modifies Buffer so that each occurrence of Ch is replaced with a space.

e. Add a procedure Compact with a declaration as follows:

procedure Compact (Buffer   : **in out** Buffer_Type;
                                  Erase_Character : **in**   Character;
                                  Fill_Character   : **in**   Character;
                                  Valid   :   **out** Buffer_Count_Type)

The procedure compacts Buffer by removing occurrences of Erase_Character. Free space opened at the end of the buffer is filled with instances of Fill_Character. On returning, the value of Valid is a count of the number of original characters that were not erased.

6.10 Let the specification of the Buffers package on page 203 be modified to use an unconstrained array type as follows:

```
package Buffers_Unconstrained is
   subtype Buffer_Count_Type is Natural;
   subtype Buffer_Index_Type is Positive ;
   type Buffer_Type is array ( Buffer_Index_Type range <>) of Character;
   ...
end Buffers_Unconstrained ;
```

Repeat Exercise 6.9.

6.11 Loop variant pragmas are not needed for many loops in SPARK programs. Under what circumstances is it appropriate to consider using a loop variant?

6.12 When a loop variant pragma is used with multiple expressions, it is possible that later expressions might "go the wrong way" as long as an earlier expression changes in the right direction. In particular, a later expression might get reset to some initial value. Explain why the loop must still eventually terminate despite this behavior. How does this relate to nested loops?

6.13 The precondition of Binary_Search does not actually need to state that the input array is sorted. A weaker, but still adequate, precondition is that the array must be partitioned by both the expressions E < Search_Item and E <= Search_Item, where E is an array element. An array is partitioned by an expression if there exists an index i such that the expression is true for every element before i and false for every element at or above i. For example, if the search item is 10, the array containing (5, 3, 10, 10, 8, 6) is suitably partitioned.

Modify the precondition on Binary_Search shown on page 167 to use this weaker condition. Does the implementation given on page 214 still satisfy the postcondition?

6.14 Consider the In_Unit_Square function on page 185. Following the style of that function, show the specification of an In_Unit_Circle function taking Float parameters and that returns +1 if the given point is in a circle with radius one centered on the origin.

6.15 The generic package Double_List discussed in Section 6.7 is incomplete. Make the package usable by adding subprograms for iterator movement and for reading and updating list elements via an iterator. Also add a Front function that returns an iterator to the first element of the list (or the sentinel if the list is empty). Add some procedures to package List_Handler in Section 6.7 to demonstrate these new capabilities. Ensure that SPARK proves your revised List_Handler free of runtime errors.

6.16 Extend Exercise 6.15 by revising package Double_List again so that it is a type package rather than a variable package. Let the maximum size of each list be given by a discriminant. Call your revised package Double_Lists with a private type List. Revise the List_Handler package to use your new package. Ensure that SPARK proves your revised List_Handler free of runtime errors.

6.17 Why is it more important to suppress assertions than runtime checks in deployed programs?

7

Interfacing with SPARK

It is often infeasible or even undesirable to write an entire program in SPARK. Some portions of the program may need to be in full Ada to take advantage of Ada features that are not available in SPARK such as access types and exceptions. It may be necessary for SPARK programs to call third-party libraries written in Ada or some other programming language such as C. Of course SPARK's assurances of correctness cannot be formally guaranteed when the execution of a program flows into the non-SPARK components. However, mixing SPARK and non-SPARK code is of great practical importance. In this chapter we explore the issues around building programs that are only partially SPARK. In Chapter 8 we look at how combining proof with testing can verify applications that are not all SPARK.

7.1 SPARK and Ada

In this section we discuss mixing SPARK with full Ada. Calling SPARK from Ada is trivial because SPARK is a subset of Ada and thus appears entirely ordinary from the point of view of the full Ada compiler. Calling full Ada from SPARK, however, presents more issues because the limitations of SPARK require special handling at the interface between the two languages.

7.1.1 SPARK *Mode*

Conceptually each part or construct of your program is either "in SPARK" or "not in SPARK." If a construct is in SPARK, then it conforms to the restrictions of SPARK, whereas if a construct is not in SPARK, it can make use of all the features of full Ada as appropriate for the construct. It is not permitted for SPARK constructs to directly reference non-SPARK constructs. For example, a subprogram body that is in SPARK cannot call a subprogram with a non-SPARK

247

declaration. However, as declarations and bodies are separate constructs, it is permitted for a SPARK subprogram body to call a subprogram with a SPARK declaration even if the body of the called subprogram is not in SPARK.

It is up to you to mark the SPARK constructs of your program as such by specifying their SPARK *mode*. This is done using the SPARK_Mode pragma or SPARK_Mode aspect as appropriate. The SPARK mode can be explicitly set to either On or Off. If the SPARK mode of a construct is not mentioned at all, then its value is taken from some appropriate enclosing construct. For library level units,[1] if the SPARK mode is not specified explicitly, it is taken to have the special value Auto. We describe the effect of automatic SPARK mode in Section 7.1.3.

You may not change the SPARK mode on a fine grained basis such as between different subexpressions of a single expression or between individual statements of a subprogram. Roughly, the SPARK mode setting can only be changed on the granularity of packages or subprograms. Specifically, there are six locations for which we can specify a SPARK mode:

- Immediately within or before a library-level package specification
- Immediately within a library-level package body
- Immediately following the **private** keyword of a library-level package specification
- Immediately following the **begin** keyword of a library-level package body
- Immediately following a library-level subprogram specification
- Immediately within a library-level subprogram body

If you desire for your entire program to be SPARK, you can change the default by specifying

pragma SPARK_Mode (On);

as a *configuration pragma* to your compiler. Such pragmas are used by the compiler to control various features of the entire compilation. The mechanism by which configuration pragmas are applied and the scope over which they operate is compiler specific. Should you use a configuration pragma to turn on SPARK mode for the entire program, you can still turn it off for specific parts of your program as necessary. The configuration pragma only changes the default, it does not prohibit you from creating a program that is a mixture of SPARK and non-SPARK code.

There are several important use cases that are supported. In this section we will examine some of these cases. In the examples that follow, we explicitly specify the SPARK mode. Later we will describe some important consistency rules on the way SPARK mode must be used and the effect of not specifying a SPARK mode explicitly.

One of the most important cases is one in which a package specification
is in SPARK and yet the corresponding package body is not in SPARK. This
allows you to call subprograms in a non-SPARK package from SPARK code. As
an example, consider the following abbreviated specification of the variable
package Interval_Tree that encapsulates an object that stores real intervals
in a structured way. A more realistic version of this package would include
additional interval tree operations.

```
package Interval_Tree
   with
      SPARK_Mode  => On,
      Abstract_State => Internal_Tree,
      Initializes    => Internal_Tree
is
   type Interval is
      record
         Low  : Float;
         High : Float;
      end record;

   -- Inserts Item into the tree.
   procedure Insert (Item : in Interval )
      with
      Global  => (In_Out => Internal_Tree),
      Depends => (Internal_Tree => (Internal_Tree, Item )),
      Post    => Size = Size'Old + 1;

   function Size return Natural
      with
      Global => (Input => Internal_Tree);

   -- Destroys the tree. After this call , the tree can be reused.
   procedure Destroy
      with
      Global => (In_Out => Internal_Tree),
      Post   => Size = 0;

end Interval_Tree ;
```

Interval trees are useful for efficiently determining if a given interval overlaps any of a set of existing intervals along with similar operations. Here, for
purposes of illustration, an interval is represented simply as a record holding
two floating point values. The specification carries the SPARK_Mode aspect set
to On to indicate that it is intended to be in SPARK. The use of On is optional;

if SPARK_Mode is mentioned at all, it is assumed to take the value On unless otherwise specified. A SPARK_Mode pragma could also have been used instead. The two forms have the same meaning. The one you use is a matter of style.

The subprogram declarations in the package specification are decorated with the usual SPARK aspects such as Global, Depends, and Post. Although this example does not illustrate it, preconditions could also be provided. These aspects are used by the SPARK tools in the usual way during the analysis of code that calls the subprograms in the package.

Here is the complete body of package Interval_Tree. This body only shows the implementation of the subprograms declared in the example specification, along with the necessary supporting type declarations.

```ada
with Ada.Unchecked_Deallocation;
package body Interval_Tree
   with
      SPARK_Mode => Off
is
   type Tree_Node;
   type Tree_Node_Access is access Tree_Node;
   type Tree_Node is
      record
         Data        : Interval ;
         Maximum     : Float;
         Parent      : Tree_Node_Access := null;
         Left_Child  : Tree_Node_Access := null;
         Right_Child : Tree_Node_Access := null;
      end record;

   -- Intantiate a procedure for deallocating node memory
   procedure Deallocate_Node is new Ada.Unchecked_Deallocation
                          (Object => Tree_Node,
                           Name  => Tree_Node_Access);
   type Tree is
      record
         Root  : Tree_Node_Access := null;
         Count : Natural := 0;
      end record;

   T : Tree;   -- The actual tree in this  variable package

   procedure Insert (Item : in  Interval ) is
      New_Node : Tree_Node_Access; -- local to Insert, global to Subtree_Insert
```

```
procedure Subtree_Insert (Pointer : in not null Tree_Node_Access) is
begin
   if Item.Low <= Pointer.Data.Low then
      if Pointer.Left_Child = null then
         Pointer.Left_Child := New_Node;
         New_Node.Parent := Pointer;
      else
         Subtree_Insert (Pointer.Left_Child);
         Pointer.Maximum :=
            Float'Max (Pointer.Maximum, Pointer.Left_Child.Maximum);
      end if;
   else
      if Pointer.Right_Child = null then
         Pointer.Right_Child := New_Node;
         New_Node.Parent := Pointer;
      else
         Subtree_Insert (Pointer.Right_Child);
         Pointer.Maximum :=
            Float'Max (Pointer.Maximum, Pointer.Right_Child.Maximum);
      end if;
   end if;
end Subtree_Insert;

begin
   New_Node := new Tree_Node'(Data => Item,
                              Maximum => Item.High,
                              others  => <>);
   if T.Root = null then
      T.Root := New_Node;
   else
      Subtree_Insert (T.Root);
   end if;
   T.Count := T.Count + 1;
end Insert;

function Size return Natural is
begin
   return T.Count;
end Size;

procedure Destroy is

   procedure Deallocate_Subtree (Pointer : in out Tree_Node_Access) is
```

```
begin
   if  Pointer  /= null then
         Deallocate_Subtree ( Pointer . Left_Child );
         Deallocate_Subtree ( Pointer . Right_Child );
         Deallocate_Node ( Pointer );
      end if ;
   end Deallocate_Subtree ;


begin
   Deallocate_Subtree  (T.Root);
   T.Count := 0;
end Destroy;


end Interval_Tree ;
```

The tree data structure in this variable package body uses pointers[2] (access types) and dynamically allocated memory to allow the tree to grow as large as necessary during program execution. As these constructs are not legal in SPARK, the package body is explicitly declared to be not in SPARK by setting the SPARK_Mode aspect to Off. Setting the SPARK mode of the body explicitly is required in this case. Because the package's specification is explicitly marked as being in SPARK, the tools will assume the body is as well unless told otherwise.

Because the package body is not in SPARK, it is not necessary to refine the abstract state declared in the specification. Furthermore, the SPARK tools will not verify that the subprograms in the body conform to their declared data and flow dependency contracts nor will the tools attempt to prove that the code is free from runtime errors and that subprograms always obey their declared postconditions. The onus is on the programmer, together with proper testing, to ensure the correctness of the code.

It is important to note, however, that pre- and postconditions are part of Ada, and thus the Ada compiler will, as usual, include runtime checks that verify the postconditions (in this example), depending on the assertion policy in force at the time the package specification is compiled. If a postcondition fails, the Assertion_Error exception[3] will be raised, which would then propagate into SPARK code. This would also be true for any unhandled Constraint_Error or Storage_Error exceptions or, for that matter, any other unhandled exceptions that might be raised in the package body.

This seems problematic because SPARK code cannot define any exception handlers to deal with exceptions from the non-SPARK code it calls. One might hope that all such cases would be caught during testing, but even if not, it is still possible to call the SPARK code from a high level "main" subprogram that is not in SPARK and that includes exception handlers for any unexpected exceptions raised by low-level non-SPARK subprograms.

It would also be possible for the subprograms in the package body to catch all exceptions they might generate (aside from the Assertion_Error exceptions raised by pre- and postcondition failures) and translate them into error status codes. However, such an approach might not be ideal if the package is to also be called by non-SPARK code where exceptions handling is natural and convenient. As we show in Section 7.1.2, this can be managed by creating a special wrapper package.

The previous example illustrated a variable package, but what if you wanted to provide interval trees as a type package? That would allow the user to create multiple, independent tree objects. This can be done, as usual, by declaring a private type to represent the trees themselves along with a private section in the package specification to detail to the compiler the nature of the tree type. However, that private section requires the use of non-SPARK constructs, access types in this example. Fortunately, it is possible to mark just the private section of the specification as not in SPARK as follows:

```
private with Ada. Finalization ;
package Interval_Trees
    with SPARK_Mode => On
is
    type Interval is
        record
            Low  : Float;
            High : Float;
        end record;

    type Tree is limited private ;

    -- Inserts Item into tree T.
    procedure Insert (T : in out Tree; Item : in Interval )
        with Global => null,
            Depends => (T => (T, Item));

    function Size (T : in Tree) return Natural
        with Global => null;

private
    pragma SPARK_Mode (Off);
```

```
type Tree_Node;
type Tree_Node_Access is access Tree_Node;
type Tree_Node is
   record
      Data        : Interval ;
      Maximum     : Float;
      Parent      : Tree_Node_Access := null;
      Left_Child  : Tree_Node_Access := null;
      Right_Child : Tree_Node_Access := null;
   end record;

type Tree is new Ada.Finalization.Limited_Controlled with
   record
      Root  : Tree_Node_Access := null;
      Count : Natural := 0;
   end record;

overriding procedure Finalize (T : in out Tree);

end Interval_Trees ;
```

In this case it is necessary to use the pragma form of SPARK_Mode as Ada does not allow aspects to be applied to just the private section of a package specification. The pragma SPARK_Mode (Off) must appear at the top of the private section marking the entire private section as not in SPARK.

This example also makes use of Ada's facility for automatic finalization of objects[4] so there is no need for the programmer to call a "destroy" procedure in this case. To do this, it is necessary to with Ada.Finalization. However, because that package is only needed to support the private section, it can be introduced using the special form of the **with** clause we introduced in Section 3.5.2. The **private with** makes the package's resources only available in the private part.

It is also possible to mark individual subprograms as being in SPARK. This is useful in cases where a package specification needs to make use of non-SPARK constructs, yet some of the subprograms in the package can still be given SPARK declarations. SPARK code can then call the subprograms with SPARK declarations even though it might not be able to use all the facilities of the enclosing package.

Similarly, the bodies of subprograms in a package body can be marked as in or out of SPARK as appropriate. This allows you to use the SPARK tools on code where it makes sense to do so without creating an unnatural design by artificially avoiding full Ada features for other subprograms in the same package.

There is an important consistency rule regarding SPARK mode that says once SPARK mode is turned off, you cannot turn it back on again for any subordinate construct. To illustrate, packages are considered to have four parts:

1. The visible part of the specification
2. The private part of the specification
3. The body
4. Elaboration code in the body that appears after **begin**

The consistency rule means that if SPARK mode is explicitly turned off for one of the parts, it cannot be turned on again in a later part. For example, if the body of a package has its SPARK mode off, you cannot then turn SPARK mode back on in the elaboration code for that package.

Furthermore if SPARK mode is turned on for a part, it is assumed to be on for all following parts unless it is explicitly turned off. Thus, setting SPARK_Mode to On in the specification of a package declares all parts of the package to be in SPARK unless SPARK_Mode is explicitly set to Off for a later part.

7.1.2 *Wrapper Packages*

As previously described, it is permitted for SPARK to call code in a library package with a non-SPARK body provided the specification of that package, or at least of the subprogram being called, is in SPARK. Even if the declarations of the called subprograms are not specifically marked as being in SPARK, it may still be permitted for SPARK code to call them using automatic SPARK mode as described in Section 7.1.3.

However, errors in the non-SPARK library package are likely to be reported by way of exceptions as that is the normal method of error handling in full Ada. Thus, some means of translating exceptions into the status codes required by SPARK-style error handling is needed. Furthermore if the non-SPARK library package has a non-SPARK specification, it may still be possible with suitable translations and conversions to make it callable from SPARK. Doing these things requires constructing a wrapper package that provides a SPARK specification and contains subprograms that just forward their calls to the underlying library package.

As an example, consider the Interval_Tree package described in Section 7.1.1. That package happens to have a SPARK specification, yet exceptions arising in the body of the package may still propagate into SPARK code. To deal with this, we create a new package Interval_Tree_Wrapper with a specification very similar to that of Interval_Tree shown as follows:

```
with Interval_Tree ;
package Interval_Tree_Wrapper
   with
      SPARK_Mode   => On,
      Abstract_State => Underlying_Tree,
      Initializes    => Underlying_Tree
is

   type Interval is new Interval_Tree . Interval ;

   type Status_Type is (Success,      Insufficient_Space ,   Logical_Error );

   -- Inserts Item into the tree .
   procedure Insert (Item   : in   Interval ;
                     Status : out Status_Type)
      with
      Global  => (In_Out => Underlying_Tree),
      Depends => (Underlying_Tree => (Underlying_Tree, Item),
                  Status => Underlying_Tree),
      Post    => (Size'Old = (if Status = Success then Size - 1 else Size ));

   function Size return Natural
      with
      Global  => (Input => Underlying_Tree);

   -- Destroys the tree . After this call the tree can be reused .
   procedure Destroy
      with
      Global  => (In_Out => Underlying_Tree),
      Post    => Size = 0;

end Interval_Tree_Wrapper ;
```

The main difference between this specification and that for Interval_Tree is that a status type is introduced and subprograms that might fail – Insert in this case – are modified to return a status indication.

The wrapper package also introduces its own types for the types provided by the underlying package (type Interval in this case). This allows the wrapper package to be self-contained without its clients needing to **with** the underlying package.

Notice also that the Spark aspects for Insert are slightly different than for the underlying version of the procedure. The flow dependency contract adds a dependency of Status on Underlying_Tree. Furthermore, the postcondition is changed to assert that the size of the tree increases if and only if the subprogram returns successfully.

It would be more natural to write the postcondition as

```
Post => (if Status = Success
          then Size = Size'Old + 1
          else  Size = Size'Old);
```

However, Ada disallows use of the 'Old attribute with a prefix of a function call in a context where it might not be evaluated, such as in a branch of a conditional expression. Recall that 'Old implies the value of the prefix expression is saved when the subprogram is entered. It is undesirable to call a function when the result might not be needed. Here, Size'Old is used in both branches of the conditional expression. Nevertheless the rules of Ada forbid it in this case.

The Underlying_Tree state abstraction is intended to represent the internal tree of the underlying package. Strictly speaking, Interval_Tree_Wrapper has no internal state so declaring any Abstract_State for it is a "lie." The Spark tools will not notice the lie because the body of Interval_Tree_Wrapper is, as you will see, not in Spark and thus not examined by the tools. However, if the only access to the underlying package is through the wrapper, the lie is not really a problem because the wrapper package, in effect, assumes the internal state of the wrapped package, just as wrapping paper can be said to contain the same present as the box it wraps.

In this case, however, Interval_Tree has a Spark specification and could potentially be called directly by Spark code willing to pass exceptions through to a higher level. For the Spark tools to properly understand the relationship between that other code and the wrapper package, it is necessary to tell the truth about what the wrapper package is doing. This can be done by defining no Abstract_State on Interval_Tree_Wrapper and instead explicitly referencing Interval_Tree . Internal_Tree in the Spark aspects where Underlying_Tree is mentioned previously.

The body of the wrapper package contains relatively simple subprograms that wrap the subprograms of the underlying library package. Here is the implementation of Insert in the wrapper package:

```
procedure Insert (Item : in   Interval ;
                  Status : out Status_Type) is
begin
    Interval_Tree . Insert ( Interval_Tree . Interval (Item ));
```

```
      Status := Success;
   exception
      when Storage_Error =>
         Status :=  Insufficient_Space ;
      when others =>
         Status :=  Logical_Error ;
   end Insert ;
```

Exceptions are converted to status codes in this case, but no other work is done aside from a trivial type conversion from the wrapper's type Interval to the underlying package's type Interval . In general, the wrapper subprograms could transform the parameters in arbitrary ways before calling the underlying subprogram or transform the results of the underlying subprogram before returning.

Creating a wrapper package can be tedious and must be done carefully to prevent errors arising that the SPARK tools cannot detect. However, it has the advantage of not requiring any access to the source code of the underlying library package body.

7.1.3 *Automatic* SPARK *Mode*

So far we have discussed SPARK_Mode as a binary valued aspect that can either be On or Off. However, there is also an automatic setting that allows the SPARK tools to determine the SPARK mode of a construct on their own. This Auto setting cannot be explicitly specified; it is only implied under certain circumstances that we outline here.

An important use case of automatic SPARK mode is when you attempt to make use of existing library packages in a SPARK program. The Ada standard library is a particularly noteworthy case, but any library written without SPARK in mind is at issue. Many entities declared by such a library may be perfectly reasonable SPARK. If the tools required an explicit SPARK mode on the specification of the library, you would have to wait until the library vendor provided a SPARK-aware update to the library before you could use it in your SPARK program. That might never happen.

To see an example of automatic SPARK mode, consider the following function Contains. This function accepts a string and a character and returns true if and only if the given string contains the given character.

```
with Ada.Strings.Fixed;
function Contains (S  : in  String;
                   Ch : in  Character) return Boolean
   with SPARK_Mode => On
```

```
is
    Search_String  :  String  (1  ..  1)  :=  (others  =>  Ch);
    Result_Index   :  Natural;
begin
    Result_Index  :=  Ada.Strings.Fixed.Index  (Source  => S,
                                                 Pattern => Search_String,
                                                 From    => S'First);
    return  Result_Index  /= 0;
end Contains;
```

This function is in its own compilation unit and is thus a library level function that is not nested inside any package. Its SPARK_Mode is explicitly set to On. However, it makes use of a function Index from the Ada standard library package Ada.Strings.Fixed. This function searches a string for a specified substring and returns the index where the substring appears or zero if it does not appear.

However, the library level specification of Ada.Strings.Fixed does not contain an explicit SPARK_Mode setting and is thus processed in automatic SPARK mode. The tools determine that the declaration of function Index is in SPARK and thus allow that function to be called from SPARK code. The tools synthesize data and flow dependency contracts for the function as described in Section 4.5. However, the body of Ada.Strings.Fixed is not analyzed and, thus, the tools are not able to synthesize the Global aspect of function Index and produce a warning to this effect. By default, this warning prevents the tools from attempting to prove the body of Contains.

The documentation for function Index makes it clear that it does not read nor write any global data. The assumption made by the SPARK tools is thus true for it. The tools can be run in such a way as to continue even if warnings are issued, and that is appropriate to do in this case. However, one verification condition is not proved. In particular, passing S'First to Index may raise Constraint_Error because in the case when S is empty, the bounds may be outside the range of the Positive subtype.

One way to handle this is to treat the empty string as a special case. Alternatively, we decide to prohibit calling Contains on empty strings by adding a precondition:

```
with  Ada.Strings.Fixed;
function Contains2 (S  :  in  String;
                    Ch :  in  Character)  return  Boolean
    with
        SPARK_Mode => On,
        Pre => S'Length > 0
```

```
is
    Search_String  :  String  (1  ..  1)  :=  (others  => Ch);
    Result_Index   :  Natural;
begin
    Result_Index  :=  Ada.Strings.Fixed.Index (Source  => S,
                                                Pattern => Search_String,
                                                From    => S'First);
    return  Result_Index /= 0;
end Contains2;
```

In this version all verification conditions are proved.

There is one additional detail to consider when using library packages in this manner. The Index function may raise various exceptions depending on the values of its arguments. Thus, as when calling any code that is not in SPARK, we need to be mindful of the possibility that exceptions may be raised despite the fact that no runtime errors will arise from the body of Contains2 itself (provided its precondition is honored). We can ensure no exceptions are raised by encoding the preconditions of Index directly into the SPARK code as an assertion. Furthermore, the postcondition of Index can be expressed as an assumption.

```
with Ada.Strings.Fixed;
function Contains3 (S  :  in  String;
                    Ch :  in  Character) return  Boolean
    with
        SPARK_Mode => On,
        Pre        => S'Length > 0,
        Post       => Contains3'Result = (for some I in S'Range => S (I) = Ch)
is
    Search_String  :  String  (1  ..  1)  :=  (others  => Ch);
    Result_Index   :  Natural;
begin
    -- An empty search string causes Index to raise  Pattern_Error
    -- A starting point for the search that is out of bounds raises Index_Error
    pragma Assert (Search_String'Length > 0 and S'First in S'Range);
    Result_Index  :=  Ada.Strings.Fixed.Index (Source  => S,
                                                Pattern => Search_String,
                                                From    => S'First);
    -- Index returns zero if it does not find the string or else it returns
    -- a position in the string where the pattern starts
    pragma Assume
        ( if  Result_Index  = 0 then
            (for all  J in S'Range => S (J) /= Ch)
```

```
      else
        ( Result_Index  in  S'Range and then  S (Result_Index) = Ch));
      return  Result_Index  /= 0;
   end Contains3;
```

This example illustrates how pre- and postconditions for library subprograms can be provided, in effect, without modifying the source code of the library packages. Of course a wrapper package around Index could also be used to provide pre- and postconditions in a more natural way.

We note that this example is unrealistic in the sense that if you really wanted to write a function like Contains3, it could be trivially done using Ada's quantified expressions directly:

```
function Contains4 (S  :  in  String;
                    Ch :  in  Character) return  Boolean is
  ( for  some  J in S'Range => S(J) = Ch);
```

However, the example illustrates the general approach to using automatic SPARK mode to call library subprograms that were not written with SPARK in mind.

7.2 SPARK and C

SPARK has an important role to play in safety-critical embedded systems where failure of the software can cause major loss of investment or serious injury. However, most embedded systems are written today in the C programming language – a language notorious for being difficult to use correctly. Yet despite this, a large amount of carefully built and very well tested C code exists that SPARK developers might want to reuse.

To make use of an existing C library from SPARK, you first need an Ada compiler that has an "associated" C compiler. In the case of the GNAT Ada compiler, one such C compiler is gcc, but there can potentially be many C compilers that would be compatible with a given Ada compiler. In general, it is necessary for the Ada compiler to be aware of the C compiler so that data layout and calling conventions can be properly matched whenever information crosses from Ada to C and vice versa. Also, the Ada compiler must match the facilities in package Interfaces .C, described shortly, with the facilities provided by the associated C compiler.

Although many of the details that arise when interfacing SPARK and C are outside the scope of this book, we now show an example that illustrates several important points. The Ada standard mandates certain features for any

implementation that wishes to provide a C interface, and we endeavor to use just
those features. Individual Ada implementations can provide additional features
that are not required by the standard and, hence, are less portable. We make use
of one such additional feature that we will highlight later.

Our example is contrived but is realistic enough to be illustrative. Suppose
there is an existing C library that manages message packets in some kind of
communication system. We focus first on the C header file that declares certain
types and two example functions:

```c
#ifndef MESSAGE_H
#define MESSAGE_H

    #include <stddef.h>

    typedef unsigned short nodeid_t;        // 16 bit network node ID numbers.
    typedef unsigned long  sequenceno_t;    // 32 bit packet sequence numbers.

    struct PacketHeader {
        nodeid_t        source_node;
        nodeid_t        destination_node;
        sequenceno_t sequence_number;
    };

    enum error_code {
        SUCCESS = 1, INVALID_DESTINATION, INSUFFICIENT_SPACE
    };

    // Returns the Fletcher checksum of the given buffer.
    unsigned short compute_fletcher_checksum(const char *buffer, size_t size);

    // Installs the given header into the buffer. Returns an error code as
    // appropriate. If an error is detected the buffer is left unchanged.
    enum error_code install_header (
        char *buffer,
        size_t size,
        const struct PacketHeader *header);

#endif
```

In this hypothetical system, each node in the "network" is represented by a
16-bit node identifier. Message packets have headers consisting of the source
and destination node addresses and a unique sequence number. A function for
computing the Fletcher checksum over a data array is given. Here, the array
is treated in the usual C style as a pointer to the first element and a separately

provided size. A second function is declared that copies a header structure into a packet buffer, providing some checks to ensure the sanity of the operation.

This example illustrates the use of type aliases (C's `typedef` declaration), structures, arrays, enumeration types, and functions that take these parameters in a natural C style. The implementation of the example functions is straight-forward but not shown here as it is not important for our purposes. In some cases the implementation of the library functions may not be available anyway. However, any C programmer who wishes to use the library will have access to the header file(s) that describe it.

The first step is to write a Spark package specification that declares the necessary types and subprograms. In effect, we translate the C header file to Ada following certain rules described in the Ada standard and extended by your specific Ada compiler. We will show the specification in stages starting with the type declarations:

```
with Interfaces .C;
package Messages
    with SPARK_Mode => On
is
    type Node_Id_Type is new Interfaces .C. unsigned_short ;
    type Sequence_Number_Type is new Interfaces.C.unsigned_long;

    type Error_Code is (Success,    Invalid_Destination , Insufficient_Space )
        with Convention => C;
    for Error_Code use (1, 2, 3);

    type Packet_Header_Type is
        record
            Source_Node       : Node_Id_Type;
            Destination_Node : Node_Id_Type;
            Sequence_Number : Sequence_Number_Type;
        end record;
        with Convention => C;

end Messages;
```

The Ada standard does not require every Ada compiler to support an interface to C. However, if a compiler does support such an interface, it must also provide package Interfaces .C, which contains, among other things, definitions of types that match the built-in types used by the associated C compiler. For example, Interfaces .C.int has the same size and range of values as the associated C compiler's type int. This approach is necessary because there is no assurance, for example, that the Ada type Integer is compatible with the C type int. It happens that with the GNAT and gcc compilers the two types are compatible, but for maximum portability it is better to use the types in Interfaces .C.

The previous package specification, written with SPARK_Mode on, starts by introducing types for the node identifiers and sequence numbers. The names do not have to be the same as in the C header file; they only need to be used appropriately in the following declarations. In the original C, nodeid_t and sequenceno_t are aliases for C built-in types and can be mixed freely with other unrelated variables having those same types. However, the definitions in package Messages are for entirely new types that cannot be accidentally mixed. This is more robust and is an example of Ada's ability to increase the type safety of a preexisting C interface.

The enumeration is defined as an Ada enumeration with the Convention aspect set to C. This informs the Ada compiler that objects of that type should be represented compatibly with the associated C compiler's handling of enumerations. The ability to set the Convention aspect on an enumeration type is the only GNAT extension we use in this example. Because the C header file defines the enumeration starting at one instead of the default of zero, package Messages uses an *enumeration representation clause* to specify the values of the enumerators in a matching way.[5]

Finally, the C structure is modeled as an Ada record, again using the Convention aspect of C to ensure that the Ada compiler lays out the record in a manner that matches the associated C compiler's expectations for structures.

Armed with these type definitions we can now write declarations for the two C functions in our example. We will start with the checksum computing function because, being a pure function, it is easy to represent in SPARK:

```
function Compute_Fletcher_Checksum
        ( Buffer  :  in  Interfaces .C. char_array ;
          Size    :  in  Interfaces .C. size_t )  return  Interfaces .C. unsigned_short
    with
        Global        => null,
        Import        => True,
        Convention    => C,
        External_Name => "compute_fletcher_checksum" ;
```

The C version of this function takes an array of characters and does not modify that array as evidenced by the const in the declaration of the buffer parameter in the C header file. Package Interfaces .C contains a declaration of an unconstrained array type holding C-style characters. Thus, the first parameter of the function is of this type and has mode in. The Ada compiler will pass the actual parameter by its address as expected by the C function.

The aspects associated with the declaration include the Import aspect set to True, indicating that the function is actually written in a foreign language. The Convention aspect specifies which language is used. It is not necessary, or even legal, to write a body (in Ada) for an imported subprogram.

The External_Name aspect specifies the name of the function as created by the C programmer. The language C is case sensitive so this allows us to give the function an Ada-friendly name using mixed case while still connecting the declaration to the correct underlying C function.

In addition, the Global aspect indicates that the function does not modify any global data. As with packages that wrap non-Spark Ada code, the Spark tools cannot verify the truth of this assertion because they cannot analyze the C body of the function. Again, the onus is on the programmer to get it right. Presumably, the programmer read the documentation for the C library before writing the Global aspect. In effect, the programmer is transferring information from the C library documentation into a form that can be understood by the Spark tools.

Before considering the second function in the C header file, it is worthwhile to step back and reflect on the package specification we have created so far. Although the specification is in Spark, it makes visible use of various entities in package Interfaces .C. This informs everyone that the body of the package is written in C and thus exposes what should ideally be a hidden implementation detail. Furthermore, the clients of this package are forced to deal with the types in Interfaces .C to use the subprograms provided by the package even though clients should know nothing about C. In effect, the "C-isms" from the implementation of this package are leaking out into the rest of the program.

It is often useful to distinguish between thin and thick bindings to an existing library. A *thin binding* is a nearly literal translation of the existing library interface with little or no effort made to change the architecture or design of that interface. In contrast a *thick binding* is a reworking of the existing library interface to take good advantage of features in the client environment.

Our work so far uses Ada features to distinguish the types Node_Id_Type and Sequence_Number_Type from each other, but it is otherwise a thin binding. We can thicken the binding both to provide a more natural interface to Spark clients and to completely hide all use of Interfaces .C. To do this we must create a wrapper package. The following specification shows one possibility:

```
pragma SPARK_Mode(On);
package Messages_Wrapper is
   type Checksum_Type is mod 2**16;
```

```
   function Compute_Checksum (Data : in String) return Checksum_Type;
end Messages_Wrapper;
```

No mention of Interfaces .C appears in this specification. Furthermore, because Ada arrays know their size, there is no reason for this function to take an additional size parameter as is common for C functions. Here is the body of this package:

```
pragma SPARK_Mode(On);
with Interfaces .C;
package body Messages_Wrapper is
   use type Interfaces .C. size_t ;    -- needed for  visibility  in precondition

      function Compute_Fletcher_Checksum
              (Buffer  :  in   Interfaces .C. char_array ;
               Size    :  in   Interfaces .C. size_t ) return  Interfaces .C. unsigned_short
        with
           Global        => null,
           Import        => True,
           Convention    => C,
           Pre           => Size = Buffer'Length,
           External_Name => "compute_fletcher_checksum" ;

      function Compute_Checksum (Data : in String) return Checksum_Type is
         -- Copy the Ada string Data into the  C string  Buffer
         Buffer :  Interfaces .C. char_array :=
                       Interfaces .C.To_C (Item => Data,
                                           Append_Nul => False);
         Result :  Interfaces .C. unsigned_short ;
      begin
         -- Call the C function whose Ada specification  is  above
         Result := Compute_Fletcher_Checksum (Buffer => Buffer,
                                              Size  => Buffer'Length);
         -- Return the Result converted to Checksum_Type;
         return Checksum_Type (Result);
      end Compute_Checksum;
end Messages_Wrapper;
```

The declaration of the imported C function now appears in the body instead of in a specification of its own. Appropriate type conversions are done to match the natural Ada types used by the wrapper package to the C-like types provided by Interfaces .C. The body of the preceding package is in SPARK, and the SPARK tools successfully prove that it is free of runtime errors. Thus, the type conversion from, for example, Interfaces .C.unsigned to Checksum_Type will always succeed without raising Constraint_Error. Furthermore, the precondition specified on the imported declaration will always be satisfied.

Writing a wrapper package is more work than just writing a specification with imported declarations, but it has the advantage of completely hiding the use of C inside the body of the wrapper package. The GNAT compiler has a command line option, -fdump-ada-spec, that automatically converts a C header file into an approximately correct Ada package specification. The binding created by this option is very thin and may require some adjustments before it even compiles. However, this feature provides a quick way to get started writing a thicker binding such as we just described.

Writing a SPARK declaration for the second C function in our example (install_header) is tricky. Because this C function modifies its parameter buffer, we cannot provide a direct SPARK function declaration. Recall that SPARK functions may not modify their parameters. Instead, we must write a SPARK procedure declaration that passes the buffer as an **in out** parameter and returns the status of the operation as an **out** parameter. This solution requires us to write a helper subprogram that calls the underlying C function install_header and returns the status through a parameter rather than as a function return value. The helper subprogram could be written in C or, alternatively, in full Ada. Here is the C version of the helper subprogram:

```
void  install_header_helper  (
   char  * buffer ,
   size_t  size ,
   const struct PacketHeader *header,
   enum error_code *status)
{
   // Call function  install_header  and save return value in  local  result
   enum error_code result  =  install_header ( buffer ,  size ,  header);
   // Copy result  to "out"  parameter
   *status = result ;
}
```

This function must be compiled with the associated C compiler and linked into the final program. However, it does not require any access to the source code of the original library function it wraps.

We can now write an Ada declaration as a procedure using the helper function:

```
-- Needed to make operators used in postcondition  directly  visible .
use type Interfaces .C. size_t ;
use type Interfaces .C.char;
use type Interfaces .C. char_array ;
procedure Install_Header ( Buffer   : in out Interfaces .C. char_array ;
                            Size    : in      Interfaces .C. size_t ;
                            Header  : in      Packet_Header_Type;
                            Status  :      out Error_Code)
     with
        Global  => null,
        Depends => (Buffer =>+ (Size, Header), Status => (Size, Header)),
        Post    => (if Status /= Success then
                       Buffer = Buffer'Old
                    else
                       ( for  all  J  in  Buffer ' First  + 12 .. Buffer ' Last  =>
                                 Buffer (J) = Buffer'Old (J))),
        Import      => True,
        Convention  => C,
        External_Name => " install_header_helper" ;
```

The buffer parameter is declared with mode **in out** because the logic of the C function is such that it returns the buffer with some of its elements unchanged. Thus, the buffer should be fully initialized before calling the procedure (the SPARK tools will ensure this is true). Notice also that the header record is passed as an ordinary **in** parameter. The Ada compiler will pass it to the underlying C function using a pointer as the C function expects. In this case the Ada procedure is given a natural name, but the External_Name aspect points the declaration to the helper function rather than the original.

The declaration includes several SPARK aspects to specify the data dependency and flow dependency contracts. A postcondition is also provided. As before, these contracts cannot be checked by the SPARK tools. In fact, because postconditions are ordinarily compiled into the body of the subprogram to which they apply, you might expect that even the postcondition would not be checked at runtime because the body of the procedure in this case is actually a C function. However, the GNAT Ada compiler will generate a stub for the declaration that surrounds the actual call to the C function, and that includes postcondition runtime checks. Thus, Assertion_Error might be raised at runtime, as usual, depending on the assertion policy in force.

Preconditions are handled similarly. Although the SPARK tools will endeavor to prove that any precondition is satisfied at each call site, the GNAT-generated stub also includes runtime checking for preconditions as described previously. The compiler's ability to create these stubs enhances the assurances of correctness obtained when testing mixed Ada/C programs.

In any case, assuming the underlying C function is correct, perhaps verified via testing, the SPARK tools will use the contracts on the declaration to help prove properties of the code that calls the procedure. This is another example of bringing information that might be in the C library documentation forward into the code itself.

As we mentioned previously, the helper subprogram could also be written in full Ada. The idea would be to write an imported declaration for the underlying C function that has an **in out** parameter, as allowed in full Ada 2012. A helper procedure could call the imported C function and perform essentially the same steps as the C helper above. In particular, it could write the value returned by the underlying function into an **out** parameter.

The helper procedure could be placed in its own package, or in a package serving as a thick binding to the C library as previously described, with pre- and postconditions applied to the helper procedure instead of to the imported declaration. However the body of the helper procedure cannot be in SPARK as it must use a non-SPARK declaration. We leave the details of this implementation as an exercise for the reader.

7.3 External Subsystems

In the previous sections we saw that a system need not be entirely written in SPARK. By providing SPARK interfaces to non-SPARK code, we can still make use of the analysis tools provided by SPARK. In this section we look at a higher level approach to interacting with hardware devices and other software subsystems that are external to our SPARK program. These *external subsystems* are by definition outside the control of our program and thus have behaviors the program can not fully anticipate. When SPARK is being used, it is especially important to properly model this situation so the SPARK tools can account for it. External variables and external state abstractions provide the necessary models.

7.3.1 *External Variables*

Memory mapped variables provide one method that programs use to interact with hardware.[6] The basic idea is that particular memory addresses resolve to hardware registers rather than to random access memory. Thus, a program can access hardware registers through ordinary variables. In Ada, memory mapped variables are defined by the Volatile and Address aspects. With the addition of SPARK aspects describing the external properties of memory mapped variables, we can use the SPARK tools to analyze the program's use of these variables.

If the external subsystem reads the value of a memory mapped variable at a time of its own choosing, that variable is said to have an *asynchronous reader*. Similarly, if the external subsystem updates a variable at a time of its own choosing, that variable is said to have an *asynchronous writer*. Notice that the terms asynchronous reader and asynchronous writer are from the point of view of the external subsystem. It is the external subsystem that is reading and writing.

SPARK provides two Boolean aspects to specify either or both of these possibilities:

Async_Readers: Any object for which Async_Readers is true may be read at any time (asynchronously) by hardware or software outside the program.

Async_Writers: Any object for which Async_Writers is true may be changed at any time (asynchronously) by hardware or software outside the program.

Async_Readers has no effect on either flow analysis or proof analysis and thus serves mostly a documentation purpose. Async_Writers has no effect on flow analysis but does have an effect on proof analysis. The proof tool takes into account that two successive reads of the same variable may return different results.

SPARK provides two related Boolean aspects that do control the flow analysis of external objects:

Effective_Reads: Indicates that the program's reading the value of a volatile variable has an effect on the external hardware or software subsystem. Effective_Reads can only be specified on a variable that also has Async_Writers set.

Effective_Writes: Indicates that the program's assigning a value to the variable has an effect on the external hardware or software subsystem. Effective_Writes can only be specified on a variable that also has Async_Readers set.

Both Effective_Reads and Effective_Writes have an effect on flow dependencies. Reading the former or writing the latter is modeled as having an effect on the value of the variable.

We typically set Effective_Reads to true for devices that provide a stream of input values such as mass storage devices and serial ports and to false for reading from devices such a sensors for which there is no significant relation between successive values. We typically set Effective_Writes to true.

Let us look at a simple example of how Effective_Reads change flow analysis.[7] In the following code fragment, Volatile_Value is a volatile variable for which Async_Writers is true. The hardware or software outside the program can change this volatile variable at any time.

```
if  Count = 0 then
    My_Value := Volatile_Value ;
end  if ;
My_Value := Volatile_Value ;
```

Does the value of My_Value depend on the value of Count? If Effective_Reads is true, then My_Value will depend on Count. For example, when reading characters from a buffer, Count determines whether My_Value ends up with the first or second character. With Effective_Reads set to false, My_Value will not depend on Count. For example, when reading from a temperature sensor, My_Value will contain the most recent temperature.

The Ada language provides the concept of Volatile objects. Such objects behave as if all four of the SPARK aspects are true. SPARK allows you to refine the behavior of the program by specifying some subset of those aspects in cases where it makes sense to do so.

Let us look at some examples. Here is a definition package that defines a modular type and a single 8-bit volatile variable mapped to memory address $FFFF0000_{16}$:

```
with System.Storage_Elements;
package Numeric_Display
    with SPARK_Mode => On
is
    type Octet is mod 2**8;

    Value : Octet
        with
            Size      => 8,  -- Use exactly 8 bits for this  variable
            Volatile  => True,
            Address   => System.Storage_Elements.To_Address(16#FFFF0000#);

end Numeric_Display;
```

The variable Value is a single 8-bit memory mapped register at a specific memory address. This register controls a standard seven segment LED display. The register is given the Ada Volatile aspect, which means it has both asynchronous readers and writers. Furthermore, reads and writes are always effective. Consider the following program fragment that makes use of this memory mapped register:

```
Numeric_Display.Value := 0;
Numeric_Display.Value := 1;
```

Normally, flow analysis would warn us that the first assignment statement is unused. However, because the volatile variable Value has an asynchronous reader and writes to it are effective, this code does not generate a flow error. Each update is processed by the external system (a hardware device in this case).

Suppose now that the program wishes to read back the value in the control register. Variable X is type Numeric_Display.Octet:

```
X := Numeric_Display.Value;
X := Numeric_Display.Value;
```

This code also does not generate a flow error because the register is assumed to potentially change values between each read and each read is effective (could change the state of the hardware).

However, this characterization of our device is overly aggressive. Because the device does not change the value in the control register at all, reading it twice in succession will always produce the same value. Nor does reading the register controlling an LED display change that display. Consider instead the following declaration of the memory mapped register:

```
Value : Octet
    with
        Size  => 8,  -- Use exactly 8 bits for this variable
        Volatile         => True,
        Async_Readers   => True,
        Effective_Writes => True,
        Address => System.Storage_Elements.To_Address(16#FFFF0000#);
```

Because two of the SPARK aspects are explicitly provided, the other two SPARK aspects default to false. The declaration is as if we wrote

```
Value : Octet
    with
        Size  => 8,  -- Use exactly 8 bits for this variable .
        Volatile         => True,
        Async_Readers   => True,
        Effective_Writes => True,
        Async_Writers   => False,
        Effective_Reads  => False,
        Address => System.Storage_Elements.To_Address(16#FFFF0000#);
```

The meaning of this can be summarized as follows:

- *Async_Readers => True.* There is external hardware that may read Value at any time.
- *Effective_Writes => True.* Values assigned to Value have an effect on the external hardware.
- *Async_Writers => False.* There is no external hardware that writes to Value.
- *Effective_Reads => False.* It is a flow problem to read Value multiple times without the program doing any intervening writes.

This refined description of how the external register works is more robust than our original because it catches errors that using just Volatile would not. For example, flow analysis of this double assignment now tells us that the first assignment is unused:

```
X := Numeric_Display.Value;
X := Numeric_Display.Value;
```

7.3.2 External State Abstractions

Information hiding is an important principle of design. By hiding our design decisions, we can more easily change those decisions. For example, in the previous section we used a memory mapped variable to allow our program to display values on a seven segment LED display. Should we need to move this application to a processor that used port-based I/O rather than memory mapped I/O, we would probably need to change many parts of that program. By hiding the details of the hardware connection, we would only have to change the module containing those details.

SPARK provides *external state abstractions* to hide the details of the external interface. Here is a package specification that describes the properties of our external LED display while hiding the memory mapped external variable in the package body. We also provide a procedure that translates the ten digits into individual display segments.

```
package LED_Display
   with Spark_Mode    => On,
        Abstract_State => (LED_State
                              with External => (Async_Readers  => True,
                                                Effective_Writes => True))
is
   subtype Digit_Type is Integer range 0 .. 9;
```

```
   procedure Display_Digit (Digit : in Digit_Type)
     with
        Global => (Output => LED_State);

end LED_Display;
```

The Abstract_State aspect defining the abstract state LED_State has more options than those you saw in Section 4.3.[8] Procedure Display_Digit references this abstract state in its Global aspect.

The declaration of LED_State includes the option External, which tells us that the actual state is maintained in hardware devices and/or other software subsystems that are external to our Spark program. Finally, the two external properties Async_Readers and Effective_Writes are given for this external state object. These are the same properties we used with volatile variables in the previous section. Like a volatile variable, if none of the four properties is specified, all four properties are assumed to be true. And, as is the case here, if one or more properties are defined, the undefined properties are assumed to be false.

Here is the body of package LED_Display where we refine the abstract state LED_State, define the external variable that connects us to the hardware, and implement the procedure Display_Digit :

```
with System.Storage_Elements;
package body Led_Display
   with SPARK_Mode => On,
        Refined_State => (LED_State => Value)
is
   type Octet is mod 2 ** 8;

   Value : Octet
     with
        Size  => 8,  -- Use exactly 8 bits for this variable
        Volatile        => True,
        Async_Readers   => True,
        Effective_Writes => True,
        Address => System.Storage_Elements.To_Address(16#FFFF0000#);

   -- Segments 'a' through 'g' are in order from least to most significant bit.
   -- Active high.
   Patterns : constant array (Digit_Type) of Octet :=
              (2#0011_1111#, 2#0000_0110#, 2#0101_1011#, 2#0100_1111#,
               2#0110_0110#, 2#0110_1101#, 2#0111_1101#, 2#0000_0111#,
               2#0111_1111#, 2#0110_0111#);
```

```
procedure Display_Digit ( Digit  :  in  Digit_Type)
   with Refined_Global  => (Output => Value)
is
begin
   Value := Patterns ( Digit );
end Display_Digit ;
```

```
end LED_Display;
```

We refined our abstract state LED_State to the volatile variable Value. We can refine an abstract state into several different concrete or abstract states. However, SPARK requires that all the external properties specified for our abstract state are realized in the refined state. These realizations of properties may be done by a single refined object as we did here or by a combination of objects. Should an external abstract state have no properties given, you must refine it into one or more objects that together realize all four external properties.

Let us look at a more complex example that uses an external state abstraction. The following package provides an interface to a single serial port. It provides procedures for opening and closing the port and procedures for reading and writing single bytes.

```
with Interfaces ;
package Serial_Port
   with
      SPARK_Mode  => On,
      Abstract_State => (Port_State, (Data_State with External )),
      Initializes    => Port_State
is
   -- Types for configuring serial parameters.
   type Baud_Type       is (B2400, B4800, B9600, B19200);
   type Parity_Type     is (None, Even, Odd);
   type Data_Size_Type  is (Seven, Eight);
   type Stop_Type       is (One, Two);

   -- Type for serial port data
   type Byte is new Interfaces .Unsigned_8;

   -- Type used to convey error codes.
   type Status_Type is (Success, Open_Failure, IO_Failure );

   -- Returns Open_Failure if port is already open or if the open fails .
   procedure Open (Baud     :  in  Baud_Type;
                   Parity :  in   Parity_Type;
```

```
                    Data_Size  : in  Data_Size_Type;
                    Stop       : in  Stop_Type;
                    Status     : out Status_Type)
     with
        Global   => (In_Out => Port_State),
        Depends => ((Port_State, Status) =>
                      (Port_State, Baud, Parity, Data_Size, Stop));


     -- Returns IO_Failure if port is not open or if the underlying I/O fails.
     procedure Read (Item   : out Byte;
                     Status : out Status_Type)
        with
          Global   => (Input => (Port_State, Data_State)),
          Depends => (Item => (Port_State, Data_State), Status => Port_State);


     -- Returns IO_Failure if port is not open or if the underlying I/O fails.
     procedure Write (Item   : in  Byte;
                      Status : out Status_Type)
        with
          Global   => (Input => Port_State, Output => Data_State),
          Depends => (Data_State => (Port_State, Item), Status => Port_State);


     -- Has no effect if port is not open. Returns no failure  indication.
     procedure Close
        with
          Global   => (In_Out => Port_State),
          Depends => (Port_State => Port_State);
end Serial_Port ;
```

The specification of the package is in SPARK and declares two state abstractions. The first, Port_State, models the serial port hardware itself. It tracks if the port is open, the serial parameters that are in use and any other related information such as permissions or system level errors. This state is initialized in some way by the underlying system so the package declares that Port_State is automatically initialized.

The other state abstraction, Data_State, represents the external subsystem to which the serial port is connected and is thus declared to be an external state abstraction. Because none of the four external properties are specified, they all default to true. The external subsystem is assumed to do I/O asynchronously with the serial port and that, furthermore, all reads and writes to the port are effective. In particular, two successive reads from the port may return different values, and writing the same value to the port twice in succession is certainly useful.

The subprograms in the package are decorated with data and flow dependency contracts as usual, written in terms of the two state abstractions. When writing these contracts, it is important to keep clearly in mind what the state abstractions represent. For example, consider the contracts on the Read procedure:

```
-- Returns IO_Failure if port is not open or if the underlying I/O fails .
procedure Read (Item   : out Byte;
                Status : out Status_Type)
   with
      Global  => (Input => (Port_State, Data_State)),
      Depends => (Item => (Port_State, Data_State), Status => Port_State);
```

The Read procedure reports an error if the port is not open, and that information is part of Port_State. Furthermore, Read checks error information reported by the underlying runtime system, which is also contained in Port_State. Thus, the procedure inputs from Port_State and, furthermore, Port_State is used to derive both the value of Item and the resulting Status.

In addition, Read also inputs from the Data_State because it reads a value from the external subsystem connected to the serial port. That value is used to derive the output Item but does not participate in setting Status.

You might imagine that the body of Serial_Port contains one or more volatile variables connected to the serial port hardware. However, in this example, we decided to implement a version that runs under the Windows operating system. Instead of refining our external state to hardware variables, we make calls to the Windows application programming interface (API).

The body of Serial_Port is not in SPARK. It makes use of APIs that use non-SPARK features such as access types. The body of Serial Port is written in Ada. However, it could be coded in C, in which case our specification would require Import and Convention aspects on the declared subprograms as described in Section 7.2. As usual, this requires that the programmer review the SPARK aspects in the package specification carefully as their refinement will not be checked by the SPARK tools.

To illustrate how a higher level package might use the low level interface to an external subsystem, consider the following abbreviated specification of a package Terminal. It is used to provide more convenient access to a standard serial terminal connected to the serial port.

```
with  Serial_Port ;
package Terminal
   with Spark_Mode => On
is
   type Status_Type is (Success,  Insufficient_Space ,  Port_Failure );
```

```
procedure Get_Line (Buffer     : out String;
                          Count  : out Natural;
                          Status : out Status_Type)
      with
         Global => (Input => (Serial_Port.Port_State,
                                   Serial_Port .Data_State)),
         Depends => ((Buffer, Count, Status) => (Buffer,
                                       Serial_Port . Port_State,
                                       Serial_Port .Data_State));
end Terminal;
```

This specification only shows a single procedure, Get_Line, that reads a carriage return terminated string of characters from the terminal and installs them into the given buffer. It returns an error indication if it runs out of space before getting a carriage return character or if the underlying serial port reports an I/O error.

The procedure is decorated with SPARK data and flow dependency contracts written in terms of the state abstractions of the underlying serial port. This appears to be a violation of information hiding: the specification otherwise does not mention the serial port at all, leading one to suppose that it could support other kinds of communications media.

However, despite syntactic appearances, the use of the serial port is not hidden by this package. For example, it is important to open the serial port before calling Get_Line; the dependency of Get_Line on the port state must be declared. Thus, SPARK serves to make explicitly visible dependencies that are semantically visible in any case.

The body of package Terminal is straight forward and shown here in its entirety:

```
with Ada.Characters. Latin_1 ;
package body Terminal
      with Spark_Mode => On
is
      use type Serial_Port .Status_Type;

      procedure Get_Line (Buffer : out String;
                          Count  : out Natural;
                          Status : out Status_Type) is
         Value         : Serial_Port .Byte;
         Port_Status : Serial_Port .Status_Type;
      begin
         Buffer := (others => ' ');
         Count := 0;
         Status := Success;
```

```
loop
   pragma Loop_Invariant (Count <= Buffer'Length);

   -- Check to be sure there is space remaining in the buffer.
   if Count = Buffer'Length then
      Status := Insufficient_Space ;
      exit ;
   end if ;

   Serial_Port .Read (Value, Port_Status );

   -- Check to be sure a byte was successfully read.
   if Port_Status /= Serial_Port .Success then
      Status := Port_Failure ;
      exit ;
   end if ;

   -- We are done if a carriage return is read.
   exit when Character'Val (Value) = Ada.Characters.Latin_1 . CR;

   -- Convert Value (a Byte) to a character and append to Buffer
   Buffer ( Buffer ' First + Count) := Character'Val (Value);
   Count := Count + 1;
   end loop;
   end Get_Line;

end Terminal;
```

The main loop contains a loop invariant pragma that is needed to prove that no buffer overflows will occur. Notice that package Terminal adds useful functionality, completely in SPARK, to the interface of an external subsystem even though direct access to the subsystem is outside of SPARK. The strategy followed here was to wrap the external subsystem in a minimalistic package with a non-SPARK body and then implement as much functionality as possible in SPARK packages that use the subsystem wrapper package.

There are actually two problems with the implementation of Get_Line as previously shown, despite SPARK being able to prove the procedure free of runtime errors. See Exercise 7.13 for more information.

7.3.3 Hierarchical External State Abstractions

In Section 4.3.3 we showed how a hierarchy of state abstractions can help simplify a system with complex state. A hierarchy of state abstractions can also be used to simplify a system with complex external state. Let us look at an example.

Air density is perhaps the single most important factor affecting aircraft performance. Density altitude is a commonly used measure of air density. It is the altitude, relative to standard atmosphere conditions, at which the air density would be equal to the indicated air density at the place of observation. The density altitude at a location may be computed from the current temperature, air pressure, and humidity. Here is a specification for a package that uses external sensors to measure these three components and determine the density altitude:

```
package Density_Altitude
    with SPARK_Mode   => On,
         Abstract_State => (Density_State with External => Async_Writers)
is
    type Feet is range −5_0000 .. 100_000;

    procedure Read (Value : out Feet)
        with Global   => (Input => Density_State),
             Depends => (Value => Density_State);
end Density_Altitude ;
```

This package encapsulates an abstract external state from which the density altitude is returned by a call to procedure Read. The abstract state, Density_State, is given the single external property Async_Writers. This property tells us and SPARK that Density_State will be updated by components external to our system. As the other three properties (Async_Readers, Effective_Writes, and Effective_Reads) are not listed, they default to false.

We refine Density_State and the Global and Depends aspects of procedure Read in the package body:

```
with Density_Altitude . Temperature_Unit,
     Density_Altitude . Pressure_Unit ,
     Density_Altitude . Humidity_Unit;
package body Density_Altitude
    with SPARK_Mode => On,
         Refined_State  => (Density_State => (Temperature_Unit.Temp_State,
                                              Pressure_Unit . Press_State ,
                                              Humidity_Unit.Humid_State)) is
    procedure Read (Value : out Feet)
        with Refined_Global   => (Input => (Temperature_Unit.Temp_State,
                                            Pressure_Unit . Press_State ,
                                            Humidity_Unit.Humid_State)),
```

```
            Refined_Depends => (Value => (Temperature_Unit.Temp_State,
                                          Pressure_Unit . Press_State ,
                                          Humidity_Unit.Humid_State))
   is
      Temperature : Temperature_Unit.Degrees;
      Pressure    : Pressure_Unit . PSI;
      Humidity    : Humidity_Unit.Percent;
   begin
      Temperature_Unit.Read (Temperature);
      Pressure_Unit . Read (Pressure);
      Humidity_Unit.Read (Humidity);
      Value := Feet (Float (Temperature) + -- A stub for the real
                     Float (Pressure) +    -- equation that calculates
                     Float (Humidity));    -- density altitude
   end Read;

end Density_Altitude ;
```

Density_State is refined into abstract states defined in three private child packages, one for each of our input sensors. The Refined_Globals and Refined_Depends are also refined into those abstract states. Values are read from each of the sensors and the density altitude is calculated.

Here is the specification of the private child package for humidity:

```
private package Density_Altitude . Humidity_Unit
   with Spark_Mode    => On,
        Abstract_State => (Humid_State
                              with External => Async_Writers,
                                   Part_Of  => Density_State)
is
   type Percent is range  0 .. 100;

   procedure Read (Value : out Percent)
      with Global  => (Input => Humid_State),
           Depends => (Value => Humid_State);

end Density_Altitude . Humidity_Unit;
```

The abstract state Humid_State of package Humidity_Unit has two options: Part_Of and External. The Part_Of option tells us and SPARK that the abstract state Humid_State is a constituent of the abstract state Density_State. The external property Async_Writers matches that of the abstract state Density_State that it is refining. At least one of the constituents of Density_State must have the external property specified for that abstract state.

Here is the body of the private child package for humidity:

```
with System.Storage_Elements;
package body Density_Altitude.Humidity_Unit
    with Spark_Mode    => On,
         Refined_State => (Humid_State => Humid_Sensor)
is
    Humid_Sensor : Percent
      with Volatile       => True,
           Async_Writers  => True,
           Address        => System.Storage_Elements.To_Address (16#A1CAF0#);

    procedure Read (Value : out Percent)
      with Refined_Global  => (Input => Humid_Sensor),
           Refined_Depends => (Value => Humid_Sensor)
    is
    begin
        Value := Humid_Sensor;
    end Read;

end Density_Altitude.Humidity_Unit;
```

Here, the abstract state Humid_State is refined to the concrete external variable Humid_Sensor. Again, at least one constituent of the refined abstract state must have the same external property as the abstract state. The private child packages for the temperature and pressure sensors are nearly identical to the one for pressure.[9] Our job is done – all abstract states have been refined to concrete variables.

Summary

- Constructs such as packages and subprograms can be either "in SPARK" or "not in SPARK." The parts of your program that are in SPARK only use the facilities allowed by SPARK and obey SPARK's other restrictions.
- The SPARK_Mode aspect or pragma controls which constructs are to be processed as SPARK. By default SPARK_Mode is off, meaning that the compiler treats your entire program as Ada.
- SPARK_Mode can be turned on by default using a configuration pragma. Otherwise it can be turned on for a given construct using either the SPARK_Mode aspect or the SPARK_Mode pragma.

- The value of SPARK_Mode cannot be changed over small-scale constructs such as subexpressions of an expression or individual statements in a subprogram. SPARK_Mode can only be changed at the granularity of larger constructs such as subprograms and packages.
- It is permitted for code in SPARK to call libraries written in some other language such as C provided the programmer writes a SPARK declaration for each foreign operation. The programmer takes responsibility for ensuring that the library actually conforms to the SPARK aspects declared by the programmer; the SPARK tools cannot check them.
- When calling C from SPARK, it is sometimes necesary to write a small helper function that gathers the return value of the underlying C function and returns it as an "out" parameter. This allows you to write the interface to the function as a procedure and work around SPARK's restriction on functions with out parameters.
- Access to information external to the program such as external hardware subsystems is possible by declaring external variables. Commonly, a package is created that wraps the external subsystem with abstract state declared as an external variable.
- By default external variables are assumed to have asynchronous readers and writers, meaning that the external subsystem accesses those variables at a time outside the program's control.
- By default external variables are assumed to always have effective reads and writes, meaning that each read of the external variable may produce a new value and that every write is significant, even if the same value is written twice in succession.
- External variables with other combinations of asynchronous readers and writers and effective reads and writes can be declared to handle specialized circumstances.
- Hierarchical external state abstractions provide a way to simplify complex external states.

Exercises

7.1 What are the advantages of allowing parts of a program to not be in SPARK? What are the dangers of doing so?

7.2 The Ada compiler defaults to having SPARK_Mode off. Why? When writing a high-integrity program, you would normally want as much of the program to be in SPARK as feasible. How could you arrange for that to happen in a convenient and robust way?

7.3 Which of the following are permitted and which are disallowed? Here A
   and B are the names of two subprograms. They could be either procedures
   or functions or one of each.
   a. A's body is in SPARK and calls B, which has a SPARK declaration and a
      SPARK body.
   b. A's body is in SPARK and calls B, which has a SPARK declaration and a
      non-SPARK body.
   c. A's body is in SPARK and calls B, which has a non-SPARK declaration
      and a non-SPARK body.
   d. A's body is not in SPARK and calls B, which as a SPARK declaration and
      a SPARK body.
   e. A's body is not in SPARK and calls B, which has a SPARK declaration
      and a non-SPARK body.
   f. A's body is not in SPARK and calls B, which has a non-SPARK declaration
      and a non-SPARK body.

7.4 It is not permitted for a subprogram to have a non-SPARK declaration and
   a SPARK body. Why would this be disallowed?

7.5 Add a function Check_Overlap to package Interval_Tree described in Section 7.1.1 with the following profile:

   function Check_Overlap(Item : **in** Interval) **return** Boolean;

   The function should return True if the given interval overlaps with at least
   one interval in the tree, otherwise it should return False. Your function
   should run in $O(\log n)$ time and have appropriate SPARK aspects.

7.6 Suppose you write a package with a non-SPARK body and a SPARK specification. Which of the following aspects that may appear on the subprogram declarations in the specification would actually be checked and
   when would that checking occur?
   a. Global
   b. Depends
   c. Pre
   d. Post

7.7 The wrapper package presented on page 266 shows imported declarations
   in the body of the wrapper package. Is it necessary for those declarations
   to be in the body or could they continue to be in a package specification of
   their own? If they could be in their own specification, modify the wrapper
   package presented to show how it would look. If they must appear in the
   body, explain why.

7.8 Write a full Ada version of the C helper function presented on page 267. An outline of how to proceed can be found at the end of Section 7.2. You may find it useful or appropriate to complete package Messages_Wrapper started on page 265. (Hint: The imported declaration of the underlying C function can be made local to the helper procedure. Thus, only the helper procedure needs to have SPARK_Mode set to Off.)

7.9 Pick a small C library that you have already written. Write a SPARK specification for your library and a demonstration program, in SPARK, that uses your library.

7.10 Repeat Exercise 7.6 for the case in which the package body is really a C library.

7.11 Define the phrases *effective read* and *effective write*. Why is it necessary to sometimes specify that reads and writes of external variables are always effective?

7.12 Write a package DIP that wraps a memory mapped register holding the state of eight DIP switches the user can adjust to provide input to your program. Your package should provide a subprogram for reading the switches and an appropriately declared external state abstraction.

7.13 The implementation of Get_Line in package Terminal suffers from two problems. First, a buffer of size zero will always cause the Insufficient_ Space error to be returned. However, it should be possible to pass a zero-sized buffer successfully provided the user enters a blank line in response. Second, if the buffer is returned completely filled with characters, there is no way to distinguish between the case when the line is exactly the length of the buffer and when the user is trying to enter too much data. Fix these problems while maintaining SPARK's proof of freedom from runtime error.

8

Software Engineering with SPARK

In the preceding chapters we have concentrated on the details of the SPARK language. In this chapter, we look at a broader picture of how SPARK might be used in the context of a software engineering process. The SPARK 2014 Toolset User's Guide (SPARK Team, 2014b) lists three common usage scenarios:

1. Conversion of existing software developed in SPARK 2005 to SPARK 2014
2. Analysis and/or conversion of legacy Ada software
3. Development of new SPARK 2014 code from scratch

We start by examining each of these scenarios in more detail, discussing the interplay between proof and testing, and then presenting a case study to illustrate some issues arising when developing new SPARK 2014 code from scratch.

8.1 Conversion of SPARK 2005

Converting a working SPARK 2005 program to SPARK 2014 makes sense when that program is still undergoing active maintenance for enhanced functionality. The larger language and the enhanced set of analysis tools provided by SPARK 2014 offer a potential savings in development time when adding functionality to an existing SPARK 2005 program.

As SPARK 2014 is a superset of SPARK 2005, the conversion is straight forward. Section 7.2 of the *SPARK 2014 Toolset User's Guide* (SPARK Team, 2014b) provides a short introduction to this conversion. Appendix A of the *SPARK 2014 Reference Manual* (SPARK Team, 2014a) has information and a wealth of examples for converting SPARK 2005 constructs to SPARK 2014. Explanations and examples are provided for converting subprograms, type (ADT) packages, variable (ASM) packages, external subsystems, proofs, and

more. Should you need to constrain your code to the SPARK 2005 constructs but wish to use the cleaner syntax of SPARK 2014, you may use
pragma Restrictions (SPARK_05) to have the analysis tools flag SPARK 2014
constructs that are not available in SPARK 2005.

Dross et al. (2014) discuss their experiences with converting SPARK 2005 to
SPARK 2014 in three different domains. AdaCore has a SPARK 2005 to SPARK
2014 translator to assist with the translation process. At the time of this writing,
this tool is available only to those using the pro versions of their GNAT and
SPARK products.

We illustrate a simple example of converting a SPARK 2005 package to SPARK
2014. The package encapsulates a circular buffer holding temperature data, for
example, from an analog to digital converter. The SPARK 2005 specification is
shown as follows:

```
with Data_Types;
--# inherit Data_Types;
package Temperature_Buffer05
  --# own Contents;
is
    type Temperature_Record is
      record
          Time_Stamp : Data_Types.Time_Type;
          Value      : Data_Types.Temperature_Type;
      end record;

    -- Adds a new item to the buffer.
    procedure Put (Item :  in  Temperature_Record);
    --# global in out Contents;
    --# derives Contents from Contents, Item;

    -- Returns True if buffer is not empty.
    function Has_More return Boolean;
    --# global in Contents;

    -- Retrieves the oldest item from the buffer.
    procedure Get (Item :  out  Temperature_Record);
    --# global in out Contents;
    --# derives Contents from Contents &
    --#         Item      from Contents;
    --# pre Has_More (Contents);

    -- Initializes the buffer.
```

```
procedure Clear;
--# global out Contents;
--# derives Contents from ;
```

end Temperature_Buffer05;

The abstract state of this variable package is declared in SPARK 2005 by way of "own variables" in the specification. Annotations, in the form of Ada comments, provide the data and flow dependency contracts in a largely intuitive way. Of particular interest is the precondition on procedure Get that requires Has_More to return true. It is not permitted to get an item from the buffer if it is empty.

In SPARK 2005 the use of Has_More in the precondition is abstract because SPARK 2005 annotations are not executable. Any functions used in pre- and postconditions must be pure, therefore, SPARK 2005 requires that the abstract state read by the function be passed as an explicit parameter.

The body of the package starts by refining the abstract state and declaring the constituents of that state:

```
package body Temperature_Buffer05
   --#own Contents is Buffer, Count, Next_In, Next_Out;
is
   Buffer_Size  : constant := 8;
   type Buffer_Index_Type is mod Buffer_Size;
   type Buffer_Type is array (Buffer_Index_Type) of Temperature_Record;
   Buffer : Buffer_Type;

   type Buffer_Count_Type is range 0 ..  Buffer_Size ;
   Count    : Buffer_Count_Type; -- Number of items.
   Next_In  : Buffer_Index_Type; -- Next available slot .
   Next_Out : Buffer_Index_Type; -- Next item to extract.
```

The use of a modular type for Buffer_Index_Type causes buffer indexes to wrap around automatically and simplifies the programming. In this case the buffer never fills; old data is pushed out as new data is entered.

The implementation of function Has_More and procedure Get follows:

```
function Has_More return Boolean
--# global in Count;
is
begin
   return Count > 0;
end Has_More;
```

```
procedure Get (Item :  out Temperature_Record)
−−# global in Buffer;  in out Count, Next_Out;
−−# derives Item      from Next_Out, Buffer &
−−#        Count      from Count          &
−−#        Next_Out from Next_Out;
is
begin
   Item := Buffer (Next_Out);
   Next_Out := Next_Out + 1;
   Count := Count − 1;
end Get;
```

As with SPARK 2014, the data and flow dependencies are refined in terms of their constituents. The code itself is straightforward. However, the SPARK 2005 tools have difficulty proving that the assignment statement Count := Count − 1 does not cause a runtime error. It does not because the precondition forbids Get from being called unless Count > 0. However, the SPARK 2005 tools do not understand the behavior of Has_More and need to be taught that behavior using techniques we do not detail here. This is necessary despite the fact that Has_More is implemented in the body of the package where, in principle, the tools can see it.

The following SPARK 2014 version of the package specification is a straightforward translation of the SPARK 2005 version:

```
with Data_Types;
package Temperature_Buffer14
   with
      SPARK_Mode => On,
      Abstract_State => Contents
is
   type Temperature_Record is
      record
         Time_Stamp : Data_Types.Time_Type;
         Value      : Data_Types.Temperature_Type;
      end record;

   −− Initializes the buffer.
   procedure Clear
      with
         Global  => (Output => Contents),
         Depends => (Contents => null);

   −− Adds a new item to the buffer.
```

```
procedure Put (Item :  in  Temperature_Record)
  with
    Global  => (In_Out => Contents),
    Depends => (Contents =>+ Item);


-- Returns True if buffer is not empty.
function Has_More return Boolean
  with Global => (Input => Contents);


-- Retrieves the oldest item from the buffer.
procedure Get (Item :  out  Temperature_Record)
  with
    Global  => (In_Out => Contents),
    Depends => (Contents =>+ null, Item => Contents),
    Pre => Has_More;

end Temperature_Buffer14;
```

The body refines the abstract state using the Refined_State aspect. However, of particular interest is the implementation of Has_More and Get:

```
function Has_More return Boolean is (Count > 0)
  with Refined_Global => (Input => Count);


procedure Get (Item :  out  Temperature_Record)
  with
    Refined_Global => (Input => Buffer, In_Out => (Count, Next_Out)),
    Refined_Depends =>
      (Item     => (Next_Out, Buffer),
       Count    =>+ null,
       Next_Out =>+ null)
  is
  begin
    Item := Buffer (Next_Out);
    Next_Out := Next_Out + 1;
    Count := Count - 1;
  end Get;
```

The Has_More function is an expression function so its implementation is used to synthesize its postcondition. The SPARK 2014 tools do not need to have the meaning of Has_More explained separately. As a result, the SPARK 2014 tools prove procedure Get free of runtime errors without additional complications.

This example illustrates that the conversion of SPARK 2005 to SPARK 2014 may allow certain simplifications to be made in the code or in the proofs. It is not just a matter of translating SPARK 2005 annotations to SPARK 2014 aspects. In addition, the SPARK 2014 tools use generally more powerful theorem provers; some verification conditions that were difficult with SPARK 2005 may be easier with SPARK 2014. As a result, it may be possible to simplify or eliminate certain loop invariants or write the code in the more natural way.

Finally, the richer language provided by SPARK 2014 offers the possibility of refactoring a SPARK 2005 program to take advantage of that richness. The Temperature_Buffer example presented earlier comes from an embedded system that also buffers other kinds of readings. It would be natural to make all of the buffers instances of a single generic unit. However, earlier versions of SPARK did not support generics. Of course, how much rewriting of a legacy system is appropriate will depend on the situation. However, if it is deemed worthwhile to update the software to SPARK 2014, it may also be worthwhile to reorganize and even redesign parts of the software to take advantage of SPARK 2014's larger set of features.

8.2 Legacy Ada Software

The preferred use of SPARK is in a *constructive analysis* style in which we create a program whose units contain a full set of contracts specified by the aspects discussed in Chapters 4 and 6. As we saw in Chapter 7, SPARK provides the means to mix SPARK code with non-SPARK code through the use of contracts on the specifications of non-SPARK code. Commonly, the non-SPARK code is written in Ada or C.

SPARK 2014 has the capability to analyze preexisting Ada code where no SPARK contracts are given. This *retrospective analysis* is made possible by the ability of the SPARK tools to synthesize a set of data dependency contracts and flow dependency contracts directly from the source code of a program unit (see Section 4.5). These synthesized contracts can be used to analyze legacy Ada code or during the early development of SPARK code in which contracts have not yet been included.

The synthesized contracts are safe over-approximations of the real contracts. For example, they assume that *all* outputs are dependent on *all* inputs. Because it is unlikely that the body of the subprogram meets all of the synthesized contracts, the SPARK tools do not generate warnings or checks when the body does not respect the synthesized contracts. The synthesized contracts are used to verify proper initialization and respect of any dependency contracts in the callers of the subprogram.

Section 6.8.1 of the *SPARK 2014 User's Guide* describes how contracts are synthesized for

- a non-SPARK subprogram – one with Spark_Mode => Off;
- a SPARK subprogram with no data or flow contracts;

- a SPARK subprogram with only data contracts; and
- a SPARK subprogram with only flow contracts.

As mentioned in the previous paragraph, the aspects that the SPARK tools synthesize are almost always more general than those we would write. However, when no data or flow contracts are given on a SPARK subprogram, the tools generate precise data and flow dependencies by using path-sensitive flow analysis to track data flows in the subprogram body. These synthesized contracts accurately describe the code whether or not that code is correct.

Section 7.3 of the SPARK*2014 Toolset User's Guide* (SPARK Team, 2014b) provides some guidance to using the SPARK tools to analyze legacy Ada code as a first step prior to performing a full or partial conversion to SPARK. Even without the intention of converting legacy Ada code to SPARK, the tools can help us find errors in our Ada code. Take, for example, the following contrived package specification and body:

```
package Unused_Parameter with SPARK_Mode => On is

   procedure Avg (A :  in   Natural;
                  B :  in   Natural;
                  C :  out Natural );
end Unused_Parameter;
```

```
package body Unused_Parameter with SPARK_Mode => On is

   procedure Avg (A :  in   Natural;
                  B :  in   Natural;
                  C :  out Natural) is
   begin
      C := (A + A) / 2;
   end Avg;

end Unused_Parameter;
```

Here we made a mistake in the body by typing (A + A) rather than (A + B). The SPARK Examine tool reports that B is not used. This analysis is not provided by the GNAT compiler. Here is another simple package:

```
package Overflow with SPARK_Mode => On is

   procedure Avg (A :  in   Natural;
                  B :  in   Natural;
                  C :  out Natural );
end Overflow;
```

```
package body Overflow with SPARK_Mode => On is

   procedure Avg  (A :  in    Natural;
                   B :  in    Natural;
                   C :  out  Natural)  is
   begin
      C := (A + B) / 2;
   end Avg;

end Overflow;
```

This time the Examine tool reports no problems. However, the Prove tool reports that the line

```
C := (A + B) / 2;
```

may overflow. It is possible that the values of A and B are so large that their sum exceeds that of the largest value the accumulator can hold. This error is still present in implementations of the binary search and merge sort algorithms in many introductory programming books even after being pointed out by Pattis in 1988. While one probably would not think to test this case, our proof tool was quick to discover it. With a little algebra, we can reorganize the expression to

```
C := A + (B − A) / 2;
```

Now the Prove tool reports no possible runtime error.

Let us look at a larger example of using SPARK to analyze preexisting Ada code. We would like to verify that no runtime errors will be raised in the package Bingo_Basket that we presented in Section 3.4. Here is its specification with the addition of the aspect to make it in SPARK:

```
with Bingo_Numbers; use Bingo_Numbers;
package Bingo_Basket with SPARK_Mode => On is

   function Empty return Boolean;

   procedure Load    -- Load all the Bingo numbers into the basket
      with
         Post => not Empty;

   procedure Draw (Letter  : out Bingo_Letter;
                   Number : out Callable_Number)
```

```
  -- Draw a random number from the basket
  with
        Pre => not Empty;

end Bingo_Basket;
```

When we run the SPARK Examine tool we see the following messages concerning the package body (code on page 84):

Phase 1 of 2: generation of Global contracts . . .
Phase 2 of 2: analysis of data and information flow . . .
bingo_basket.adb:34:07: warning: no Global contract available for "Reset"
bingo_basket.adb:34:07: warning: assuming "Reset" has no effect on global items
bingo_basket.adb:36:26: warning: no Global contract available for "Random"
bingo_basket.adb:36:26: warning: assuming "Random" has no effect on global items

It is obvious that the Examine tool is not happy with our use of the generic random value generator from the Ada library. Our solution here is to factor out the code involving operations from the library and put it into a private child package. We mark the specification as in SPARK and the body as not in SPARK:

```
private package Bingo_Basket.Random with Spark_Mode => On is
    function Random_Number return Callable_Number;
end Bingo_Basket.Random;

with Ada.Numerics.Discrete_Random;
package body Bingo_Basket.Random with SPARK_Mode => Off is

    package Random_Bingo is new Ada.Numerics.Discrete_Random
                        (Result_Subtype => Callable_Number);

    -- The following object holds the state of a random Bingo number generator
    Bingo_Gen : Random_Bingo.Generator;

    function Random_Number return Callable_Number is
    begin
        return Random_Bingo.Random (Gen => Bingo_Gen);
    end Random_Number;

begin
    -- Initialize the random number generator from the system clock
    Random_Bingo.Reset (Gen => Bingo_Gen);
end Bingo_Basket.Random;
```

Here is the revised body of package Bingo_Basket with all Ada library usage done in calls to the child package:

```ada
with Bingo_Basket.Random;
package body Bingo_Basket with SPARK_Mode => On is

   type Number_Array is array (Callable_Number) of Callable_Number;
   The_Basket : Number_Array; -- A sequence of numbers in the basket
   The_Count : Bingo_Number; -- The count of numbers in the basket

   procedure Swap (X : in out Callable_Number;
                   Y : in out Callable_Number) is
      Temp : Callable_Number;
   begin
      Temp := X; X := Y;  Y := Temp;
   end Swap;

   function Empty return Boolean is (The_Count = 0);

   procedure Load is
      Random_Index : Callable_Number;
   begin
      -- Put all numbers into the basket (in order)
      for Number in Callable_Number loop
         The_Basket (Number) := Number;
      end loop;
      -- Randomize the array of numbers
      for Index in Callable_Number loop
         Random_Index := Bingo_Basket.Random.Random_Number;
         Swap (X => The_Basket (Index),
               Y => The_Basket (Random_Index));
      end loop;
      The_Count := Callable_Number'Last;  -- all numbers now in the basket
   end Load;

   procedure Draw (Letter  : out Bingo_Letter;
                   Number : out Callable_Number) is
   begin
      Number   := The_Basket (The_Count);
      The_Count := The_Count - 1;

      -- Determine the letter using the subtypes in Bingo_Definitions
      case Number is
```

```
          when B_Range => Letter := B;
          when I_Range => Letter := I;
          when N_Range => Letter := N;
          when G_Range => Letter := G;
          when O_Range => Letter := O;
        end case;
      end Draw;
  end Bingo_Basket;
```

With all of the code that uses the Ada library moved out to a child package, the SPARK Examine tool finds no problems with this package. Nor does the proof tool report any problems. We are now confident that package Bingo_Basket has no runtime errors and that procedure Load's postcondition that the basket is not empty always holds.[1] We were tempted to add Abstract_State and Initializes aspects to the specification of Bingo_Basket.Random. However, our goal here is the analysis of legacy Ada code, not the conversion of Ada to SPARK.

When analyzing legacy code, we suggest beginning with the lowest level packages in your program – those that do not depend on other units. Add SPARK_Mode => On to each package specification and run the SPARK examine tool on it to see a listing of potential errors. Correct any errors reported by the examination. Then add SPARK_Mode => On to the body and examine it. As we did with package Bingo_Basket, you will see warnings for any standard Ada library operations you use. To obtain a deeper analysis, move such operations to their own package whose body is not in SPARK. You can then repeat the process for the next level of program units.

8.3 Creating New Software

SPARK is best applied to the development of new software. Starting from scratch provides the opportunity to make use of the SPARK tools from the development of the architectural design through the detailed implementation.

Test Driven Development (TDD) is a popular, evolutionary approach to software development that combines test-first development (in which you write a test before you write just enough code to fulfill that test) and refactoring (a disciplined restructuring of code). With SPARK's ability to combine proof with testing, we can extend TDD to an even more rigorous approach we call *Verification Driven Development* (VDD).[2] With VDD, we write contracts before we write the code to fulfill them. Data dependency and flow dependency contracts can be verified early on. Verification of freedom from runtime errors and of pre- and postconditions can be done once the code is written. Designing to meet your verification goals is a powerful approach to creating quality software.

Software design is all about the decisions a software engineer makes between the gathering and verification of requirements and the creation of code to implement those requirements. A design is the specification of a group of software artifacts or modules.

Many different design methodologies have been devised to guide us in making the many decisions involved. Section 7.1 of the *SPARK 2014 Toolset User's Guide* (SPARK Team, 2014b) gives the following overall view of developing SPARK programs from scratch:

1. Begin by creating a set of package specifications that describe the architectural design of the system. Include contracts with each specification that describe the abstract state encapsulated by each package. Use subprogram contracts to specify global dependencies on the abstract state and dependency contracts to specify information flow in each subprogram. Preconditions and postconditions may be added to these high-level packages to describe high-level properties such as safety and security.

2. Identify the SPARK packages with the SPARK_Mode aspect. At this stage the high-level package structure can be analyzed with the Examine tool before any executable code is implemented.

3. Implement the package bodies making use of top-down decomposition. Start with the top-level subprogram specifications and implement the bodies by breaking them down into lower-level subprograms, each with appropriate contracts. You can continuously run the Examine tool during each iteration of this process.

4. As each subprogram is implemented, you can verify it by proof or testing. Testing contracts with assertion checking enabled provides us with confidence that our contracts are written correctly. Proof then shows absence of runtime errors and that the contracts are met.

5. Once verification is complete, the executable can be compiled with assertion checks either enabled or disabled depending on the policy chosen by the project.

In the following sections we look at a more detailed approach to designing SPARK programs. The INFORMED[3] design method was developed especially for applying the strengths of SPARK during this crucial stage. This introduction to INFORMED is based on the technical report *INFORMED Design Method for SPARK* (SPARK Team, 2011). Chapter 13 *SPARK: The Proven Approach to High Integrity Software* (Barnes, 2012) provides another discussion of the INFORMED method. Although the examples in both the technical report (SPARK Team, 2011) and book (Barnes, 2012) are SPARK 2005, the principles apply equally well to SPARK 2014.

8.3.1 *Design Principles*

The properties of a good design are reasonably well known:

Abstraction is the separation of the essential features of an entity from the details of how those features actually work. It is our major tool for dealing with complexity.

Encapsulation is the inclusion of one entity within another entity so that the included entity is not apparent. The concept of class, in which data and operations are combined to form a single component, is a prime example of encapsulation in object-oriented design. Encapsulation provides a clear separation between specification and implementation – a necessary tenet of the contract model of programming. The package is SPARK's major construct for encapsulation.

Information hiding is the principle of segregation of the design decisions in a system that are most likely to change. It protects other parts of the program from extensive modification when the design decision is changed. Information hiding is closely related to abstraction as it is the details of how things work that we want to hide. Hiding unnecessary details allows us to focus on the essential properties of an entity.

Information hiding is related to but different than encapsulation. Encapsulation puts things into a box. Whether that box is opaque or clear determines whether the information is hidden or not. The private type is SPARK's major construct for information hiding.

Coupling is a measure of the connections between entities. Highly coupled objects interact in ways that make it difficult to modify one object without modifying the other. High levels of coupling may be a result of poor abstractions or inadequate encapsulation. Weak or loose coupling is desirable.

In SPARK, the appearance of a package name in a **with** clause represents loose coupling (use of a service). The appearance of a package name in a data dependency contract (global aspect) or a flow dependency contract (depends aspect) indicates stronger coupling.

Cohesion is a measure of focus or purpose within a single entity. It is the degree to which the elements of a module belong together. Having high cohesion in our modules makes it easier for us to understand them and make changes to them. Having unrelated abstract state variables in a SPARK package is an indicator of low cohesion.

Hiding unnecessary details allows us to focus on the essential properties of an entity. However, the state of an entity is an essential property that should not be hidden – we cannot reason in the absence of state information. The state of an object is defined by its implementation. Because inspecting the implementation of an object to ascertain state information breaks the contract model, we must include this information in the object's specification. We accomplish this task by including Abstract_State aspects. These aspects provide the appropriate level of abstraction of state information that is needed to reason about the effect of operations on an object without having or needing the details of how the state is represented. Managing state information in this way is an important piece of the INFORMED design method.

8.3.2 *Design Elements*

INFORMED uses concepts from both object-oriented design (OOD) and functional design. OOD techniques are used to establish the architecture of the system. This architecture is expressed as a main program and framework of packages with contracts. Of particular importance is the assignment of state to these packages. With this information, we can use the SPARK tools to analyze the data dependency and flow dependency at an early stage.

We use classic functional decomposition to implement the operations within our objects. We can again make use of SPARK tools to check that the desired properties of our design are being maintained, our code is free of runtime errors, and any functional properties expressed by postconditions are met.

Main Programs

Main programs frequently have a form similar to the following program. The system is initialized and then a loop (often infinite) does all of the processing required.

```
with A, B, C;
procedure Main
    with Spark_Mode => On,
        Global    => -- references to states in packages A, B, and C,
        Depends   => -- references to states in packages A, B, and C
is
    procedure Initialize    is ...
    procedure Do_Something is ...
begin
    Initialize;
    loop
        Do_Something;
    end loop;
end Main;
```

The Initialize and Do-Something procedures are likely decomposed into several procedures, each responsible for some individual mode of the system's behavior. For example, one Do-Something procedure may be responsible for controlling the temperature in a vessel while another is responsible for controlling the pressure.

The most important parts of this generalized main program are the two aspects that specify the data dependencies and flow dependencies of the system. These aspects generally refer to the abstract state of the packages that are withed rather than to specific variables.

Packages

In Chapter 3 we organized packages into four groups: (1) definition packages, (2) utility packages, (3) type packages, and (4) variable packages. INFORMED adds a few more to this classification scheme.

Variable Packages. Contain states that should be revealed through an Abstract-State aspect. We use the name of the abstract state in the Global and Depends aspects of our main program and/or other units that use the package. Encapsulation and information hiding are maintained because no details of the internal state need be revealed. Refined-State allows us to specify a number of more detailed state items within the package body.

We may compose variable packages. Thus, a bicycle object could contain a frame object and two wheel objects. The abstract state of the bicycle may be refined into the abstract states of its components. SPARK private child packages allow the logical nesting or embedding of variable packages without the need to physically embed the packages that represent them.

Type Packages. Do not have state and therefore do not have Abstract-State aspects. As described in Section 3.3, a type package provides the name of a type that may be used in the declaration of objects in other units. This type may be a concrete type (as illustrated by the first version of our bounded queue on page 73) or a private type (as illustrated by the second version of our bounded queue on page 78).

Type packages are used to implement abstract data types. For private types, the package must also provide a set of operations that may be performed on objects of that type. Concrete types come with their own predefined set of operations, which may be extended by the declaration of additional operations with parameters of that type.[4]

Variables of the types declared in type packages are declared at the point of use and passed as parameters to the operations provided by the type package.

Because this localizes state at the point of variable declaration, type packages provide a mechanism for the reduction of information flow and, hence, coupling. The INFORMED report uses the phrase "instance of a type package" for a variable of a type declared in a type package.

INFORMED describes a more specialized type package called a *type package declaring concrete types*. This form of type package is equivalent to the definition package we described in Section 3.1.

Utility Packages. Provide shared services to other packages. These packages never contain state (otherwise they would be variable packages). Any types declared in a utility package should be simple concrete types rather than abstract data types (otherwise they would be type packages). The INFORMED report provides examples of where utility packages are appropriate and where they are not.

Boundary Variable Packages. Are a special kind of variable package that provide interfaces between our system and the elements outside of it. The entity to which our SPARK program communicates might be some kind of hardware sensor or actuator. Section 7.3 discusses the nature of external subsystems found commonly in embedded applications.

These external subsystems make use of external variables that represent streams of data arriving from or being sent to the external system so they are characterized by a **with** External in their abstract state aspects.

Boundary Variable Abstraction Packages. Are used to place an abstraction layer between the external variables of a system and their users. This approach eliminates direct exposure of any external variables, shielding the higher level units from the details of the external variables. Boundary variable abstraction packages use SPARK's state refinements to provide this indirect access to the external variables.

The abstraction may hide the fact that more than one external variable is involved in providing the inputs or may hide some other processing that is taking place. The abstraction may also hide other local state (such as previous values) that are not external variables. The INFORMED technical report provides an example of using a single boundary variable abstraction package to encapsulate two different buttons that may be pressed by a user. This package is refined into two boundary variable packages implemented as private child packages. Accompanying this example in the INFORMED report is a very important guideline concerning boundary variable abstraction packages – never mix input and output external variables in a single abstraction. This mixing leads to confusing information flow results where inputs incorrectly appear to depend on values previously sent as outputs. Use a separate abstraction for each external variable as was done in package Serial_Port in Section 7.3.2.

Finally, we note that a variable abstraction package need not include any hidden external variables. The external entity to which our SPARK program communicates might be an API of some library, operating system, or cooperating software system.

8.3.3 *Principles of the INFORMED Design Approach*

The INFORMED technical report lists five guiding design principles.

1. Application-Oriented Aspects

SPARK aspects provide an expression of the behavior of the software independently of the actual code. This description is more useful if it is expressed in problem domain terms rather than in implementation terms. For example, we prefer to see the terms *fuel valve* rather than digital-to-analog converter #3.

2. Minimal Information Flow

To reason about the behavior of a system, we need to reason about the information that flows through it. Such reasoning is simplified if the information flows are minimized. Moving data from one part of the system to another increases the information flow complexity as measured by the Global and Depends aspects. Methods for minimizing information flow include

* Minimizing propagation of unnecessary details;
* Localizing and encapsulating of state information;
* Avoiding making copies of data; and
* Using an appropriate hierarchy of packages.

3. Clear Separation of the Essential from the Inessential

Software designers have to reconcile many, sometimes conflicting, constraints. When such conflicts arise, the designer should make the essential functionality of the system the highest priority.

For example, although it might ease the testing of a system by making certain data global, it is preferred that this inessential aspect of the design be located in the place that ensures minimal information flow. Additional code, clearly identified by comments and flow analysis as not being necessary for the essential functionality of the system, can provide access to the data at test time.

4. Careful Selection of the SPARK Boundary

Careful thought should be given to defining the boundary between what is in SPARK and what is not. This boundary is far more fluid with SPARK 2014 with its goal of supporting verification through a combination of proof and testing than it is with SPARK 2005.

5. Use Static Analysis Early

The packages making up the design should be examined as early as possible with the SPARK tools. Early use of these tools is facilitated by using abstractions, deferring implementation details, and making appropriate use of Spark_Mode => Off. The analysis should continue as the design evolves. This constant checking of design choices provides assurance that our aims are met.

8.3.4 *INFORMED Design Steps*

The INFORMED report includes a suggested sequence of six steps for constructing a SPARK application.

1. Identification of the system boundary, inputs, and outputs.
2. Identification of the SPARK boundary within the overall system boundary.
3. Identification and localization of system state.
4. Handling of the initialization of state.
5. Handling of secondary requirements.
6. Implementing the internal behavior of components.

Design is an iterative process so there is usually considerable looping, backtracking, and feedback among the steps within the following steps.

1. *Identification of the system boundary, inputs, and outputs*

The SPARK system being designed is typically part of a larger system that has interactions with the outside world. The first step is to delineate this boundary and identify the physical inputs and outputs. These are the environmental quantities that impact or are impacted by the system's behavior. They are described as *monitored* and *controlled* variables in the Four-Variable Model of Parnas and Madey (1995), which describes the interactions between a computer system and the environment. This model is illustrated in Figure 8.1.

2. *Identification of the SPARK boundary*

After identifying the boundary of our overall system, we give thought as to where to place the boundary of the SPARK portions of our application – that is, what parts are in SPARK and what parts are not. Selection of the boundary

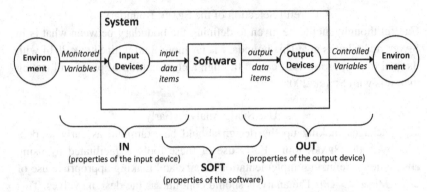

Figure 8.1. The four-variable model (adapted from Parnas and Madey, 1995).

variable packages and boundary variable abstract packages is one way to define the SPARK boundary. The input and output values provided by the abstract state of these packages are the input data items and output data items of the Parnas model illustrated in Figure 8.1. Figure 8.2 shows the flow of information through these packages to and from the non-SPARK software and environment defined by the Parnas four-variable model. The INFORMED report gives examples of systems that contain multiple SPARK systems within an overall system.

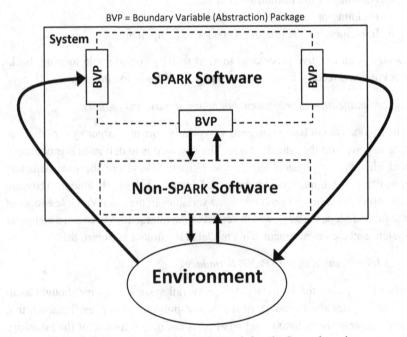

Figure 8.2. Boundary variable packages define the SPARK boundary.

The identification of the styles of verification that will be applied to each component identified at this point is a crucial part of VDD. Proof will certainly play a large role in the verification of SPARK units, and runtime assertion checking will help us verify Ada units. Units written in other languages will need to be tested. We must determine the depth of analysis required of each unit. The recommendations given in Section 8.4 provide guidance in planning the verification at the boundaries between SPARK and non-SPARK units.

3. *Identification and localization of state*

The identification of state that is required in our system and determining where to place that state information are central to meeting the INFORMED design method's goals. As such, the report categorizes the different ways that packages can be used for the management, concealment, and communication of state.

Most nontrivial systems store values in variables and therefore have "history" or state. In the absences of state, calling an operation with a particular set of values always returns the same answer. On the other hand, the result of calling an operation that uses state may also depend on some complex history of all previous calls of that procedure. The INFORMED report emphasizes that the selection of appropriate locations for this state is probably the single most important decision that influences the amount of information flow in the system. You must decide (1) what must be stored, (2) where should it be stored, and (3) how should it be stored.

What must be Stored? Some static data storage is almost always required, but the amount should be minimized as far as possible. You should avoid duplicating data by storing it in a single place and make it available to other units through "accessor functions."

Classification of state is a crucial part of INFORMED. States may be classified into groups such as essential, inessential, input, output, and so on. The *golden rule of refinement* tells us to only refine concrete states as constituents of the same abstract state if they are of the same classification and initialization mode.

Integrity levels for safety (level A, B, etc.) or security (classified, unclassified, top-secret, etc.) are good candidates for state classes. The golden rule of refinement is especially important here – never refine together states that are of different integrities. If you have separation properties, such as making sure that top-secret and unclassified material are kept separate, you need to design that separation into your state hierarchy.[5]

Where should it be Stored? The INFORMED reports gives us several guidelines. Data stored inside the main program does not appear in its data flow or information flow dependency contracts. This has the unfortunate effect of removing all of the information describing the flow of data. Therefore, it is more appropriate to place this data within variable packages or boundary variable packages. The main program then includes the abstract states of these packages in its global and depends aspects. Of course, within the packages we will refine the abstract states into combinations of concrete state variables and abstract state variables of lower level packages with state.

How should it be Stored? The INFORMED report describes a number of ways to store state:

- In a variable package at library level (global state)
- In a variable package embedded within another variable package (hierarchical state refinement)
- In a variable package that is a private child of another variable package (the preferred approach to hierarchical state refinement)
- In a variable package embedded within the main program
- As an instance of type defined in a type package
- As a concrete Ada variable

State should be localized as much as possible. It should be avoided entirely where a local variable within a subprogram will suffice. Variables declared in subprograms (other than the main program) exist only for the life of a call to that subprogram. Type packages give us extra freedom in to locate items with complex state as locally as possible.

We advise that when you need only a single instance of an object with state that you use a variable package and use type packages when multiple copies are required. The use of variable packages can be extended to those situations with a small finite number of objects. For example, it might be better to encapsulate three buttons within a single control panel package rather than to define a button type package.

4. *Handling of the initialization of state*

After identifying and determining the location of states, our next consideration is on how the various states will be initialized. There are two approaches to initialize state:

- a. Initializing during program elaboration. This initialization includes the assignment of initial values accompanying variable declarations and the execution of statements in a package's elaboration part (see Section 3.4.1).
  We discussed default initialization in Section 4.4. The use of the Initializes aspect provides an important piece of information to the SPARK

tools to ensure that states within a variable package are not used prior to their initialization.

b. Initializing during program execution. The main program can assign values directly to concrete Ada variables and call initialization procedures to initialize the state of variable packages or objects declared from types in type packages.

5. *Handling of secondary requirements*

The third principle of the INFORMED design approach is to have a clear separation of the essential and inessential requirements. INFORMED defines *secondary* requirements as those that are not derived from the core functional requirements. Secondary does not mean unimportant, but rather that they should be accommodated in ways that do not distort the "purity" of design through state and information flow. Read-only variables, data logging and test points, and caching are three examples of secondary requirements discussed in Apppendix B of the INFORMED report (SPARK Team, 2011).

6. *Implementation of the internal behavior of components*

After identifying the components of our architecture such as variable packages, type packages, and boundary variable packages, we can create specifications with contracts. We can perform early static analysis on these specifications.

Next, we need to implement the desired behavior of each object. The first step, as usual, is to decompose this behavior into smaller INFORMED components. For example, a variable package for a control panel might be decomposed into a number of boundary variable packages – one for each component on the panel. When we have taken decomposition as far as we can, we can use a standard top-down refinement process to decomposed behaviors into appropriate subprograms. We can include contracts with each subprogram specification and continue to run the Examine tool before implementing the bodies. As the bodies of the subprograms within a particular package are completed, we can run the Proof tool to check for potential runtime errors or postcondition violations.

The INFORMED report (SPARK Team, 2011) includes three case studies to illustrate the design method. Although these designs are in SPARK 2005, the ideas translate easily to SPARK 2014. We illustrate this approach with a security-related case study in Section 8.5.

8.4 Proof and Testing

As we discussed in Section 1.1.2, testing is the primary means for verifying and validating software. Testing can only show us that the program is "correct" for the cases actually tested. A good tester picks the most appropriate test cases to discover faults. Industry standards such as DO-178 (RTCA, 2011a) and ISO/IEC/IEEE 29119 provide guidance on appropriate testing techniques.

In Chapter 6 we looked at how to use SPARK to prove correctness properties of programs. If we can prove that our program is correct, then we have total confidence that it will work in all cases covered by the assertions. Formal verification gives stronger guarantees than testing. New verification standards provide guidance on using proof. For example, The DO-333 standard, a supplement on formal methods for the DO-178C standard, states, "Formal methods might be used in a very selective manner to partially address a small set of objectives, or might be the primary source of evidence for the satisfaction of many of the objectives concerned with development and verification" (RTCA, 2011b).

In addition to providing stronger guarantees, the cost of proof can be less than the cost of testing. This is particularly true for the most critical software for which coverage criteria require a lot of testing (Moy et al., 2013). A clear example of savings was seen in the use of SPARK for the mission computer of the C130J aircraft. Lockheed reported an 80 percent savings over their projected cost for testing and certification of more than 100,000 lines of code (Amey, 2002).

However, there are times when proof is not the best option:

- Our entire program is not amenable to proof. Parts of our program may need to use Ada constructs such as exceptions or access types that are not legal in SPARK. Parts of our programs may be written in another language such a C (see Section 7.2).
- It may be very expensive or even impossible to provide formal descriptions of all the desired properties of a package. Interactive packages are particularly difficult to formalize.
- Software validation[6] is not specifically addressed by formal contracts. Testing remains the best way to validate software.

By combining proof and testing, we get the best of both worlds. We can combine methods by dividing our application into pieces (packages or subprograms) and applying either proof or testing to each separate piece. As the verification chain is only as strong as its weakest link, our goal is to obtain verification at least as good as can be accomplished with testing alone, but at a lower cost. Comar, Kanig, and Moy (2012) provide an excellent discussion of combining formal verification and testing. This paper is available through AdaCore's GEM series.

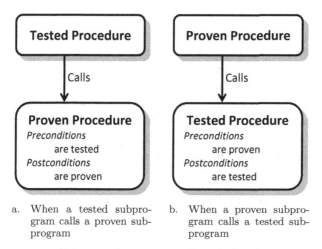

a. When a tested subpro-
    gram calls a proven sub-
    program

b. When a proven subpro-
    gram calls a tested sub-
    program

Figure 8.3. Verifying preconditions and postconditions when combining proof and testing.

SPARK's contracts provides an ideal mechanism for combining proof with testing in such a divided program. How we verify the contracts depends on the relationship between the subprograms in our application:

• When a proven subprogram calls another proven subprogram, the preconditions and postconditions of the called subprogram are verified by proof.
• When a tested subprogram calls another tested subprogram, the preconditions and postconditions of the called subprogram need to be verified by test.
• When a tested subprogram calls a proven subprogram, the preconditions of the proven subprogram need to be verified by test and the postconditions of the proven subprogram are verified by proof (see Figure 8.3a). Calls from different tested subprograms to the same proven subprogram must have the proven subprogram's preconditions tested separately.
• When a proven subprogram calls a tested subprogram, the preconditions of the tested subprogram are verified by proof and the postconditions of the tested subprogram need to be verified by test (see Figure 8.3b).

The 80/20 ratio so common in software engineering seems to fit the model of combined proof and testing. About 80 percent of the subprograms in a typical high integrity program can be "easily" proven, and 80 percent of the remaining subprograms can be "easily" tested. That leaves 4 percent of the subprograms in the difficult-to-verify category.

By setting a switch in our Ada 2012 compiler, the preconditions and postconditions we have written in our subprograms will be checked at runtime.

This simplifies our testing work. We need only develop and run an appropriate set of test cases. An exception is raised whenever an assertion check fails.

The GNATtest tool in combination with the GNAT specific aspect Test_Case may be used to build and run a complete testing harness. This tool is based on AUnit, the Ada version of the xUNIT family of unit test frameworks.

Finally, it is worth saying that irrespective of how you intend to verify your operations, testing can help identify potential issues with proofs and proof can help identify potential issues with tests. If you cannot prove a postcondition, try testing it. You may find that the error is in the contract, not in the code.

8.5 Case Study: Time Stamp Server

In this section we outline a realistic case study to illustrate the use of SPARK in the construction of new software. The latest source for this case study, with additional documentation, can be found on GitHub (Chapin, 2014).

Our application is a secure time stamp server, which we call *Thumper*, implementing the time stamp protocol specified in RFC-3161 (Adams et al., 2001). For the sake of brevity, certain details of the protocol are not fully supported. However, the implementation is complete enough to demonstrate many features of SPARK. In this section we describe the protocol, sketch the architecture of Thumper, and discuss the role SPARK plays in its implementation.

8.5.1 *Time Stamp Protocol*

The time stamp protocol is simple in concept. It provides a way for some person, such as Alice, to obtain a small, cryptographic token that proves a particular document in her possession existed on or before a specific time. Alice can present this token to another person, Bob, for later verification.

More concretely, suppose Alice is a student at a university and Bob is an instructor. Bob requires that a certain assignment be completed by a certain date and time. Alice finishes the assignment and obtains the time stamp token. She then submits her work to Bob via e-mail. Unfortunately, because of some network problem, her message does not arrive in Bob's mailbox until after the due date. Alice can then use the time stamp to prove to Bob that she did, in fact, complete the assignment on time.

The time stamp protocol makes use of three cryptographic concepts that we briefly review here. For more information, consult any textbook on cryptography such as Mao (2004) or Stallings (2014).

A *cryptographic hash* is a relatively small value that can be used to represent a larger document. If a change is made to the document, the hash will, with very high likelihood, be different. A cryptographic hash is similar to a checksum except that it is computationally infeasible for anyone to find a document that generates a particular hash value or modify a document in such a way as to generate the same hash value. When a high quality cryptographic hash algorithm is used, it is also computationally infeasible to find two different documents that generate the same hash value, a property sometimes called *strong collision resistance*.

A *public/private key pair* is a related pair of keys such that material encrypted by the public key can only be decrypted by the corresponding private key. Typically, a user keeps the private key secret but distributes the public key widely allowing people the user does not know to send encrypted messages that only the user can read.

A *digital signature* is a unit of data attached to a message obtained by processing a cryptographic hash of that message with the signer's private key. The signature can be verified by anyone using the corresponding public key. A successful verification shows both that the message was unmodified, because any modification would (with high likelihood) change the hash, and that the signer is authentic because only the owner of the private key can make a signature that is verifiable with the corresponding public key.

Here is how Alice obtains a time stamp for one of her documents using a time stamp server:

1. Alice computes a cryptographic hash H of her document.
2. Alice sends H to the server.
3. The server appends the current time to H and then digitally signs the combination. The result is the time stamp.
4. The server returns the time stamp to Alice.
5. Alice verifies the time stamp by checking the time it contains is reasonable, the hash it contains is still H, and the digital signature on the time stamp is valid.

Later Alice submits her document together with its time stamp to Bob. Bob computes the hash H of the document and verifies that it agrees with the hash in the time stamp. He also verifies the server's digital signature. If Bob believes the server has not been compromised and trusts the server to have an accurate time, he must agree that Alice's document existed at or before the time mentioned in the time stamp.[7]

Even though Alice holds the time stamp, she cannot defeat this protocol. Modifying her document after obtaining the time stamp will change its hash. If she tries to tamper with the time stamp itself to change either the hash or time stored in it, she will invalidate the server's signature. Notice that Alice does not need to reveal her document to the server (only a hash of it), authenticate to the server, or trust the server in any way because she verifies the time stamp when she receives it.

8.5.2 *Architecture, Design, and Implementation*

Clearly, both Alice and Bob would make use of a specialized client program to simplify the handling of the time stamps and the required cryptographic operations. However, here we are only concerned with the time stamp server, Thumper.

During the design and implementation of Thumper we will make two important security-related assumptions. We assume all files stored on the host file system are private to Thumper. This includes especially Thumper's private key. Furthermore, we assume the time returned by the host operating system is correct. Ensuring these assumptions is a problem of system administration rather than of software design and implementation.

Thumper is conceptually simple. It waits for a time stamp request message from the network, computes the desired time stamp, and returns it. Thumper then waits for the next request message. Invalid request messages cause Thumper to generate an error response. However, RFC-3161 has many requirements for precisely how messages are to be formatted. In particular the Distinguished Encoding Rules (DER) of Abstract Syntax Notation 1 (ASN.1) (International Telecommunication Union, 2002) are used.

RFC-3161 is not prescriptive about how messages are to be transported. Thumper uses the User Datagram Protocol (UDP). This is reasonable because both the request and the response are small enough to fit into a single UDP datagram. Thus, there are no concerns about ordering multiple packets or about acknowledgments. The response serves as the acknowledgment to the request. Furthermore, Thumper is an iterative server that processes only one request at a time. This simplifies the implementation and is reasonable because the time required to process a request is small. Also, clients can in no way slow down the operation of the server by, for example, refusing to send required information after the initial request is made.

Thumper makes use of three major supporting services:

- The network
- A cryptography library
- A serial number generator

Thumper abstracts these services into their own packages. The network package provides subprograms for sending and receiving UDP datagrams. We use a non-SPARK Ada library provided by the compiler vendor, GNAT.Sockets. The cryptography package provides a subprogram for making digital signatures. It is built on top of a C library provided by a third party, OpenSSL (OpenSSL Project, 2014a).

RFC-3161 requires that each time stamp created by the server be marked with an integer serial number. Furthermore, the serial number must be unique over the life of the server's deployment; even if the server is shut down and restarted it cannot use serial numbers from previous runs. We implement this requirement by generating serial numbers randomly using a pseudo-random number generator with a large period (2^{64}), seeded by the server's boot time. Although this admits the possibility of creating two time stamps with the same serial number, the probability of doing so is vanishingly small. The serial number generator package makes use of the Ada standard library.

In Section 8.3.4 we presented the six steps of the INFORMED design process. Here we walk through those steps showing how they can be applied to Thumper:

1. *Identification of the system boundary, inputs, and outputs*

The simple structure of Thumper makes this step relatively easy. The server as a whole reads messages from and writes messages to the network. It must also read its private key from the host file system. Finally, we identify a secondary requirement of writing a log file where messages about errors encountered can be stored.

It is possible that a future version of Thumper may have other inputs and outputs. For example, we considered providing remote management through a web interface or the ability to store generated time stamps in a database for auditing purposes. However, security sensitive applications such as Thumper benefit from being as simple as possible. Every input increases the attack surface of the system and makes maintaining security more difficult. Consequently, the current version of Thumper does not support these additional features. For similar reasons, all of Thumper's "configurable" parameters are hard coded; no configuration file is used.

2. *Identification of the SPARK boundary*

The INFORMED design method emphasizes the importance of clearly delineating the boundary between the SPARK and non-SPARK sections of the system. Deciding when to not use SPARK is as important as deciding when to use it. The first step in identifying this boundary is to identify your *verification goals*. These goals represent what you wish to accomplish by using SPARK, and they guide your decision about how to partition your program into SPARK and

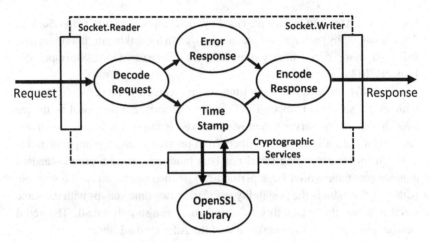

Figure 8.4. Architecture of the SPARK components of Thumper.

non-SPARK sections. In the case of Thumper we identify our verification goals as ensuring freedom from runtime error when processing client input along with ensuring that an invalid or inappropriate time stamp is never returned to the client.

From a security point of view, the critical path through Thumper is that traversed by the messages received from the client on their way to becoming responses sent back to the client. We assume input messages may be malicious and purposely malformed with the intent of crashing the server or coaxing the server to generate an invalid time stamp. In contrast, Thumper's initialization and secondary logging feature are not critical because they do not depend on client input and can thus be reasonably written in full Ada.

Figure 8.4 shows the architecture of the SPARK components of Thumper. The boundary between the SPARK and non-SPARK code is marked by several boundary variable packages that encapsulate the connection to the non-SPARK components. The packages Network.Socket.Reader and Network.Socket.Writer wrap the compiler vendor's network library and provide simplified interfaces. They also hide the underlying network library to prevent vendor specific names from leaking into the rest of the program. A future version of Thumper may use a different networking library or even a different transport mechanism for messages; the SPARK components do not need to know about such changes.

For pragmatic reasons we choose to use the OpenSSL library for Thumper's cryptographic needs. This is not ideal and is particularly worrisome in light of OpenSSL's history of security problems (OpenSSL Project, 2014b). Unfortunately, at the time of this writing no open source cryptographic library supporting digital signature algorithms and written in verified SPARK is available to us. Because OpenSSL is written in C and lies outside of SPARK, we use a boundary variable package Cryptographic_Services that allows SPARK to access OpenSSL's services. It hides all the required C interfacing as well as Thumper's private key in its (non-SPARK) body.

SPARK is used in Thumper, as shown in Figure 8.4, to decode the incoming request messages, check their validity, and encode either an error response or a time stamp response as appropriate. Because of the complexity involved in processing DER encoded ASN.1 messages, there are plenty of opportunities for errors in this process, and we endeavor to show that no runtime exceptions can be raised by Thumper's code.

   3. Identification and localization of state

The boundary variable packages Network.Socket.Reader and Network.Socket. Writer contain external state abstractions that represent the flow of messages from and to the network, respectively.

   The specification of the Reader package is as follows:

```
pragma SPARK_Mode(On);

with Messages;
with Network.Addresses;

package Network.Socket.Reader
  with Abstract_State =>
    (Input_Message_Stream with External =>(Async_Writers  => True,
                                           Effective_Reads  => False))
is
    type Status_Type is (Success,  Failure );

    −− This procedure receives a datagram.
    −− It also returns the source address.
    procedure Receive (Message : out Messages.Network_Message;
                       From    : out Addresses.UDPv4;
                       Status  : out Status_Type)
      with
      Global  => (Input => Input_Message_Stream),
      Depends => ((Message, From, Status) => Input_Message_Stream);
end Network.Socket.Reader;
```

The Messages package is a utility package written in SPARK that provides basic data types and few helper subprograms for manipulating bounded messages of raw data. The package Network.Addresses is a type package written in SPARK that provides an abstract type for UDP addresses. Notice that although the body of this package is implemented in terms of a vendor-provided library, no evidence of that fact is visible here.

The stream of messages coming from the network is modeled using an external state abstraction Input_Message_Stream. The external state abstraction has Async_Writers set to True because messages can appear at any time for reasons outside of Thumper's control. In particular, multiple calls to Receive in succession might return different results. On the other hand, Effective_Reads is set to False because reading a message has no influence on the external system sending them. This is particularly true in the case of the UDP protocol where there is no connection between the sender and receiver of a datagram.

The specification of the Writer package is as follows:

```
pragma SPARK_Mode(On);

with Messages;
with Network.Addresses;


package Network.Socket.Writer
   with Abstract_State =>
     (Output_Message_Stream with External =>(Async_Readers   => True,
                                             Effective_Writes  => True))
is
   type Status_Type is (Success,  Failure );

   -- This procedure sends a datagram to the given  destination  address.
   procedure Send (Message :  in   Messages.Network_Message;
                   To       :  in   Addresses.UDPv4;
                   Status   :  out Status_Type)
      with
        Global   => (In_Out => Output_Message_Stream),
        Depends =>
          (Output_Message_Stream =>+ (Message, To),
           Status  => (Output_Message_Stream, Message));
end Network.Socket.Writer;
```

Here the stream of outgoing messages is modeled using another external state abstraction Output_Message_Stream. In this case, Async_Readers is set to True indicating that some external system is reading the outgoing messages at a time unrelated to Thumper's activities. Also, Effective_Writes is set to True, indicating that every message potentially influences the external system reading them.

Some of the flow dependences on the Send procedure are not immediately obvious. For example, why should the output message stream depend on itself?

This arises because it is possible, in principle, for the output message stream to be temporarily unusable as a result of a filled network queue in the underlying operating system. In that case, sending may fail and the output message stream's state would not be changed. The output message stream returned by the procedure thus depends on the output message stream given to the procedure.

It is important to remember that the contracts used with these boundary variable packages are not verified by SPARK because the bodies of these packages are outside of SPARK and not analyzed by the tools. Careful review of these contracts is thus required if SPARK is to have a proper understanding of the real data and information flows involved.

Following the guideline in the INFORMED report (SPARK Team, 2011), we do not use a single state abstraction to model both input and output streams simultaneously. Using a single state abstraction would confuse analysis. For example, the SPARK tools might conclude that the messages read from the network are somehow related to the messages sent to the network.

There are two variable packages containing state to consider. The first is the pseudorandom number generator used to create serial numbers. Its specification is as follows:

```
pragma SPARK_Mode(On);

package Serial_Generator
  with
    Abstract_State  => State,
    Initializes     => State
is
  type Serial_Number_Type is mod 2**64;

  procedure Next (Number : out Serial_Number_Type)
    with
      Global  => (In_Out => State),
      Depends => ((State, Number) => State);

end Serial_Generator ;
```

The second package containing state is the cryptographic services package that holds the server's private key used to make digital signatures. Its specification is as follows:

```
pragma SPARK_Mode(On);

with Hermes;
```

```
package Cryptographic_Services
  with
      Abstract_State => Key
is
    type Status_Type is (Success, Bad_Key);

    procedure Initialize (Status : out Status_Type)
      with
          Global   => (Output => Key),
          Depends => ((Key, Status) => null);

    function Make_Signature (Data : in   Hermes.Octet_Array)
                              return Hermes.Octet_Array
        with Global => (Input => Key);

end Cryptographic_Services ;
```

Here, Hermes is a package, entirely written in SPARK, containing ASN.1 encoding and decoding facilities. The type Octet_Array in that package holds raw data intended to be part of a DER encoded ASN.1 data stream.

The body of Cryptographic_Services contains all the necessary code to interface to the OpenSSL library, but the use of that library is not visible here. If at some future time a suitable SPARK cryptographic library becomes available, only the body of Cryptographic_Services would need to be updated to use it.

We note that the state held by the two packages described here have significantly different security levels. The key held by Cryptographic_Services is obviously security sensitive information. In contrast, the state of the pseudo-random number generator is much less sensitive because it is only used to derive serial numbers on response messages. It is thus appropriate to store these states in different variable packages rather than, for example, creating a single package to hold all the state in one place.

4. Handling of the initialization of state

The previously described state is initialized in different ways. The network packages are children of Network.Socket, a non-SPARK package that encapsulates a single UDP socket. The specification of Network.Socket is as follows:

```
with Network.Addresses;
private with GNAT.Sockets;
package Network.Socket is
```

```
Network_Error : exception;

procedure Create_And_Bind_Socket (Port : in Addresses.Port_Type);

private
    Socket : GNAT.Sockets.Socket_Type;
end Network.Socket;
```

The procedure Create_And_Bind_Socket initializes the two network streams. It reports failures by way of raising the Network_Error exception, a translation of the vendor specific exception GNAT.Socket_Error. The variable Socket declared in the private section of this package is visible to the (non-SPARK) bodies of the Reader and Writer packages. Here we use a parent package to provide private resources to the two child packages. In reality both message streams use the same underlying socket, yet this organization makes it possible to abstract the streams into different packages as we described earlier.

The Serial_Generator package is initialized at elaboration time, as evidenced by the Initializes aspect on its specification. It uses the system time at start-up to seed the pseudorandom number generator. The Cryptographic_Services package is initialized by the main program by way of a special initialization procedure. It reads the private key from the file system and stores it internally for future use.

5. *Handling of secondary requirements*

At this time Thumper has only one secondary requirement: to create a log of any external errors that arise during operation. We are not concerned with initialization errors. If Thumper fails to initialize, it terminates at once with an appropriate message; such errors do not need to be logged. However, there might be problems receiving or sending on the network and such problems should be recorded to alert the operator and assist with troubleshooting.

The logger is another boundary variable package, not shown in Figure 8.4, with a specification as follows:

```
pragma SPARK_Mode(On);
package Logger
    with
        Abstract_State =>
            (Log_Stream with External => (Async_Readers  => True,
                                          Effective_Writes => True)),
        Initializes  => Log_Stream
is
```

```
    procedure Write_Error (Message : in  String)
      with Global  => (Output => Log_Stream);
```

end Logger;

At elaboration time this package initializes itself by opening a suitable log file.

6. *Implementation of the internal behavior of components*

What remains, of course, is implementing the bodies of the packages mentioned so far along with the core logic of the program. Here we describe a few of highlights of the implementation.

Thumper's main program is not in SPARK. It is mostly concerned with initialization and dealing with any initialization errors. It then calls a procedure Service_Clients where the core functionality of the system resides. The main program, in its entirety, follows:

```
with Ada.Exceptions;
with Ada.Text_IO;

with Cryptographic_Services ;
with Network.Socket;
with SPARK_Boundary;

use Ada.Exceptions;

procedure Thumper_Server is
   use type Cryptographic_Services .Status_Type;

   Crypto_Status :  Cryptographic_Services .Status_Type;
begin
   -- Be sure the key is  available .
   -- This initializes  Cryptographic_Services . Key
   Cryptographic_Services . Initialize  (Crypto_Status);
   if  Crypto_Status /= Cryptographic_Services .Success then
      Ada.Text_IO.Put_Line
         ("*** Unable to  initialize  the cryptographic  library :  missing key?" );
   else
      -- Set up the socket.
      -- This  initializes  the network streams (both input and output).
      Network.Socket.Create_And_Bind_Socket (318);

      SPARK_Boundary.Service_Clients;  -- Infinite loop  services  requests
   end if ;
```

```
exception
   when Ex : Network.Socket.Network_Error =>
      Ada.Text_IO.Put_Line
         ("*** Unable to  initialize  network: " & Exception_Message(Ex));
end Thumper_Server;
```

The package SPARK_Boundary corresponds to the dashed box in Figure 8.4. The Service_Clients procedure executes the material inside that box in an infinite loop, making use of the (boundary) variable packages we described earlier. The specification of SPARK_Boundary is shown as follows:

```
pragma SPARK_Mode(On);

with  Cryptographic_Services ;
with  Logger;
with  Network.Socket.Reader;
with  Network.Socket.Writer;
with  Serial_Generator ;

use Network.Socket;

package SPARK_Boundary is

   procedure  Service_Clients
      with
         Global  =>
            (Input  =>
               (Reader.Input_Message_Stream,  Cryptographic_Services . Key),
            In_Out  =>
               (Logger.Log_Stream,
                Writer. Output_Message_Stream,
                Serial_Generator . State )),
         Depends =>
            (Logger.Log_Stream =>+
               (Reader.Input_Message_Stream, Writer. Output_Message_Stream,
                Cryptographic_Services . Key,  Serial_Generator . State ),
            Writer. Output_Message_Stream =>+
               (Reader.Input_Message_Stream,
                Cryptographic_Services . Key,
                Serial_Generator . State ),
            Serial_Generator . State =>+ Reader.Input_Message_Stream);

end SPARK_Boundary;
```

Notice that the **with** statements exactly mention those packages that are either boundary variable packages or packages containing state. These **with** statements are necessary so that the various abstract states can be used in the data and flow dependency contracts on Service_Clients .

The presence of the logger complicates the dependency contracts. This is unfortunate because the logger is a secondary requirement, and one might prefer that it did not clutter the essential information. Unfortunately, the SPARK tools require that flows to (and, in general from) the logger's state be properly declared as for any other flows.

Some of the flows are surprising. In particular the dependency of the output message stream on itself. This arises because Service_Clients ultimately calls the Send procedure in the Writer package. As explained previously, this procedure might leave the output message stream unchanged. In addition if Service_Clients only gets errors when trying to receive a request, it will never even attempt to write to the output message stream. Thus the output message stream must be an In_Out global item. These details were not fully appreciated when the contracts on Service_Clients were first written. Some adjustments were made during the implementation of Service_Clients as these issues came to light.

It is interesting to note that the flow dependency contract helps with security review. Because attackers can manipulate the input message stream, any items that depend on that stream need to be carefully secured. In this case all outputs are potentially attackable. Of particular interest is the log stream. Is it possible for an attacker to send a malformed request in such a way as to cause a malformed log message to crash the server? This question is particularly interesting in light of the fact that the body of package Logger is not in SPARK. Similarly, could an attacker somehow manipulate the state of the serial number generator by sending appropriately malformed requests?

The Service_Clients procedure itself contains an infinite loop as shown:

```
procedure Service_Clients is
   use type Reader.Status_Type;
   use type Writer.Status_Type;

   Client_Address     : Network.Addresses.UDPv4;

   Network_Request  : Messages.Network_Message;
   Request_Message  : Messages.Message;
   Read_Status      : Reader.Status_Type;

   Response_Message : Messages.Message;
   Network_Response : Messages.Network_Message;
```

```
   Write_Status       : Writer.Status_Type;
begin
   loop
      Reader.Receive (Message => Network_Request,
                      From    => Client_Address,
                      Status  => Read_Status);

      if  Read_Status /= Reader.Success then
         Logger.Write_Error(" Failure reading request message!");
      else
         Request_Message := Messages.From_Network (Network_Request);
         Timestamp_Maker.Create_Timestamp (Request_Message, Response_Message);
         Network_Response := Messages.To_Network (Response_Message);

         Writer.Send (Message => Network_Response,
                      To      => Client_Address,
                      Status  => Write_Status);

         if  Write_Status /= Writer.Success then
            Logger.Write_Error (" Failure sending reply message!");
         end if ;
      end if ;
   end loop;
end  Service_Clients ;
```

The variables Network_Request and Network_Response hold raw octets of type Network.Octet received from and being sent to the network. They are records that carry a fixed size array along with a count of the number of elements in that array actually being used. The variables Request_Message and Response_Message hold raw octets of type Hermes.Octet that contain DER encoded ASN.1 data.

The functions From_Network and To_Network only do type conversions on the data from Network.Octet to Hermes.Octet and vice versa. Although it may seem pedantic to distinguish between different kinds of octets, it makes sense because data on the underlying network may have many forms. Hermes works only with DER encoded ASN.1. But in the future, time stamp messages may be encapsulated in some application protocol such as HTTP. So distinguishing between raw network data and the time stamp messages would be useful in a future version of Thumper.

The procedure Create_Timestamp converts request messages into response messages. Every request generates a response; invalid or malformed requests generate error responses. Create_Timestamp is the heart of the application and is almost purely functional. It accepts one array of octets and returns another.

However, because each generated time stamp is digitally signed and must include a unique serial number, Create_Timestamp needs to use the cryptographic key and the serial number generator. The SPARK declaration of Create_Timestamp is as follows:

```
procedure Create_Timestamp (Request_Message : in   Messages.Message;
                            Response_Message : out Messages.Message)
  with
    Global =>
      (Input  => Cryptographic_Services.Key,
       In_Out => Serial_Generator.State),
    Depends =>
      (Response_Message =>
        (Request_Message, Cryptographic_Services .Key, Serial_Generator .State),
       Serial_Generator .State =>+ null);
```

The bulk of the program is actually inside Create_Timestamp. However, the high degree of purity of the procedure – it rarely references any state – means that its implementation is, in principle, straightforward. We refer you to the Thumper site on GitHub (Chapin, 2014) for the details.

Alternate Designs

It is useful to consider some alternate designs to understand how the concepts we have developed so far apply to them. First, consider the network boundary variable packages Network.Socket.Reader and Network.Socket.Writer. These two packages encapsulate external state abstractions for input from and, respectively, output to the network. For the sake of accurate flow analysis, it is important that differen state abstractions be used for inputs and outputs. Yet creating two separate packages is not strictly necessary even if two state abstractions are to be used. It would be possible to define a single package with two state abstractions. Such an approach might seem more natural particularly in light of the fact that both state abstractions use a common underlying socket.

However, we anticipate that a future version of Thumper may wish to store generated time stamps for auditing. Such a change could be made by replacing the Network.Socket.Writer package body with a different body that also communicates with a database. This change would not affect the Network.Socket.Reader package at all. Two separate packages may seem like overkill, but it does clearly distinguish the inputs and outputs of the system, allowing one to be changed without interfering with the other.

The use of variable packages to hold the key and pseudorandom number generator state could also be changed. In particular, Cryptographic_Services and Serial_Generator could be converted to type packages that provided suitable abstract data types to hold their state. Objects of those types could be declared in the main program and passed to Service_Clients as parameters. However, this does not simplify the dependency contracts on Service_Clients very much. Cryptographic_Services . Key and Serial_Generator . State would no longer be global items, but they would still appear, as parameter names, in the flow dependency contract. Also, Thumper needs neither multiple cryptographic keys nor multiple pseudorandom number generators so the main advantage of using type packages is not required.

Summary

- The conversion of a SPARK 2005 program to SPARK 2014 is straight forward as SPARK 2014 is a superset of SPARK 2005.
- The SPARK tools may be used to perform retrospective analyses of existing Ada code where no SPARK aspects are given.
- The SPARK tools will generate safe over-approximations of data dependency contracts and flow dependency contracts directly from the source code of a program unit.
- More in-depth analyses of legacy Ada code may require moving non-SPARK code segments into child or private child packages.
- Designing to meet your verification goals is a powerful approach to creating quality software. This approach to creating new SPARK programs is called verification driven development.
- Abstraction, encapsulation, information hiding, coupling, and cohesion provide measures of good software design.
- The INFORMED design method was developed especially for applying the strengths of SPARK during this crucial stage of software development.
- The elements of an INFORMED design include variable packages, type packages, utility packages, boundary variable packages, and boundary variable abstraction packages.
- We use Abstract_State aspects to make it known that a package encapsulates state without revealing the implementation details of that state.
- Localizing state and minimizing data flow are major tenets of the INFORMED design method.
- Combining proof and testing is a powerful mechanism for verifying code. As the verification chain is only as strong as its weakest link, our goal is to obtain verification at least as good as can be accomplished with testing alone, but at a lower cost.

9

Advanced Techniques

In this chapter we examine some advanced techniques for proving properties of SPARK programs. Although the approaches we describe here will not be needed for the development of many programs, you may find them useful or even necessary for handling larger, realistic applications.

9.1 Ghost Entities

Ghost entities make it easier to express assertions about a program. The essential property of ghost entities is that they have no effect on the execution behavior of a valid program. Thus, a valid program that includes ghost entities will execute the same with or without them.

9.1.1 *Ghost Functions*

In applications where you are trying to prove strong statements about the correctness of your programs, the expressions you need to write in assertions become very complex. To help manage that complexity, it is desirable to factor certain subexpressions into separate functions, both to document them and to facilitate reuse of them in multiple assertions.

Functions that you create for verification purposes only are called *ghost functions*. The essential property of ghost functions is that they do not normally play any role in the execution of your program.[1] Ghost functions may only be called from assertions such as preconditions, postconditions, and loop invariants. They may not be called from the ordinary, non-assertive portions of your program.

As an example consider the specification of a package Sorted_Arrays that contains subprograms for creating and processing sorted arrays of integers:

```
package Sorted_Arrays is
   type Integer_Array is array( Positive range <>) of Integer;

   -- Sorts the given array.
   procedure Sort (Data : in out Integer_Array )
      with Global => null,
           Post   => (for all J in Data' First .. Data'Last − 1 =>
                       (Data(J) <= Data(J + 1)));

   -- Return index of specified Value if it exists ; zero if Value not in Data.
   function Binary_Search (Data  : in  Integer_Array ;
                           Value : in  Integer ) return Natural
      with Pre => (for all J in Data' First  .. Data'Last − 1 =>
                    (Data(J) <= Data(J + 1)));
end Sorted_Arrays ;
```

Notice that the postcondition of Sort and the precondition of Binary_Search both use the same quantified expression to assert that the array being processed is sorted. Although the expression is not exceptionally unwieldy in this case, it is still somewhat obscure and hard to read. Having it duplicated on two subprograms also hurts the package's maintainability.

Our second version of this specification introduces a ghost function to abstract and simplify the pre- and postconditions on the other subprograms. We use the Boolean aspect Ghost to indicate that the function Is_Sorted is included only for verification purposes.

```
package Sorted_Arrays2 is
   type Integer_Array is array( Positive range <>) of Integer;

   function Is_Sorted (Data : in  Integer_Array ) return Boolean
      with Ghost => True,
           Post  => (Is_Sorted'Result =
                      (for all J in Data' First  .. Data'Last − 1 =>
                        (Data(J) <= Data(J + 1))));

   -- Sorts the given array.
   procedure Sort (Data : in out Integer_Array )
      with Global => null,
           Post   => Is_Sorted (Data);
```

```
-- Return index of specified Value if it exists ; zero if Value not in Data.
function Binary_Search (Data  :  in  Integer_Array ;
                              Value :  in  Integer ) return Natural
   with Pre => Is_Sorted (Data);
end Sorted_Arrays2 ;
```

The postcondition on Sort and the precondition on Binary_Search use the Is_Sorted function rather than the lengthier quantified predicates. They are now clearer and easier to maintain.

The function Is_Sorted is decorated with a postcondition that explains its effect. One might be tempted to use a conditional expression in the postcondition as follows:

```
function Is_Sorted (Data :  Integer_Array ) return Boolean
   with Ghost => True,
      Post  => (if Is_Sorted ' Result then
                  ( for all  J in Data' First  ..  Data'Last − 1 =>
                     (Data(J) <= Data(J + 1))));
```

However, this postcondition is not strong enough. It says nothing about the array if Is_Sorted returns False. In particular, an implementation of Is_Sorted that returns False would always satisfy this postcondition (see the implication entry in Table 5.1). What is required is for Is_Sorted to return true "if and only if" the array is sorted. This equivalence is expressed in our first version with the equality of Is_Sorted ' Result and the qualified expression. To satisfy the postcondition, it is necessary for the truth value of both those things to be the same.

It is not strictly necessary to include a postcondition on Is_Sorted at all. The SPARK tools will understand that the array coming out of Sort passes Is_Sorted , and this is all that is required to send that array to Binary_Search. Exactly what Is_Sorted does is of no immediate concern.

However, exposing the details of what Is_Sorted does might allow the SPARK tools to complete other proofs elsewhere in the program more easily. For example, with the postcondition on Is_Sorted visible, the tools will "know" that the array coming out of Sort has, for example, the property

```
Data(Data' First) <= Data(Data' Last)
```

as a result of the transitivity of <=. In general it is good practice to expose as much information as feasible to the SPARK tools.

Here is a body for the ghost function Is_Sorted :

```
function Is_Sorted (Data : in Integer_Array ) return Boolean is
begin
    return ( for all J in Data'First  ..  Data'Last − 1 =>
             (Data(J) <= Data(J + 1)));
end Is_Sorted ;
```

In this case, the body is essentially a duplication of the postcondition. This is not unusual for ghost functions although it is not required or even universal. It does mean if the assertion policy is Check the test done by Is_Sorted is essentially done twice. The test is done in the body to compute Is_Sorted ' Result and then again in the postcondition. However, if the assertion policy is Ignore, assertions are not executed and the entire Is_Sorted function could be removed from the program by the compiler because it can never be used outside assertion expressions anyway.

A better alternative in this case is to write the Is_Sorted function as an expression function as follows:

```
package Sorted_Arrays3 is
    type Integer_Array  is  array( Positive  range  <>) of Integer;

    function Is_Sorted (Data : in Integer_Array ) return Boolean
    is ( for all  J in Data'First  ..  Data'Last − 1 =>
         (Data(J) <= Data(J + 1)))
      with Ghost  => True;

    −− Sorts the given  array .
    procedure Sort (Data : in out Integer_Array )
      with Global => null,
           Post   => Is_Sorted (Data);

    −− Return index of specified  Value if it  exists ; zero if Value not in Data.
    function Binary_Search (Data  :  in  Integer_Array ;
                            Value :  in  Integer ) return Natural
      with Pre => Is_Sorted (Data);

end Sorted_Arrays3 ;
```

This version has the advantage that no separate body is needed for Is_Sorted because the entire function is implemented in the package specification. Furthermore, the body of an expression function is used to automatically generate a postcondition for the function as explained in Section 6.2.3.

9.1.2 *Ghost Variables*

The aspect Ghost may be applied to variables and constants as well as to functions. Such variables may only be used in verification assertions. They are commonly used in loop invariants. As with ghost functions, the runtime behavior of a valid program is the same with or without the ghost variables. We look at an example with ghost variables and constants in the next section.

9.2 Proof of Transitive Properties

Many properties we need to prove are transitive relations. As an example of such a property and the use of ghost entities, we return to the selection sort procedure. We gave its specification in Section 1.4 and repeat it here:

```
pragma Spark_Mode (On);
package Sorters is

    type Array_Type is array ( Positive range <>) of Integer;

    function Perm (A : in Array_Type;
                   B : in Array_Type) return Boolean
    -- Returns True if A is a permutation of B
      with Global  => null,
           Ghost   => True,
           Import  => True;

    procedure Selection_Sort (Values : in out Array_Type)
    -- Sorts the elements in the array Values in ascending order
      with Depends => (Values => Values),
           Pre     => Values'Length >= 1 and then
                      Values'Last    <= Positive'Last,
           Post    => (for all J in Values' First .. Values'Last − 1 =>
                      Values (J) <= Values (J + 1)) and then
                      Perm (Values'Old, Values);
end Sorters;
```

Procedure Selection_Sort has two postconditions. The first postcondition states that the values returned are in ascending order. The second postcondition uses the ghost function Perm to state that the array returned, Values, is a permutation of the original array, Values' Old. That is, the new array is a reordering of the values in the original array. Without this second postcondition, a sort procedure that was given the integers (5, 7, 3, 3, 8) and returned (5, 5, 5, 5, 5) would be valid.

A common approach to determining whether two arrays are permutations is to sort each array and compare the sorted arrays. As we are using the permutation property to verify our sort procedure, we cannot use the sort to verify the permutation. Another approach is to count the number of each element in each array and compare the counts. As our array components are integers, this approach could require 2^{32} counters for 32-bit integer representations.

We take another approach to show that the result is a permutation of the original. Function Perm is a ghost function. The aspect Import states that the body of the function is external to the SPARK program. Rather than write a body, we will give the proof tool the mathematical rules it needs to verify our permutation postcondition. Here is the complete package body that implements our selection sort:

```
pragma Spark_Mode (On);
package body Sorters is

    function Perm_Transitive (A, B, C : Array_Type) return Boolean
        with Global => null,
             Post   => (if Perm_Transitive ' Result
                            and then Perm (A, B)
                            and then Perm (B, C)
                        then Perm (A, C)),
             Ghost  => True,
             Import => True;


    procedure Swap (Values :  in out Array Type;
                    X      :  in        Positive ;
                    Y      :  in        Positive )
        with Depends => (Values => (Values, X, Y)),
             Pre     => (X in Values'Range and then
                         Y in Values'Range and then
                         X /= Y),
             Post => Perm (Values'Old, Values)    and then
                     (Values (X) = Values'Old (Y) and then
                     Values (Y) = Values'Old (X) and then
                     ( for all J in Values'Range =>
                        ( if J /= X and J /= Y then Values (J) = Values'Old (J))))
    is
        Values_Old : constant Array_Type := Values
            with Ghost => True;
        Temp : Integer ;
```

```ada
begin
   Temp       := Values (X);
   Values (X) := Values (Y);
   Values (Y) := Temp;
   pragma Assume (Perm (Values_Old, Values));
end Swap;


-- Finds the index of the smallest element in the array
function Index_Of_Minimum (Unsorted : in Array_Type) return Positive
   with Pre  => Unsorted'First <= Unsorted'Last,
        Post => Index_Of_Minimum'Result in Unsorted'Range and then
                  (for all J in Unsorted'Range =>
                     Unsorted (Index_Of_Minimum'Result) <= Unsorted (J))
is
   Min : Positive ;
begin
   Min := Unsorted'First ;
   for Index in Unsorted'First  .. Unsorted'Last loop
      pragma Loop_Invariant
        (Min in Unsorted'Range and then
        (for all  J in Unsorted'First  .. Index - 1 =>
           Unsorted (Min) <= Unsorted (J)));

      if Unsorted (Index) < Unsorted (Min) then
         Min := Index;
      end if ;
   end loop;
   return Min;
end Index_Of_Minimum;


procedure Selection_Sort (Values : in out Array_Type) is
   Values_Last : Array_Type (Values'Range)
      with Ghost => True;
   Smallest : Positive ;  -- Index of the smallest value in the unsorted part
begin -- Selection_Sort
   pragma Assume (Perm (Values, Values));
   for Current in Values'First  .. Values'Last - 1 loop
      Values_Last := Values;
      Smallest := Index_Of_Minimum (Values (Current .. Values'Last ));

      if Smallest /= Current then
```

```
       Swap (Values => Values,
             X      => Current,
             Y      => Smallest);
    end if ;

    pragma Assume (Perm_Transitive (Values'Loop_Entry, Values_Last, Values ));

    pragma Loop_Invariant (Perm (Values'Loop_Entry, Values ));
    pragma Loop_Invariant    -- Simple partition property
      (( for all J in Current .. Values'Last =>
           Values (Current) <= Values (J)));
    pragma Loop_Invariant    -- order property
      (( for all J in Values' First .. Current =>
           Values (J) <= Values (J + 1)));
  end loop;
  end Selection_Sort ;
end Sorters ;
```

The heart of the permutation verification is in procedure Swap starting on line 14. Its postcondition states that (1) the resulting array is a permutation of the original array; (2) the values at index locations X and Y were swapped; and (3) the rest of the values in the array are unchanged.

We know that swapping two elements in an array creates a permutation of the original array. However, the SPARK tools do not know this fact. We use pragma Assume on line 34 with the ghost function Perm to state this fact. After swapping two elements, the SPARK tools will assume that the result is a permutation of the original. We used the ghost constant Values_Old to hold a copy of the original array. We could not use Values'Old as the 'Old attribute can only be used in postconditions.[2]

Next we have to tell the SPARK tools that after multiple element swaps the final array is a permutation of the original array. This is a transitivity property: if A and B are permutations and B and C are permutations, then A and C are permutations. We use another ghost function, Perm_Transitive defined on lines 4–11, to express this transitivity. The postcondition of this function states the transitivity property. A function postcondition should always mention the result of the function so we have also included it. As the postcondition is all we need for our proof, we included the aspect Import so we do not have to write a body for this function.

The pragma Assume on line 78 tells the proof tools that after each swap, the result is still a permutation of the original. The three parameters of the call to Perm_Transitive in this pragma are the original array (its value prior to the start of the loop), the array before the last swapping, and the current array. We use the ghost variable Values_Last to hold a copy of the array prior to swapping elements.

There is still one more fact we need to give to the proof tools: an array is a permutation of itself. This fact is given in the **pragma** Assume on line 67.

As usual, we need to help the proof tools prove our postconditions by writing invariants for our loops. While you may only write one invariant for each loop, you may use multiple Loop_Invariant pragmas as long as they are consecutive. The three pragmas on lines 80–86 could be written as a single pragma using the conjunctive operator **and then** as was done in the function Index_Of_Minimum. Notice how the loop invariants in both Selection_Sort and Index_Of_Minimum support their postconditions.

The approach taken in this example may be applied to any proof requiring a transitivity property. Let us look at a more general example. In the specification,

- declare the property for which there is transitivity as a ghost function without a body and
- use that property in the postcondition of the change operation you wish to prove maintains that property.

See if you can pick out these two steps in our sorting package specification (page 330).

In the package body,

- declare the transitivity relation as a ghost function without a body (see lines 4–11 of the sorting package body),
- add a **pragma** Assume to the beginning of the change operation body to state that the property applies to itself (see line 67 of the sorting package body),
- declare a ghost variable (see lines 63–64 of the sorting package body) and assign the current value to it prior to applying a change (see line 69), and
- add a **pragma** Assume with the transitive relation ghost function after carrying out a change to indicate that the property applies to the current value (see line 78 of the sorting package body).

Let us look at a simpler example that illustrates this approach.[3] Procedure Change makes some modification to its parameter X with the postcondition that the transitive property, given by procedure Property, holds.

```
package Transitive
   with SPARK_Mode => On
is

   function Property (X, Y : in Natural) return Boolean
      with Global => null,
```

```
          Ghost  => True,
          Import => True;

   procedure Change (X : in out Natural)
      with Post => Property (X'Old, X);


end Transitive ;
```

Here is the body of this package. Notice that we have no idea about the meaning of Property, just that it is transitive.

```
package body Transitive
  with SPARK_Mode => On
is

   function Prop_Transitive (A, B, C : in Natural) return Boolean
   -- Define the  transitivity  of Property
      with Global  => null,
           Post    => (if Prop_Transitive ' Result
                          and then Property (A, B)
                          and then Property (B, C)
                       then Property (A, C)),
           Ghost  => True,
           Import => True;

   procedure Shift (X : in out Natural)
      with Post => Property (X'Old, X)
   is
   begin
      -- Tell the proof tool that Property holds after  this  operation
      pragma Assume (Property (X, X / 2));
      X := X / 2;
   end Shift ;

   procedure Change (X : in out Natural) is
      X_Last : Natural
         with Ghost => True;
   begin
      -- Tell the proof tool that the Property applies to an unchanged value
      pragma Assume (Property (X, X));
      for I in 1 .. 10 loop
         pragma Loop_Invariant (Property (X'Loop_Entry, X));
         X_Last := X;
         Shift (X);
```

```
      -- Tell the proof tool that
      --   because the Property holds for X'Loop_Entry and X_Last and
      --   the Property holds for X'Last and X then the property
      --   must hold for X'Loop_Entry and X
      pragma Assume (Prop_Transitive (X'Loop_Entry, X_Last, X));
   end loop;
 end Change;

end Transitive ;
```

Until recently, the default theorem provers were not able to complete the proof of our selection sort. And they took a while to prove our simpler transitive property example. However, the Z3 theorem prover was able to prove both of these packages in a very short amount of time. See Section 9.3.2 for a brief discussion of alternative theorem provers.

9.3 Proof Debugging

As a programmer you have no doubt learned a variety of techniques for finding and fixing bugs in your programs. You have probably also learned that program debugging can be difficult and requires significant practice. Special debugging tools exist to simplify finding and removing bugs, yet such tools also require practice to use well.

When you start to formally verify your programs using SPARK you need to develop skills for a new kind of debugging: proof debugging. If a proof is unsuccessful, how do you find out what is wrong and how do you fix it? Of course, if the proof is unsuccessful because the program has an error, fixing the error is a necessary first step. It is a surprisingly easy step to overlook –

- If a proof fails, check carefully that the code is right before trying to fix the proof.

Even before reviewing the code itself, it is worth stepping back to be sure the formal specification of that code is correct. For example, you may have implemented a subprogram properly, but if you stated the postcondition wrong, it may not prove. Here the problem is not in your implementation but in your specification of what the subprogram is intended to do. It is surprisingly easy to overlook this step as well –

- If a proof fails, check carefully that your assertions state what you intend.

However, a proof might fail even on a correctly specified and implemented code because of insufficient information in your program or because of limited theorem prover technology. In this section we talk about various methods of proof debugging that help you diagnose such cases and fix them. However, be aware that like any debugging activity, proof debugging requires practice and experience. The best way to learn how to do it is to work through many troublesome proofs.

9.3.1 *Proof Workflow*

Imagine that you have just completed a package of SPARK code that successfully compiles as Ada and that successfully passes examination and so is free of flow issues. You are now ready to prove the code is free of runtime errors and that it obeys its pre- and postconditions and other assertions. Unfortunately when you run the SPARK tools, you find that some proofs fail. How should you proceed?

The automatic theorem prover that backs the SPARK tools requires a certain amount of time to complete the proof of each verification condition. Unfortunately it is not possible, in general, to set a specific limit on how much time is required. Verification conditions that are false will never prove no matter how long the theorem prover works (assuming the theorem prover is sound). But even verification conditions that are true may not be provable by any given theorem prover or, even if they are, may require a very long time for the proof to complete.

The problem with allowing the theorem prover to work for a long time is that many failing verification conditions will require you to wait an inordinate amount of time for the proving process to finish. For example, if your package has fifty verification conditions of which ten fail to prove and you set your theorem prover to work for a maximum of sixty seconds on each verification condition, you may have to wait ten minutes to get past the failing verification conditions – in addition to whatever time the prover spends on the other proofs. This makes the process of editing and reproving your code tedious because each time you try to prove your code you must wait for all the failing verification conditions to time out.

The SPARK tools mitigate this problem to some extent by caching proof results on a per-subprogram basis. If you edit only one subprogram in your package, it is only that subprogram that is reprocessed. The proofs (failed or otherwise) done in the unchanged subprograms are not recomputed. However, this is not as helpful if you are working in a complex subprogram with many failing verification conditions. Thus, your first line of defense when trying to prove complicated code is to avoid complex subprograms –

- Split complicated subprograms into several simpler ones.

In addition to taking better advantage of the SPARK tools' proof caching features, this also tends to reduce the complexity of the verification conditions by reducing the number of paths in each subprogram, thus, speeding up their processing. As an additional bonus, it can make your program easier for a human to understand as well.

We recommend at first using a relatively short timeout, say five seconds, on the theorem prover. This will abort the prover on failing verification conditions quickly and gives you a quicker turnaround time in your editing cycle. Unfortunately this also means some proofs will fail that might succeed if given more time. As you work with your code and fix "easy" failing proofs by, for example, adding necessary preconditions or loop invariants, you can gradually increase the prover's timeout. It is reasonable to spend twenty or even thirty seconds on each verification condition as the number of failing verification conditions declines, depending on your patience. The longer timeout by itself may allow other proofs to succeed with no additional work on your part –

- Start with a short timeout on the prover, but increase it as the number of failing verification conditions drops.

Sometimes you will encounter a verification condition that can be proved using an exceptionally long timeout of, perhaps, many minutes. It may be possible to prove such a verification condition more quickly by changing your code. Using extremely long timeout values should only be done as a last resort. However, if nothing else is working and you are confident that your code is actually correct, trying a timeout value of ten or twenty minutes or more may be successful.

Of course it also helps if your development system is fairly powerful. Ten seconds on one machine might get more work done than two minutes on another. In addition, the SPARK tools support multicore systems. You can set the number of processors used by GNATprove with a switch on the command line or in the GNAT project properties.

In the version of the SPARK tools available at the time of this writing, each verification condition is analyzed by a single thread. Running, for example, four threads at once allows the tools to process four verification conditions in parallel, but each verification condition by itself is not accelerated. A single verification condition that requires many minutes to prove will still require many minutes regardless of how many threads you use –

- Use your multi-core processor to make long timeouts more tolerable by allowing the SPARK tools to work on several difficult proofs simultaneously.

9.3.2 *Alternate Theorem Provers*

At the time of this writing, the SPARK tools actually use two theorem provers each time you launch a proof: CVC4 (New York University, 2014) and Alt-Ergo (OCamlPro, 2014). You can also download and install other provers. Different provers have different strengths and weaknesses. You may find some verification conditions provable by one prover but not others. In fact, this is the reason the SPARK tools ship with two provers that are used together. Yet even if two provers both discharge a verification condition, there might be considerable difference in the time required or memory consumed to do so. Furthermore, theorem proving is an evolving technology so the capabilities and performance of provers used in the future are likely to be better than that available today.

As an example, until recently we were not able to prove the selection sort given in Section 9.2 with these two provers, even with very long timeouts. We discovered that the Z3 theorem prover (Bjørner, 2012) could prove this procedure with a very short timeout. However, a new version of CVC4 was also able to prove this code –

- Try using alternate theorem provers to see how they fare against your difficult verification conditions.

Section 9.2 of the *SPARK 2014 Toolset User's Guide* (SPARK Team, 2014b) provides information on using alternative theorem provers. GNATprove can use any theorem prover that is supported by the Why3 platform.[4] To use another prover, it must be listed in your .why3.conf configuration file. The command `why3config --detect-provers` can be used to search your PATH for any supported provers and add them to your .why3.conf configuration file. Any prover name configured in your .why3.conf file can be used as an argument to switch `--prover` when running GNATprove from the command line or entered into the "Alternate prover" box when running GNATprove from GPS. You can specify that multiple provers be used by listing their names separated by commas.

Theorem provers all endeavor to be sound in the sense that they should never claim to have proved a false verification condition. Thus if any one prover claims to have discharged a verification condition, it is reasonable for you to say it has been proved. This does assume, of course, that all the provers you use are themselves error free. Using multiple provers increases the size of your *trusted computing base*, defined here as the body of software that needs to be correct for you to have faith in the validity of your proofs. Clearly that is a disadvantage of using multiple provers, but we feel that the advantages of doing so generally outweigh the disadvantages.

9.3.3 *General Techniques*

The previous discussion is mostly about different ways to run the tools. In this and the following subsections we talk about ways to modify your program to help difficult proofs go through. Here we make a few general observations that can be helpful to consider. In the later subsections we discuss more active techniques of proof debugging –

- Use types and subtypes that are as specific as possible.

Types such as Integer or Float are almost never the right choice. Instead you should define types that encode as much information about your problem as possible and then use those types. The built-in subtypes Natural and Positive are sometimes appropriate, but often you can do better than that. For example:

```
subtype Class_Size_Type   is Natural  range 0 .. 500;
subtype Header_Size_Type is  Positive range 20 .. 40;
subtype Student_ID_Type is  String(1 .. 9);
subtype Extended_Integer  is Very_Longs.Very_Long(20);
```

Many proofs are greatly simplified if the SPARK tools have knowledge about the constraints that are really being used. For example, computing the average $(A + B)/2$ of two Positive values may overflow, but computing the average of two Class_Size_Type values will not because the computation is done in Class_Size_Type's base type (likely Integer). Similarly, proving that X/Y does not entail division by zero is trivial if Y's subtype does not allow the zero value. While tight constraints may make certain proofs more complicated, in the long run they simplify the overall proving process tremendously. A corollary of this rule is that unconstrained types, such as unconstrained array types, tend to make the proofs harder. Although they can be very useful for writing general purpose code, do not use them unless they are really necessary –

- Verification is typically easier if the code is less general.

Many subprograms are written with assumptions about the nature of their inputs. The SPARK tools cannot know these assumptions unless you make them explicit using preconditions. Suitable preconditions will often allow difficult proofs in the subprogram's body to go through because more information is now available to the tools when analyzing the body. Of course, strong preconditions do add proof obligations at the call site, but probably those are proofs that should have been done anyway –

- Add strong preconditions.

Preconditions and tightly specified subtypes are really two ways of saying the same thing. Both entail bringing more information into a subprogram body.

Preconditions can express relationships between inputs and are thus more general and have a heavier weight. It is usually better to use subtypes when it is possible to do so and resort to preconditions for the situations in which Ada's subtyping is insufficiently expressive.[5]

Many subprograms with loops will need loop invariants to be fully proved. Writing good loop invariants can be tricky. However, if you find difficult verification conditions inside or past a loop, it is likely that a loop invariant is what you need. Of course, loop invariants also add their own proof obligations, but that is often a necessary cost for getting the other proofs to work –

- Add loop invariants.

You can get any verification condition to prove by adding an appropriate Assume pragma. You might convince yourself that the assumption you want to make is always valid and so be tempted to do this –

- Avoid using Assume.

See Section 6.3.3 for a discussion about why the Assume pragma is dangerous. That said, Assume does have a role to play in the proof debugging process as we describe in the next section and in conveying to the SPARK tools information that would ordinarily be outside their knowledge such as when we proved transitive properties in Section 9.2.

9.3.4 *Containing Proof Problems*

Although uninhibited use of the Assume pragma can be dangerous, we now describe a powerful way to use it temporarily while debugging a failing proof. The procedure can be described with three steps:

1. As always, when trying to fix a failing proof, try to understand why the code looks correct to you. For example, imagine trying to explain to someone else why the code is correct.
2. Temporarily add an Assume pragma to the code that embodies your understanding of what makes the code correct. Adjust your assumption until the SPARK tools are able to complete the previously failing proof.
3. If the assumption still looks reasonable to you after any adjustments you made to it, try changing it to an Assert pragma. If the SPARK tools are able to prove the assertion, you are done. If not, try changing the assumption, or moving the assumption to a different place, or even repeating the process by using a second assumption to assist with proving the newly placed assertion.

In some cases you may find the only way to get a difficult proof to succeed is to make assumptions that are entirely unreasonable. This is a strong indication that there may, in fact, be something wrong with your code or with your assertions. The nature of the assumption you have to make, and where you have to make it, can help you find the fault.

We recommend using assumptions for this process rather than assertions directly because the SPARK tools will not attempt to prove an assumption and that speeds up the analysis of your program. If instead you used an assertion immediately and if the tools failed to prove both the assertion and the original verification condition, you end up waiting twice as long before you can try again. This is particularly an issue if you are using long timeouts. Just be sure you convert the assumption into an assertion before you are done.

This approach could be called *backward tracing* because it involves starting at the failing proof and moving backward through the code until you find the assertion(s) you need. For example, suppose the program contained an assignment statement such as

```
X := A/B;
```

Suppose the proof that B $/=$ 0 is failing. You can "fix" this proof by using an assumption such as

```
pragma Assume (B /= 0);
X := A/B;
```

Of course, as soon as you convert the assumption to an assertion that assertion will immediately fail to prove and you will have gained nothing. However, if you move backward through the program flow, you may be able to find a place where you can say something more meaningful. For example, showing a bit more context in our hypothetical program gives

```
B := F(X);
if  B <= 0 then
    C := G(X) + 1;
    pragma Assume (C /= 1);
    B := C - 1;
end if ;
X := A/B;
```

In this case if the **if** block is skipped, B must be greater than zero. Otherwise, if we assume C receives a value that is not one from the expression G(X) + 1, all is well. In this case converting the assumption to an assertion may still fail to prove, but the exercise perhaps reveals that G's postcondition is inadequately specified. For example, you might find yourself saying, "That is not a problem because G always returns a positive value and any positive value plus one cannot be one." The fix to the failing proof might be as simple as adding a postcondition to G such as

```
Post => G'Result > 0;
```

Of course the real problem might be that G's result type is not declared appropriately. Perhaps it was declared as Integer but instead should be Positive, or even better, some more constrained subtype of Positive.

This example is simple and highly contrived. However, it illustrates the general approach of exploring the paths leading to the troublesome proof by injecting suggestive assumptions into those paths until the proof can be made to work. The assumptions can then be converted to assertions or at least guide other changes that need to be made in the program. As hinted here, the method can often reveal problems in remote parts of the program or help you uncover faults you missed.

Another similar approach that could be called *forward tracing* entails starting at the beginning of the program flow, adding assertions (not assumptions) that are "obviously" true, and working toward the failing proof. Each assertion that you add can contain progressively more information and be readily proved using the assertions before it, until the amount of information available to the tools by the time the flow reaches the failing verification condition is sufficient to complete the difficult proof. This approach is similar to proving a difficult theorem in mathematics by first proving a series of increasily strong lemmas that ultimately make the final proof straightforward. Adding assumptions or assertions in this way is the proof debugging equivalent of adding debugging print statements to your program.

As with ordinary debugging, finding the problem is really only the first step toward solving it. Often the more difficult step is deciding on the most appropriate fix. Should more suitable types be declared and used? Should a runtime test be added using a conditional statement? Should pre- or postconditions be adjusted? All of these choices have the potential to affect significant parts of your program. For example, adding a stronger postcondition on a procedure will increase the burden of proof inside that procedure. If that, in turn, requires the procedure to have a stronger precondition, more proof obligations may be created throughout the code base.

9.3.5 *Partitioning Unproved Code*

Sometimes completing the proof of certain verification conditions is infeasible for one reason or another. Yet you may still have confidence about the code in question as a result of rigorous testing, code review, or other reasons. Having program units with failing proofs is unsightly. It can also be hazardous because you become insensitive to the repeated ignorable messages from the tools. If the messages change or a new message appears that is not ignorable, you may not notice. Thus, it is highly desirable to have program units partitioned into those that prove cleanly and those that are not intended to be SPARK.

The SPARK tools do provide a means for suppressing warnings using **pragma** Warnings and for justifying failed proofs using **pragma** Annotate. See the *SPARK 2014 Toolset User's Guide* (SPARK Team, 2014b) for more information. Of course, suppressing messages should be done cautiously and only after careful review or concentrated testing provides evidence of correctness.

In cases where a larger block of code contains numerous unproved verification conditions, or is even outside of SPARK, it may be more appropriate to factor the unproved code into a separate unit. This can help draw attention to the difficult code as a subject for future review. The Ada feature of private child packages is particularly useful in this context. We illustrate the technique with a simple example.

In an earlier version the SPARK tools did not have a good understanding of the effect of the bit manipulation operations.[6] As a result, proving verification conditions related to those operations was often problematic.

Suppose one wanted to create a package implementing serveral network protocols. It would be reasonable to organize such a potentially large package as a collection of child packages working together. The top-level parent package might include declarations of interest to the entire system such as declarations of fundamental types representing the basic units of data flowing over the network. A partial specification of such a package Network follows:

```
package Network
    with SPARK_Mode => On
is
    type Octet        is mod 2**8;
    type Double_Octet is mod 2**16;
end Network;
```

Children of this package might implement various network protocols such as, for example, TCP, UDP, or application protocols like SMTP. Assume that various helper subprograms that are useful when implementing multiple protocols are factored out into a child package Network.Helpers. For sake of illustration, suppose that package contained a procedure Split16 that separated a 16-bit value into an 8-bit most significant octet and an 8-bit least significant octet. One might attempt to write that procedure as follows:

```
package body Network.Helpers0
   with SPARK_Mode => On
is

   function Shift_Right (Value :  in  Double_Octet;
                            Count :  in  Natural) return Double_Octet
      with Import => True,
           Convention => Intrinsic;

   procedure Split16 (Value :  in   Double_Octet;
                       MSB :  out Octet;
                       LSB  :  out Octet) is
   begin
      MSB := Octet (Value and 16#00FF#);
      LSB := Octet (Shift_Right (Value, 8));
   end Split16;
end Network.Helpers0;
```

Of course, a realistic package Network.Helpers would likely contain many other subprograms of varying complexity. Function Shift_Right has two aspects. The Boolean aspect Import tells us and the tools that the body of this function is defined in a foreign language that is imported into our Ada program. The aspect Convention names the foreign language. In Section 7.2 we used Convention => C to say that the body of a subprogram was written in C. In this case, the Convention specified is Intrinsic . This convention means that the body of the subprogram is provided by the compiler itself, usually by means of an efficient code sequence (usually a single machine instruction), and the user does not supply an explicit body for it. Intrinsic operations available with the GNAT compiler are listed in Section 2.10.2 of the *GNAT User's Guide* (GNAT, 2015b).

The desire is to write as much of the network protocol implementations in SPARK as possible. However, the older version of the SPARK tools had difficulty proving, for example, that the conversion of Value and 16#00FF# to an Octet will not raise Constraint_Error because it did not understand the significance of the masking operation. All the tools saw was that the type being converted, Double_Octet, might have a value that would not fit into Octet. Similar comments apply to the use of Shift_Right to find the least significant byte. To get around this, we can move the problematic constructs into a separate package as follows:

```
pragma SPARK_Mode(On);
private package Network.Bit_Operations is
```

```
-- Returns the least  significant  byte  in  a  16-bit value.
function TakeLSB_From16 (Value : in Double_Octet) return Octet
   with
      Inline => True,
      Global => null;

-- Returns the most  significant  byte  in  a  16-bit value.
function TakeMSB_From16 (Value : Double_Octet) return Octet
   with
      Inline => True,
      Global => null;
end Network.Bit_Operations;
```

The aspect Inline applied to the two functions in this package specification requests that the compiler replace subprogram calls with copies of the subprogram. This substitution typically improves the execution time and stack memory usage but increases the size of the program. Here is the body of this package:

```
pragma SPARK_Mode(Off);
package body Network.Bit_Operations is

   function Shift_Right (Value : in Double_Octet;
                         Count : in Natural) return Double_Octet
      with
      Import => True,
      Convention => Intrinsic;

   function TakeLSB_From16 (Value : in Double_Octet) return Octet is
   begin
      return Octet (Value and 16#00FF#);
   end TakeLSB_From16;

   function TakeMSB_From16 (Value : in Double_Octet) return Octet is
   begin
      return Octet ( Shift_Right (Value, 8));
   end TakeMSB_From16;

end Network.Bit_Operations;
```

This package has a specification with SPARK_Mode set to On so that it can be used from SPARK code. However, the body has SPARK_Mode set to Off as a

way of explicitly saying that its code is not subject to proof. The Network.Helpers
package is now

```
with Network.Bit_Operations;
use  Network.Bit_Operations;
package body Network.Helpers
   with SPARK_Mode=> On
is
   procedure Split16 (Value : in   Double_Octet;
                      MSB   : out Octet;
                      LSB   : out Octet) is
   begin
      MSB := TakeMSB_From16 (Value);
      LSB := TakeLSB_From16 (Value);
   end Split16;
end Network.Helpers;
```

This new version proves easily as all the types match without conversions.

Notice that Network.Bit_Operations is a private child package. This is stated
by the use of **private** in its specification. Private children are commonly used
in Ada as a way of factoring out internal support facilities from a collection of
related packages. See Section 3.5.1 for more information. Here we use a private
child to encapsulate the unprovable code needed by some other package(s)
allowing the bulk of the code base to be proved cleanly.

9.3.6 *When All Else Fails*

If you are completely unable to get a verification condition to prove after trying
the techniques described in this section, you can instead resort to testing to
explore the issue. We discuss this in Section 8.4. Here, the value of SPARK is in
the focus it provides. The unproved verification conditions must be carefully
covered by test cases, whereas tests to cover the proved aspects of the code are
less critical and can be given a lower priority –

• Use testing to cover unproved verification conditions.

9.4 SPARK Internals

In this section we give an overview of how the SPARK tools work internally. Our
intention is not to provide a detailed description of the theory and operation of
the tools, but rather to give you a sense of what they are doing so you can be a

more effective tool user. We also hope to interest you in learning more about how to use the advanced techniques made possible by the SPARK architecture.

We illustrate the internal operation of the tools by way of a short example. Consider a package Workspaces that contains a number of utility subprograms for manipulating unconstrained arrays of natural numbers. An abbreviated specification for that package might be as follows:

```
pragma SPARK_Mode (On);
package Workspaces is
    type Workspace_Type is array ( Positive range <>) of Natural;
    function Generate_Workspace (Size :  in  Positive ) return Workspace_Type;
end Workspaces;
```

The function Generate_Workspace returns an array of the specified size initialized in a specific way. In particular, all array elements in the first half of the array are initialized to their index values, and all array elements beyond the halfway point are initialized with the same values in descending order. For example, a call to Generate_Workspace(6) returns the array (1, 2, 3, 3, 2, 1).

To keep the example simple from a verification standpoint we do not provide a postcondition for the function. However, we will verify that our implementation is free of runtime errors. Our first attempt at an implementation follows:

```
pragma SPARK_Mode (On);
package body Workspaces is

    function Generate_Workspace (Size :  in  Positive ) return Workspace_Type is
        Workspace : Workspace_Type(1 .. Size) := (others => 0);
    begin
        for J in 1 .. Size / 2 loop
            Workspace (J) := J;
            Workspace ((Size + 1) − J) := J;
        end loop;
        return Workspace;
    end Generate_Workspace;

end Workspaces;
```

The SPARK tools are unable to prove that the computation of Size + 1 will not overflow. This attempted proof shows a real problem with the implementation. Because Natural'Last is the same as largest value of Natural's base type (using GNAT's default overflow options), adding one to Size might, in fact, cause an overflow. But what proof are the tools actually trying to complete and how are they trying to do it?

The SPARK tools make use of a program verification system called Why3 (Bobot et al., 2011). The Why3 tools accept as input a language called WhyML that provides many facilities similar to other ML family languages such as Standard ML or Objective Caml. WhyML programs have executable semantics and could, in principle, be run like any other program.

WhyML was developed as an intermediate language for software verification. WhyML augments the usual ML language elements with extensive features for expressing pre- and postconditions, loop invariants, and other assertions similar to the ones available in SPARK. WhyML also supports the ability to specify and use various *theories* about the properties of types and data structures. The Why3 system includes a predefined library of theories for commonly used entities.

The main SPARK tool, GNATprove, translates each unit it analyzes into a collection of WhyML modules, with one module for each subprogram analyzed. This module, along with extensive supporting material, is written into a file (`workspaces.mlw` for our example) in the proof folder for the project. By default the proof folder is the `gnatprove` folder in the project's build output folder.

As an example of some of the supporting material created for SPARK programs, consider the following WhyML module describing the Ada built-in type Natural:

```
module Standard__natural
  use import " _gnatprove_standard" . Main
  use import " int" . Int
  use          " _gnatprove_standard" . Integer

  type natural " bounded_type"
  function  first :  int  = 0
  function  last :  int  = 2147483647
  predicate in_range (x  :  int )  =
    ( (  first  <= x ) /\ ( x <= last ) )

  clone  export  " ada__model" . Static_Discrete  with
  type t  = natural,
  function  first  = first ,
  function  last  = last,
  predicate in_range  = in_range
end
```

Here, various library theories are imported, including some provided by the SPARK tools to supplement those available in the stock Why3 platform. A type natural is introduced along with functions returning the lower and upper bound of that type. In addition, a predicate is defined that takes an integer and returns true if the integer is in the bounds of the type. We note that in WhyML integers have arbitrary precision and thus model true mathematical integers. Finally, the Static_Discrete theory is cloned with the type natural substituted for Static_Discrete's type t and similarly for functions first and last and predicate in_range. The result is a full logical description of the Ada type Natural as a discrete type.

All standard Ada types are provided in this way in addition to types defined in the program itself. In this example, this includes the unconstrained array type Workspace_Type, which is described by cloning a library Unconstr_Array theory. Anonymous types used in the program are given tool-generated names and described as well. In the example, the dynamic subtype used to specify the bounds on the array Workspace is given the name TTworkspaceSP1 and described by cloning a library Dynamic_Discrete theory.

The WhyML module created to check contracts and freedom from runtime errors of the SPARK function Generate_Workspace appears in workspaces.mlw after all the supporting definitions. The SPARK tools do not format the WhyML in a human-friendly way, making the code difficult to read. However, WhyML is intended to be producible by humans as some users of the Why3 system write WhyML directly. With more natural names and better formatting, it is clearer that the WhyML program is a translation of the SPARK subprogram with all checks made explicit.

The following fragment of WhyML is taken from the module created from Generate_Workspace. To promote readability, the names have been greatly simplified and the formatting arranged suggestively.

```
1   workspace :=
2     Array__1 . set
3       (! workspace)
4
5     ( let  workspaces_0 =
6       (( "VC_OVERFLOW_CHECK"
7         ( integer . range_check_ (( positive . to_int ( size )) + 1))) − !j)
8       in
9       (( assert
10        { ( "VC_INDEX_CHECK"
11          ((( integer . to_int  workspace_first ) <= workspaces_0) /\
12           (workspaces_0 <= (integer. to_int  workspace_last )))) };
13        workspaces_0)))
14
15     ( natural . of_int (! j ));
```

Understanding WhyML also requires a familiarity with the syntax and semantics of ML-like languages in general. The preceding expression was generated from the SPARK assignment statement

```
Workspace ((Size + 1) − J) := J;
```

The code creates a new version of the Workspace array by using a function set to set one of the elements of the existing array. In ML-like languages function arguments are separated by spaces, here shown as blank lines. The first argument on line 3 is the existing Workspace array. The name workspace is actually a kind of pointer, and the ! operator is used to dereference that pointer.

The second argument to the function on lines 5–13 is the result of a "let expression" that creates a temporary variable workspaces_0 initialized by (Size + 1) − J and ultimately just evaluates to that variable on line 13. GNATprove inserted an overflow check into the evaluation of Size + 1 using a range-checking helper function. Finally, before workspaces_0 is returned, an assertion is used to check that its value is in the range of the array's index subtype.

The third argument to the set function on line 15 is just the value of J used on the right-hand side of the original assignment statement. Notice that no check is needed here because the type of J at the SPARK level guarantees its value must be in range of the array element.

The Why3 tools can convert WhyML directly into code in the Objective Caml programming language. Thus, GNATprove together with the Why3 tools constitute a kind of SPARK to OCaml compiler. However, of greater interest to us is the use of theorem provers. The Why3 tools extract from the WhyML "proof tasks" based on the requested checks and using other information in the program (not shown in the previous example). These proof tasks are then processed by Why3 into a form that can be read as input by a theorem prover. This processing is guided by a Why3 driver.

Different theorem provers have different requirements on the kinds of logics they can accept as input. It is the job of the Why3 driver to transform the proof tasks extracted from the WhyML program into a form suitable for the prover being driven.

In this case the overflow check fails to prove because overflow might, in fact, occur. The code is easily fixed by rearranging the order of operations in the expression (Size + 1) − J to (Size − J) + 1. This change results in correponding changes to the generated WhyML that allow the proof to succeed.

Why use an intermediate verification system such as Why3? Why not just generate proof tasks directly from the SPARK code in a format suitable for the theorem prover to process? In fact, that is exactly what the SPARK 2005 tools did. However, the architecture of SPARK 2014 is much more flexible and extensible. It can also capitalize better on advances in proof technology. For example, to support a new theorem prover one only needs to create a suitable Why3 driver for it. This could even be done by a third party; no changes to GNATprove are required. The SPARK tools ship with Why3 drivers for several popular theorem provers, and this is the basis of how the tools support multiple provers.

Also, it is possible to directly interact with the underlying tools at the Why3 level. Consider, for example, asking the SPARK tools to prove a mathematical property about trigonometry functions such as the Pythagorean identity

Sin(X)*Sin(X) + Cos(X)*Cos(X) = 1.0

Even if we set aside the difficulties associated with floating point arithmetic, it is not a simple matter to write suitable (provable) postconditions for Sin and Cos that would allow the above to be proved. The Pythagorean identity is a consequence of an underlying mathematical theory relating the two functions. To illustrate, suppose Cos was declared as follows:

```
function Cos(X : Float) return Float
  with Post => Sin(X)*Sin(X) + Cos'Result*Cos'Result = 1.0;
```

The body of Cos might be something like[7]

```
function Cos(X : Float) return Float is
begin
  return Sqrt(1.0 − Sin(X)*Sin(X));
end Cos;
```

It might be possible to prove the given postcondition of such an implementation, provided a suitable postcondition for Sqrt was available, but clearly Sin cannot be written in a similar way or else the two functions would be infinitely mutually recursive. Instead, some other implementation of Sin would be necessary, say based on the Taylor series expansion of $\sin(x)$. The relationship between such an implementation and the Pythagorean identity is not obvious; the connection requires an appeal to broader mathematical concepts.

Yet the Pyhagorean identity is an example of a basic relationship that might be quite useful in proving other properties of your program. How can you tell the SPARK tools about such relationships?

One way it can be done is to provide an *external axiomatization*. This is, in effect, a handwritten Why3 theory that describes the desired properties. The Why3 tools will use this theory like any other, allowing proofs to succeed that otherwise might not. However, care is needed when using this technique because an error in the Why3 theory might introduce unsoundness and allow false conclusions to be proved as well as true ones. As we cautioned in Section 6.3.3, if even one false conclusion can be proved, then all conclusions can be proved. In this respect, careless use of external axiomatizations has much in common with careless use of the Assume pragma. See Section 9.5 of the *SPARK 2014 Toolset User's Guide* (SPARK Team, 2014b) for more information about external axiomatizations.

In addition to manually injecting human written WhyML into the proving process, it is also possible to conduct human proofs at this level as well. In particular, the SPARK tools ship with Why3 drivers supporting the Coq and Isabelle proof assistants. This may allow you to discharge some difficult proofs that elude fully automated theorem provers. However, the use of a proof assistant obviously requires you to be familiar with that tool as well. See Section 9.2.3 of the *SPARK 2014 Toolset User's Guide* (SPARK Team, 2014b) for more information about configuring Coq for use with SPARK.

Finally, there are other software verification systems that use Why3 as an intermediate verification system. One system of particular interest is Frama C with the WP plug-in for C programs. Using a common intermediate verification language opens the possibility of seamless mixed language verification. In many embedded systems applications in which SPARK and C are often used together, the possibility of doing full verification across the SPARK-C boundary is very enticing.

The techniques mentioned here are advanced and, outside of this section, we have not discussed them in this book. However, they do illustrate that the architecture of SPARK 2014 sets the stage for more advances and developments in the future. This is an exciting time to be involved in the formal verification of software, and SPARK is at the forefront of the field.

Notes

1 Introduction and Overview

1. In 1997 the SEI replaced the Software CMM with the Capability Maturity Model Integration (CMMI).
2. When using the (GPS) – integrated development environment or GNATbench (the Ada plug-in for Eclipse), the check and flow analyses are combined into the *examine* command.

2 The Basic SPARK Language

1. The variable Letter, declared as subtype Uppercase defined on page 45, has a domain of the 26 uppercase letters.
2. A different identifier with the same name.
3. Assignment and equality testing are not available for Ada's limited types. A limited type is a type that includes the reserved word **limited** in its definition or in the definition of a component of a composite type.
4. With SPARK, each instantiation is individually verified.

3 Programming in the Large

1. Ada's operators are and, or, xor, =, /=, <, <=, >, >=, +, - , &, *, /, rem, mod, **, abs, and not.
2. This sharing of private data is similar to the *friend class* notion found in some object-oriented programming languages.
3. Elaboration order is a significant problem in C++ and Java, programs where it is commonly called the *static initialization order fiasco* on programmer forums.

4 Dependency Contracts

1. Roughly, a *static expression* is an expression that can be evaluated by the compiler. See the Ada Reference Manual (2012), Section 4.9, for more details.

2. It does mean an ineffective value computed by the caller might appear effective if it participates as an input in a flow dependency that does not actually exist.
3. See the *SPARK 2014 Toolset User's Guide* (SPARK Team, 2014b).

5 Mathematical Background

1. Arguments in this context are usually called *conjectures* (potential theorems).
2. The operator $\in$ is for set membership. The expression $x \in U$ is read "x is a member of the set of all humans alive today."

6 Proof

1. For an explanation of Ada's exceptions and exception handlers, see Dale and McCormick (2007) or Barnes (2014).
2. Examination of the subprogram may also fail if it is not sufficiently implemented to honor its data and flow dependency contracts.
3. The older SPARK 2005 does have some support for tasking.
4. The assume assertion is special. See Section 6.3.
5. The N-th Fibonacci number, $F(N)$, is given by $F(N-1) + F(N-2)$, where $F(0) = 0$ and $F(1) = 1$ are base cases.
6. In this example, the procedure only searches arrays of exactly 100 integers. In Section 6.7 we show a generic version of this procedure that is more general.
7. Recall that limited types cannot be copied.
8. *Inline expansion* is a process in which the compiler replaces subprogram calls with copies of the subprogram. This substitution typically improves the execution time and stack memory usage; however, it also increases the size of the program. The aspect Inline is used to request this expansion.
9. At the time of this writing SPARK does not support type invariants. However, support is planned for a future version of SPARK.
10. At the time of this writing SPARK does not support dynamic predicates. However, support is planned for a future version of SPARK.
11. For example, 192.168.56.2.
12. The algorithm can be supplemented to deal with single digit divisors (Knuth, 1998), but we do not do so here.
13. Secure hash algorithms are used with, for example, digital signature algorithms to provide strong data integrity checks.

7 Interfacing with SPARK

1. *Library level* means that the program unit is not nested within another program unit. It may be compiled separately and referenced in with and use clauses.
2. For an explanation of Ada's pointers, see Dale and McCormick (2007) or Barnes (2014).
3. For an explanation of Ada's exceptions and exception handlers, see Dale and McCormick (2007) or Barnes (2014).
4. For an explanation of Ada's automatic finalization, see Dale and McCormick (2007) or Barnes (2014).
5. For a full treatment of using Ada to interact with hardware, see McCormick, Singhoff, and Hugues (2011).

6. McCormick et al. (2011) provide a complete discussion on interacting with hardware in Ada.
7. Thanks to Angela Wallenburg, Altran UK, and Yannick Moy, AdaCore, for this example.
8. The complete syntax for abstract state aspects is given in Section 7.1.4 of the *Spark 2014 Reference Manual* (SPARK Team, 2014a).
9. All of the source code for this example is available on the http://www.cambridge.org/ us/academic/subjects/computer-science/programming-languages-and-applied-logic/building-high-integrity-applications-spark?format=PB.

8 Software Engineering with SPARK

1. The postcondition was not proven when function Empty was written as an ordinary function. The SPARK tools do not generate postconditions for subprograms. The proof succeeded when a postcondition was added to the body of the ordinary function. Because the result of an expression function is taken as that function's postcondition, it is worthwhile to use expression functions rather than ordinary functions whenever possible.
2. Thanks to Rod Chapman for suggesting the name Verification Driven Development.
3. The name of the method is loosely derived from the concept of using information flow as the central tool in the design of the objects or entities making up the system. INFORMED is an acronym for **IN**formation **F**low **OR**iented **ME**thod of **D**esign.
4. For example, defining a record type implicitly defines equality and field selection operations. We might add an additional operation such as less than or equal to.
5. The Heartbleed Bug in the popular OpenSSL library was, in part, a result of combining sensitive data with nonsensitive data in the same buffer object.
6. The classic colloquial definitions: Verification – are we building the product right? Validation – Are we building the right product?
7. Bob must also believe that the various cryptographic algorithms used are secure.

9 Advanced Techniques

1. Ada assertions are executable when the assertion policy is set to Check. So when the assertion policy is set to Check, ghost functions may be executed.
2. A future version of SPARK may allow 'Old to be used in Assume pragmas.
3. Thanks to Johannes Kanig.
4. See http://why3.lri.fr/\#provers for a complete list of compatible provers.
5. Also keep subtype predicates in mind, although at the time of this writing Dynamic_ Predicate is not supported by SPARK.
6. This limitation has since been partially removed, and work is ongoing to improve the SPARK tools further in this area.
7. A real implementation would need to choose the positive or negative square root depending on the value of x.

References

Ada Conformity Assessment Authority. 2012. *Ada Reference Manual, ISO/IEC 8652:2012 (E)*. 3rd edn.

Adams, C., Cain, P., Pinkas, D., and Zuccherato, R. 2001 (August). *RFC-3161: Internet X.509 Public Key Infrastructure Time-Stamp Protocol (TSP)*. Freemont, CA: Internet Engineering Task Force.

Aho, Alfred V., Lam, Monica S., Sethi, Ravi, and Ullman, Jeffrey D. 2007. *Compilers Principles, Techniques, & Tools*. 2nd edn. Boston, MA: Addison Wesley.

Amey, Peter. 2002. Correctness by Construction: Better Can Also Be Cheaper. *CrossTalk, the Journal of Defense Software Engineering*, **15**(3), 24–28.

Ammann, Paul, and Offutt, Jeff. 2008. *Introduction to Software Testing*. Cambridge: Cambridge University Press.

Barnes, John. 2012. SPARK: *The Proven Approach to High Integrity Software*. http://www.altran.co.uk, UK: Altran Praxis.

Barnes, John. 2014. *Programming in Ada 2012*. Cambridge: Cambridge University Press.

Beizer, Boris. 1990. *Software Testing Techniques*. New York: Van Nostrand Reinhold.

Ben-Ari, Mordechai. 2009. *Ada for Software Engineers*. 2nd edn. London: Springer-Verlag.

Bjørner, Nikolaj. 2012. Taking Satisfiability to the Next Level with Z3. Pages 1–8 of: Gramlich, Bernhard, Miller, Dale, and Sattler, Uli (eds), *Automated Reasoning*. Lecture Notes in Computer Science, vol. 7364. Berlin: Springer.

Black, Rex. 2007. *Pragmatic Software Testing: Becoming an Effective and Efficient Test Professional*. Indianapolis: Wiley.

Blair, Michael, Obenski, Sally, and Bridickas, Paula. 1992. *Patriot Missile Defense: Software Problem Led to System Failure at Dhahran, Saudi Arabia*. Tech. rept. GAO/IMTEC-92-26. Washington, DC: United States General Accounting Office.

Bobot, François, Filliâtre, Jean-Christophe, Marché, Claude, and Paskevich, Andrei. 2011. Why3: Shepherd Your Herd of Provers. In: *In Workshop on Intermediate Verication Languages* (pp. 53–64). Wroclaw, Poland.

Chapin, Peter. 2014. *Thumper*. https://github.com/pchapin/thumper.

Chapman, Roderick, Botcazou, Eric, and Wallenburg, Angela. 2011. SPARKSkein: A Formal and Fast Reference Implementation of Skein. Pages 16–27 of: *Proceedings of the 14th Brazilian Conference on Formal Methods: Foundations and Applications.* SBMF'11. Berlin: Springer-Verlag.

Chapman, Roderick, and Schanda, Florian. 2014. Are We There Yet? 20 Years of Industrial Theorem Proving with SPARK. Pages 17–26 of: Klein, Gerwin, and Gamboa, Ruben (eds), *Interactive Theorem Proving.* Lecture Notes in Computer Science, vol. 8558. Switzerland: Springer International Publishing.

Comar, Cyrille, Kanig, Johannes, and Moy, Yannick. 2012. *Integrating Formal Program Verification with Testing.* Tech. rept. AdaCore. http://www.adacore.com/uploads_gems/Hi-Lite_ERTS-2012.pdf.

Croxford, Martin, and Chapman, Roderick. 2005. Correctness by Construction: A Manifesto for High-Integrity Software. *CrossTalk, the Journal of Defense Software Engineering,* **18**(12), 5–8.

Dale, Nell, and McCormick, John. 2007. *Ada Plus Data Structures: An Object-Oriented Approach.* 2nd edn. Sudbury, MA: Jones and Bartlett.

Dale, Nell, Weems, Chip, and McCormick, John. 2000. *Programming and Problem Solving with Ada 95.* 2nd edn. Sudbury, MA: Jones and Bartlett.

Davis, Noopur, and Mullaney, Julia. 2003. *The Team Software Process (TSP) in Practice: A Summary of Recent Results.* Tech. rept. CMU/SEI-2003-TR-014 ESC-TR-2003-014. Software Engineering Institute, Carnegie Mellon University, Pittsburgh, PA.

DeRemer, Frank, and Kron, Hans. 1975. Programming-in-the-Large Versus Programming-in-the-Small. Pages 114–121 of: *Proceedings of the International Conference on Reliable Software.* New York: Association for Computing Machinery.

Dross, Claire, Efstathopoulos, Pavlos, Lenss, David, Mentré, David, and Moy, Yannick. 2014. *Rail, Space, Security: Three Case Studies for SPARK 2014.* http://www.spark-2014.org/uploads/erts_2014.pdf.

Dutertre, Bruno. 2014. Yices 2.2. Pages 737–744 of: Biere, Armin, and Bloem, Roderick (eds), *Computer-Aided Verification (CAV'2014).* Lecture Notes in Computer Science, vol. 8559. Heidelberg, Germany: Springer.

Eisenstadt, Marc. 1997. My Hairiest Bug War Stories. *Communications of the ACM,* **40**(4), 30–37.

English, John. 2001. *Ada 95: The Craft of Object-Oriented Programming.* http://www.adaic.org/resources/add_content/docs/craft/html/contents.htm.

Epp, Susanna S. 2010. *Discrete Mathematics with Applications.* 4th edn. Pacific Grove, CA: Brooks/Cole Publishing.

Gersting, Judith. 2014. *Mathematical Structures for Computer Science.* 7th edn. New York: W.H. Freeman.

GNAT, 2015a. GNAT Reference Manual, http://docs.adacore.com/gnat_rm-docs/html/gnat_rm/gnat_rm.html

GNAT, 2015b. GNAT User's Guide, http://docs.adacore.com/gnat_ugn-docs/html/gnat_ugn/gnat_ugn.html

Hall, Anthony, and Chapman, Roderick. 2002. Correctness by Construction: Developing a Commercial Secure System. *IEEE Software,* **19**(1), 18–25.

Humphrey, Watts. 2000. *Introduction to the Team Software Process.* SEI Series in Software Engineering. Boston, MA: Addison Wesley.

Humphrey, Watts. 2004. *Security Changes Everything.* Keynote address presented at the ACM SIGAda Annual International Conference, November 14–18, Atlanta, GA.

Humphrey, Watts. 2006a (January). *Defective Software Works.* News at SEI. http://www.sei.cmu.edu/library/abstracts/news-at-sei/wattsnew20041.cfm.

Humphrey, Watts. 2006b (February). *Security Changes Everything.* News at SEI. http://www.sei.cmu.edu/library/abstracts/news-at-sei/wattsnew20042.cfm.

International Telecommunication Union. 2002 (July). *Information Technology – ASN.1 Encoding Rules: Specification of Basic Encoding Rules (BER), Canonical Encoding Rules (CER), Distinguished Encoding Rules (DER).* Geneva, Switzerland.

Jones, Capers. 2000. *Software Assessments, Benchmarks, and Best Practices.* Addison-Wesley Information Technology Series. Boston: Addison Wesley.

Jones, Capers. 2012 (September). *Software Quality in 2012: A Survey of the State of the Art.* Software Quality Group of New England. http://sqgne.org/presentations/2012-13/Jones-Sep-2012.pdf.

Jones, Capor. 2013. *Software Defect Origins and Removal Methods.* Tech. rept. Narragansett, RI: Namcook Analytics LLC.

Jorgensen, Paul. 2008. *Software Testing: A Craftsman's Approach.* 3rd edn. Boca Raton, FL: Auerbach Publications.

Kaner, Cem, Falk, Jack, and Nguyen, Hung Quoc. 1999. *Testing Computer Software.* 2nd edn. Indianapolis, IN: Wiley.

Knight, John, DeJong, Colleen, Gibbs, Matthew, and Nakano, Luis. 1997 (September). Why Are Formal Methods Not Used More Widely? In: Holloway, Michael, and Hayhurst, Kelly (eds), *Proceedings of the Fourth NASA Langley Formal Methods Workshop* pp. 1–12. Hampton, VA: NASA.

Knuth, Donald. 1998. *The Art of Computer Programming: Seminumerical Algorithms.* Vol. 2. Boston, MA: Addison-Wesley.

Mao, Wenbo. 2004. *Modern Cryptography Theory and Practice.* Upper Saddle River, N.J.: Pearson.

Marsh, William, and O'Neill, Ian. 1994. *Formal Semantics of* SPARK. Tech. rept. Bath, England: Program Validation (available from Altran Praxis).

McCormick, John. 1997. Forum Letter. *Communications of the ACM*, **40**(8), 30.

McCormick, John W., Singhoff, Frank, and Hugues, Jérôme. 2011. *Building Parallel, Embedded, and Real-Time Applicatins with Ada.* Cambridge, England: Cambridge University Press.

Mills, Harlan, Dyer, Michael, and Linger, Richard. 1987. Cleanroom Software Engineering. *IEEE Software*, **4**(5), 19–25.

Moy, Yannick, Ledinot, Emmanuel, Delseny, Herve, Wiels, Virginie, and Monate, Benjamin. 2013. Testing or Formal Verification: DO-178C Alternatives and Industrial Experience. *IEEE Software*, **30**(3), 50–57.

NASA. 2011 (January). *National Highway Traffic Safety Administration Toyota Unintended Acceleration Investigation.* Technical Assessment Report TI-10-00618. Washington, DC: NASA Engineering and Safety Center.

New York University. 2014. *CVC4: The SMT Solver.* http://cvc4.cs.nyu.edu/web/.

National Institute of Standards and Technology. 2002 (May). *The Economic Impacts of Inadequate Infrastructure for Software Testing.* Planning Report 02-3. Washington, DC: NIST.

OCamlPro. 2014. *The Alt-Ergo Theorem Prover.* http://alt-ergo.lri.fr/.

OpenSSL Project. 2014a. *OpenSSL Cryptography and SSL/TLS Toolkit.* https://www.openssl.org/.

OpenSSL Project. 2014b. *OpenSSL Vulnerabilities.* https://www.openssl.org/news/vulnerabilities.html.

Parnas, David Lorge, and Madey. 1995 (January). Functional Documents for Computer Systems. *Science of Computer Programming,* **25**(1), 41–61.

Pattis, Richard E. 1988. Textbook Errors in Binary Searching. *SIGCSE Bulletin,* **20**(1), 190–194.

Paulk, Mark C. 2009. A History of the Capability Maturity Model for Software. *ASQ Software Quality Professional,* **12**(1), 5–19.

Radio Technical Commission for Aeronautics (RTCA). 2011a. *DO-178C Software Considerations in Airborne Systems and Equipment Certification.* RTCA and European Organisation for Civil Aviation Equipment (EUROCAE).

Radio Technical Commission for Aeronautics (RTCA). 2011b. *DO-333, Formal Methods Supplement to DO-178C and DO-278A.* RTCA and European Organisation for Civil Aviation Equipment (EUROCAE).

Riehle, Richard. 2003. *Ada Distilled: An Introduction to Ada Programming for Experienced Computer Programmers.* Tech. rept. Salinas, CA: AdaWorks Software Engineering.

Rosen, Kenneth. 2011. *Discrete Mathematics and Its Applications.* 7th edn. New York: McGraw-Hill.

SPARK Team. 2011 (September). *INFORMED Design Method for SPARK.* Bath, England. http://docs.adacore.com/sparkdocs-docs/Informed.htm.

SPARK Team. 2014a. SPARK *2014 Reference Manual.* New York: AdaCore. http://docs.adacore.com/spark2014-docs/html/lrm/.

SPARK Team. 2014b. SPARK *2014 Toolset User's Guide.* New York and Paris: AdaCore. http://docs.adacore.com/spark2014-docs/html/ug/.

Stallings, William. 2014. *Cryptography and Network Security, Principles and Practice.* 6th edn. Upper Saddle River, N.J: Pearson.

Wikibooks. 2014. *Ada Programming.* http://en.wikibooks.org/wiki/Ada_Programming.

Index

∃, 145
∀, 145
∈, 356

abstract data type, 73, 300
abstraction, 298
Ada reference manual, 18
Ada, interfacing with, 247
Addition, 142
aggregate
  array, 51
  record, 55
antecedent, 137
argument, 141
arithmetic operators, 44
array, 47
  attributes, 51
  constrained, 49
  unconstrained, 49
aspect, 13, 76
  Abstract_State, 111
  Address, 270, 271
  Async_Readers, 270
  Async_Writers, 270
  Contract_Cases, 184
  Convention, 264, 265, 345
  Default_Value, 125
  Depends, 105
  Effective_Reads, 270
  Effective_Writes, 270
  External_Name, 265, 268
  Ghost, 327
  Global, 31, 100, 265
  Import, 265, 331, 333, 345

Initial_Condition, 171
Initializes, 112
Inline, 176, 346
Post, 76, 167
Pre, 77, 164
Refined_Depends, 117
Refined_Global, 117
Refined_Post, 174
Refined_State, 116
Size, 271
Spark_Mode, 101
synthesized, 291
Volatile, 270, 271
Assert pragma, 189
Assert_And_Cut pragma, 196
assertion policy, 163
assertions, 9, 155, 163
Assume pragma, 198, 333
Async_Readers, 270
Async_Writers., 270
asynchronous reader, 270
asynchronous writer, 270
attribute, 42, 51
  'First, 42, 51
  'Image, 42, 43
  'Last, 42, 51
  'Length, 51
  'Loop_Entry, 204
  'Old, 77, 169, 186
  'Pred, 42
  'Range, 51
  'Result, 78, 170, 186
  'Succ, 42
  'Value, 42, 107

binder, 95
binding
    thick, 265
    thin, 265
bound variable, 145
boundary variable abstraction package,
        301
boundary variable package, 301

C, interfacing with, 261
call tree, 161
calling conventions, 261
Case Analysis, 142
case expression, 25
case statement, 23
casting. *See* type conversion
child package, 87
circular dependency, 95
clean room, 7
cohesion, 298
compilation unit, 68
concatenation, 50
conclusion, 141
conditional expression, 23
configuration pragma, 248
conjecture, 356
Conjunction, 142
connective, 136
consequent, 137
constituents, 115
Constraint_Error, 161
constructive analysis, 128, 291
context clause, 19
context item, 19
    limited with clause, 93
    private with clause, 92, 254
    use clause, 21, 68, 71
    use type clause, 71
    with clause, 19, 68
contract, 13, 76, 163
    data dependency, 100
    flow dependency, 105
    refined, 116
    synthesis, 127, 291
contract programming, 162
Contract_Cases aspect, 184
Contrapositive, 142
controlled variable, 303
Convention aspect, 264, 265,
        345
conversion. *See* type conversion

correct by construction, 7
correct, definition of, 8
coupling, 298
cryptographic hash, 310
cut point, 196

data dependency contract, 100
data layout, 261
data type, 32
declarative part, 20, 29, 93
declarative region, 30
default value aspect, 125
definition package, 69, 301
dependent expression, 24
depends aspect, 105
digital signature, 311
discriminant
    private type, 80
    record, 56
Disjunctive Syllogism, 142
dynamic predicate, 180

effective computation, 99
Effective_Reads, 270
Effective_Writes, 270
elaboration, 86, 93
    circular dependency, 95
encapsulation, 68, 298
enumeration representation clause, 264
erroneous execution, 156
error
    external, 155
    logical, 155
    runtime, 156
exclusive or, 137
existential quantifier, 145
expression function, 31
external axiomatization, 352
external error, 155
External option, 274, 281
external property, 274
external state abstraction, 273
external subsystems, 269

false coupling, 121
flow dependency contract, 104
for loop, 26, 43
formal methods, 7
formal verification, 8
function, 31
    expression, 31

generic
    formal
        subprograms, 62
        types, 59
    package, 36, 80
    parameter, 59, 80
    proof of, 224
    subprogram, 59
ghost function, 173, 326
ghost variable, 330
global, 30
Global aspect, 31, 100
golden rule of refinement, 305

hash, cryptographic, 310
header files, 262
homograph, 30
Hypothetical Syllogism, 142

if expression, 24
if statement, 22
inclusive or, 137
indexing, 47
inference rules, 142
    Addition, 142
    Case Analysis, 142
    Conjunction, 142
    Contrapositive, 142
    Disjunctive Syllogism, 142
    Hypothetical Syllogism, 142
    Modus Ponens, 142
    Modus Tolens, 142
    Simplification, 142
information hiding, 69, 78, 298
INFORMED, 297
    design elements, 299
    design steps, 303
    principles of, 302
Initial_Condition aspect, 171
Initializes aspect, 112
Inline aspect, 176, 346
interfacing with
    Ada, 247
    C, 261
Intrinsic, 345

key, public/private, 311

library unit, 68
limited with clause, 93
local, 30

logical equivalence, 140
logical error, 155
logical operators, 22, 44
logical statement, 11, 135
loop parameter, 27
loop statement, 25
    for scheme, 26, 43
    while scheme, 26
Loop_Invariant pragma, 201
Loop_Variant pragma, 212
loose coupling, 298

main procedure, 29
model number, 35, 38
Modus Ponens, 142
Modus Tolens, 142
monitored variable, 303
mutually dependent units, 93

name precedence, 30
Natural, 46
null range, 27
null statement, 160

option
    External, 274, 281
    Part_Of, 124, 281
or
    exclusive, 137
    inclusive, 137
overloading
    operators, 58
    subprograms, 57

package, 69
    boundary variable, 301
    boundary variable abstraction, 301
    child, 87
    definition, 69, 301
    generic, 36
    initialization of, 86
    nested, 121
    private child, 89, 124
    public child, 89
    type, 73, 300
    utility, 71, 301
    variable, 83, 300
package state, 110
parameter
    association, 20
    mode, 29

Part_Of option, 124, 281
Patriot missile, 38
Positive, 46
postcondition, 76, 167
poststate, 169
pragma, 13
    Assert, 189
    Assert_And_Cut, 196
    Assume, 198, 333
    Loop_Invariant, 201
    Loop_Variant, 212
    Spark_Mode, 101, 254
precondition, 77, 164
predefined exceptions
    constraint error, 161
    program error, 157
    storage error, 160
    tasking error, 160
predicate, 144
    dynamic, 180
    static, 181, 182
premise, 141
prestate, 169
private child package, 89, 124
private part, 80
private type, 69, 78
private with clause, 92, 254
procedure, 28
Program_Error, 157
programming language, C, 261
proof obligation, 162
property
    Async_Readers, 270
    Async_Writers, 270
    Effective_Reads, 270
    Effective_Write, 270
proposition, 135
propositional connective, 136
public child package, 89

range, 27
Refined_Depends aspect, 117
Refined_Global aspect, 117
Refined_Post aspect, 174
Refined_State aspect, 116
refinement, 115
    golden rule of, 305
relational operators, 22
representation clause, enumeration,
    264

reserved word, 19
retrospective analysis, 128, 291
rules of inference. *See* inference rules
runtime error, 156

scope, 30
Simplification, 142
singleton, 83
slicing, 48
sound argument, 144
spark mode, 248
Spark_Mode aspect, 101
Spark_Mode pragma, 101, 254
state abstraction, 111
    external, 273
statement. *See* logical statement
static predicate, 181
static verification, 8
Storage_Error, 160
String, 53
subprogram, 27
subtype, 45
    Natural, 46
    Positive, 46
subtype predicate, 179
synthesis of contracts, 127, 291

Tasking_Error, 160
tautology, 139
test driven development, 296
thick binding, 265
thin binding, 265
transitivity, 333, 334
trusted computing base, 339
type
    array, 47
        constrained, 49
        unconstrained, 49
    atomic, 33
    composite, 33
    derived, 57
    discrete, 40
    enumeration, 40
    integer
        modular, 44
        signed, 43
    parent, 57
    private, 69, 78
    real, 35
        decimal, 39

fixed point, 37
  floating point, 35
  record, 55
  scalar, 34
  string, 53
type conversion, 20, 44
type invariant, 178
type package, 73, 300

unbound variable, 145
undefined behavior, 156
universal quantifier, 145
universe of discourse, 144
use clause, 21, 68, 71
use type clause, 71
utility package, 71, 301

valid argument, 141
variable package, 83, 300
VC. *See* verification condition
verification condition, 143, 162
verification driven development, 296, 305
verification goals, 313
visibility, 91
  direct, 91
  with clause, 91
visible part, 80

while loop, 26
with clause, 19, 68
  limited, 93
  private, 92, 254

Printed in the United States
by Baker & Taylor Publisher Services